Music and the Making of Portugal and Spain

Music and the Making of Portugal and Spain

Nationalism and Identity Politics in the Iberian Peninsula

Edited by
MATTHEW MACHIN-AUTENRIETH,
SALWA EL-SHAWAN CASTELO-BRANCO,
AND SAMUEL LLANO

UNIVERSITY OF
ILLINOIS PRESS
Urbana, Chicago, and Springfield

This book was funded in part, including the Open Access edition, by the European Research Council funded grant "Past and Present Musical Encounters across the Strait of Gibraltar" (MESG__758221).

© 2023 by the Board of Trustees
of the University of Illinois
All rights reserved
1 2 3 4 5 C P 5 4 3 2 1
∞ This book is printed on acid-free paper.

Library of Congress Cataloging-in-Publication Data Names:
Machin-Autenrieth, Matthew, editor. | Castelo-
    Branco, Salwa El-Shawan, editor. | Llano, Samuel, editor.
Title: Music and the making of Portugal and Spain :
    nationalism and identity politics in the Iberian peninsula
    / edited by Matthew Machin-Autenrieth, Salwa el-Shawan
    Castelo-Branco, and Samuel Llano.
Description: Urbana : University of Illinois Press, 2023. |
    Includes bibliographical references and index.
Identifiers: LCCN 2023006237 (print) | LCCN 2023006238
    (ebook) | ISBN 9780252045325 (hardback) | ISBN
    9780252087448 (paperback) | ISBN 9780252054853 (ebook)
Subjects: LCSH: Music—Political aspects—Spain. | Music—
    Political aspects—Portugal. | Nationalism in music. |
    Music and state—Spain. | Music and state—Portugal. |
    National songs—Spain—History and criticism. | National
    songs—Portugal—History and criticism. | Sound recording
    industry—Spain—History—20th century. | Sound
    recording industry—Portugal—History—20th century.
Classification: LCC ML3917.I14 M87 2023 (print) | LCC
    ML3917.I14 (ebook) | DDC 780.946--dc23/eng/20230210
LC record available at https://lccn.loc.gov/2023006237
LC ebook record available at https://lccn.loc.gov/2023006238

The Open Access edition is licensed under a Creative
Commons Attribution-Non-Commercial-No Derivatives
4.0 International License: https://creativecommons.org/
licenses/by-nc-nd/4.0/.
Open Access Version ISBN: 978-0-252-05529-4

Contents

Acknowledgments ix

Introduction: Sounding Nation and Region
in Portugal and Spain 1

> *Matthew Machin-Autenrieth,*
> *Salwa El-Shawan Castelo-Branco, and Samuel Llano*

**PART I: MUSIC, STATE PROPAGANDA,
AND AUTHORITARIAN REGIMES**

Chapter 1: Patriotic, Nationalist, or Republican?
The Portuguese National Anthem 29
> *Paulo Ferreira de Castro*

Chapter 2: The Battle for the Greatest Musical Emblem:
The National Anthem and the Symbolic
Construction of Francoist Spain 46
> *Igor Contreras Zubillaga*

Chapter 3: Portuguese Rural Traditions as Cultural Exports:
How Modernism and Transnational Connections
Shaped the New State's Folklore Politics 63
> *Vera Marques Alves*

**PART II: SOUND TECHNOLOGIES
AND THE NATION**

Chapter 4: Recording *zarzuela grande* in Spain in the Early Days
of the Phonograph and Gramophone   83
Eva Moreda Rodríguez

Chapter 5: The Invisible Voices of the Early Recording
Market in Portugal   100
Leonor Losa

Chapter 6: Radio, Popular Music, and Nationalism in
Portugal in the 1940s   118
Pedro Moreira

Chapter 7: Protest Song and Recording in the Final Stages
of the Estado Novo in Portugal (1960–1974)   135
Hugo Castro

**PART III: NEGOTIATING THE STATE,
NATION, AND REGION**

Chapter 8: Towards a Critical Approach to Flamenco
Hybridity in Post-Franco Spain: Rock Music,
Nation, and Heritage in Andalusia   155
Diego García-Peinazo

Chapter 9: Portuguese Rock or Rock in Portuguese?
Controversies Concerning the "Portugueseness"
of Rock Music Made in Portugal in the Early 1980s   172
Ricardo Andrade

Chapter 10: Indie Music as a Controversial Space on
Spanish Identity: Class, Youth, and Discontent   189
Héctor Fouce and Fernán del Val

Chapter 11: Catalonia vs Spain: How Sonorous Is Nationalism?   205
Josep Martí

PART IV: MUSICAL HERITAGIZATION AND THE STATE

Chapter 12: Intangible Cultural Heritage and State Regimes in Portugal and Spain   227
> *Salwa El-Shawan Castelo-Branco*
> *and Cristina Sánchez-Carretero*

Chapter 13: Sounding the Alentejo: Portugal's *Cante* as Heritage   247
> *Salwa El-Shawan Castelo-Branco*

Chapter 14: Flamenco Heritage and the Politics of Identity   267
> *Cristina Cruces Roldán*

Contributors   287

Index   293

Acknowledgments

In putting together a volume such as this one, there are always numerous people and institutions who have contributed in some way. This volume was first proposed as the result of the symposium "Music, Nation, and Region in the Iberian Peninsula: (Re)Sounding History, Identity, and Heritage," hosted by the Faculty of Music, University of Cambridge in June 2017 and funded through The Leverhulme Trust. The editors would like to thank the University of Cambridge and The Leverhulme Trust for supporting the event, which in turn led to the production of this book. Moreover, we would like to thank the presenters who took part, some of whom have now contributed to this volume. The editors also recognize the support of the European Research Council: through Machin-Autenrieth's ERC Starting Grant "Past and Present Musical Encounters across the Strait of Gibraltar" (MESG_758221) work on this volume, and its conversion into an open access format, was possible. The editors extend their gratitude to the University of Illinois Press and particularly Laurie Matheson and Jennifer Argo for their continued support and patience. We also would like to thank Raquel Campos for her translation of Cristina Cruces Roldán's chapter. Finally, and by no means least, the editors thank the chapter contributors for showcasing their wonderful research and working so closely with us in bringing the volume together.

Music and the Making
of Portugal and Spain

Introduction

Sounding Nation and Region in Portugal and Spain

MATTHEW MACHIN-AUTENRIETH,
SALWA EL-SHAWAN CASTELO-BRANCO,
AND SAMUEL LLANO

The Spectre of Nationalism in the Iberian Peninsula

The recent waves of xenophobia and populism across the globe have shown that nationalism, having undergone significant changes from at least the nineteenth century until today, continues to be a major force driving social, political, economic, and religious movements. The reasons for nationalism's continuing dominance cannot be attributed only to xenophobia, however, and are indeed multiple and complex. One could point out the prevalence of anxieties arising from social and economic change and mass migration in recent decades. Experts and the media predicted that the intensification of globalization in the 1990s would herald the weakening or even the demise of the nation-state (Biddle and Knights 2007, 1). However, due to fears that national values and identity are being threatened, globalization has in fact strengthened movements that appeal to polarized notions of the indigenous and the foreign. This situation has been aggravated by the economic crisis prior to, and exacerbated by, the COVID-19 pandemic. The scapegoating of immigrants has given rise to movements that seek to control national boundaries and that mobilize essentialist constructions of national identity and racial purity. In Portugal and Spain, there has been a rise in nationalism, populism, and anti-immigration rhetoric especially with the

2 INTRODUCTION

mobilization of political movements on the far-right, such as Vox and Chega. Meanwhile, regionalist movements and non-state nationalisms have challenged both the nation-state and globalization, by complicating the local/global binary, most notable in recent upsurges in Catalan separatism.

Music is implicated in this strained climate, as it is frequently mobilized by different actors to reinforce national sentiment. Music has become the target of significant state-level cultural policies that seek to construct selected genres and practices as "national heritage," often in articulation with UNESCO's Intangible Cultural Heritage (ICH) paradigm. Music redraws social boundaries and creates spaces in which the perceived and imagined limits of communities are negotiated. Music writes and rewrites memories, and musical genres and practices are reclaimed as heritage by a range of communities in the name of the nation or the region, or by transnational and supranational organizations. This book considers the diverse and yet intersecting histories, identities, and heritage practices that characterize music in Portugal and Spain,[1] guided by questions such as: what can the interrelated study of music in these two states reveal about the relationship between projects of national and regional identity building? How is music instrumentalized by an array of actors in the service of nationalism at state and sub-state levels? How do musical nationalisms intersect with wider European and global networks and influences? How have state and international heritage regimes contributed to nationalist and regionalist projects? Finally, how can the study of musical nationalisms in Portugal and Spain revert the dominance of interpretive paradigms derived from the study of central-European geographies, and, in so doing, lead us to rethink how musical nationalisms have been theorized?

The contributors to this book address these questions from a range of transdisciplinary perspectives that cover different historical and contemporary contexts and genres. One central theme is the role of the state and the music industries in demarcating which musical manifestations come to sound notions of Portuguese or Spanish identity. Here, a key area of focus is the often-contested ways in which music was strategically adapted to align it with the ideological agendas and heritage regimes of the Salazar and Franco authoritarian regimes. The book also examines the impact in Portugal and Spain of UNESCO's ICH paradigm in the early twenty-first century, and the tensions between institutional and community involvement in processes of heritagization. Finally, the volume examines how the articulation between music and nationalism is nuanced by different local contexts and musical scenes. Drawing on a range of case studies including local recording networks, "national style" in popular music, music's role in political protest, and state and international heritage regimes, the volume explores how music embodies and contributes to historical and contemporary regionalisms and nationalisms.

Scholarly Context

This book draws on a large body of scholarship in Portugal and Spain that has consolidated since the institutionalization of music studies in both countries from the 1980s onwards. Numerous scholars have analyzed how music is instrumentalized by different political regimes and groups to construct and to negotiate a sense of national or regional belonging. Much of this work has been written in Portuguese or Spanish, although there has also been an increase in English-language publications. This book departs from a tendency in research on music in the Iberian Peninsula to look for expressions of the nation and the region exclusively in "folklore" or in the cultural production of national elites—including composers, critics, and institutions such as symphony orchestras and philharmonic societies. In contrast, we take a broad approach that considers all domains of music-making capable of creating consensus or division around ideas of national or regional identity. The book thus challenges the division dominant in scholarship between popular and elite genres, showing the multiple ways in which the nation and the region are imagined musically. A unique feature of the volume is that it focuses on a range of understudied genres in popular music and sound practice, departing from the tendency to restrict the study of nationalism to "art" music or genres such as fado and flamenco that have become iconic through the effects of cultural policy, mass tourism, and globalization.

The chapters in this volume address wider musicological debates around nationalism, modernity, the mediatization of music, and heritage. There is an abundance of scholarship that addresses the intricate relationship between music and nationalism, which would be impossible to summarize here. However, most relevant to the theoretical thrusts of this volume are seminal texts by scholars such as Matthew Gelbart (2009), who explores how the rise of the concepts of folk and art music, parallel to the development of early formulations of the nation in eighteenth-century Europe, was tied to the involvement of music scholars, song collectors, and the printing press in a nostalgia-fuelled project of salvage ethnography analogous to the "invention of tradition" (Hobsbawm 1983). The works of Jane Fulcher (1999; 2005), Katherine Bergeron (1998), Katharine Ellis (2005; 2013) on nineteenth- and twentieth-century musical culture in France, and Pamela Potter's study of music and musicology in 1930s and 1940s

4   INTRODUCTION

Germany (1998), have pioneered the study of European music nationalisms from an analytical perspective.

The lengthy and substantial introductions to *Western Music and Its Others* (Born and Hesmondhalgh 2000), *Music and the Racial Imagination* (Bohlman and Radano 2000), and *Beyond Exoticism* (Taylor 2007) have explained how the construction of the idea of Europe through music from the Early Modern period has relied on a range of strategic forms of representation and appropriation of the musical idioms of constructed racial and cultural Others that lie outside and inside Europe's borders. Finally, Bohlman's *Music, Nationalism, and the Making of the New Europe* (2011) interweaves historical research and ethnography in his analysis of "national" and "nationalist" constructions of belonging in Europe and how music from a range of folk, popular, and "state" (e.g., anthems, military marches) genres are instrumentalized in the formation and negotiation of national identities. He notes, "as we listen to the music of Europe and its nations [. . .] we experience both the historical past and the ethnographic present, and the ways they interact as music and nationalism combine in the making of modern Europe" (xviii). In a similar way, our volume draws together historical research and the ethnographic present to examine how music reinforces but also blurs the boundaries of nationhood in Portugal and Spain.

In music studies, the Iberian Peninsula has been relatively neglected for multiple reasons that include the predominance of the English language as the academic *lingua franca* and a tendency among scholars to regard central Europe as the powerhouse from which the very idea of the nation emerged in the eighteenth century. So-called "peripheral" nations in Europe are rarely considered as laboratories where new insights into the ontologies and functions of the nation can be developed. Rather, they are usually treated as residual geographies, onto which can be applied the insights gained through the study of the "ur-nations" of central Europe. This "central-Europe-centric" approach misses the relevant ways in which Europe's "peripheral" geographies can complicate, enrich, and challenge the knowledge gained through the study of "central" geographies (Llano 2012; Taruskin 1997). By giving visibility to scholarship previously accessible only to Portuguese- and Spanish-speaking scholars, this book aims not so much to vindicate the right of music scholarship on Portugal and Spain to participate in these broader debates—no sound mind could object to this happening—but to spell out the ways in which these geographies contribute to our understanding of the relationship between music, nationalism, and regionalism.

A key contribution in this regard is the book's departure from analytical models where music is understood according to a local/national/global framework,

Sounding Nation and Region in Portugal and Spain

where sub-national territories are often conflated with the local. In their volume on music and national identity, Biddle and Knights seek to "reintroduce the national dimension in a productive and critical manner as the missing middle term of the local/global syllogism in order to reconsider how nation-states and social units like them might operate as [. . .] a 'mediator' of the two outer terms" (2007, 2). We agree with this assertion but expand our approach to consider the role of regional (or sub-national) territorial entities. While the concept of *nation* may constitute the overarching framework, we do not take it as a "fixed" entity but one that is mutable and malleable. Another important contribution is the book's focus (above all in Part II) on the mediatization of music, most notably how the production and dissemination of music through recording technology and radio, and the local, regional, national, and transnational networks and enterprises that emerge as a result, are implicated in wider debates around national identity and modernity, especially at moments of political and societal change. An understudied area of focus here is the mobilization of popular music in the context of national identity politics and ideas about modernity (Bermúdez and Pérez 2009; García Peinazo 2017; Martínez and Fouce 2013; Silva 2016).

Finally, this book intersects with current debates around music and processes of "heritagization," especially in ethnomusicology, anthropology, and critical heritage studies. We take heritagization to mean the process by which a musical genre, and the social and cultural contexts associated with that genre, are defined, and categorized as national or regional heritage. This is usually a top-down process where state organizations identify heritage "items," classify and categorize them, and implement safeguarding policies. Such a process has become particularly prevalent since the adoption of UNESCO's Convention for the Safeguarding of the Intangible Cultural Heritage in 2003. As Bendix, Eggert, and Peselmann point out, the state-level implementation of international heritage regimes "brings forth a profusion of additional heritage regimes, endowing actors at state, regional and local levels with varied levels of power over selective aspects of culture that prior to the UNESCO initiatives had rarely seen attention or control on the part of the state" (2012, 14). Our aim, therefore, is to examine how the heritagization process plays out in Portugal and Spain, focusing on how actors implement regional, national, and international heritage regimes, as well as to consider reactions from communities to this process and the identity politics that emerge as a result. The chapters that focus on heritage (Part IV) contribute to a growing body of work that deals with the heritagization of music at both institutional and community levels (Howard 2012; Machin-Autenrieth 2017; Norton and Matsumoto 2020).

Portugal and Spain in Perspective: Methodological Challenges

This book follows music in the Iberian Peninsula across its different journeys to and from the local, regional, national, European, and global. This task is not without its challenges. Recent debates about the goals and identity of "Iberian studies" have shed light on some of the epistemological and methodological challenges faced by this academic field. Joan Ramón Resina warns that the study of the cultures of the Iberian Peninsula could lead to a "bi-cefalic confusion of the peninsula with two sovereignties" (2013, 12). In view of this hazard, our book considers the realities and movements that challenge the state and that break down the binary of Portugal/Spain. Second, there is a risk that in studying the region in relation to the state not only is another binary reinforced, but the state also becomes the sole prism through which all regional and national realities are analyzed. The mutual support that Catalan and Portuguese nationalisms have found in each other, the mirroring and mutual borrowing of nationalist tropes between Portugal and Galicia, or the rise of pro-federalist tendencies in the Iberian Peninsula from the late nineteenth century onwards (Núñez Seixas 2013), are all indications that a complex web of interests has existed for at least the last two centuries. These different movements have been united by the fact that "Castilian rule, with its intrinsically homogenizing and annexionist tendencies, was seen as a threat to the survival of other Iberian cultures and a burden to the future of Spain" (86). Finally, the study of cultural diversity in Spain and Portugal could give rise to what Resina calls a "tokenist" view (13) that celebrates diversity without considering the power relations and asymmetries lying below its surface.

To avoid fetishizing the diverse cultures of Spain and Portugal, this book does not directly compare between them. Comparison normally relies on categories of knowledge and systems of values produced by the one who compares. Cultures are not discrete units that can be compared but changing modalities that engage with one another in diverse ways. The different territories of the Iberian Peninsula are not considered as specimens of a preconceived idea of nation or region but rather as changing realities. Likewise, musical practices in the Portuguese and Spanish nations and regions are not compared on equal terms but rather as contingent upon shifting and mutually influencing social and political processes that problematize the very idea of music and its relationship with territoriality.

Notwithstanding these challenges, Portugal and Spain share similar political histories, experience of authoritarian regimes, links between folklore and national ideology, the tourist exploitation of fado and flamenco, uses of protest

Sounding Nation and Region in Portugal and Spain

song, and comparable geopolitical and economic relations with the rest of Europe. Therefore, the Iberian Peninsula is a particularly rich site for examining how music making might nuance our understanding of nationalism. While, with a few exceptions (Castelo-Branco and Moreno Fernández 2018; Castelo-Branco, Moreno Fernández, and Medeiros 2022), this dialogical approach may be missing in scholarship on music in the Iberian Peninsula, there are precedents in other fields, particularly in history and anthropology. Mar-Molinero and Smith (1996) have pioneered the study of non-state nationalisms in Portugal and Spain since the nineteenth century, albeit with a predominant focus on Spanish case studies. Roseman and Parkhurst (2008) take a broader and more balanced perspective on the social and political meanings that are ascribed to physical spaces in the Iberian Peninsula from the late nineteenth century. The authors consider a range of case studies around the topics of colonial spaces and national identity, fascism and the politics of memory, regionality, and cultural politics and globalization.[2] It is this approach that intertwines case studies from both Portugal and Spain around shared analytical themes that characterizes our volume.

Chronologies of Music and the Nation in Portugal and Spain

While we recognize the long and complex musical histories that characterize Portugal and Spain, beginning in the Early Modern period, this book corresponds to a period that spans the late nineteenth century to the present day, coinciding with the expansion of mass media and debates on national identity in the public sphere. The chapters focus on four key periods: 1) the late nineteenth and early twentieth centuries as nationalisms intersected with debates around modernity, national regeneration, and cosmopolitanism; 2) the period of authoritarian regimes when hypernationalism exerted significant influence on cultural policy; 3) the transition to democracy and the subsequent resignification of national and regional identities within the framework of the European Union; and 4) the twenty-first century and the development of state-led heritage regimes informed by UNESCO's ICH paradigm, and the strengthening of regionalist and sub-nationalist movements. In this section, we sketch these periods and summarize how music has been implicated in conversations about territorial identity. Before doing so, we offer a broad historical overview of the emergence of the Portuguese and Spanish *nations*.

The birth of the Spanish state is usually traced back to the territorial unification of part of the Iberian Peninsula brought about by the so-called Catholic Monarchs, following the forced conversion or expulsion of all Muslims and

8   INTRODUCTION

Jews in 1492 and the joining of the Kingdoms of Aragon and Castile under the same crown. Amid political and social turmoil and a dynastic succession in 1714, the following centuries witnessed the implementation of a series of policies of cultural and linguistic homogenization—including ethnic cleansing through the persecution of Gitanos (Roma) (Charnon-Deutsch 2004)—but which faced notable challenges such as a series of Catalan revolts against the Spanish state during the seventeenth century (Kamen 2008). The Spanish state continued to show signs of weakness in the nineteenth century (Álvarez Junco 2001), with Carlism posing the biggest challenge to the centralizing project undertaken by the liberals from the early 1800s. Originally a movement in defense of the right to rule of King Ferdinand VII's pro-absolutist brother Carlos, Carlism became a full-fledged reactionary ideology that fueled the defense of foral privileges in the Basque provinces (which form the Basque Country and Navarra today) and that seriously challenged the Spanish state during the three so-called Carlist Wars of the nineteenth century.[3] Carlism branched out into different reactionary movements that lay at the root of both Basque nationalism at the turn of the twentieth century and, ironically, of Franco's ultra-centralist national-Catholic doctrine during the dictatorship.

The rise of Catalan cultural nationalism from the mid-nineteenth century and its morphing into a full-fledged political movement a few decades later complicated this map. Catalan nationalism opened the eyes of Spain's successive governments to the fact that non-state nationalisms were affected by a range of ideologies from across the political spectrum. The Primo de Rivera (1923–1930) and Franco (1939–1975) dictatorships seriously thwarted the trajectories of non-state nationalisms, but these movements came back with renewed force following the restoration of democracy in 1975. The mapping of Spain as a state of autonomies (*comunidades autónomas*) sanctioned in the 1978 Constitution has created a legal framework propitious to the gradual increase of devolution, with "faster routes" being awarded to *comunidades* or so-called "historic nations," such as the Basque Country, Catalonia, and Galicia (Roseman and Parkhurst 2008, 10). The impact on Spanish politics of the situation in Catalonia and the Basque Country has been notorious from the early 1980s (Balfour and Quiroga 2007). The alliances forged with the political leaders of these two *comunidades* have been key to the formation of the successive Spanish governments in the wake of various elections. The recent rise of irredentism in Catalonia is perhaps the topic that most clearly divides Spanish public opinion and is one of the most serious challenges faced by the central government at the time of writing.

Portugal has been described as one of the "oldest nations" in Europe. The

Kingdom was established in 1143 and its territorial boundaries have remained stable since 1249 when King Afonso III conquered the south from Muslim occupation. Portugal's existence as an autonomous kingdom until the establishment of a republican regime in 1910 was interrupted for sixty years (1580–1640) when the country was ruled by the Spanish crown. The regaining of independence from Spain is still commemorated as an important moment for the "celebration of national identity" (Monteiro and Pinto 2011, 58). As elsewhere in Europe, nationalist discourses by intellectuals and artists in Portugal go back to the nineteenth century. However, the terms of the nationalist debate in Portugal and Spain in the modern era have been quite distinct (Mar-Molinero and Smith 1996, 1). In Portugal, nationalist discourses were initially associated with the Liberal Revolution of 1820 following the French invasion (1807–1811) leading to the flight of the court to Brazil and British military presence. Unlike Spain, Portugal's claim to nationhood has historically remained unchallenged. However, the definition of the constitutive elements of Portuguese "national culture" was a concern among nineteenth-century intellectual and artistic elites (Sobral 2003, 1106). Diverse nationalist discourses that reflect different intellectual and political orientations have emerged (1106). Historical narratives have focused on the origins of the nation, its ascent and decay, and the relative weight of its racial and ethnic makeup, especially the racialized opposition between North and South (Sobral 2004, 259–60, 267–77). In addition, many scholars have emphasized regional differences through sound documentation, descriptive monographs, and folklorized representations of regional costumes, music, and dance repertoires by formally structured groups labelled *ranchos folclóricos* (Castelo-Branco 2017; Holton 2003).

Musical Nationalism in Portugal and Spain in the late nineteenth and early twentieth Centuries

The late nineteenth and early twentieth centuries constitute a crucial period for understanding the intersection between music and debates about national identity across Europe. In Portugal, the decades between 1880 and 1930, which marked the end of the monarchy and the first republican regime (1910–1926), have been dubbed as the era of the "invention of Portugal," as a movement for "Portuguesefying culture" was configured by intellectuals and artists with a "modern" and cosmopolitan outlook (Ramos 1994, 565–95). This period saw the "invention" of national symbols such as the flag and national anthem, events exalting historical figures and "achievements," the rise of interest in "heritage," and the creation of cultural artifacts embodying "Portugueseness" (565–95).

The British ultimatum fueled Portuguese national sentiment, as it demanded the retreat of Portuguese armed forces from the territories that correspond to Zimbabwe and Malawi today and that were previously claimed by the crown as part of Portugal's colonial Empire. The acceptance of British demands by the Portuguese government was regarded as a humiliating defeat and intensified republican opposition to the monarchy.

As Ferreira de Castro discusses in Chapter 1, in 1911 the Republican regime adopted "A Portuguesa," a patriotic march composed by Alfredo Keil (1850–1907) as Portugal's national anthem. The patriotic fervor in the wake of the British ultimatum inspired "nationalist" compositions such as the landmark symphony *À Patria (To the Fatherland)*. Written by José Viana da Mota in 1894 to 1895, *À Patria* "acquired through time the status of a foundational moment of modern Portuguese music" (Ferreira de Castro 2014, 212), and of a "nationalist manifesto" (Cascudo 2000, 214), along with the works of composers such as Alfredo Keil, Augusto Machado, Alexandre Rey Colaço, Rui Coelho, and Luís de Freitas Branco (Ferreira de Castro 1991, 157–62). The efforts of these composers were framed by a debate between supporters of nationalism or cosmopolitanism in music (1991, 165; Artiaga and Silva 2010). This period was also marked by a debate between "Germanists," who supported the German ideal of "absolute music," and "Italianists," or advocates of Italian music, which Germanists considered to be decadent and excessively emotional (Artiaga and Silva 2010, 855).

Similarly, the late nineteenth and early twentieth centuries in Spain were characterized by debates about national identity and which cultural symbols should be employed to construct "Spanishness." Tensions between competing republican and monarchical interests, the question of autonomous representation for the "historic nations," and the demise of Spain's imperial ambitions with the loss of its last colonies in 1898 (labelled the *desastre*) provided a fractious backdrop for the development of musics that could represent the nation. As shown by Carol Hess (2001), the rivalry that grew in the late nineteenth century between musicians supportive of the French avant-garde (Debussy, Ravel, and Stravinsky) and those who embraced German romanticism (Wagner and Strauss) was exacerbated by the First World War. These skirmishes mapped onto broader cultural and ideological battles between *aliadófilos* and *germanófilos*, who aimed to break Spain's official neutrality by forging military and cultural alliances with France and Germany respectively. In the long run, composers supporting the French avant-garde, represented in Spain by Manuel de Falla (1875–1946) and critic Adolfo Salazar (1890–1958) among others, gathered critical and popular support thanks to having formulated a compelling version of Spanish music nationalism based on a rich dialogue with contemporary French composers.

Sounding Nation and Region in Portugal and Spain

This dialogue, which had already begun with Enrique Granados (1867–1916) and Isaac Albéniz (1860–1909), was not devoid of polemics, however, because of its reliance on aesthetic blueprints molded by a long tradition of exoticizing Spain in French and European music (Llano 2012).

As shown by Gerhard Steingress (2006), the same tension between the ideas of the indigenous and the foreign manifested in the realm of popular music through the circulation of flamenco troupes between different international destinations, most notably Paris, and the expansion of an entertainment industry constructed around flamenco and popular musics (Llano 2018). The celebration in Granada (1922) of a competition (*concurso*) of *cante jondo* ("deep song," which refers to a repertoire of traditional flamenco), organized by Falla and poet Federico García Lorca (1898–1936), reinforced a growing chasm between modernizing and traditionalist trends in flamenco that continues to this day. Debates between outward-looking, modern formulations of Spanish music, and fiercely nationalistic and traditionalist ones mapped onto similar conceptions of the Spanish "nation." The Franco dictatorship somehow smothered these debates, as it sent into exile a considerable portion of the Spanish avant-garde, although musical expressions that challenged the regime's traditionalist aesthetics (Moreda Rodríguez 2017) found their space in the margins and became mainstream as the regime gradually opened up to "foreign" cultural influx from the late 1950s (Contreras Zubillaga 2021). The cultural and ideological struggles that underpinned these competing musical aesthetics also shaped Spain's tortuous road towards finding a national anthem (see Chapter 2), a national symbol that continues to divide public opinion.

This period was also characterized by the search for the "roots of the nation," where folk and popular music gained more popularity among audiences. In Portugal, the notions of the *popular*, *cultura popular*, and *música popular* were resignified by different political regimes and cultural agents (musicians, the media, scholars) and mobilized for political action by nation-building projects, local and regional political movements, and opposition movements (Castelo-Branco 2013). Deriving from the notion of *povo* (literally, the "folk")—an essentialized and idealized "collective subject" (Hall 1981, 237)—these concepts are grounded in relations of power between "elite or dominant culture and the culture of the periphery" (233), and condense attributes of authenticity, primordiality, and antiquity (Castelo-Branco and Cidra 2010; Castelo-Branco 2020). *Cultura popular* constituted the main object of the then-emerging fields of ethnography and philology. It encompassed language, oral literature, and vernacular cultural practices and representations (including music, dance, and ritual) that were mobilized as symbols of Portuguese national identity (Leal 2000, 18). *Música popular* attracted the interest of musicians and collectors, who published piano vocal transcriptions for the urban aristocracy and bourgeoisie, such as the three-volume *Cancioneiro de músicas populares* (Neves and Campos 1893; 1895; 1898).

Like Portugal, Spanish intellectuals and folklorists at this time were increasingly interested in documenting folk or "rural" song practices all over Spain. They were influenced by Herderian cultural nationalism coming from Germany via the doctrine of Krausism, which led to the emergence of a number of folksong collections (*cancioneros*). This research fed into an emergent Spanish musicology and compositional crossovers between the folk and art music domains. Perhaps most noteworthy here is the composer and musicologist Felipe Pedrell (1841–1922) who believed strongly that the answer to Spain's "renewal" at the turn of the twentieth century lay in the documentation and appropriation of folklore in art music composition (Hess 2001, 17–18). Pedrell's distinction between "*música natural*" ("folk music") and "*música artificial*" ("art music"), and his desire for interaction between the two, influenced several notable composers and musicologists such as Manuel de Falla and Higini Anglés (1888–1969) (Llano 2012, 82–89). Isaac Albéniz interpreted Pedrell's advice as an exhortation to use folklore from the different regions of Spain to construct "Spanish" music nationalism as a mosaic of different musical cultures (Clark 2002). Yet as Martí points out, much early folk music research especially in the peripheral "nations" of Catalonia and the Basque Country, "had a clearly nationalistic character" (1997, 109). As such, folk music research in Spain and the appropriation of folk practices in the art music domain were implicated in wider territorial struggles across the country between regionalist and centralist positions. In the aftermath of the *desastre* in 1898 and *regeneracionista* debates around the right path for Spain's national "regeneration," "composers, critics and musicologists were in broad agreement that the only way out of Spain's state of cultural 'decadence' was the creation of a kind of music that would reflect a particular 'Spanishness'" (Pérez-Zalduondo 2007, 217). Yet, there was never complete consensus on *which* music could best represent this "Spanishness."

There is one genre, however, that is most often associated with an iconic "Spanishness": flamenco. Consolidated in the mid-nineteenth century as a commercial genre in professional theatres (*cafés cantantes*) across Spain, yet deeply linked to subcultural urban communities and Gitanos in Andalusia, flamenco became a sonic marker for Spanish identity both at home and abroad (Holguín 2019; Steingress and Baltanás 1998; Washabaugh 2012). On the back of wider European (and particularly French) fascination with the "exotic," flamenco came to represent a Spanish nation that was objectified yet marginalized culturally and politically in Europe. The exoticization of Spain led to well-documented debates

Sounding Nation and Region in Portugal and Spain

around the dominance of Andalusian cultural stereotypes, such as flamenco and "Gypsy-ness," in representations of "Spanishness" (Charnon-Deutsch 2004; Christoforidis and Kertesz 2018; Llano 2018). On the one hand, flamenco became a highly consumed form of popular culture across Spain, so much so that a host of composers, artists, and intellectuals sought to reclaim its status as a "folk art," which for some was representative of an Andalusian cultural autonomy. On the other hand, flamenco was vilified and cast as a backward cultural form that should not represent Spanish national culture, demonstrated by the so-called *anti-flamenquismo* movement (Llano 2018).

A similar process occurred with fado in Portugal, a tradition that has also become a national icon. Fado emerged in the 1840s in taverns and brothels in Lisbon's poor working-class neighborhoods that also attracted aristocrats, intellectuals, and bohemians (Nery 2012, 62–65). From the mid-nineteenth century, it penetrated the salons of the aristocracy and the middle classes. It also reached a wider audience through outdoor fiestas marking the religious calendar, saint days, carnival, secular celebrations, and bullfighting parties. It was also regularly featured in the review theatre (*teatro de revista*), operetta, and musical comedies. In the early twentieth century, fado was mediatized through commercial recordings, while new performance venues were established that featured celebrated fado singers and guitarists and attracted a middle-class audience, leading to the gradual professionalization of fado performance. During this period, fado was controversial among intellectuals. Some were hostile towards a genre that they saw as "decadent" and "sentimental." Others defended fado's social role in Lisbon's poor neighborhoods and its use as a medium for political expression during the unstable years of the republican regime (215).

Expanding the geographical frame of reference, it is also important to consider how Portuguese and Spanish nation building through music was linked to international trends around the commercialization of popular/folk musics. This is particularly evident in the context of sound recordings and the emergence of locally embedded recording industries. Their emergence was interconnected with international networks and debates around modernity and the regeneration of national music culture. As Losa shows in Chapter 5, an urban market for commercial music recordings emerged in Portugal in this context and was consolidated by the 1910s as its connections to the outside world developed. Sound recordings of popular and art musics gradually became part of the consumption habits of the urban middle classes. In Chapter 4, Moreda Rodríguez examines similar issues in the context of Spain's emerging recording industry at the end of the nineteenth century through the prism of vernacular genres. She explores how the distribution of early recordings of genres such as the *zarzuela grande*

14 INTRODUCTION

beyond their place of origin was implicated in wider national identity debates in Spain around the relationship between technology and national regeneration.

Music and Authoritarian Regimes

The national identity debates that characterized the late nineteenth and early twentieth centuries paved the way for the emergence of authoritarian regimes in Portugal and Spain, which had an indelible impact on the uses of music in national representation.[4] The expressive practices of rural and urban working classes, which represented the foundational element of national and regional identities, anchored the nationalist ideology and cultural politics of the authoritarian regimes that ruled Portugal (1933–1974) and Spain (1939–1975). Both António de Oliveira Salazar's Estado Novo (New State),[5] and Francisco Franco's fascist regime were underpinned by traditionalist Catholicism, corporatist nationalism (an administrative system that guaranteed state control over all sectors of social and economic life), state economic interventionism, and colonialism.

In Portugal, the Estado Novo's cultural policy, designated "Politics of the Spirit" (*Política do Espírito*) was forged by António Ferro (1895–1956) and implemented through the Secretariado de Propaganda Nacional, founded in 1933, renamed Secretariado Nacional da Informação, Cultura Popular e Turismo in 1944, and headed by Ferro until 1949. The "Politics of the Spirit" aimed at constructing national identity according to Salazar's ideological cornerstones and promoting the regime's image in Portugal and abroad. It was anchored on a conceptual and programmatic distinction between "*alta cultura*" (high culture), "*cultura popular*" (popular culture), and *espectáculos* (shows) (Nery 2010). A range of governmental agencies assured state control over expressive culture by defining aesthetic ideals, institutionalizing folkloric representations of regional costumes, and censoring cultural production and performance, among other measures. Major institutions in the domain of music such as the State Radio (see Chapter 6), the National Conservatory, and the São Carlos National Theater were directed by agents or sympathizers of the regime. The 1940 Exposition of the Portuguese World (Exposição do Mundo Português), which commemorated the double centenary of the founding of the nation in 1140 and the restoration of its independence from Spain in 1640, mobilized composers to write "nationalist" works for the occasion and showcased music and dance from rural areas and the former African colonies (Artiaga and Silva 2010, 862; Ferreira de Castro 1991, 167, 169). Composers either supported the regime and its initiatives or remained marginal. Fernando Lopes-Graça (1906–1994), the most prominent nationalist composer in twentieth-century Portugal, was a staunch opposer to the Estado

Novo, having been imprisoned and prohibited from holding a position that he had won as professor at the National Conservatory.

Similarly in Spain, music took on an explicitly political role as Francoist institutions sought to align musical production with the ideological image of "New Spain." Alongside the founding of key institutions such as the Instituto Español de Musicología in 1943, the regime worked to control music production through education, the formation of state-endorsed ensembles and orchestras, and music journalism and criticism (Moreda Rodríguez 2017). The dictatorship carried out a purge of political and cultural institutions that reached as far as the network of music conservatories and implemented strict censorship policies that expunged the nation's musical output of any "foreign" elements such as urban popular music, genres associated with republicanism, and the use of regional languages.[6] In addition, the Franco regime propped up the career of Father Federico Sopeña, a Catholic priest and member of the fascist party Falange Liberal with musical training. He was appointed to the Comisaría de Música, the regime's chief musical institution responsible for the management of the Orquesta Nacional de España; directed the Madrid Conservatoire (1951–1956); and was elected member of the Academy of Beaux Arts from 1958 and Comisario de Música (1971–1972). Above all, Sopeña was Spain's most prolific and influential music critic, a musical factotum indeed, who worked hard to promote and to impose what Moreda Rodríguez (2017, 52) has described as a traditionalist aesthetics of "feeling, emotion and sincerity (as opposed to dehumanization)," which were aligned with the goals of the Franco regime and best epitomized by his protege Joaquín Rodrigo's *Concierto de Aranjuez* (1939). While not overtly opposed to Spain's avant-garde currents, Sopeña's traditionalist aesthetics were nonetheless inimical to the modernist credo embraced by many of the anti-Francoist composers who were exiled during the Civil War.

The Estado Novo and the Franco regime institutionalized the production of folklorized staged representations of regional rural music, dance, and costumes by amateur folklore groups. In Portugal, as Alves argues in Chapter 3, a distinct medium for national self-definition was engendered by the Estado Novo through the state-sponsored professional dance company Bailados Portugueses Verde Gaio (VG), founded in 1940. This company enacted "modern" aestheticized representations of "tradition" consisting of scenes and choreographies set to original compositions. In Spain, the Franco regime set upon itself the impossible task of subsuming the country's diverse array of regional folk song and dance under the rubric of a unified, national tradition. As Moreda Rodríguez argues, traditional music "had to be adapted to the new understandings of Spanish identity promoted by the regime" (2017, 107). Through increased emphasis on

16 INTRODUCTION

selective collection, stylization, and centralized distribution, the regime sought to bring together Spain's regional diversity into a unified body of folk culture that could be harnessed for ideological ends (2017; Ortiz 1999). Similar to the *Ranchos folclóricos* of Portugal, the *Coros y danzas de España*, founded by the Women's Section of Franco's Falange Party in 1939, instrumentalized folkloric representations for ideological indoctrination and as a code for interpreting the nation (Castelo-Branco and Branco 2003; Ortiz 1999; Jordan 2020; Moreda Rodríguez 2017). Given the diversity of regional folkloric traditions across the country, the *Coros y danzas* embraced an ideology of Spanish folklore as the expression of national unity through diversity.

Music, Democracy, and Heritage

While distinct in many ways, the transitions to democracy triggered by a revolutionary process in Portugal in 1974 and the death of Franco in Spain in 1975 heralded new eras of political and social freedom.[7] Both countries sought to modernize their economies and societies, adopting values and lifestyles associated with the more "developed" Western European countries. Music overlapped with the profound changes promoted by the opposition to authoritarian rule and implemented during the transitions to democracy. Notions of the "popular" (in contrast to folk or traditional musics) as denoting the oppressed working classes were central to the discourse of intellectuals, musicians, and political activists who opposed authoritarian rule.

In Portugal, for some folklorists and collectors, *música* or *canção popular* denoted "authentic," archaic rural musics, and song made by and for "the people," presumably untouched by Ferro's "politics of the spirit." However, as Castro shows in Chapter 7, politically engaged musicians working within distinct aesthetic paradigms resignified *música popular* as a site for ideological and aesthetic combat. A protest song movement was launched in the mid-1940s by the aforementioned composer Fernando Lopes-Graça, which gained momentum in the 1960s and 1970s through the creation of a new discursive field labelled *música popular portuguesa* by Portuguese musicians who mostly belonged to the left of the political spectrum (most notably José Afonso and Adriano Correia de Oliveira). *Música popular portuguesa* was characterized by a cosmopolitan aesthetic and the use of poetry and music to fight against the dictatorship and to promote democracy following the revolution. Their creative work, largely enabled by the record company Orfeu, was a site for imagining a new society and a new nation ruled by values of freedom, equity, and democracy (Castelo-Branco 2020).

In Spain, artists of the singer-songwriter movement (*canción de autor*) were important agents in the transition to democracy through their determination

Sounding Nation and Region in Portugal and Spain

to deconstruct the hegemony of the Franco regime (Ayats and Salicrú-Maltas 2013; Pérez Villalba 2007). Inspired by other international musical movements, singer-songwriters sought to galvanize opposition to the Franco regime among the working classes and students, which eventually led, in the late 1960s, to a backlash from the state in the form of strict censorship of these artists' outputs. Some artists also adopted staunch regionalist positions to facilitate the struggle for administrative autonomy in regions such as Andalusia, Catalonia, and the Basque Country. *Rock radikal vasco* became a platform for the disenfranchised working-class youth of the Basque Country to express their dissatisfaction with the restoration of democracy and with what they regarded as moderate policies of devolution designed by the central government (Sánchez Ekiza 2013). In Andalusia, so-called *Rock andaluz* became a platform for the promotion and negotiation of a distinctive Andalusian cultural identity (García Peinazo 2017; Chapter 8). In Catalonia, artists such as Ramon Pelegero Sanchis "Raimón" and Lluis Llach used song as a political vehicle for advancing Catalonia's political and cultural autonomy in the dying years of the Franco regime, as part of the *Nova Cançó* movement (Ayats and Salicrú-Maltas 2013). The bottom-up negotiation of national and regional identity, as well as issues around class and political affiliation through popular music, continue into present-day political and territorial debates. For example, debates around Catalan independence continue to this day most notably with the divisive holding of an independence referendum in 2017 (see Chapter 11).

With democratization has also come the configuration and implementation of top-down state international-heritage regimes in both Iberian countries (see Chapter 12) where music is mobilized by national and sub-national institutions to promote territorial identity, cultural tourism, and "nation and region branding." Following the 1974 revolution in Portugal, fado faced hostility as a national symbol, especially from left-wing intellectuals and politicians, due to its associations with the authoritarian regime. However, the genre was resignified as an expression of Portugueseness, and new lyrics and styles were introduced.[8] In the 1990s and 2000s, a new generation of fado musicians revitalized the genre, creating hybrid styles and disseminating the genre through the "world music" circuit. In 2011, fado was inscribed on UNESCO's Representative List of the ICH of Humanity, reinforcing the perception and promotion of the genre as the sonic embodiment of Portuguese national identity both at home and abroad. At the same time, the folklore movement institutionalized and promoted by Salazar's regime was resignified and supported by municipal governments in an effort to consolidate and to promote local and regional identities (see Chapter 13).

Flamenco has followed a similar trajectory. During the Franco regime, flamenco was adapted as an emblem of national culture, especially on the back of tourism as Spain opened up to the international stage in the 1950s. In the era of democracy, flamenco's international presence and articulation as a Spanish cultural product has strengthened, especially through state intervention, tourism, and the "world music" industry. But unlike fado, flamenco has become caught up with the politics of decentralization in Spain. Since Andalusia was granted autonomy in the early 1980s, flamenco has become the target of significant institutional intervention and development through the regional government (Aix Gracia 2014; Machin-Autenrieth 2017; Washabaugh 2012). This process has been heightened by flamenco's inscription on UNESCO's Representative List of the ICH of Humanity in 2010, which, while spearheaded by the Spanish state, was fundamentally an Andalusian initiative. It is the intersection between the regional politics that underpin an international heritage declaration and community responses to the heritagization process that Cruces Roldán examines in Chapter 14. As indicated above, however, one of the aims of this volume is to move beyond a tendency in studies of music on the Iberian Peninsula to focus on flamenco and fado as key symbols of national identity and heritage. As such, Castelo-Branco's research (Chapter 13) focuses on the lesser-known genre of *cante* in the Alentejo region, examining its institutionalization as a regional icon by the Estado Novo, its resignification following the 1974 revolution, and its branding as ICH following its inscription on UNESCO's Representative List of the ICH of Humanity in 2014.

Structure of the Book

The book is structured into four parts. In Part I, "Music, State Propaganda, and Authoritarian Regimes," the authors explore how the state has appropriated music for agendas of nationalist propaganda from the late nineteenth century, with a particular focus on the authoritarian regimes of the mid-twentieth century. The section begins with two chapters (Ferreira de Castro and Contreras Zubillaga) that address the complex political and ideological circumstances surrounding the institutionalization of the Portuguese and Spanish national anthems. The authors uncover the micro-histories surrounding the formation of these anthems as national symbols and vehicles of state propaganda. In doing so, they reveal the heterogenous nature of the dictatorships and the ways in which music reveals multiple political and ideological affiliations. The next chapter deals with the role of folk and popular music in the consolidation of state power. Alves

Sounding Nation and Region in Portugal and Spain

examines how "folk" music and dance were appropriated by the Salazar regime in the construction of an idyllic, rural image of Portuguese identity.

Part II, "Sound Technologies and the Nation," examines how recording industries were implicated in, and contributed to, the mediatization of identities in the Iberian Peninsula. The authors focus on localized readings of the recording industry (from the late nineteenth century to the 1970s), exploring how local actors, networks, and businesses engaged with and influenced prevailing national debates. Moreover, the authors consider how such local networks intersected with the transnational phonographic industry at large. Here, the authors bring studies of music on the Iberian Peninsula into dialogue with a broader interdisciplinary focus on sound studies, listening, and the socio-political analysis of recording technologies. Moreda Rodríguez focuses on the emergence of the recording industry in Spain in the early twentieth century, offering insights on how recordings were involved in debates around national identity and regeneration. Losa's chapter examines the advent of recorded music and its impact on Portuguese society, exploring the role of local markets in debates around modernization at the turn of the twentieth century. Moreira considers the role that the official radio station of the Estado Novo played in fostering an "imagined community" of listeners amenable to the regime's long-term goals of social control. Finally, Castro considers the relationship between protest song and phonographic production and mediatization during the final years of the Salazar dictatorship.

Part III, "Negotiating the State, Nation, and Region," explores how music has served alternative visions of nationalism. In particular, and more apparent in the Spanish context, the section foregrounds musical manifestations of regionalism and sub-state nationalism. The spectre of national identity in the Iberian Peninsula has resurfaced in contemporary political and cultural debates, most notably encapsulated in the Catalonian independence crisis. Exploring the role of both sub-state institutions and grassroots movements, the contributors all situate music as a powerful vehicle for reframing the meaning of nationalism from distinct historical and political perspectives. García-Peinazo considers the role of flamenco hybridization among Andalusian rock bands during the transition to democracy (1969–1982) in the context of topical debates around what it meant to be Andalusian. Also focusing on the national symbolism of rock music, Andrade considers the "boom" of rock music in Portugal during the 1980s and related debates around the construction and significance of the category of socalled "Portuguese rock." The final two chapters consider contemporary issues around the relationship between popular music, class, regional, and national identities in Spain. In their chapter, Fouce and del Val consider the role of indie music in the articulation of class and youth discontent, especially in the wake of the financial crisis and wider protest movements (such as the *indignados*) in the twenty-first century. Finally, Martí analyzes the musical and sonic practices that have characterized the ideological battle between Spanish and Catalan nationalisms since the independence crisis of 2017.

The final section, "Musical Heritagization and the State," focuses on how music has been instrumentalized by governmental institutions to consolidate national and regional identities. It considers the impact of national and international heritage regimes on policies of safeguarding and musical sustainability, with a particular focus on the role of UNESCO's 2003 Convention for the Safeguarding of the Intangible Cultural Heritage. Contributors consider how music has been selected, promoted, and managed as heritage on the Iberian Peninsula. The chapters explore the processes and ideologies involved in the recognition of selected musical practices as "national or regional heritage," the (re)appropriation of heritagized practices at the regional level, as well as the tensions between institutional and community involvement in processes of "heritagization." In their comparative chapter, Castelo-Branco and Sánchez-Carretero offer a critical perspective on state and international heritage regimes in democratic Portugal and Spain, and consider the impact of UNESCO's Convention on heritage discourse and praxis. The remaining two chapters focus on specific case studies from Portugal (Castelo-Branco) and Spain (Cruces Roldán). Castelo-Branco examines the heritagization of *cante* in the Alentejo region through different heritage regimes implemented by the authoritarian regime and following the establishment of democracy, culminating in its inscription on UNESCO's Representative List of the ICH of Humanity in 2014. Adopting a historical and ethnographic approach, Castelo-Branco analyses the processes of selection, recontextualization, display, transformation, categorization, branding, and commodification that have emerged as a result of *cante*'s recognition as Portuguese heritage. In the Spanish context, Cruces Roldán considers the circumstances surrounding flamenco's heritagization in Andalusia before and after the tradition's recognition as ICH in 2010. The chapter explores the regional politics surrounding flamenco's heritagization as well as the somewhat ambivalent attitudes and criticism of this process from within the flamenco community.

The different essays in this book will demonstrate that the making of Portugal and Spain through music has been, and continues to be, a complex process, in which the authority and identity of the state is permanently being challenged and redefined. The different case studies show that boundaries are mobile and porous and that the construction of the diverse musical identities studied in this volume cannot be properly understood without considering the exchanges that constantly cross and redefine those boundaries. The persistence of nationalism today, and the recent rise of extreme forms of nationalism and xenophobia, therefore, do not do justice to the complex histories and identities that the essays in this volume highlight. Thanks to its semantic malleability and its capacity to transgress boundaries, music is a privileged medium to explore these complex histories and identities, offering us a more complete picture of the ways in which Portuguese and Spanish national identities might be culturally manifested and negotiated, both in the past and in the present.

Notes

1. This volume emerges from the symposium "Music, Nation, and Region in the Iberian Peninsula: (Re)Sounding History, Identity, and Heritage," held at the Faculty of Music, University of Cambridge (June 22–23, 2017).

2. See also María Cátedra (2001).

3. Until 1841 (Navarre) and 1876 (Álava, Gipuzkoa, and Biscay), Spain's Basque-speaking territories had their own jurisdiction, territorial statutes, and their own bodies for political representation (the Juntas Generales or "Representative Assemblies"), which regulated their own internal tax systems, according to their *fueros* (charters). Following the 1876 abolition of the *fueros*, the Basque provinces have continued to enjoy enhanced control over tax collection in the form of successive economic agreements with Spain's central government (Payne 2000, 95–98).

4. For a comparative approach to music and propaganda under authoritarian regimes across the globe, see Buch et. al. (2017).

5. Salazar ruled Portugal from 1933 to 1968 when he was succeeded by Marcelo Caetano until the 1974 revolution.

6. For further information on music during the Franco regime, see Contreras Zubillaga (2021); Moreda Rodríguez (2017); Pérez-Zalduondo and Germán Gan Quesada (2013); and Pérez-Zalduondo (2011).

7. In Spain, the beginning of the transition to democracy was marked by Franco's death in 1975, though in reality the social activism and cultural revolution that marked the latter years of the regime are sometimes understood as the beginning of the transition (Pérez Villalba 2007). In Portugal, Salazar's regime was overturned by a coup d'état on April 25, 1974, which was followed by a period of political and social instability known as the Processo Revolucionário em Curso (Ongoing Revolutionary Process, PREC), which lasted until the approval of the Portuguese constitution in 1976.

8. For more on fado's contemporary relationship with Portuguese national identity, see Gray (2013), Elliot (2010), and Nery (2012).

References

Aix Gracia, Francisco. 2014. *Flamenco y poder: Un estudio desde la sociología del arte*. Madrid: Fundación SGAE.

Álvarez Junco, José. 2001. *Spanish Identity in the Age of Nations*. Manchester: Manchester University Press.

INTRODUCTION

Artiaga, Maria José, and Manuel Deniz Silva. 2010. "Música erudita." In *Enciclopédia da música em Portugal no século XX*. Vol. 3. Edited by Salwa Castelo-Branco, 854–70. Lisbon: Círculo de Leitores/Temas e Debates.

Ayats, Jaume, and Maria Salicrú-Maltas. 2013. "Singing Against the Dictatorship (1959–1975): The *Nova Cançó*." In *Made in Spain: Studies in Popular Music*, edited by Héctor Fouce and Silvia Martínez, 28–41. London: Routledge.

Balfour, Sebastian, and Alejandro Quiroga. 2007. *The Reinvention of Spain: Nation and Identity since Democracy*. New York: Oxford University Press.

Bendix, Regina, Adiyta Eggert, and Arnika Peselmann, eds. 2012. *Heritage Regimes and the State*. Göttingen, DE: Universitätsverlag Göttingen.

Bergeron, Katherine. 1998. *Decadent Enchantments*. Berkeley: University of California Press.

Bermúdez, Silvia, and Jorge Pérez. 2009. "Introduction: Spanish Popular Music Studies." *Journal of Spanish Cultural Studies* 10, no. 2: 127–33.

Biddle, Ian, and Vanessa Knights, eds. 2007. *Music, National Identity and the Politics of Location: Between the Global and the Local*. Abingdon, UK: Ashgate.

Bohlman, Philip V. 2011. *Music, Nationalism, and the Making of New Europe*. 2nd ed. New York: Routledge.

Bohlman, Philip V., and Ronald M. Radano, eds. 2000. *Music and the Racial Imagination*. Chicago: The University of Chicago Press.

Born, Georgina, and David Hesmondhalgh. 2000. "Introduction: On Difference, Representation and Appropriation in Music." In *Western Music and Its Others: Difference, Representation, and Appropriation in Music*, edited by Georgina Born and David Hesmondhalgh, 1–58. Berkeley: University of California Press.

Buch, Esteban, Igor Contreras Zubillaga, and Manuel Deniz Silva, eds. 2017. *Composing Music for the State: Music in Twentieth-Century Dictatorships*. Abingdon, UK: Ashgate.

Cascudo, Teresa. 2000. "A década da invenção de Portugal na música erudita (1890–1899)." *Revista Portuguesa de Musicologia* 10: 181–226.

Castelo-Branco, Salwa El-Shawan. 2013. "The Politics of Music Categorization in Portugal." In *The Cambridge History of World Music*, edited by Philip Bohlman, 661–77. Cambridge: Cambridge University Press.

———. 2017. "Rancho Folclórico." *Bloomsbury Encyclopedia of Popular Music of the World: Genres: Europe*, edited by Paolo Prato and David Horn, 619–20. London: Bloomsbury.

———. 2020. "Orfeu and the Changing Meaning of the 'Popular': Aesthetics and Discourses." Paper presented at the 2020 Virtual Annual Meeting of the Society for Ethnomusicology, October 28, 2020.

Castelo-Branco, Salwa, and Rui Cidra. 2010. "Música popular." In *Enciclopédia da música em Portugal no século XX*. Vol. 3. Edited by Salwa Castelo-Branco, 875–78. Lisbon: Círculo de Leitores/Temas e Debates.

Castelo-Branco, Salwa El-Shawan, and Jorge Freitas Branco, eds. 2003. *Vozes do povo: A Folclorização em Portugal*. Lisbon: Celta Editora & Etnográfica Press. https://books.open edition.org/etnograficapress/537.

Castelo-Branco, Salwa El-Shawan, and Susana Moreno Fernández. 2018. *Music in Portugal and Spain: Experiencing Music, Expressing Culture*. Oxford: Oxford University Press.

Castelo-Branco, Salwa El-Shawan, Susana Moreno Fernández, and António Medeiros, eds. 2022. *Outros celtas: Celtismo, modernidade e música global em Portugal e Espanha.* Lisbon: Tinta-da-China.

Cátedra, María, ed. 2001. *La mirada cruzada en la Península Ibérica: Perspectivas desde la antropología social en España y Portugal.* Madrid: Catarata.

Charnon-Deutsch, Lou. 2004. *The Spanish Gypsy: The History of a European Obsession.* University Park: The Pennsylvania State University Press.

Christoforidis, Michael, and Elizabeth Kertesz. 2018. *Carmen and the Staging of Spain.* Oxford: Oxford University Press.

Clark, Walter Aaron. 2002. *Isaac Albéniz: Portrait of a Romantic.* Oxford: Oxford University Press.

Contreras Zubillaga, Igor. 2021. *"Tant que les revolutions ressemblent à cela": L'avant-garde musicale espagnole sous Franco.* Paris: Horizons d'attente.

Elliot, Richard. 2010. *Fado and the Place of Longing: Loss, Memory and the City.* Farnham, UK: Ashgate, Routledge.

Ellis, Katherine. 2005. *Interpreting the Musical Past: Early Music in Nineteenth-Century France.* New York: Oxford University Press.

———. 2013. *The Politics of Plainchant in fin-de-siècle France.* Abingdon, UK: Ashgate.

Ferreira de Castro, Paulo. 1991. "O Século XX." In *História da Música,* edited by Rui Vieira Nery and Paulo Ferreira de Castro, 148–82. Lisbon: Imprensa Nacional Casa da Moeda.

———. 2014. "Quão musical é a República?" In *Pensar a Repúblicao 1910–2010,* edited by Ana Paiva Morais et. al. Lisbon: Almedina.

Fulcher, Jane F. 1999. *French Cultural Politics and Music: From the Dreyfus Affair to the First World War.* New York: Oxford University Press.

———. 2005. *The Composer as Intellectual: Music and Ideology in France, 1914–1940.* New York: Oxford University Press.

García-Peinazo, Diego. 2017. *Rock Andaluz: Significación musical, identidades e ideología en la España del tardofranquismo y la Transición (1969–1982).* Madrid: Sociedad Española de Musicología.

Gelbart, Matthew. 2009. *The Invention of "Folk Music" and "Art Music": Emerging Categories from Ossian to Wagner.* Cambridge: Cambridge University Press.

Gray, Ellen. 2013. *Fado Resounding: Affective Politics and Urban Life.* Durham, NC: Duke University Press.

Hall, Stuart. 1981. "Notes on Deconstructing 'The Popular.'" In *People's History and Socialist Theory,* edited by Raphael Samuel, 227–40. New York: Routledge.

Hess, Carol A. 2001. *Manuel de Falla and Modernism in Spain, 1898–1936.* Chicago: University of Chicago Press.

Hobsbawn, Eric. 1983. "Introduction: Inventing Traditions." In *The Invention of Tradition,* edited by Eric Hobsbawn and Terence Ranger, 1–14. Cambridge: Cambridge University Press.

Holguín, Sandie. 2019. *Flamenco Nation: The Construction of Spanish Identity.* Madison: The University of Wisconsin Press.

Holton, Kimberley. 2003. *Performing Folklore: Ranchos Folclóricos from Lisbon to Newark.* Bloomington: Indiana University Press.

Howard, Keith, ed. 2012. *Music as Intangible Cultural Heritage: Policy, Ideology and Practice in the Preservation of East Asian Traditions.* Farnham, UK: Ashgate.

Jordan, Daniel. 2020. "Sección Femenina: Documenting and Performing Spanish Musical Folklore During the Early Franco Regime (1939–1953)." *Music and Letters* 101, no. 3: 544–66.

Kamen, Henry. 2008. *Imagining Spain: Historical Myth and National Identity*. New Haven, CT: Yale University Press.

Leal, João. 2000. *Etnografias portuguesas (1870–1970): Cultura popular e identidade nacional*. Lisbon: Publicações Dom Quixote.

Llano, Samuel. 2012. *Whose Spain? Negotiating Spanish Music in Paris, 1908–1929*. Oxford: Oxford University Press.

———. 2018. *Discordant Notes: Marginality and Social Control in Madrid, 1850–1930*. New York: Oxford University Press.

Machin-Autenrieth, Matthew. 2017. *Flamenco, Regionalism and Musical Heritage in Southern Spain*. London: Routledge.

Mar-Molinero, Clare, and Angel Smith, eds. 1996. *Nationalism and Nation in the Iberian Peninsula: Competing and Conflicting Identities*. Oxford: Berg.

Martí, Josep. 1997. "Folk Music Studies and Ethnomusicology in Spain." *Yearbook for Traditional Music* 29: 107–40.

Martínez, Sílvia, and Héctor Fouce, eds. 2013. *Made in Spain: Studies in Popular Music*. London: Routledge.

Monteiro, Nuno G, and António Costa Pinto. 2011. "Cultural Myths and Portuguese National Identity." In *Contemporary Portugal: Politics, Society and Culture*, 2nd ed. Edited by António Costa Pinto, 55–72. Boulder, CO: Social Science Monographs.

Moreda Rodríguez, Eva. 2017. *Music Criticism and Music Critics in Early Francoist Spain*. New York: Oxford University Press.

Nery, Rui Vieira. 2010. "Políticas culturais." In *Enciclopédia da música em Portugal no século XX*, edited by Salwa Castelo-Branco, 1017–30. Lisbon: Círculo de Leitores/Temas e Debates.

———. 2012. *A History of Portuguese Fado*. Lisbon: Imprensa Nacional Casa da Moeda.

Neves, César das, and Gualdino Campos. 1893, 1895, 1898. *Cancioneiro de Músicas Populares*. 3 vols. Porto: Empresa Editora.

Norton, Barley, and Naomi Matsumoto, eds. 2020. *Music as Heritage: Historical and Ethnographic Perspectives*. London: Routledge.

Núñez Seixas, Xosé M. 2013. "Iberia Reborn: Portugal through the Lens of Catalan and Galician Nationalism (1850–1950)." In *Iberian Modalities: A Relational Approach to the Study of Culture in the Iberian Peninsula*, edited by Joan Ramón Resina, 83–98. Liverpool: Liverpool University Press.

Ortiz, Carmen. 1999. "The Uses of Folklore by the Franco Regime." *The Journal of American Folklore* 112, no. 446: 479–96.

Payne, Stanley G. 2000. "Catalan and Basque Nationalism: Contrasting Patterns." In *Ethnic Challenges to the Modern Nation State*, edited by Shlomo Ben-Ami, Yoav Peled, and Alberto Spektorowski, 95–107. Houndmills, UK: MacMillan Press.

Pérez Villalba, Esther. 2007. *How Political Singers Facilitated the Spanish Transition to Democracy, 1960–1982: The Cultural Construction of a New Identity*. Lewiston, NY: The Edwin Mellen Press.

Pérez-Zalduondo, Gemma. 2007. "Racial Discourses in Spanish Musical Literature, 1915–1939." In *Western Music and Race*, edited by Julie Brown, 216–29. Cambridge: Cambridge University Press.

———. 2011. "Music, Totalitarian Ideologies and Musical Practices under Francoism (1938–1950)." *Diagonal Journal of the Center for Iberian and Latin American Music.* http://www.cilam.ucr.edu/diagonal/issues/2011/index.html.

Pérez-Zalduondo, Gemma, and Germán Gan Quesada, eds. 2013. *Music and Francoism.* Turnhout, BE: Brepols.

Potter, Pamela M. 1998. *Most German of the Arts: Musicology and Society from the Weimar Republic to the End of Hitler's Reich.* New Haven, CT: Yale University Press.

Ramos, Rui. 1994. *A segunda fundação: 1890–1920. História de Portugal.* Vol. 6. Edited by José Mattoso. Lisbon: Círculo de Leitores.

Resina, Joan Ramón. 2013. "Introduction: Iberian Modalities: The Logic of an Intercultural Field." In *Iberian Modalities: A Relational Approach to the Study of Culture in the Iberian Peninsula*, edited by Joan Ramón Resina, 1–20. Liverpool: Liverpool University Press.

Roseman, Sharon. R, and Shawn S. Parkhurst, eds. 2008. *Recasting Culture and Space in Iberian Contexts.* New York: State University of New York.

Sánchez Ekiza, Karlos. 2013. "Radical Rock: Identities and Utopias in Basque Popular Music." In *Made in Spain: Studies in Popular Music*, edited by Héctor Fouce and Silvia Martínez, 42–52. London: Routledge.

Silva, João. 2016. *Entertaining Lisbon: Music, Theater, and Modern Life in the Late 19th Century.* New York: Oxford University Press.

Sobral, Manuel. 2003. "A formação das nações e o nacionalismo: Os paradigmas explicativos e o caso Português." *Análise Social* 37, no. 165: 1093–1126.

———. 2004. "O norte, o sul, a raça, a nação—representações da identidade nacional portuguesa (séculos XIX-XX)." *Análise Social* 37, no. 171: 255–84.

Steingress, Gerhard. 2006. *y Carmen se fue a París: Un estudio sobre la construcción artística del género flamenco (1833–1865).* Córdoba, ES: Almuzara.

Steingress, Gerhard, and Enrique Baltanás, eds. 1998. *Flamenco y nacionalismo: Aportaciones para una sociología política del flamenco.* Seville: Universidad de Sevilla, Fundación el Monte.

Taruskin, Richard. 1997. *Defining Russia Musically.* Princeton: Princeton University Press.

Taylor, Timothy. 2007. *Beyond Exoticism: Western Music and the World.* Durham, NC: Duke University Press.

Washabaugh, William. 2012. *Flamenco Music and National Identity in Spain.* Abingdon, UK: Ashgate.

PART I

Music, State Propaganda, and Authoritarian Regimes

1

Patriotic, Nationalist, or Republican?

The Portuguese National Anthem

PAULO FERREIRA DE CASTRO

Marches, anthems, and songs have always constituted popular means of self-representation for socio-political movements, drawing on the power of music to energize and ritualize words and gestures, in keeping with ancestral practices rooted in religion and war. In particular, national anthems fulfil a role akin to a country's flag as patriotic symbols, enabling individuals to take part in collective performances of nationhood, and thus to experience, or exhibit, a sense of belonging and social cohesion. As noted by Benedict Anderson (1991, 145), national anthems make us aware of the power of unisonance: "No matter how banal the words and mediocre the tunes, there is in this singing an experience of simultaneity [. . .], the echoed physical realization of the imagined community." Countless authors, working from different epistemological perspectives, have emphasized that singing or listening to national anthems tends to generate a feeling of unity, pride, and patriotism (Mach 1994; Csepeli and Örkény 1997; Mayo-Harp 2001; Kolstø 2006; Gilboa and Bodner 2009; Kelen 2014; Waterman 2019), occasionally going as far as describing anthems as "modern totems (in the Durkheimian sense)—signs that bear a special relationship to the nations they represent, distinguishing them from one another and reaffirming their identity boundaries" (Cerulo 1993, 244).

Not surprisingly, the scholarly literature on national anthems tends to emphasize their function as "part of the paraphernalia of national packaging, the iconography that many of us inherit and which we come to regard as both normal and normative" (Waterman 2019, 6). Detailed analyses of individual works, especially from a musical point of view, have been less prevalent, however, owing perhaps to the belief that the meaning of national anthems arises almost exclusively from their performative value. Even though this dimension should not be overlooked, my purpose is to examine "A Portuguesa"—the Portuguese national anthem since 1911—as a poetic and musical artifact, by discussing some aspects of the text, its relation to genre and historical precedents, as well as the particular political context of its creation and reception, with a view to assessing the relevance of the work for the self-image of the Portuguese nation. This approach differs somewhat from the extant literature on "A Portuguesa,"[1] which remains tied to a narrow local historical perspective and has not yet begun to address the wider questions of identity construction and symbolic representation through the association of words, music, and performance.

Archetypes

It is probably fair to say that national anthems do not constitute a specific musical genre except in a very loose sense, drawing as they do from a range of codified musical typologies. In this respect, the term "anthem" can be misleading, as it seems to imply a generic consistency that is often lacking in what should rather be called a special repertoire, mostly defined by its uses. Any discussion of national anthems should therefore consider those typologies in their variety, and so it is worth briefly examining some of the historical models for comparison with the Portuguese anthem. One of the oldest, and in many ways an archetypal specimen, is the British "God Save the King/Queen," the origins of which remain a matter of dispute. Its first documented public performances date back to 1745 at the Drury Lane and Covent Garden theaters in London. These performances inaugurated a theatrical connection with national anthems that has survived to this day: the interaction between actors and audience in a form of collective self-spectacle. It is worth noting that the melody of "God Save the King/Queen" was used as the basis for national anthems in various countries, including Denmark, Sweden, Switzerland, Russia, the United States, and some German states (Boyd 2001, 660). This illustrates a curious paradox, noted by Philip Bohlman among others (2011, xviii): national anthems do not necessarily foreground "nationalist" (or even "national") musical characteristics, if by "nationalist" one understands—in Romantic fashion—distinctive traits considered "typical" of a particular country (usually derived from folk music), relying instead on trans-national semiotic features.[2] Experiencing a sense of

1. Patriotic, Nationalist, or Republican?

togetherness through song does not in itself constitute a nationalist statement. In this sense, one could go as far as to claim that the musical expression of "generic" patriotism (as the celebration of community and civic virtue) is primarily cosmopolitan in nature, a reflection, perhaps, of the anxiety often involved in self-exoticisation (Bohlman 2011, 115).

But music, however cosmopolitan, is not semiotically neutral, contrary to what F. Gunther Eyck, a historian of national anthems, seems to imply by stating that "the notes would be empty shells without the words to which they resound" (1995, xv; also see Castro 2009, 265–69). Expressive musical gestures and modes of temporality, rather than specifically concerned with ethnic idiosyncrasies, seem to be defining features of many national anthems, and "God Save the King/Queen" again provides a good illustration of this principle. The work takes the form of a hymn, or a prayer, for the preservation of the monarch. It belongs to the sub-group of compositions based on triple meter. Its slow and majestic rhythm, reminiscent of the royal ceremonial, together with its smooth melodic movement, suggestive of the musical practices of a congregation, make it especially appropriate to celebrate a monarch of the *ancien régime*. As Wye Allanbrook notes, "it makes sense that meter [. . .] should take on an important role in an aesthetic which connects emotion with motion. Since meter is the prime orderer of [. . .] movement, its numbers are by no means neutral and lifeless markers of time, but a set of signs designating a corresponding order of passions, and meant in execution to stir their hearers directly by their palpable emanations in sound" (1983, 14). Thus, it comes as no surprise that the metric and melodic configuration of "God Save the King/Queen" should correlate so obviously with the quality of physical movement inherent in the representation of royalty, and thus, indexically, with a certain "trans-historical" image of British majesty.

Majesty, however, became less attractive as a symbolic marker in the wake of the French Revolution. The choice of musical typologies for patriotic use clearly reflects the political and cultural changes of the era, as the former monarchic stasis gave way to the representation of collective energy and goal-directed motion, conceived as the embodiment of a new sense of agency possessed by the newly empowered citizens. Accordingly, the majority of nineteenth-century and later anthems share the musical typology of the march, in duple or quadruple meter and a moderate-to-fast tempo, with an energetic, potentially heroic character that makes them often indistinguishable from regimental marches. Thus, whether explicitly or not, national anthems often take the form of symbolic celebrations of military valour and virility, in which the distinction between the citizen and the soldier is often blurred. "La Marseillaise," a product of the

PAULO FERREIRA DE CASTRO

Revolutionary Wars eventually adopted as the French national anthem,[3] perfectly illustrates this paradigm, providing a model for the anthems of several other nations (Boyd 2001, 655; Daughtry 2003, 44–45), including, as we shall see, the Portuguese Republic.

Musical Symbols of the Monarchy

Before we discuss "A Portuguesa," a survey of earlier Portuguese anthems may provide some useful background. The first composition to approach the status of a national anthem in the absolutist era was the so-called "Hino Patriótico" ("Patriotic Hymn"), also known as the "Hino do Príncipe" or "Hino Português" ("The Prince's Hymn" or "Portuguese Hymn"), with music extracted from the cantata *La speranza, ossia l'augurio felice*, composed by Marcos Portugal in 1809 to commemorate the birthday of the Prince Regent (the future King D. João VI, then resident in Brazil, following the first Napoleonic invasion of Portugal in 1807).[4] The "Hino" is typical of an era when the idea of love for the fatherland was essentially indistinguishable from loyalty to the sovereign, although it also seems to have been used as an expression of patriotic sentiment following the defeat of the French army by Anglo-Portuguese forces (Neves 1893, 92). This anthem, in common time and in the key of B-flat major, was based on the alternation of verse and refrain that would prove the standard template for its successors.[5] Bearing the tempo indication "Andante majestoso," it was preceded by an introduction in dotted rhythms. These rhythmic figures were reminiscent of the topic of the Ouverture as befitted the expression of royal pomp, already by then inflected by a more prosaic military direction (Monelle 2000; 2006). The text, which proclaimed the devotion of the royal subjects to prince and fatherland (*pátria*), vowed a fierce combat against the "cruel enemy" that "advance[d] in vain": the (unnamed) French invader. Curiously, the relatively florid line of the choral refrain is marked by inflections more typical of operatic or salon vocality than of the battlefield, and the overall impression is that of an ad hoc grafting of the patriotic text onto a generic musical canvas.

The national anthem in use (albeit with interruptions) from the establishment of the liberal regime in 1834 to the fall of the monarchy in 1910 was the composition that came to be known as the "Hino da Carta" ("Hymn of the Charter"), following the granting of the Constitutional Charter in 1826.[6] In all likelihood, the piece was composed (as "Hino Constitucional," or "Constitutional Hymn") in Rio de Janeiro, in March 1821, by Prince D. Pedro, the future first Emperor of Brazil and the first Portuguese constitutional king, whose passion for music inspired him to try his hand at composition. Incidentally, one could say that the symbolic dimension of the "Hino da Carta" is the exact reversal of that of the "Hino Patriótico": in the earlier case, the anthem had been presented to the sovereign as the nation's offering, whereas now the anthem was meant as the king's own gift to the nation. In both cases, however, the nation was defined in terms of the loyalty of its subjects to their king. Some uncertainty remains regarding the chronology of the "Hino da Carta," aggravated by the different titles under which the work circulated throughout the nineteenth century (Neves 1893, 42–44; Andrade 1967, 140–43; Valentim 2008, 19–21, 175–77). According to music historian Ernesto Vieira, the anthem was sung for the first time at the São Carlos Theatre (the Lisbon Opera) "a few days after its arrival in Lisbon," on January 6, 1827, in an orchestral version by João Evangelista Pereira da Costa (1900, 154). However, this most likely erroneous statement is contradicted by Francisco da Fonseca Benevides, who, in his historical study of the São Carlos Theatre, asserts that "it was on the 24th of August 1821 that the 'Hino da Carta' was played at the São Carlos Theatre for the first time—the hymn composed by D. Pedro IV in honour of the 1820 Revolution" (1883, 124), which seems more likely, the confusion of titles notwithstanding.

The "Hino da Carta" is written in common time, in E-flat major, and, like its predecessor, it is structured around the simple alternation of verse and choral refrain, preceded by an introduction based on fanfare figures, with the expressive indication "Marcial." While it is hard to overlook the literary platitude of the original text, it is interesting to note the reference to the "divine" nature of the Constitution in its opening lines, no doubt a means to make it more palatable to a predominantly Catholic population.[7] The music is also extremely banal in its rhythmic monotony (ubiquity of the "military" figure dotted quaver-semiquaver in anacrusis) and in the stereotypical character of the melodic and harmonic structure. These features attest not only to the modest musical talent of the composer-king but also to the way in which Portuguese liberalism would choose to portray itself, for many decades thereafter, with music obviously rooted in the military parade ground. Judging by these two examples, it seems that the Portuguese monarchy was not particularly fortunate in its choice of musical symbols.

An Anthem for the Republic

The Portuguese Republic, proclaimed on October 5, 1910, was also to face the question of musical self-representation. The most emblematic piece in this regard, the march "A Portuguesa" by Alfredo Keil and Henrique Lopes de Mendonça, however, was in fact the result of a gradual appropriation process rather

34 PAULO FERREIRA DE CASTRO

than a deliberate republican creation. The history of "A Portuguesa" can be said to encompass three successive functions: 1) as a protest song and a token of patriotic unity, in the wake of the British Ultimatum of 1890, the event that immediately sparked its composition;[8] 2) as an anthem adopted by the republican movement, especially after the unsuccessful Porto Revolution of January 31, 1891; and 3) as the Portuguese national anthem, instituted by decree of the National Constituent Assembly of June 19, 1911. Inspired by the theme of the resurgence of the fatherland after a long period of decadence (a *topos* of *fin-de-siècle* culture, which had found ample musical expression among Portuguese artists and composers),[9] Alfredo Keil (1850–1907) probably composed his march in late January 1890, before requesting the poet, playwright, and naval officer Henrique Lopes de Mendonça (1856–1931) to provide the appropriate verses.[10] It is worth noting that Keil had previously composed a cantata entitled *Patrie!* (premiered with great success in Lisbon on June 6, 1884) to a French libretto that seems to foreshadow the patriotic scenario of "A Portuguesa" in its melodramatic and dualistic schematism—the blunt opposition between "us" and "them." Following is the description of the final scene, according to the Portuguese libretto distributed at the time of the premiere:

> In a last cry of enthusiasm, and listening only to the voice of the fatherland, they swear to defend the honor of the standard that will lead them to victory, sweeping away from the homeland the sacrilegious footsteps of the invaders like a destructive and holy windstorm. At the sound of a warrior's hymn, the youth, full of enthusiasm and aspiring to glory, march fearlessly and proudly in front of the temple, saluting the crowd that admires them.[11]

This para-operatic description almost sounds like an outline of the scenario implicit in "A Portuguesa," despite important differences between the two in terms of ideological motivation: in the context of the British Ultimatum, a competition among European colonial powers for the possession of Africa was now simply recast as the defense of the fatherland under imminent danger. At any rate, the melodramatic roots of Keil and Lopes de Mendonça's patriotic imagination are well evidenced: their patriotic march remains an eloquent example of the theatricalization, if not the operatization, of Portuguese civic conscience as collective self-spectacle in the late nineteenth century. Its prototypes could easily be found in Verdi or Meyerbeer.

In an article dated November 1, 1910, in the daily *Diário de Notícias*, Lopes de Mendonça narrated his version of the genesis of "A Portuguesa." According to his testimony (no doubt tinged by the ideological fervor inspired by the then-recent regime change), the composer's original intention had been to give his work the

1. Patriotic, Nationalist, or Republican?

widest possible circulation, so as not to "let the enthusiasm of the people cool down," and in order to give voice to the people's grievances against the monarchy. In the same article, the author also gave an account of the admittedly ungrateful task of having had to write the words to a previously composed piece:

> It was in close agreement with Keil, almost always at his home, that I composed the words, bar by bar, constantly accommodating the verse not only to the musical context, but also to the intentions of each phrase, setting a syllable to every note that he pulled out of the piano, with the aim, common to us both, of removing from the text the slightest glimpse of monarchical feeling. The heart of the people was already sincerely republican, and ours beat in unison with theirs.

The title—"A Portuguesa" (directly echoing "La Marseillaise")—was apparently adopted at the poet's suggestion, "as being likely to bring together the patriotic aspirations of all Portuguese."[12]

It was under the title "A Portuguesa" that the anthem acquired immediate popularity throughout the country, disseminated through leaflets, musical scores, newspapers, and ornamental and decorative objects of all kinds. One must not forget the fundamental role played by theaters in the dissemination of the anthem, a natural outcome of the theatrical and operatic imagery behind its creation (and a well-rooted practice since the time of "God Save the King/Queen," as we have seen). For example, "A Portuguesa" was performed as the concluding number of the play *As cores da bandeira* (*The Flag's Colors*), by Lopes de Mendonça, at the Rua dos Condes Theatre in March 1890, a practice soon imitated on other stages. Moreover, it was at a concert held at the São Carlos Theatre on March 29, 1890, that Keil and Lopes de Mendonça's anthem was to receive its most prestigious consecration, sung by the then *prime donne* and by a choir consisting of Lisbon students. The program also included some popular excerpts from the operatic repertoire with libertarian connotations (such as the chorus of Hebrew slaves from Verdi's *Nabucco*) and Keil's own cantata *Patrie!*[13] This global operatic environment may also explain the composer's original choice of the "bright" key of G major for his anthem, bringing the melody to a climax on a high B more appropriate to the trained voices of opera singers than to those of the common citizen.

As soon as April 26, 1890, however, composer and poet felt the need to distance themselves from any partisan appropriation of their work, as revealed in a letter to the press:

> We adopted, as a sufficient pledge for [its] reception [. . .] a complete aloofness from the internal political strife [. . .]. Faced with the shame of an affront [. . .],

we wished that, under the influence of a patriotic chant, a single cry should spontaneously emerge from Portuguese lips, a vehement and energetic cry that would resonate abroad as the affirmation of a living nationhood, a unanimous clamor that would lift the despondent spirits [. . .]. That cry was: Long live Portugal! (*O Século*, April 27, 1890)

Whatever the original intention of its creators, "A Portuguesa" quickly became the favorite song of students and young military men engaged in the 1890–91 patriotic demonstrations in the country's main urban centers, which were generally imbued with the spirit of rebellion against the institutions of the monarchical state, accused of pusillanimity and subservience to foreign interests. It was mainly after the republican revolt of January 31, 1891, in Porto that "A Portuguesa" saw its status confirmed as a symbol of the mobilization against an increasingly discredited monarchy.[14] This turn of events contributed to discrediting Keil in court circles, a fact bitterly resented by the composer, as is evident from several passages of his unpublished correspondence. In fact, the Portuguese Republic was eventually proclaimed on October 5, 1910, to the strains of "A Portuguesa," played by military bands in the streets of the capital (Ramos 2001, 475). The work was finally adopted as the official national anthem by decree of the National Constituent Assembly in 1911 concurrently with the new republican red and green flag. Ironically, Keil was no longer alive to witness this somewhat equivocal triumph, which he probably did not anticipate.[15]

Text and Intertext

The reception of "A Portuguesa" as an artistic achievement has been diverse. Like any similar composition, its value as a patriotic icon has inevitably prevailed over a "purely aesthetic" evaluation, which is of limited relevance in such contexts. The work can be considered a compelling semiotic artifact that is particularly rich in intertextual resonances (a feature it shares with other national anthems; see Geisler 2005, xxv). Let us examine some of these aspects.[16]

At first glance, the affinities between "A Portuguesa" and its prototype, "La Marseillaise," can hardly be overlooked. Having composed his work in the absence of a pre-existing poetic text, it is reasonable to suppose that Keil may have used the French anthem as a formal template for his own composition (a hypotext, in Gérard Genette's terminology; 1982, 13). Incidentally, the choice also reflects the predominance of French models in the fashioning of political symbolism among Portuguese intellectuals of Keil's generation. The poetic structure of both pieces is very similar, consisting of a *couplet* made up of two four-line stanzas, followed by a five-line stanza (a choral refrain). They also

1. Patriotic, Nationalist, or Republican?

possess a virtually identical rhyme scheme, differing only in that the Portuguese text uses heptasyllabic verses (the so-called *redondilha maior*, the most popular of Portuguese poetic meters) instead of the French octosyllables and hexasyllables—a fact that does not prevent the almost perfect prosodic match between the two melodies, at least before the refrain.

The affinities between the two pieces are not limited, however, to macrostructural aspects. Even more than the common key (G major, according to a manuscript draft that has been identified as the original version of Keil's composition),[17] the rhetorical parallel established through the inflection to minor mode at equivalent moments in both pieces is immediately apparent: "Mugir ces féroces soldats" ("The Howling of These Fearsome Soldiers"), in "La Marseillaise"; and "Ó Pátria, sente-se a voz" ("O Fatherland, the Voice is Heard"), in "A Portuguesa." In both cases, the passage in the minor mode has the effect of maximising the contrast with the aggressive refrains that follow in each of the anthems—"Aux armes, citoyens!" ("To arms, citizens!") / "Às armas, às armas!" ("To arms, to arms!")—and that are marked by a triumphant return to the major mode. On the other hand, both anthems begin with the exact same rhythmic formula: semiquaver-dotted quaver-semiquaver in anacrusis, corresponding to the text "Allons, enfants" ("Let us go, children") / "Heróis do mar" ("Heroes of the sea"), before the first downbeat, from which point the contour of the melodies diverges (ascending in the French anthem, descending in the Portuguese). Interestingly, the refrain of "A Portuguesa" contains—in the passage corresponding to the verse "Sobre a terra, sobre o mar" ("On the Land, on the Sea")—an almost exact musical quotation from the earlier "Hino da Maria da Fonte," or "Hino do Minho" ("Hymn of Maria da Fonte," or "Hymn of Minho"), composed by Ângelo Frondoni (1812–1891), whose popularity in certain quarters made it a potential rival to "A Portuguesa" as a national anthem after the proclamation of the Republic.[18] Even more evident—in keeping with Keil's explicit intention to introduce in his composition "some slight but significant reminiscences of our main anthems and popular songs"[19]—are the fado-like inflections in the minor-mode section ("Ó Pátria, sente-se a voz," referred to above). These inflections are motivated by the nostalgic character of the text, which evokes the memory of the ancestors emerging "entre as brumas da memória" ("among the mists of memory"), thus echoing the widespread (albeit historically unsustainable) belief that fado's roots are ancestral and stand for the most genuine expression of the national soul.[20] In light of Lopes de Mendonça's pro-republican statements quoted above, the melodic affinities between the fado-inspired phrase and the beginning of the monarchic "Hino da Carta," which are made even more evident by the common rhetorical invocation to the Fatherland ("Ó Pátria"), are somewhat surprising—unless one interprets the allusion as a way to identify the monarchy symbolically with the bygone past.

However, the most significant implication of Keil's attempts to find an adequate Portuguese color for his composition is probably that it adds a nativist inflection to patriotic expression. The anthem was no longer a generic extolling of civic or military virtue alone, as in previous anthems of a "cosmopolitan" type, but a specific foregrounding of national identity according to a Romantic sense of ethnicity that was conceived as the basis for national transformation and regeneration. Almost imperceptibly, the musical representation of the national slides into a nationalist agenda (in Bohlman's sense), as if the rebirth of the Portuguese nation were predicated on a renewed awareness of its specific difference (also in the "totemic" sense mentioned by Cerulo, above): in other words, a return to "deep" and "true" origins. Also relevant here is the curious harmonic treatment given to the initial verse of Keil's composition, "Heróis do mar, nobre povo," via the "weak" progression (I)-II^7-III-VI^7-V$^{6/5}$dim-I (reinforced by *piano* dynamics), a progression that was relatively unusual in a patriotic song in the local tradition, usually restricted to tonic-dominant alternation. This progression lends a "poetic" tinge to the otherwise emphatic scansion of the verses, and was probably conceived by the composer as the expression of the ineffable Portuguese *saudade*, made more explicit by Lopes de Mendonça's words.[21] It should also be remembered that, among the criticisms levelled against "A Portuguesa" by the champions of the "Hino da Maria da Fonte," there were accusations that Keil's anthem lacked "cheerfulness" and "brilliance," which may be related to the somewhat doleful effect of the opening phrase (Neuparth 1910). In fact, from a melodic point of view, the setting of the first stanza tends to shift the tonic to a non-accented position within the bar, thus saving the strongest metric and harmonic emphasis for the second verse of the second stanza, and above all, for the beginning of the refrain, at that point underlined by the *fortissimo* choral interjection. The refrain climaxes on the highest note of the entire composition (a third above the tonic), on the word "Pátria." The symbolism of the passage could not be more obvious.

The original version of "A Portuguesa" presented one major obstacle to its wider popularization, in that its overall melodic range (a thirteenth between the lowest and highest notes) made it relatively unsuitable for the untrained voices of ordinary citizens. (By way of comparison, "La Marseillaise" hardly exceeds the octave; "God Save the King/Queen" does not quite reach it). This fact, as well as the proliferation of melodic and rhythmic variants (some resulting from the somewhat imperfect match between words and music, others arising from the instrumental, rather than vocal, origins of the melody), led to the creation of an official committee in March 1956, tasked with establishing a definitive version of the national anthem. The revised version (in C major, a key more suitable for medium-range voices) differs from the original mainly in that its melodic range is slightly reduced and there are rhythmic variations. It was published—unfortunately without accompaniment or dynamic indications, thus inviting permanent disfigurement—in the *Diário do Governo* (*Government Gazette*), 1st Series, no. 199 (September 4, 1957), and it is this version that remains in force. Around the same time, the composer Frederico de Freitas made a new orchestration of the work. A later version for chorus and orchestra (1977), by Joly Braga Santos, remains virtually unknown.

A Case of Symbolic Inertia?

As a conclusion, one may ask: what is the specifically republican content of "A Portuguesa" as a poetic and musical object? In my view, as may be inferred from the above, such content is slight. The Portuguese Republic did not seem to attempt a symbolic expression of its own in this domain, preferring to adopt a pre-existing composition, associated with republicanism by way of historical vicissitudes. In itself, however, this composition mainly illustrates the nineteenth-century topoi of national reawakening. It capitalized on nostalgia for a mythical past (the Golden Age of the "heroes of the sea"), a kind of default position for Portuguese nationalism, rather than any specific program for a more promising future: its implicit temporality appears more circular than teleological. The choice of this anthem could arguably be regarded as symptomatic of the more reactive than affirmative ideological character of Portuguese republicanism itself, as well the movement's roots in Romanticism. In Lopes de Mendonça's words, at stake was the restoration of the chimerical "esplendor de Portugal" (the "splendour of Portugal") rather than the struggle for freedom, democracy or modernization, especially insofar as the symbolism of the "cannons" against which the anthem exhorts its citizens to march ("contra os canhões, marchar, marchar") remains enigmatic once the original subtext has been forgotten.[22] The rhetoric of the text adopts a tone of exhortation, rather than self-determination, with the voice of the poetic subject arising from an indefinite, transcendent location. For example, compare the Portuguese "levantai hoje de novo" ("rise today once more"), a second-person plural imperative, with "allons, enfants de la Patrie" in the French anthem, which, in the first-person plural, euphorically celebrates the collective *we* from the very first verse of the composition. Despite the skill shown by the composer in manipulating the almost subliminal references to his predecessors' compositions (as well as to fado) in the name of national unity and historical continuity, it can be said that the musical setting is essentially predicated on the contrast between a sense of loss and a generic call to bravery and self-sacrifice. This call is embodied, once again, in military topics: a thinly disguised frustration arising from thwarted colonial ambitions stylized as a fight for the nation's survival.

That the republican movement should have sought to appropriate for itself a sentiment shared by many Portuguese citizens, particularly exacerbated by the atmosphere of the *fin de siècle*, was only to be expected. The fact that the new regime, however, did not feel the urge to devise a poetic and musical symbology of its own, beyond a mere rallying cry against an undefined enemy, remains a source of perplexity. Equally surprising is the fact that neither did the authoritarian regime of Salazar and Caetano (1933–1974) attempt to replace "A Portuguesa" with a new national anthem, probably because the poetic and musical rhetoric of Keil and Lopes de Mendonça's work could comfortably be accommodated within the regime's own mystique of national regeneration and colonialist ideology. This suitability became particularly patent after the eruption of Portugal's "Overseas War" ("Guerra do Ultramar") in Angola in 1961 (followed by similar conflicts in Guinea-Bissau and Mozambique), which was emphatically recast, according to official rhetoric, as a fight for the preservation of the nation's integrity. In fact, as we have seen, the so-called Estado Novo ("New State") actually confirmed the official status of the anthem as a means to enhance its own political legitimacy as the agent of historical continuity with the Portuguese imperial "mission." Ultimately, through this historical inertia, the Portuguese national anthem reveals the seeming inability of the modern state (including the post-1974 democratic state) to develop a paradigm of civic ritual clearly emancipated from the military ceremonial matrix and its associated chauvinism—more often transferred, nowadays, to the sports arena, as a thinly-disguised symbolic transposition of the battlefield.[23] Even in the absence of an obvious threat to the nation's identity, the fate of "A Portuguesa" ultimately remains tied to a social and political narrative that thrives on the antagonistic relation to the inimical, albeit imaginary, Other, and the abstract, ahistorical faith in "victory at all costs." In an age in which collective symbols are being questioned around the world in the name of emancipatory and inclusive values, it might be worth pausing to ask whether a call to arms, even of a symbolic nature, is the best possible celebration of the modern nation—and, more important, what could come to replace it. For the time being, this must remain an open question.

1. Patriotic, Nationalist, or Republican? 41

Notes

1. See below, at the end of the section "An Anthem for the Republic."

2. It would be hard to disagree with Richard Taruskin's view that "it is not likely that consensus will ever be reached on [the] precise meaning [of nation and nationalism], since different definitions serve differing interests" (2001, 689). For his part, Carl Dahlhaus emphasized that national music (*Nationalmusik*) almost always emerges as an expression of a politically motivated need, especially in situations where collective identity is perceived to be under threat (1989, 38). Compare also the contrast between the national and the nationalist according to Bohlman (2011, 60). The distinction between patriotism and ethnically-grounded nationalism is articulated in Taruskin (2001, 694–95).

3. Originally published as "Chant de guerre pour l'armée du Rhin" ("War Song for the Rhine Army"), Rouget de Lisle's "La Marseillaise" (1792) was recognized as a "chant national" in 1795, and although its popularity fluctuated throughout the nineteenth century, its status as a national anthem was definitively confirmed in 1879 under the Third Republic.

4. Marcos Portugal (1762–1830) was one of the most prolific Portuguese composers of his time. His operas in the Italian style brought him considerable international acclaim. As Master of Music and Composer of the Royal Chamber, he joined the court in Rio in 1811 (for further biographical information, see Marques 2012). A version of the anthem for voices and military band dated 1810 bears the title "Hymno patriotico Da Nação portugueza A Sua Alteza Real o Príncipe Regente N. S" (P-Ln, cic-77-a).

5. References to musical scores in this essay (other than "A Portuguesa") are principally based on the collection *Hinos nacionais portugueses* published by Sassetti in the mid-nineteenth century (P-Ln, M. P. 449 A).

6. The period between the French invasions of Portugal (1807–1811) and the establishment of the constitutional monarchy was marked by extreme political instability. In the aftermath of the Peninsular Wars, leaving Portugal under British tutelage, aspiration to political liberalism and discontent with foreign influence erupted in the Porto Revolution of 1820, precipitating the return of D. João VI from Rio in 1821 and the adoption of the first Constitution the following year. This was replaced by a more moderate Constitutional Charter in 1826, granted by the new King D. Pedro IV, who almost immediately abdicated in favour of his daughter D. Maria II. The latter's reign was troubled by the bitter conflict between liberal and absolutist factions, culminating in a civil war (1832–1834) and the return of D. Pedro to the political arena, as the champion of liberal forces.

7. Following the accession to the throne of D. Maria II, the anthem received a new text, in praise of D. Pedro. For a facsimile of this version, see http://purl.pt/16561.

8. The Ultimatum, delivered to Portugal on January 11, 1890, by the British government, forced the retreat of the Portuguese army from disputed African territories between the colonies of Angola and Mozambique known as the "Rose-coloured Map." By acquiescing to British demands, the Portuguese government became the object of widespread criticism, and the whole episode was regarded as a national humiliation, fostering republican opposition to the monarchy. On the history of the republican movement in Portugal, see Catroga (2010).

9. On the subject of nationalism in late nineteenth-century Portuguese music, see Castro and Nery (1991, 154–65) and Cascudo (2000).

10. The son of a German tailor established in Lisbon, Alfredo Keil rose to prominence in the Portuguese artistic milieu of the 1880s and 1890s as a composer and painter. He went on to compose *Serrana* (1899), usually credited as the first "nationalist" Portuguese opera, on account of its popular setting and its borrowings from folk music. For further information, see Cascudo (2001).

11. Original in a private collection. All translations from Portuguese are the author's.

12. "Como nasceu a 'Portuguesa,'" *Diário de Notícias*, November 18, 1910. The article is reproduced as part of the entry on Alfredo Keil in Silva and Aranha (1911, 334–37).

13. According to the program, "A Portuguesa" closed the first part of the performance. The various stanzas were shared among the *prime donne* Bulicioff, Corsi, Pasqua, and Tetrazzini. Keil's march had previously been played by an ensemble of military bands and fanfares on March 10, at a "Great literary and musical soirée" at the Real Coliseu de Lisboa, organized by the Associação Música 24 de Junho (a musicians' professional association) and by the Executive Committee of Navy Aspirants, as part of a fund-raising campaign for the acquisition of war vessels. See "Em volta da 'Portuguesa,'" *Arquivo Nacional* 4, no. 165 (March 6, 1935): 148–50.

14. A manuscript copy of "A Portuguesa" of uncertain date (P-Ln, M. M. 345/3), bears the mention: "In Portugal this march is considered a republican hymn since the Porto Revolution. Therefore, regimental bands cannot play it."

15. On further aspects of the history of "A Portuguesa" and its reception, see also Machado (1957); Leite (1978); Medina (1999); Freitas (2000); and Ramos (2001).

16. The main sources consulted for "A Portuguesa" were the Neuparth and Imprensa Nacional editions (undated). For a facsimile of the latter (P-Ln, cic-79-a), see http://purl.pt/15292.

17. This draft (currently inaccessible) is given in facsimile in Peres (1935, 416).

18. "Maria da Fonte" was the name given to a popular uprising (from the name of its purported instigator), originating in the province of Minho, against the authoritarian central government in 1846. The expression "nobre povo" ("noble people") in the opening verse of "A Portuguesa" also suggests a borrowing from the "Hino da Maria da Fonte."

19. This is according to a leaflet (in a private collection) sent to the newspapers in 1890, announcing that the Neuparth publishing house would deliver the score of the "patriotic song" to the provinces free of charge.

20. Fado ("fate") is an urban song genre, developed since the second third of the nineteenth century, especially typical of the bohemian quarters of Lisbon. Although a relatively modern phenomenon, it has played an important role in the construction of the national mystique. The double reminiscence of the French anthem and fado in "A Portuguesa" is corroborated by Ernesto Vieira, who claims to have received this information from the composer himself (1914, 215). For more on fado, see Nery (2010).

21. Often regarded as the ultimate Portuguese idiosyncrasy, *saudade* can be defined as a state of melancholic longing for something or someone, often accompanied by a feeling of irreparable loss or the impossibility to attain the object of desire.

22. There seems to be no written evidence in support of the purported use of the alternative text "contra os bretões" ("against the Britons") at some point in the anthem's history.

23. Political resistance to the Estado Novo regime gave rise to a rich repertoire of protest songs (for an overview, see Côrte-Real 2010). One such song, "Grândola, vila morena" ("Grândola, Swarthy Town"), by the singer-songwriter José ("Zeca") Afonso (1929–1987), gained great popularity as a result of having been chosen to be broadcast on the radio in the early hours of April 25, 1974, as one of the signals for the start of the democratic revolution. The song has since enjoyed something of the status of a national symbol of protest and solidarity, not unlike "A Portuguesa" in the pre-republican period. But no single twentieth-century protest song has been "canonized" to the same degree at the national level.

References

Allanbrook, Wye Jamison. 1983. *Rhythmic Gesture in Mozart*. Chicago: University of Chicago Press.

Anderson, Benedict. 1991. *Imagined Communities: Reflections on the Origin and Spread of Nationalism*. London: Verso.

Andrade, Ayres de. 1967. *Francisco Manuel da Silva e seu tempo*. Vol. 1. Rio de Janeiro: Tempo Brasileiro.

Benevides, Francisco da Fonseca. 1883. *O Real Teatro de S. Carlos de Lisboa*. Lisbon: Tipografia Castro Irmão.

Bohlman, Philip V. 2011. *Music, Nationalism, and the Making of the New Europe*. 2nd edition. New York: Routledge.

Boyd, Malcolm. 2001. "National Anthems." In *The New Grove Dictionary of Music and Musicians*. Vol. 17. Edited by Stanley Sadie, 654–87. London: Macmillan.

Cascudo, Teresa. 2000. "A década da invenção de Portugal na música erudita (1890–1899)." *Revista Portuguesa de Musicologia* 10: 181–226.

———. 2001. "Alfredo Keil, compositor." In *Alfredo Keil,1850–1907*, edited by António Rodrigues, 337–53. Lisbon: IPPA.

Castro, Paulo Ferreira de. 2009. "Figuras da temporalidade na música erudita portuguesa na transição do séc. XIX para o séc. XX." In *Expressões da analogia*, edited by Maria Luísa Couto Soares et. al, 265–78. Lisbon: Colibri.

Castro, Paulo Ferreira de, and Rui Vieira Nery. 1991. *História da música (Sínteses da cultura portuguesa)*. Lisbon: Imprensa Nacional-Casa da Moeda.

Catroga, Fernando. 2010. *O Republicanisno em Portugal: Da formação ao 5 de Outubro de 1910*. Alfragide, PT: Casa das Letras.

Cerulo, Karen A. 1993. "Symbols and the World System: National Anthems and Flags." *Sociological Forum* 8, no. 2: 243–71.

Côrte-Real, Maria de São José. 2010. "Canção de intervenção." In *Enciclopédia da música em Portugal no século XX*. Vol. 1. Edited by Salwa Castelo-Branco, 220–28. [Lisbon]: Círculo de Leitores-Temas e Debates.

Csepeli, György, and Antal Örkény. 1997. "The Imagery of National Anthems in Europe." *Canadian Review of Studies in Nationalism* 24, no. 1–2: 33–41.

Dahlhaus, Carl. 1989. *Nineteenth-Century Music*. Translated by J. Bardford Robinson. Berkeley: University of California Press.

Daughtry, J. Martin. 2003. "Russia's New Anthem and the Negotiation of National Identity." *Ethnomusicology* 47, no. 1: 42–67.

Eyck, F. Gunther. 1995. *The Voice of Nations: European National Anthems and Their Authors.* Westport, CT: Greenwood Press.

Freitas, Frederico de. 2000. "Hino nacional." In *Enciclopédia Verbo luso-brasileira de cultura.* Vol. 14. Edited by João Bigotte Chorão, 1048–51. Lisbon: Verbo.

Geisler, Michael E. 2005. "What Are National Symbols—and What Do They Do To Us?" In *National Symbols, Fractured Identities: Contesting the National Narrative*, edited by Michael E. Geisler, xiii-xlii. Middlebury, CT: Middlebury College Press.

Genette, Gérard. 1982. *Palimpsestes: La littérature au second degré.* Paris: Seuil.

Gilboa, Avi, and Ehud Bodner. 2009. "What Are Your Thoughts When the National Anthem Is Playing? An Empirical Exploration." *Psychology of Music* 37, no. 4: 459–84.

Kelen, Christopher. 2014. *Anthem Quality: National Songs—A Theoretical Survey.* Bristol: Intellect.

Kolstø, Pål. 2006. "National Symbols as Signs of Unity and Division." *Ethnic and Racial Studies* 29, no. 4: 676–701.

Leite, Teixeira. 1978. *Como nasceu* "A Portuguesa." Lisbon: Terra Livre.

Mach, Zdzislaw. 1994. "National Anthems: The Case of Chopin as a National Composer." In *Ethnicity, Identity and Music: The Musical Construction of Place*, edited by Martin Stokes, 61–70. Oxford: Berg.

Machado, F[ernando] Falcão. 1957. "A Portuguesa." *Labor* 166: 5–19.

Marques, António Jorge. 2012. "Portugal [Portogallo], Marcos [Marco] António (da Fonseca)." In *Dicionário Biográfico Caravelas—Núcleo de Estudos da História da Música Luso-Brasileira.* https://www.yumpu.com/pt/document/read/16639529/marcos-portugal-caravelas-nucleo-de-estudos-da-historia-da.

Mayo-Harp, Maria Isabel. 2001. "National Anthems and Identities: The Role of National Anthems in the Formation Process of National Identities." MA thesis, Simon Fraser University.

Medina, João. 1999. "Que fazer do chamado 'Hino Nacional'? Estudo crítico sobre a letra de Henrique Lopes de Mendonça para o Hino Nacional português." *Clio* 4: 117–41.

Monelle, Raymond. 2000. *The Sense of Music.* Princeton: Princeton University Press.

———. 2006. *The Musical Topic: Hunt, Military and Pastoral.* Bloomington: Indiana University Press.

Nery, Rui Vieira. 2010. "Fado." In *Enciclopédia da música em Portugal no século XX.* Vol. 2. Edited by Salwa Castelo-Branco, 433–53. [Lisbon]: Círculo de Leitores-Temas e Debates.

Neuparth, J[úlio]. 1910. "Crónica musical." *Diário de Notícias*, October 26, 1910.

Neves, César das. 1893. *Cancioneiro de músicas populares.* Vol. 1. Porto: Tipografia Ocidental.

Peres, Damião et al., 1935. *História de Portugal* [Edição monumental]. Vol. 7. Barcelos, PT: Portucalense Editora.

Ramos, Rui. 2001. "O cidadão Keil: 'A Portuguesa' e a cultura do patriotismo cívico em Portugal no fim do século XIX." In *Alfredo Keil, 1850–1907*, edited by António Rodrigues, 475–509. Lisbon: IPPA.

Silva, Inocêncio Francisco da, and Brito Aranha. 1911. *Dicionário bibliográfico português.* Vol. 20 [13 of Supplement]. Lisbon: Imprensa Nacional.

Taruskin, Richard. 2001. "Nationalism." In *The New Grove Dictionary of Music and Musicians.* Vol. 17. Edited by Stanley Sadie, 689–706. London: Macmillan.

1. Patriotic, Nationalist, or Republican?

Valentim, Maria José Borges. 2008. "A produção musical de índole política no período liberal (1820–1851)." MA thesis, NOVA University of Lisbon.

Vieira, Ernesto. 1900. *Dicionário biográfico de músicos portugueses*. Vol. 2. Lisbon: Tipografia Matos Moreira e Pinheiro.

———. 1914. "Alfredo Keil." *Eco musical* 4, no. 170, July 23, 1914.

Waterman, Stanley. 2019. "National Anthems and National Symbolism: Singing the Nation." In *Handbook of the Changing World Language Map*, edited by Stanley D. Brunn and Roland Kehrein. Cham, CH: Springer. https://doi.org/10.1007/978-3-319-73400 -2_102-1.

2

The Battle for the Greatest Musical Emblem

The National Anthem and the Symbolic Construction of Francoist Spain

IGOR CONTRERAS ZUBILLAGA

Many different political groups, including "Alfonsist" monarchists,[1] Traditionalist Communion Carlists, the Fascist-oriented party Falange, large sections of the army, and the Church, participated in and supported the coup against the government of the Second Spanish Republic on July 17, 1936. The ideological differences among the army generals at the head of putschists meant the movement lacked a well-defined political profile. Their goal was to seize control of the State in one swift move, to create a military government inspired by the early years of Miguel Primo de Rivera's dictatorship (1923–1925), and to solve the country's severe political problems. Notwithstanding their profound differences, all rebel generals shared two basic ideals: they supported a centralist and historicist form of Spanish nationalism that was firmly opposed to any form of decentralization or secessionism; and they shared vague anti-communist feelings that rejected communism *stricto sensu*, liberal democracies, socialism, and anarchism alike (Moradiellos 2000, 40; Losada Málvarez 1990, 25–35). While the political project that was to emerge from the coup was initially uncertain, all the rebels rapidly embraced a ferociously messianic form of nationalism saturated by myths and symbols. This led to the development of a salvationist rhetoric that made constant reference to the need to save the motherland, a goal that became the ultimate motivation and justification for the coup (Saz 2003).

2. The Battle for the Greatest Musical Emblem

The different political and social forces that supported the movement were no less heterogeneous than its leadership. The only common ground for Traditionalist Carlists, "Alfonsist" monarchists, Falange, and the Church was their loath of democracy, liberalism, the Popular Front, and communism. However, the goals they intended to achieve by supporting the coup could not have been more different. Their common denominator was their fierce nationalism, which encouraged them to come together and to overlook their differences to save the motherland. The war, which was an unexpected outcome and the result of the rebel's initial failure to make the coup work, compelled these heterogeneous forces to group together for the long haul.

Once it was clear that the war was going to be long, Franco's government began to consolidate its power base through measures such as the organization of, and legislation for, national symbols (Núñez Seixas 2006, 320–27). This chapter focuses on the institutionalization of one of the key symbols of early Francoism: the national anthem. As we shall see, Franco's government did not create a new national anthem but used an existing one, the "Marcha granadera" ("March of the Grenadiers"), coercing Spaniards to unite under it. As Esteban Buch argues, "the trajectory [. . .] of anthems, marches, flags, and banners is like a gravitational field that ends up capturing the history of that which they symbolise, provided, naturally, that these are symbols that work. The draws of all states, political movements, even of clubs and institutions are full of failed symbols, of aborted marches" (2004). In the context of the Spanish anthem, the final outcome of this process is clear: the "Marcha granadera" did not only represent Francoist Spain during the nearly four decades in which the regime was in power, but it has also survived the dictator's death to become part of the nascent democratic system that followed. Before the national anthem was formally recognized by all, however, it needed to overcome the opposition of one of the most powerful ideological factions within the regime: the Falange. This chapter examines the disputes surrounding the "Marcha granadera," and the ways in which Franco's government overcame reticence towards it and consolidated its symbolic hegemony as the national anthem. This study follows the trail left by previous works on the symbolic construction of Francoist Spain (Box 2010; 2014), emphasizing the role played by specialists such as musicologist Nemesio Otaño (1880–1956). As Gabriella Elgenius (2011) argues, processes of national construction imply the negotiation, updating, and endorsement of symbols in an ongoing process of reinvention. Historian Carmen Ortiz (1999) has studied the ways in which the Franco regime seized traditional poetic forms—lyric and especially epic—as a means to legitimize the political winners of the Civil War and to inculcate in the popular masses a heroic cult surrounding Franco.

IGOR CONTRERAS ZUBILLAGA

By focusing on the national anthem, I examine the ways in which the dictatorship used military music which, according to Philip Bohlman, aims to generate "moments of unisonality" (2004, 146), and to exalt Franco's personality, thus in turn reinforcing his charisma.

The Return of an Anthem
That Was Never Fully Gone

In a decree issued on February 27, 1937, Franco's Government established the "Marcha granadera" as the national anthem of the insurgents. This march replaced the national anthem of the Second Republic—the "Himno de Riego"— in the territories where the coup succeeded, and in those progressively taken over by Franco's troops. According to the 1937 decree, "national music" was to return through the military coup, as the "Marcha granadera" would be heard in all "squares, churches, and cathedrals," raising the enthusiasm of the "good Spaniards" who longed for a country that was "great, free, and traditional" (BOE 1937a, 548). Franco's government looked to the past in search of the new anthem, rather than create something new, as it had done with other symbols (Box 2010, 286–317).[2] In this sense, the use of the word "traditional" in the decree was an accurate way to describe the "Marcha granadera." Although this was the first time it was officially established as the national anthem, this piece was already part of Spain's history. In 1768, under Charles III's reign, the Granadera, which had originally been used by Grenadier elite infantry units, was established as "Spain's honor march," to honor members of the royalty, the military authorities that represented them, and the Eucharist (Fernández de Latorre 1999).

Like other military tunes, this march is based on an arpeggiated major chord, making it suitable to solemnize special occasions in the eyes of many contemporary observers. The march's institutional role was consolidated throughout the nineteenth century. From 1836, the "Marcha granadera" became known as the "Marcha real" ("Royal March"), owing to its close and explicit links to the throne and the Church (Lolo 2000, 415). It was to be listened to with a deferential and respectful attitude—standing and with hats off—but was not conceived to be sung, and therefore had no lyrics, in a clear departure from traditional anthems (Buch 2002). This particularity illustrated the conservative Spanish elites' mistrust of popular patriotism, and fitted the elites' hierarchical, disciplined, and non-participative notion of citizenship.

The "Marcha real" became institutionalized and was disseminated by the State as part of attempts in Spain, and other European kingdoms, to merge monarchy and nation from the mid-nineteenth century onwards. In this way,

2. The Battle for the Greatest Musical Emblem 49

it ceased being just a march and acquired a status closer to that of a national anthem. At this point, some monarchists warned that the absence of lyrics was a serious shortcoming, particularly if the march was to become a vehicle for patriotism. It was not until the 1920s, however, in the context of Miguel Primo de Rivera's strongly nationalistic dictatorship—which promoted official symbols and suppressed non-state nationalisms—that lyrics were officially commissioned. In 1927, in celebration of the 25th anniversary of Alfonso XIII's coronation—who had supported Primo de Rivera's coup—the Catholic and conservative author Eduardo Marquina (1879–1946) was asked to write several poems for the King to choose from. Marquina was not new to glorifying Spain's history, having previously produced plays such as *Las hijas del Cid* (*El Cid's Daughters*, 1908), based on the adventures of Rodrigo Díaz de Vivar "El Cid," the hero *par excellence* in nationalist narratives of Spanish history, and *En Flandes se ha puesto el sol* (*The Sun Has Set in Flanders*, 1910), inspired by the final days of the Spanish rule in the Netherlands. In response to his new commission, Marquina presented twelve poems pregnant with historical myths, landscapes, and ancestral legacies. The King chose three to suit the "Marcha granadera": "La bandera de España" ("Spain's Flag"), a salute to the colours of the flag; "España guiadora" ("Spain the Guider"), about the willingness to die for Spain; and "¡Viva España!" ("Long Live Spain!"), dedicated to the twenty nations that use Spanish as their national language.

A performance of the March with the new lyrics premiered on a programme that was broadcast in several Spanish cities by Unión Radio to commemorate the King's 25th anniversary, following several speeches, including one by Miguel Primo de Rivera (Moreno Luzón and Núñez Seixas 2017, 182). A few days later, the anthem was sung by the royal family during a thanksgiving mass in the palace, and this soon became the custom. Afterwards, the sung anthem became a regular feature in events attended by the dictator or the King. It was also incorporated into the repertoire of several musical ensembles, such as the Coral Vallisoletana and the Unión Patriótica choir, and was recorded during a live performance with a view to distributing and popularizing it (Moreno Luzón and Núñez Seixas 2017, 182).

However, Marquina's verses were not printed in any decree or government order. The reason for this may have been that, from the beginning, conservative circles harbored doubts about the suitability of the verses chosen for the "Marcha real," while Catholic institutions disliked the lack of religious references. Miguel Primo de Rivera himself promoted alternative lyrics, penned by the writer and president of the Cádiz-based Unión Patriótica, José María Pemán (1897–1981). These lyrics focused on the sense of pride that, he claimed, had guided Spanish history and should also guide its future. These verses had no more success than Marquina's, however, and, at the time Primo de Rivera's regime ended in 1930, the "Marcha real" still had no lyrics, and continued to be sung only occasionally and not in an official capacity. The search for other anthems continued, focusing on songs deemed capable of expressing nationalist sentiment, such as the "Marcha de Cádiz"—extracted from the *zarzuela Cádiz* by Federico Chueca (1846–1908) and Joaquín Valverde (1846–1910) (Nagore 2011, 840–41)—and the *pasodoble La banderita* (Moreno Luzón 2018).

The greatest rival for the "Marcha real" was without doubt the "Himno de Riego," which Moreno Luzón and Núñez Seixas have described as the Spanish equivalent to the revolutionary "La Marselleise" (2017, 417). This piece was written on the initiative of Rafael del Riego, who led the mutiny against Ferdinand VII in 1820 and was a symbol of the liberal revolution that restored the Spanish Constitution of 1812. Conceived as a means to raise the spirits of the troops at the beginning of the revolt, this anthem not only became one of the most famous patriotic anthems of the period but was also, according to Moreno Luzón and Núñez Seixas, "the closest thing to a national anthem Spain had during the 19th century" (2017, 37). The anthem was regarded in this way as early as April 1820, and in April 1822 was officially elevated to the status of "honor march," the same rank enjoyed by the *granaderos*, by an excited liberal parliamentary majority that emphasized its Spanish "indigenous" character (Nagore 2011, 827–34). The lyrics, written by the military officer Evaristo Fernández de San Miguel, merged nationalistic and liberal principles without any reference to the King or to religion. The "Himno de Riego" exhorted the troops—referred to in the lyrics as "sons of El Cid"—to heed the call of the motherland and to break free from the chains that constrained them, under the leadership of their *caudillo*. The absolutist victory in 1823 brought back the emblems of the monarchy—among them the "Marcha real"—that exalted the Church and the King above the liberal nation.

The "Himno de Riego" never really ceased being perceived as a partisan anthem that represented only the radical liberals, and this perception seriously hampered its wider acceptance. Not even during the Second Republic did its use become fully consolidated, with supporters of the republican-socialist coalition headed by Manuel Azaña being divided over it. Some of its detractors denounced its "anachronism," its inability to represent the recent revolution, and "the high significance of our democratic and modern republican regime" (Moreno Luzón and Núñez Seixas 2017, 206). Others deemed it of poor quality and somewhat populist. The government therefore hesitated, and, despite making it the national anthem, it did so only provisionally, while final regula-

2. The Battle for the Greatest Musical Emblem 51

tions were being enacted to determine the "national march" (Diario Oficial del Ministerio de la Guerra 1931).

The "Marcha real," for its part, became a weapon in the hands of the monarchist sectors. With King Alfonso XIII in exile, monarchists adopted a radical counter-revolutionary stance as soon as the Republic was proclaimed. In response to this threat, the constitutional parliament passed the National Defence Act (October 1931)—inspired by the analogous 1922 act in Germany—which punished the use of alternative symbols to represent the nation. The first article listed a series of "acts of aggression against the Republic," including the "exaltation of the monarchic regime and of those people that are thought to represent it; and the use of symbols to allude to one or the other" (Gaceta de Madrid 1931), such as the "Marcha real." For the enemies of the republican regime, this persecution shrouded the "Marcha real" in a halo of martyrdom. However, this did not make it any more acceptable to some of its Francoist detractors.

Partisan Music Versus State Music

Franco's supporters used multiple anthems and songs, as illustrated by the aforementioned decree of February 1937 (BOE 1937a). This order, in addition to declaring the "Marcha real" the new national anthem—which Franco's government insisted on referring to by the name of "Marcha granadera"—equally recognized as national chants the anthem of the Fascist-oriented party Falange, "Cara al sol," the anthem of the traditionalist and legitimist Carlist movement, "Oriamendi," and the anthem of the *Legión*. All these anthems were to be listened to "at the official events in which they are played, while standing, as an homage to the Motherland and in remembrance of the Crusade's glorious fallen" (BOE 1937a, 549). These requirements were aimed at recognizing the different political factions that had come together under Francoism, while giving the "Marcha granadera" a pre-eminent position among the symbolic emblems of the state.

These four anthems are quoted in *Amanecer en los Jardines de España* (*Sunrise in the Gardens of Spain*), composed in 1937 by Ernesto Halffter. Halffter was in Lisbon when the Spanish Civil War started and expressed his support for Franco's side from this city (Silva 2010). Commissioned by the National Delegation of Press and Propaganda, this piece was included in an album alongside a speech by Franco (Contreras Zubillaga, 2021).[3] The title of the work is inspired by *Noche en los jardines de España*, by his mentor Manuel de Falla. *Amanecer en los Jardines de España* follows a clear narrative related to the Civil War. It begins with the funeral sequence *Dies Irae*, rendered *pianissimo* by the brass section in a low tessitura, representing the death of the Second Republic, and ends with a climax on the notes of the "Marcha granadera," the emblem of the New Spain, led by a solo violin, representing the "leader" around which all other instruments should rally in a "new light" of orchestral clarity.

Despite the pre-eminent role of the "Marcha granadera" in Halffter's work, and despite claims made in the February 1937 decree regarding the rise of a popular and spontaneous expression of support in favour of the new anthem, this tune was practically absent during the initial months of the Civil War.[4] Rather, the dominant anthem in the rebel camp during the mobilization brought about by the coup was "Cara al sol" (Cruz 2005, 170), which continued to compete with the "Marcha granadera" to become Spain's national anthem. A telling incident occurred on March 1, 1937, during the official "re-premiere" of the national anthem: after the Italian ambassador Roberto Cantalupo presented his credentials in Salamanca, Franco stood on the balcony to salute the crowd, while the music band began playing the "Marcha granadera." At this moment, a group of Falangists began to sing "Cara al sol" loudly (Vegas Latapié 1987, 157–58). The official press did not comment on the incident. The conservative and monarchist newspaper *ABC*, in fact, recounted the emotion of the audience as they reportedly heard the "Marcha granadera" being restored as the official anthem (Anon. 1937a, 9–11).

A few months later, however, the same newspaper covered another incident concerning the "Marcha granadera," in Seville this time (Anon. 1937b, 11). The success of the July 17 coup in Seville represented a great symbolic victory for the rebels given its status as capital of Andalusia and its revolutionary history (Jackson 1965, 237). According to *ABC*, at the end of a concert in which the national anthem was played, a young lady noticed that one member of the audience did not stand up and raise his right arm. When she invited him to do so and show due respect, he claimed to have an injured foot as an excuse. After other people and, finally, the authorities intervened, it became clear that the man's intention was simply to disobey the order to stand up and make the fascist salute (April 25, 1937 [BOE 1937b]).

The veiled criticism of this kind of behavior in the press, and its insistent calls to comply with the government's orders and show respect for the national anthem, suggests that these incidents were not exceptional. *ABC* repeatedly published a message under the heading "Respect for the national anthem." According to the note, the "Spanish" and "traditional" nature of the "Crusade"—the name with which the Spanish Catholic Church referred to the Civil War to legitimize the cause of Franco's side—required that no anthem other than the "Marcha granadera" should be sung, and implied that doing otherwise was tantamount to showing contempt for Spain. The text exhorted all Spaniards to not only listen

2. The Battle for the Greatest Musical Emblem

to the national anthem standing and with due respect but also to become its zealous guardians too, and to impose respect on those who, "owing to cynicism, rebelliousness or spiritual weakness," disrespected the anthem (Anon. 1937c, 9). The number of times this message was published in a newspaper as widely read as was *ABC* during the summer of 1937—no less than fifteen—suggests that the July incident regarding the "Marcha granadera" was not a mere anecdote.

Members of the fascist-oriented Falange party clearly expressed their opposition to the new anthem. As noted at the beginning of this chapter, there existed significant ideological differences among the political groups that participated in and supported the coup against the government of the Second Spanish Republic. These differences pointed to the very heart of the definition of Spain and could be summed up in the binary opposition restoration/revolution. According to Zira Box (2010, 30), these differences translated into a fight between attempts to politicize religion, championed by the monarchical sectors, the conservative right, and the Church, on one side, and a Falangist project of sacralization of the nation on the other. The militants of the Falange were not willing to accept a hymn historically linked to the monarchy, to which, moreover, some attributed a foreign origin, alleging that it was originally a gift from the King of Prussia to Spain's Charles III.

The most common way to express contempt for the national anthem by some Falangists was to remain seated and to refuse to perform the fascist salute. An order given to the Sección Femenina (Female Section, the women's branch of the Falange), intercepted by military censors in March 1937, explicitly commanded members not to show any respect for the "Marcha granadera," arguing that the Falange recognized no anthem but "Cara al sol." The note forbade members of the Sección Femenina from standing up for, "let alone saluting," any other anthem (Rodríguez Jiménez 2000, 271). The Falange's resistance towards the "Marcha granadera" contrasted with the scarce hostility it showed towards the imposition by Franco's government of the red and yellow flag, which did not prompt the Falange to defend its own red and black flag. This different attitude suggests that the Falange attached to "Cara al sol" substantially more symbolic value than to the flag. In contrast to the red and black flag, which was a legacy of the fascist organization Unión de Ofensiva Nacional-Sindicalista (with which Falange merged in 1934), "Cara al sol" had been created by a group of intellectuals that included José Antonio Primo de Rivera, founder of the Falange turned into "martyr" after being imprisoned by the Republicans and shot in November 1936.

The different versions of the process that led to the composition of "Cara al sol" all stress the role played by José Antonio in its composition. They corroborate the story according to which the Spanish fascist anthem was the result of a meeting that came to gain legendary status within the Falangist imagination (Suárez-Pajares 2016). According to Falangist writer Agustín de Foxá (1906–1959), who co-authored the lyrics, several party members asked José Antonio to write an anthem they could sing after their rallies. The latter summoned several Falangist writer-friends to pen the lyrics for a march that had been composed by Juan Tellería (1895–1949).

The result is an anthem that summarizes Falangist values close to fascism, such as national character, youth, the cult of the leader and the fallen, and the palingenetic myth of the nation being reborn after a period of decadence. According to de Foxá, the sun in the title and the opening verse symbolizes the direct, ardent, and impetuous character of Falangists: "We do everything under the light of the sun; that's the way you go to war, with the sun on your face, without blinking; that's the way we look at Spanish history blinding us" (1939). The reference in the lyrics to "The shirt that was yesterday embroidered in red" contained an oblique allusion to the two most important women in every young male Falangist's life: his mother and his girlfriend, comrades in the struggle. The line "Death will find me, and I shall not see you again" summarized José Antonio's notion of death: "the hero does not seek death, as one commits suicide. He simply accepts it as part of his duty. Because Falange's military ethos is to look at death face to face, and to give one's life for the Motherland" (de Foxá 1939). The stars in the second stanza—"I shall stand next to my stern comrades who stand guard over the stars, and are always present in our toils"—are a metaphoric reference to fallen Falangists standing guard in heaven. The line "If they tell you that I fell, I shall be at my post there," describes the destiny awaiting all Falangists: to join the host of the fallen, who remain close to the living. These lines were followed by José Antonio's prophetic verses—"Victorious flags will return with the happy stroll of peace"—reflecting a prescient intuition of Franco's sword, which would bring victory to the national-syndicalist cause. Victory, however, could not be achieved without pain, death and, finally, resurrection: "Pain opens the door to life," wrote de Foxá, just as "the soil must be broken up to reap its harvest." The five arrow-like roses, the organization's emblem, were the symbol of the "generous and fertile" blood spilt by heroic Falangists. The final verses— "The spring, coming from the sky, the earth and the sea, will laugh again. Get up squads! To victory! In Spain, the sun is coming out!"—foretell the triumph of national-syndicalism and the coming of a new age of peace and happiness, far from "the sad nostalgic autumns of liberal romanticism" and the "hard winters of Moscow," in De Foxá's words.

"Cara al sol" was a collective work that bore the signature of the fallen leader and represented the whole Falangist imaginary. "Cara al sol" could be sung with raised arms by the ecstatic crowd, satisfying fascism's emphasis on the aesthetic of mass events and ceremonial symbols. As such, it was difficult for the Falangists to accept that "Cara al sol" could play only a secondary role, especially relative to a march without lyrics whose only prop seemed to be tradition. The Falange aspired to turn its own symbols into the emblems of the New State, following the example of Fascist Italy and especially Nazi Germany.

The Re-Symbolization of the National Anthem

The Falange's attitude towards the "Marcha granadera" questioned Franco's authority, or at least so the government thought. The fascist radicalism of the Falange, so different from the Catholic, traditionalist leanings of the other forces integrating the government, adding to its revolutionary and violent style, and its cult of the state that bordered on "paganism," deeply worried all the other members of the counter-revolutionary coalition in the government. Franco's government did not remain idle before the Falangist challenge. The government launched a strategic propaganda campaign to defend the notion that the "Marcha granadera" represented, above all, Spain, and in this way sought to reduce any hostility towards the anthem and to consolidate its position. As a result of this propaganda, the anthem stopped being called the "Marcha real" and was no longer associated with the monarchy, becoming instead a symbol of "eternal" and "natural" Spain. This move was also a way to suppress any monarchist enthusiasm that might try to restore the King after the war. The French monarchist aristocrat Auguste de Beaupoil (Count of Saint-Aulaire) still believed in 1938 that Franco aspired only to act as a regent for the duration of the hostilities, and that the restoration of the red and yellow flag and the "Marcha real" were unequivocal signs of Franco's will to restore the monarchy (Beaupoil 1938, 272–73). Nothing could be further from the truth: the dictator was concerned only with consolidating his power. The monarchic groups on Franco's side were in the minority among a coalition of forces that had little if any interest in restoring the monarchy at the end of the war.

The government enjoyed the support of the Jesuit composer and musicologist Nemesio Otaño. Most of his career as an organist and choir conductor was devoted to religious music and to implementing in Spain the reform of religious music commissioned by Pius X in 1903 (García Sánchez 2009). He was arrested and jailed after the coup and set free following the swift victory of the rebels in Guipúzcoa. Following this episode, the National Delegation of Press and Propaganda used his expertise in military music, which was another of his specialities, along with folklore. In a letter to the director of the Orfeón

Donostiarra, Juan Gorostidi, Otaño claimed that Franco had requested his services to gather support for the national anthem (Otaño 1936).[5] Few people knew the "Marcha granadera" as well as Otaño. In 1921, to mark the bringing of El Cid's remains to the Burgos Cathedral, he wrote a version of the march for choir and orchestra. Alfonso XIII, who was in attendance, commissioned him to write a study about Spanish military music. This job led him to visit numerous archives and libraries, where he amassed a large volume of musical examples that, he claimed, had been submitted to the military authorities, and that he was asked to use in order to make the "Marcha granadera" more popular. Otaño revealed to his friend, Juan Gorostidi, that the hostility of the Falange towards the "Marcha Granadera" had forced Franco "to act carefully" (1936). Gorostidi wanted the issue of the anthem to be settled "spontaneously" by the majority of the population.

Far from leaving the matter to popular "spontaneous" support, Franco wanted to control public opinion through the propaganda campaign led by Otaño from late 1936 onwards, which included radio broadcasts and press articles. According to Otaño, the strategy worked. As he told Gorostidi, the misgivings of those who opposed the march receded thanks to the dissemination of his articles highlighting its military origins, and those who had criticized its monarchical links no longer dared to express their dissent openly (Otaño 1936).

Otaño set great store by giving public talks and concerts, which he organized carefully, aiming to avoid that they be regarded as a barefaced exercise in propaganda around the national anthem. His strategy was "to take things slowly," weaving a historical account of military marches from the Middle Ages to the nineteenth century and presenting musical examples that were well received thanks to their "historical importance and singular character" (Otaño 1936). The "Marcha granadera" was an "historical landmark," the pinnacle of this account, in which the Jesuit emphasized the eighteenth-century origin and military associations of the march while side-lining its links to the Bourbon monarchy and the name "Marcha real." At an event of the Orfeón Donostiarra, Otaño claimed, without entering into deeper political considerations, that the "Marcha granadera" was historically legitimized and had a proven military and ceremonial record. He added that the recovery of the march was a homage to those who had been persecuted by the Republic and all the victims of "red" repression, because it had been forbidden by the forces of the "revolution" (Otaño 1937a).

Otaño propagated these arguments through a number of public talks in different cities under the control of Franco's troops, in which the musical examples were illustrated by choirs and orchestras. Otaño was even planning a tour of

2. The Battle for the Greatest Musical Emblem 57

Portugal and Spain (Otaño 1937b). These events not only served as acts of propaganda around the anthem, but they also openly proselytized in support of Franco. In fact, the final act in these talks was always reserved for the anthem "¡Franco!, ¡Franco!," which included elements from the "Marcha granadera" (Contreras Zubillaga, 2021). In this way, a clear association was established between the ideal of "restoring" Spain and the cult of the *Generalísimo*, which was then on the rise, using the prestige of the "Marcha granadera" to exalt his personality and reinforce his charisma. From the moment he was appointed leader of the rebels, Franco had played with the symbolic associations surrounding his figure, such as the red and yellow flag and the national anthem, to increase his popularity. He ordered that his photograph be shown in all cinemas while the anthem was played. Franco identified himself with the nation subliminally, posing as the saviour of Spain and the embodiment of its virtues. This propaganda complemented his speeches, the newspaper stories that glorified his figure, his radio broadcasts, and the documentaries made about him (Sevillano 2010, 61–64; Zenobi 2011, 256–57).

Paradoxes of the National Anthem
in Early Francoist Spain

In the wake of the Civil War, the regime's apologists continued to present the "Marcha granadera" as an historical embodiment of Spain with no attachments to the monarchy. In his early work about the meaning of national symbols, published in 1941, the pro-Franco politician Antonio María de Puelles y Puelles insisted it was a mistake to link the anthem to the Crown because the march paid homage to God and people of non-royal status long before it became associated with the monarchy (Puelles y Puelles 1941, 179). The Falange's rejection of the march continued, although their demonstrations became less loud and frequent over time. A decree passed in July 1942 ordered that the anthem's pre-eminence be respected at all times (BOE 1942). This evidence ties in with Otaño's disappointment at what he thought was the authorities' disregard for the march once hostilities had come to an end. In the preface to his *Toques de guerra del ejército español* (*War Tunes of the Spanish Army*), Otaño wrote that the "Marcha granadera" had not achieved real status as an anthem because it could not be sung, as it had no official lyrics (Otaño 1939, x). He asked the competent authorities to provide lyrics with the greatest urgency (Otaño 1940a; 1940b).

As Moreno Luzón and Núñez Seixas have pointed out, the search for lyrics for the anthem became an intermittent obsession from the early twentieth century onwards, until today, when the Spanish anthem continues to be one of the very few with no lyrics (2013, 66). Otaño had proposed a text in which God was asked to protect Spain. Of all the available lyrics, however, those by José María Pemán were the most popular by some distance. They are an adaptation of those he wrote in 1928 for General Primo de Rivera. They begin with a sonorous hail to Spain and mix the glorification of Spain's imperial past ("through the blue of the sea / the route of the sun") with Spain's resurgence, through a reference to the Falangist salute ("raise your arms, sons of Spain," instead of "raise your heads," as in the 1928 lyrics). Moreover, they expressed solidarity for the labourers responsible for the country's reconstruction ("anvils and bearings sing together"), an endeavor presided over by God ("new anthems of faith"). The lyrics, therefore, combined classic topoi in Spanish nationalist discourse, such as the imperial past and colonialism in America, with the call for a new beginning, which was characteristic of the rhetoric of contemporary fascist regimes. The changes introduced by Pemán in his lyrics—and the aforementioned order mandating the fascist salute while listening to the national anthem (BOE 1937b)—were evidence that the government's counter-revolutionary coalition underwent a process of increased Fascist influence under the sway of the Falange. The latter, for its part, softened its radicalism and opened itself somewhat to the influence of Catholicism, a move which was critical for it to survive in the government.

According to the textbooks, generations of Spaniards raised under Francoism had to sing the anthem with Pemán's lyrics at school. Learning the anthem was part of the subject "Formation of the National Spirit," which was in force until the enactment of the General Education Act in August 1970. The fact that these lyrics were never officially imposed by law or decree, however, raises some doubts about the obligation to sing and to learn them. Once all power was unified around the figure of the dictator, Franco and his supporters ceased to use the anthem to gain followers for the regime. This role was left to "Cara al sol" until the final days of the regime and even beyond it. The long-lasting Franco dictatorship drew its legitimacy from the use of a set of symbols that were combined in various ways: the military, monarchist marches, the exaltation of the dictator, historical reminiscences of the Civil War, the fusion of the State's ideology with Catholicism, and Falangist paraphernalia. The national emblems that had been re-signified during the war became identified with Franco and his regime during the authorities' trips, rallies in support of the regime, popular festivities, and sports events.

Conclusions

Despite these obstacles, the "Marcha granadera" ended up representing Franco's Spain for nearly four decades. This and later debates about its adoption by the democratic regime that followed the death of Franco in 1975 have overshadowed the intricate process that led to its institutionalization. The success of a symbol that represents the Spanish nation still today makes it difficult to imagine that the anthem was at the center of an intense negotiation through which different factions tried to shape the incipient regime following the Civil War.

In this chapter, I have brought this process of institutionalization to the foreground and have examined the dynamics underlying it. The "Marcha granadera" was not spontaneously adopted by the masses that rallied behind the "national" cause but was accepted by the majority only by legal mandate. There was no voluntary and spontaneous consensus but rather a premeditated strategy to impose the "Marcha" as the national anthem. The regime's master stroke was to sever the links between the march and the Crown, presenting the "Marcha granadera" as the natural symbolic embodiment of Spain. This severance was not accidental but rather was meant to undermine the monarchists' prominent position following the coup; to identify the dictator with traditional national symbols; and to legitimize a regime that was not only not a monarchy but, in fact, replaced it symbolically in several ways.

The process that led to the imposition of the anthem during the Civil War acted as a backdrop to the political struggles that characterized the regime until the end in different ways. The central players in this struggle over the anthem were the Falangists. As one of the main factions within the movement, the Falangists sternly resisted sanctioning a symbol that they did not see as their own. Thus, the history of the national anthem expresses the heterogeneity of the National Movement and is a privileged window through which to examine the conflicts and internal dynamics of the regime.

Notes

1. A coalition of Catholic right-wing parties under the CEDA (*Confederación Española de Derechas Autónomas*).

2. The rebels reinstated the two-colored flag (red and yellow), to the detriment of the Second Republic's three-colored version (red, yellow, and purple). The purple had been added in remembrance of Castile's *Comuneros*, one of Spanish liberals' favourite myths.

3. *Amanecer en los jardines de España* by Ernesto Halffter, Columbia C 3901/3810–3. The other side of the record contains Franco's "Alocución a la Nueva España" ("Address to the New Spain").

4. The city of Pamplona, in which Carlists and the "Alfonsist" monarchists were in the majority, was the exception to this situation during the July 18 coup, when the use of the "Marcha granadera" was widespread (Box 2010, 301).

5. According to Albano García Sánchez, Otaño was obsessed about achieving public prominence. One should be wary of this claim that the dictator had been personally involved in his appointment (2015, 341).

References

Anon. 1937a. "Con extraordinaria solemnidad presentó ayer en Salamanca sus cartas credenciales al Generalísimo, y Jefe del Estado Español, su excelencia el embajador de Italia." *ABC* (Sevilla), March 2, 1937.

———. 1937b. "Respeto obligatorio al himno nacional." *ABC* (Sevilla), June 30, 1937.

———. 1937c. "Acatamiento y respeto al himno nacional." *ABC* (Sevilla), July 2, 1937.

Beaupoil, Auguste de (Count of Saint-Aulaire). 1938. *La renaissance de l'Espagne*. Paris: Librairie Plon.

Bohlman, Philip V. 2004. *The Music of European Nationalism: Cultural Identity and Modern History*. Santa Barbara, CA: ABC-Clio World Music Handbooks.

Boletín Oficial del Estado [BOE]. 1937a. no. 131, February 28, 1937: 548–49.

———. 1937b. no. 187, April 25, 1937: 1106.

———. 1942. no. 202, July 21, 1942: 5346.

Box, Zira. 2010. *España año cero: La construcción simbólica del franquismo*. Madrid: Alianza Editorial.

———. 2014. "Símbolos eternos de España: El proceso de institucionalización de la bandera y el himno en el franquismo." In *Imaginarios y representaciones de España bajo el franquismo*, edited by Stéphane Michonneau and Xosé M. Númez Seixas, 7–23. Madrid: Casa de Velázquez.

Buch, Esteban. 2002. "Les Hymnes." In *Dictionnaire critique de la République*, edited by Vincent Duclert and Christophe Prochasson, 896–902. Paris: Flammarion.

———. 2004. "Notas sobre un grito de corazón." *La Marcha. Los muchachos peronistas* 3: 12–16. Available at http://www.ameriquelatine.msh-paris.fr/spip.php?article32.

Contreras Zubillaga, Igor. 2021. "Composing for the Francoist Side in the Spanish Civil War." In *Music and the Spanish Civil War*, edited by Gemma Pérez Zalduondo and Iván Iglesias Iglesias, 59–78. Berlin: Peter Lang.

Cruz, Rafael. 2005. "Old Symbols, New Meanings: Mobilising the Rebellion in the Summer of 1936." In *The Splintering of Spain: Cultural History and the Spanish Civil War, 1936–1939*, edited by Chris Ealham and Michael Richards, 159–76. New York: Cambridge University Press.

Diario Oficial del Ministerio de la Guerra. 1931. May 1, 1931: 267.

Elgenius, Gabriella. 2011. *Symbols of Nations and Nationalism: Celebrating Nationhood*. London: Palgrave Macmillan.

Fernández de Latorre, Ricardo. 1999. *Historia de la música militar de España*. Madrid: Ministerio de Defensa.

Foxá, Agustín de. 1939. *Canción de la Falange*. Seville: Ediciones Españolas.

Gaceta de Madrid. 1931. October 22, 1931: 420.

García Sánchez, Albano. 2009. "José María Nemesio Otaño Eguino (1880–1956): Una

2. The Battle for the Greatest Musical Emblem   61

aportación a la verdadera reforma de la música religiosa en España." *Revista de Musicología* 32, no. 1: 475–89.

———. 2015. "El músico José María Nemesio Otaño Eguino (1880–1956): Perfil biográfico, pensamiento estético y análisis de su labor propagandística y gestora (summary of PhD diss.)." *Revista de Musicología* 38, no. 1: 339–46.

Jackson, Gabriel. 1965. *The Spanish Republic and the Civil War, 1931–1939.* Princeton: Princeton University Press.

Lolo, Begoña. 2000. "El Himno." In *Símbolos de España*, edited by Faustino Menéndez Pidal de Navascués et. al, 377–477. Madrid: CEPC.

Losada Málvarez, Juan Carlos. 1990. *Ideología del Ejército Franquista (1939–1959).* Madrid: Istmo.

Moradiellos, Enrique. 2000. *La España de Franco (1939–1975): Política y sociedad.* Madrid: Síntesis.

Moreno Luzón, Javier. 2018. "La banderita: Un himno popular para un nacionalismo guerrero." In *Historia mundial de España*, edited by Xosé M. Núñez Seixas, 725–31. Barcelona: Ediciones Destino.

Moreno Luzón, Javier, and Xosé M. Núñez Seixas. 2013. "Rojigualda y sin letra: Los símbolos oficiales de la nación." In *Ser Españoles: Imaginarios nacionalistas en el siglo XX*, edited by Javier Moreno Luzón and Xosé M. Núñez Seixas, 57–103. Barcelona: RBA.

———. 2017. *Los colores de la pátria: Símbolos nacionales de la España contemporánea.* Madrid: Tecnos.

Nagore, María. 2011. "Historia de un fracaso: El 'himno nacional' en la España del siglo XIX." *Arbor. Ciencia, Pensamiento y Cultura* 187, no. 751: 827–45.

Núñez Seixas, Xosé M. 2006. *¡Fuera el invasor! Nacionalismos y movilización bélica durante la guerra civil española (1936–1939).* Madrid: Marcial Pons.

Otaño, Nemesio. 1936. "Letter to Juan Gorostidi, December 12, 1936." Archivo del Orfeón Donostiarra, caja 23, correspondencia 1936.

———. 1937a. *La Voz de España*, February 2, 1937.

———. 1937b. "Letter to Juan Gorostidi, April 6, 1937." Archivo del Orfeón Donostiarra, caja 23, correspondencia 1936.

———. 1939. Prologue to *Toques de guerra del ejército español*, v–xi. Burgos, ES: Junta de Relaciones Culturales del Ministerio de Asuntos Exteriores.

———. 1940a. "El Himno Nacional español." *Ritmo*, no. 133, April: 4–8.

———. 1940b. "El Himno Nacional y la música militar." *Ritmo*, no. 138, September: 3.

Ortíz, Carmen. 1999. "The Uses of Folklore by Franco Regime." *Journal of the American Folklore* 112, no. 446: 479–96.

Puelles y Puelles, Antonio María de. 1941. *Símbolos nacionales de España.* Cádiz: Cerón y Cervantes.

Rodríguez Jiménez, José Luis. 2000. *Historia de Falange Española de las JONS.* Madrid: Alianza Editorial.

Saz, Ismael. 2003. *España contra España: Los nacionalismos franquistas.* Madrid: Marcial Pons.

Sevillano, Francisco. 2010. *Franco: "Caudillo" por la gracia de Dios, 1936–1947.* Madrid: Alianza Editorial.

Silva, Manuel Deniz. 2010. "Ernesto Halffter." In *Enciclopédia da música em Portugal no século XX*. Vol. 2. Edited by Salwa Castelo-Branco, 605–6. Lisboa: Círculo de Leitores.

Suárez-Pajares, Javier. 2016. "El himno falangista *Cara al sol*: De la composición a la ilustración." In *Music and Figurative Arts in the Twentieth Century*, edited by Roberto Illiano, 289–322. Turnhout, BE: Brepols.

Vegas Latapié, Eugenio. 1987. *Los caminos del desengaño: Memorias políticas (II), 1936–1938*. Madrid: Tebas.

Zenobi, Laura. 2011. *La construcción del mito de Franco: De Jefe de la Legión a Caudillo de España*. Madrid: Cátedra.

3

Portuguese Rural Traditions as Cultural Exports

How Modernism and Transnational Connections Shaped the New State's Folklore Politics

VERA MARQUES ALVES

The building of national cultures is an intrinsically transnational phenomenon. In this respect, the anthropologist Orvar Löfgren writes: "the construction of national identity is a task which calls for internal and external communication. In order to create a symbolic community, identity markers have to be created within the national arena in order to achieve a sense of belonging and loyalty to the national project, but this identity also has to be marketed to the outside world as a national otherness" (1989, 12). When considering the Portuguese New State's politics of national identity and, in particular, the nationalist uses of folk culture carried out by the regime's propaganda department— the Secretariat of National Propaganda (Secretariado da Propaganda Nacional, henceforth referred to as the SPN)—most authors have failed to address how these politics related not only to the ideologies of the Salazar dictatorship but also to the cultural and political dynamics taking place outside the domestic sphere. In previous work on the SPN's ethnographic campaign during the 1930s and 1940s (Alves 2013), I examined the decisive role the international arena had on the definition of the Secretariat's folkloristic initiatives, showing how they were partly the expression of a conscious project of national self-definition vis-à-vis the outside world. In fact, when António Ferro, the journalist and writer who headed the SPN between 1933 and 1949, decided to present the country to foreign audiences through representations of its rural traditions, he was adjusting Portugal's image according to a wider disillusionment with progress and a longing for the "authentic" common among European intellectuals and artists in the years between the two World Wars (Alves 2013).

In this chapter, I examine the SPN's politics surrounding folk dance and music, focusing particular attention on the creation of a dance company intended to provide ballet performances inspired by Portuguese "folk culture." I analyze the processes by which António Ferro's initiatives in this domain were influenced by the international modernist scene, more than a decade before his appointment as the Secretariat's director. As authors such as Gelbart (2007) remind us, any understanding of the creation of "national" art forms should take into account the relationship between intellectual demands for "primordial" culture in central Europe and the search for recognition by peripheral artists and communities. For example, such a process was already true at the beginning of the eighteenth century, when the Scottish elite made highland music, previously characterized as different, wild, and natural by the English, "into their own national identity and cultural export" (2007, 29). Later, under the influence of Herder, folk culture in general, and folk music in particular, became "a ticket to international recognition on a stage dominated by others" (227).

The early twentieth century and the interwar years witnessed a similar process: to be recognized on the international stage, artists at the periphery were often compelled to present themselves as Others and their art as an authentic expression of their national identities (Llano 2013). A similar process also occurred with nations. As Samuel Llano notes, "the 'peripheral' nations attract[ed] more attention through the appeal of their 'difference' or 'exoticism'" (36). While this pattern of national identity building was prominent in European urban centers such as Paris, it also circulated between peripheral countries, thus replicating itself through multiple transnational networks. In fact, the constant movement of intellectuals, artists, and ideas between countries and continents allowed such agents to learn from each other about how to aestheticize selected folk culture elements in order to imagine their national identity as an alterity. As we will see, during the 1920s, António Ferro fully participated in these cultural dynamics, connecting with artistic groups such as the Ballets Russes or with Mexican post-revolutionary appropriations of popular art. It was in this context that Ferro first began to see how rural traditions, frequently depreciated as signs of backwardness and indigence, could be transformed into symbols of an authentic, yet up-to-date and vital national identity. In this regard, the politics

3. Portuguese Rural Traditions as Cultural Exports

of folklore subsequently launched by the SPN, far from being a mere instrument of internal propaganda, was part of a major transnational response by peripheral nations and artists to the demand for displays of cultural difference and the "authentic" in countries such as France, England, and Germany.

"Songs and Dances from the Harvest Field": The Ethnographic Campaign under Salazar's New State

> For the Blue Guide, men exist only as types. In Spain, for instance, the Basque is an adventurous sailor, the Levantine a light-hearted gardener, the Catalan a clever tradesman and the Cantabrian a sentimental highlander [. . .]. The ethnic reality of Spain is thus reduced to a vast classical ballet, a nice, neat *commedia dell'arte*, whose improbable typology serve[d] to mask the real spectacle of conditions, classes, and professions. (Barthes 1991, 75)

Although addressing the tourist's imagination of Spain, the above passage from Roland Barthes's *Mythologies* bears a striking resemblance to one of the most influential programs of national identity building carried out in Portugal during the twentieth century: the Secretariat of National Propaganda (SPN), founded in the 1930s and 1940s by the New State's propaganda department. António Ferro and his team launched an ethnographic campaign with the goal of redesigning Portugal's image as that of an enchanting country, comprised of intuitive "folk artists and peasant aesthetes" (Alves 2013). The campaign included many events and publications such as folklore competitions; books on ethnographic themes; performances inspired by rural music and dance; the creation of a dance company devoted to Portuguese historical and ethnographic themes; as well as folk art exhibits in Portugal, in the 1937 Paris International Exhibition, and in the New York World Fair in 1939 (2013).

In 1940, the SPN's folkloristic activity culminated in the commemorations for the national double centenary—the foundation of the nation-state in 1140 and its independence from Spain in 1640[1]—a large-scale event through which the New State tried to enhance its prestige and legitimacy. The climax of the celebrations was the Exhibition of the Portuguese World (*Exposição do Mundo Português*) in Lisbon. This was a major cultural event in which the SPN created a designated space for the representation of rural life and traditions under the designation of a "Regional Center" (Corkill and Almeida 2009). Here, the State's propaganda office built a replica of a rural village, displaying examples of Portuguese vernacular architecture, perfectly clean house interiors, and "happy, well behaved" peasants. During the exhibition, however, these peasants did not farm the land. Rather, they produced local crafts, sang, and danced to traditional music, or simply walked around in their beautiful Sunday attire (Alves 2013, 82–89). The Regional Center propagated an image of Portugal's rural population as graceful peasants whose existence appeared mysteriously detached from economic constraints and completely alien to the social and political conflicts that characterized modernity.

This idealized representation of life in rural areas would be continuously reaffirmed by the SPN's ethnographic campaign. In 1948, for instance, while delivering a speech at the inauguration of the Museum of Folk Art—one of the SPN's achievements, following on from previous folk art exhibitions—António Ferro took this idealization even further, displaying rural material culture as if it were a dreamlike reality: "Some might be surprised by the subtle atmosphere of this museum [. . .]. The objects—blankets, yokes, carts, clays and pottery—seem to hover above the earth, as though they are floating through an imagined fantasy world" (Ferro 1948, 25). Thus, as in the Blue Guide's depiction of the Spanish inhabitants, the Portuguese people's portrait created by António Ferro and his team "serve[d] to mask the real spectacle of conditions, classes, and professions" (Barthes 1991, 75). Peasants and artisans were depicted as intuitive, spontaneous artists, never as workers. Similarly, their handicraft was not represented as material culture, produced, and consumed in a specific economic and social context, but rather as anonymous art (Alves 2013). This orientation was of special relevance to the regime, since Salazar's dictatorship was characterized by a nationalist and traditionalist ideology that promoted an organic view of social relations, rejecting any reference to socio-economic inequalities and class struggle.[2] In this way, the SPN's gentle and idyllic portrait of rural Portugal reinforced and legitimated the regime's values.

"A Well-Coordinated Ballet":
The *Bailados Portugueses Verde Gaio*

The relevance of Barthes' ballet metaphor goes further since the SPN's close collaborators were themselves particularly fond of such an analogy. Fernanda de Castro—António Ferro's wife and a writer who was closely involved in the Secretariat's folkloristic initiatives—emphasized the ethereal portrait of Portuguese peasants using ballet as a metaphor. In her memoirs, Castro regretted "progress and its inescapable consequences," nostalgically revisiting her tours around Portugal's rural north during the 1930s. As she recalls, "people's movements [along] the country roads looked like a well-coordinated ballet" (Castro 1986, 248).[3] On this matter, she also remembered the words of the French critic Émile Vuillermoz: visiting Portugal in 1935,[4] he told her how the "décor" of that

3. Portuguese Rural Traditions as Cultural Exports 67

"rural ballet," composed by lacy yokes, colorful harnesses, and placid oxen with lyre-shaped horns, would be the envy of the most demanding stage director of all times (248). It has not been verified whether the French critic's delight with the Portuguese countryside was conveyed in these terms. We do know, however, that his statements correspond to Castro and Ferro's own imaginary view of rural Portugal. In fact, in the preceding year, Vuillermoz had seen a Portuguese folklorized dance performance, organized by the SPN (in association with the House of Portugal in Paris),[5] at the Théâtre des Ambassadeurs in Paris (Santos 1999). His observations may have also been shaped by that experience.

This performance was one of several SPN events that paved the way for the creation of a Portuguese dance troupe inspired by Diaghilev's Ballets Russes, a project cherished by Ferro since the early 1920s. However, it was not until 1940 that António Ferro turned Castro's vision of a "rural ballet" into reality by forming the first Portuguese professional dance company, the Bailados Portugueses Verde Gaio (Santos 1999). Directed by Francis Graça, a Portuguese choreographer and dancer who had collaborated with Ferro in several cultural events since 1925 (Roubaud 2003), the Verde Gaio (henceforth referred to as VG) performed a set of ballets with choreographies, designs, and music evoking a Portuguese rural atmosphere. On its inauguration, the company performed *O Muro de Derrête* (*The "Derrête" Wall*), a ballet that was based on the traditions of the saloios, the peasant inhabitants of the rural areas surrounding Lisbon. In 1941, the VG performed *O Homem de Cravo na Boca* (*The Man with a Carnation in the Mouth*), a production evoking rural festivities and pilgrimages, and *A Dança da Menina Tonta* (*The Dance of the Silly Girl*), a reinvention of northeastern customs. *Imagens da Terra e do Mar* (*Images of Earth and Sea*), with a script by António Ferro, premiered in 1943, and *Nazaré* in 1948.

In 1949, when the VG performed at the Théâtre des Champs Elysées, in Paris—a few weeks before Ferro stepped down from his position as head of the SPN—critics and journalists emphasized the folkloristic character of the company's performances (Ferro 1950, 82–91). The choreographer and dance critic Dinah Maggie applauded the music, the "wonderful and variegated costumes," as well as the folk dance movements (*Combat*, June 15, 1949). The musicologist W. L. Landowski, in turn, noted how the folk aspect of the Portuguese troupe greatly "impressed the theater audience" (*Le Parisien Liberé*, June 11, 1949). In *Franc-Tireur* (June 11, 1949), L. Algazzi praised *Imagens da Terra e do Mar* as an example of the "inventiveness and sensitivity" with which Francis Graça explored Portuguese folklore, and Victoria Acheres referred to Verde Gaio as "joyful, youthful, and marvelously colorful. More than theater dance it illustrates folk life: an ingenuous set of images, but of rare variety and richness" (*Les Lettres*

Françaises, June 16, 1949). These comments reveal another crucial aspect of the company's performances: the ways in which ethnographic materials were transformed into components of highly estheticized sceneries. In harmony with Vuillermoz's vision, as narrated by Fernanda de Castro, António Ferro and his team viewed rural culture as a set of detachable elements, able to be rearranged to form an impressive picture of the nation. Already in previous SPN folk art exhibitions, objects with the most varied functions, meanings, and cultural contexts were treated as display pieces of enchantment. And, moreover, the newspaper reports of the time leave no doubt as to the atmosphere of aesthetic and emotional involvement these initiatives were meant to create (Alves 2013).

When the SPN created the Verde Gaio, this aestheticizing approach to rural material culture was raised to a new level by converting rural artifacts into décors for the ballet. In accordance with Vuillermoz's proclaimed epiphany, António Ferro himself highlighted this metamorphosis: "Portugal [. . .] is one of the richest European countries in ballet motives. All around its territory, buried or simply forgotten, we may find an infinity of themes, of exceedingly poetic quality, which may be transformed into choreography [. . .]. With the Verde Gaio, all those ingenuous and familiar objects displayed at the Regional Center came alive: the paper flowers, the filigree, the potteries, the costumes, the blankets, the festive hats, the folk instruments, harmoniums, and *adufes*,[6] even the ballerinas' hands of the embroiders" (Ferro 1950, 18). When reading this and other speeches by Ferro, it appears as if ballet was considered the medium par excellence to represent Portuguese rural culture. The result was an intensification of the idyllic depiction of peasants already present in the SPN's folk art displays and in the Portuguese World Exhibition. In Verde Gaio, Portuguese people were portrayed as little more than imaginary, stereotyped beings, with "ballerina hands" and heavenly bodies. Like the Blue Guide commented by Roland Barthes, so too the Portuguese dance company transformed the ethnographic reality into a wonderful and colorful choreography.

"A Banner to Display in Europe and the World": The Spell of the Ballets Russes and the SPN's Folkloric Representation of the Nation

By celebrating a pastoral image of the Portuguese people, from which the industrial working classes and the urban plebe were excluded, Verde Gaio's performances were in perfect harmony with the New State's ideology. The troupe's performances, in conjunction with other folkloric events, emphasized time and again the values and concepts that sustained Salazar's dictatorship: "res-

3. Portuguese Rural Traditions as Cultural Exports 69

ignation and obedience and [. . .] a society free of politics [. . .]" (Carvalho and Pinto 2018). The formation of a professional dance company, however, was not the outcome of an ethnographic campaign designed to create consensus among the masses and, thus, perpetuate the ideologies of the regime. Indeed, some commentators noticed the unprecedented character of the initiative. For example, when writing about the 1949 Verde Gaio performance at the Théâtre des Champs Élysées, the French journalist Maurice Brillant observed that it was "unbelievable that [such a company] was born within a state department" (Ferro 1950, 90). This raises two key questions: why did António Ferro create a ballet company? Why did the SNP ground its ethnographic practices in such an overwhelming aestheticism? To understand such motivations, we must take into consideration Ferro's earlier intellectual and professional path before the establishment of the New State.

In 1917, Diaghilev's dance company performed in Lisbon, where they encountered a group of Portuguese artists and intellectuals quite aware of the artistic trends coming from Europe and especially Paris (Santos 2017). Among them was António Ferro, for whom the Russian company remained a major cultural reference over the years. Since his adolescence, Ferro was integrated in Portuguese modernist circles, becoming particularly attentive to the cultural practices emerging in the international arena, which he then tried to replicate in Portugal (Rodrigues 1995). Therefore, when he became editor of the magazine *Ilustração Portuguesa* in 1921, he tried to use his position to "style up" and modernize the Portuguese nation. Moreover, for the first time he expressed his desire to create a modern ballet company like the Ballets Russes: "Portugal may have its own ballet company, like the Russians; a modern ballet of rainbow and jester colors" (O Homem que Passa 1921, 233). In line with the legacy of Diaghilev and his circle, who "found their inspiration in the designs and colors of peasant costumes, the paintings on carts and sleighs, the carvings around windows and doors, and the myths and fables of an unassuming rural culture" (Eksteins 1990, 32), Ferro argued that the creation of a Portuguese company should also make use of rural culture materials: "In our folk dances, in our regional costumes, in our traditions, we have the raw material for wonderful stylizations; we have plenty of colors to compose a great banner to put up in Europe and in the world" (O Homem que Passa 1921, 233).

Therefore, the creation of the Verde Gaio in 1940 was the materialization of a project long dreamt of by António Ferro. If we consider some of the values and motivations that undergirded the creation of the Ballets Russes, we may understand better why this was a model that appealed so much to Ferro, ultimately leading him to found a similar dance company in Portugal. Established in 1909 by Sergei Diaghilev, the Ballets Russes revolutionized the twentieth-century art world while instrumentalizing Russian national identity. Debuting in Paris, the troupe achieved almost immediate success, and, since then, has occupied a prominent place in the imagination of intellectuals and artists all over the world (Eksteins 1990; Veroli 2013; Tregulova 2009). Such a triumph was indelibly linked to the modernism of Diaghilev's artistic endeavor, the innovative choreographies of Fokine and Nijinsky, the stunning set and costume designs, and above all, the way all these components related to each other to form a new configuration of *Gesamtkunstwerk* (Tregulova 2009, 48). Equally important to the company's success was the exoticism of its oriental themes (Eksteins 1990, 25), while at the same time its productions were convincingly displayed as authentically Russian. As Patrizia Veroli stresses, for Diaghilev and his first collaborators, Russian identity was a "myth to export" (Veroli 2013, 475). Correspondingly, the Ballets Russes were received as the true manifestation of a "primitive" Russian culture through which materialist European civilization could be redeemed (2013, 475), a point of view held by Diaghilev (Eksteins 1990, 32). In the first decades of the twentieth century, therefore, the outstanding performances of the Ballets Russes were seen in Europe as tangible proof of a unique and impressive Russian culture that was unknown to the West.

Diaghilev's dance company demonstrated how a peripheral country's image could be transformed by promoting a sophisticated cultural product which, at the same time, was clearly connected to that country's traditions, thus serving as a powerful identity marker. Ferro was clearly avid to replicate the Russian example, and he took advantage of leading the SPN to achieve this goal. However, Portugal was far from being the only country where the local modernist scene fell under the spell of the acclaimed Russian company, seeing in it a model for how to promote national identity. As Michelle Clayton states in an analysis of the impact of the Ballets Russes among South American intellectuals and artists, the Russian dance troupe "signified not only the latest modernity—seen in their explosive effect on fashion and décor—but also a modernity which harnessed and transformed the national past, transmuting Russian primitivism into the up-to-date" (2014, 37).

It is against this backdrop that we may understand Ferro's statement, published in the above-mentioned issue of *Ilustração Portuguesa*: "Portugal, my friend, will be a *Ballet Russe* [sic], or it will be nothing!" (O Homem que Passa 1921, 234). Twenty years later, still with this idea in mind, Ferro would create the dance company he conceived as a fundamental and necessary testimony of a unique, yet modern, Portuguese identity. Meanwhile, as a writer and international reporter during the 1920s, António Ferro became acquainted with

3. *Portuguese Rural Traditions as Cultural Exports*   71

other examples of the reshaping of a nation's image through the appropriation of elements of rural culture by modernist artists. In 1922, for instance, Ferro was quite impressed with the Mexican Pavilion at the Rio de Janeiro Independence Centenary International Exposition, which combined decorations of the modernist painter Roberto Montenegro with an exhibition of Mexican folk art. Several years later, referring to this event, the Portuguese journalist would stress how the "Azteca pavilion, boldly decorated by Montenegro" had been able to harmoniously contemplate both the past and the present of the country, thus completely transforming Mexico's image (Ferro 1929). In fact, the aim of Mexican participation in the Exposition was to present Mexico as a nation that had finally surpassed its endemic state of civil war and returned to a path of progress (Barbosa 2018). Popular art objects, promoted by several Mexican modernist artists, occupied a prominent place in the "Azteca Pavillion," achieving a great success among its visitors (Tenorio-Trillo 1996, 215). These rustic objects were not exhibited to compose a retrograde picture of Mexican identity. On the contrary, their appearance was an audacious novelty, promoting the image of a modern nation with a vital and exciting culture. The display of artifacts was a sequel to the Exposição de Arte Popular organized the year before in the City of Mexico, by Roberto Montenegro, Gerardo Murillo (known as Doctor Atl), and Jorge Enciso, which celebrated rural Indian crafts for the first time as an artistic expression of "authentic" Mexico (López 2010).

Mexican participation in the Brazilian exposition thus offered Ferro one more example of how folk culture could be used to present a modern version of a national identity in the international arena. With this example in mind, Ferro would later advocate that Portugal, a country with a rudimentary industry and incipient scientific and economic development, could greatly benefit from the display of its "folk art" at international exhibitions in order to create a unique image of the nation: "If we cannot bring machines, nor automobiles, nor planes, if we cannot stage our exhibitions with [. . .] train models and liners [. . .]—why not make a parade of regional arts and crafts, rugs, furniture, ceramics—everything that gives us character, all those poor little things which, after all, are the wealth of a nation's soul" (Ferro 1929).

Although Ferro did not mention Diaghilev's company in this statement, it is still the influence of the Ballets Russes that reverberates in his proposal. The interest of Mexican modernists in their country's folk art was, after all, deeply connected with their experiences of Parisian artistic circles during the second decade of the century and, particularly, with their contact with the Russian troupe. In 1917, Montenegro would even produce ten drawings of Nijinsky in black and white, highlighted in gold, and offer them to the British dance historian Cyril

Beaumont. As Rodrigo Gutiérrez Viñuales reveals, the primitivistic sensibility that emerged in the European modernist scene was integral to the interest and appreciation that Roberto Montenegro, Doctor Atl, and others displayed for their native folk arts once they returned to Mexico (2003, 100, 120).

Influenced by the work of Russian and Mexican modernists, Ferro also used ethnographic materials to give international visibility to Portugal. In fact, when examining the SPN's folkloristic initiatives during the 1930s and 1940s, it is clear that Ferro continued to pursue his proposal that Portugal should have a dance troupe inspired by the Ballets Russes, and which he conceived of as a "banner of Portugal to raise in Europe and the world" (O Homem que Passa 1921, 233). As I have shown elsewhere (Alves 2013), since its very inception the Secretariat placed great importance on activities beyond Portugal's borders, making a significant effort to disseminate abroad different displays of Portuguese ethnography. Therefore, the first Portuguese folk art exhibition organized by the SPN in 1935 was shown in Geneva during the Portuguese Fortnight taking place at the seat of the then League of Nations.[7] Subsequently, Portuguese "folk art" was exhibited in Lisbon (1936), Paris (1937), and New York (1939). World War II and its aftermath provoked a long hiatus in the pursuit of Ferro's program, but he still organized "folk art" exhibits in Spain, in 1943 and 1944, in Madrid and Seville respectively.

As with the "folk art" exhibits, Verde Gaio, formed in 1940, was not able to travel abroad for a long period, again except for Spain: in 1943, the Verde Gaio performed in Barcelona and Madrid. It was not until the end of the decade that the company travelled further abroad: in 1949, as mentioned, the VG finally performed in Paris. However, if we look back to the 1930s, we find that the SPN had already organized small-scale Portuguese folk dance and music performances abroad, in anticipation of the VG's future performances. As noted above, in 1934, António Ferro delivered a lecture at the Théâtre des Ambassadeurs, in Paris, which was accompanied by a performance by Francis and Ruth Walden, the VG's future lead dancers. Entitled *Portuguese Rhapsody*, the talk consisted of a poetic evocation of the different Portuguese metropolitan provinces and its folk traditions and was illustrated by artistic recreations of Portuguese regional dances. In 1935, the event was replicated in the Portuguese Fortnight at Geneva (Alves 2013; Santos 1999). Two years later, following the success of the folk-art exhibit at the Portuguese pavilion of the Paris International Exposition, Ferro restated his ambition to create, "like in the old Russia, a great company of national ballet," in order to show abroad some reflections of what the SPN director called "our rustic poetry" (Ferro 1937). In light of this chain of events, it is clear that the creation of the VG was the result of the profound and lasting

3. Portuguese Rural Traditions as Cultural Exports

impact of the Ballets Russes on António Ferro's own view about the possibilities of redesigning and affirming Portugal's image abroad, within a domestic ideological and political context that was particularly favorable to the development of such a program. It is also this complex set of circumstances that explains the Secretariat's ambivalence toward regional folksong and dance groups, as I will now show.

"Disinfecting Portuguese Folklore": The Folk Dance Groups and the SPN's Politics and Aesthetics of Authenticity

The formation of the Verde Gaio had another side to it: the SPN's generic disregard for regional folk dance groups. Contrary to the widespread idea that the SPN advocated for the widespread formation of such groups, only in 1947—fourteen years after the creation of the New State propaganda department—did António Ferro develop a program to accommodate them (Alves 2003; 2013). Moreover, this decision coincides with the moment when the VG was experiencing setbacks: according to the historian Pavão dos Santos (1999, 70), following the 1943 performances in Madrid and Barcelona, the Portuguese company seemed to have run out of steam. A cycle of crises resulted in Francis Graça abandoning the company in 1946 (although he returned in 1949). The following year, the SPN hired the Italian choreographer Guglielmo Morresi, who, in turn, was replaced by the Swedish Ivo Crámer in 1948. Both of them departed from the VG's original configuration, creating a new repertoire with no connection to Portuguese rural traditions (Santos 1999, 69–71). Thus, between 1946 and 1949, the SPN's troupe became less suitable to serve the role that motivated its formation, namely, to affirm Portuguese identity abroad. It seems to me that this situation finally encouraged a skeptical António Ferro to organize a series of competitions in 1947, with the purpose of selecting folk music and dance groups that could represent Portuguese traditions to a sophisticated national and foreign audience (Alves 2003; 2013). Therefore, why did the SPN disdain regional folk music and dance groups? Why did António Ferro not integrate these groups in the Secretariat's "folklore politics"? To answer these questions, we must return to a consideration of the influence of avant-garde aesthetics on Ferro.

In Portugal, the first folksong and dance groups were formed at the end of the nineteenth century (Castelo-Branco and Branco 2003). Therefore, when the New State was established, this kind of formation was already known to bourgeois audiences, a formation that offered a colorful and benign version of traditional rural dances and traditions. Some of the regime's political organizations co-opted these groups and incentivized the creation of new ones, presenting them at official events (Sardo 2009). The SPN, on the contrary, was always very skeptical about these groups. In fact, in an article in the *Diário de Notícias* from 1937, where Ferro passionately defended the creation of "a great national ballet company," he vigorously criticized extant folk dance groups and contested their proliferation throughout the country. According to the SPN's director, such folksong and dance formations were rapidly growing under the harmful influence of the urban vaudeville theater (*Teatro de revista*), adopting their "fake" versions of traditional costumes, dances, and songs. In this regard, he did not hesitate to call for the disciplining and "disinfection" of Portuguese "folklore":

> Let us study, without further delay, the means of organizing and disciplining this stream [. . .]. Let us ensure that none of these so-called regional groups [. . .] may take form in a definitive way, or display themselves, without special authorization of any department in charge of selecting them. [. . .] If this is done, we will be able not only to disinfect Portuguese folklore, but also to increase the vast richness of [. . .] our folk life." (Ferro 1937)

Following this line of reasoning, the SPN frequently tried to prevent the participation of folklore groups in festivals abroad and discouraged the formation of new groups (Alves 2003). Grounded on the alleged "fake" character of regional groups, this politics of rejection was, however, never dissociated from aesthetic criteria (Alves 2003). For the Secretariat, popular manifestations that were not consistent with the elite's sense of artistic beauty were classified as spurious traditions, incapable of representing the true essence of Portuguese "folk culture." This is quite evident in a 1944 missive written by Francisco Lage, the Secretariat's official in charge of ethnographic matters:

> There are very few, not to say rare, regional groups that deserve this Secretariat's trust in order to perform anywhere, much less to represent Portugal outside the national borders. Most of them, due to the costumes they wear and to the dances and songs they exhibit, are nothing more than distasteful inventions [. . .] completely influenced by Lisbon's popular theaters. (Alves 2003)

Over the years, the SPN replicated, time and again, the same ideas about regional folk groups in Portugal, denouncing their alleged inauthenticity and lack of "good taste." This leads us to a discussion of the Secretariat's approach to folk culture in general, and to the folk dance groups in particular, namely its overwhelming aestheticism. To shed some light on this, we must return to the impact that the modernist perspective of the Ballets Russes had on António Ferro's action.

3. Portuguese Rural Traditions as Cultural Exports 75

According to Modris Eksteins, one of the fundamental features of Diaghilev's intervention was an "aesthetic imperialism that [. . .] craved everything" related to a wider intellectual and cultural trend in which art was placed above everything else (1990, 33). This pronounced aestheticism was visible in the ways in which the Ballets Russes transformed folk traditions into audacious forms of dance art. In fact, every little detail in the troupe's performance was submitted to a highly aestheticized approach. As Patrizia Veroli emphasizes, Diaghilev's team controlled the artistic quality of all aspects of the company's performances—such as publicity, editions, and decoration of host theaters—in order to appeal to the company's target audience, an elegant and refined elite (2013, 476). These practices of exclusion and distinction were understandable in light of the thin line then separating manifestations of high culture from mass culture and of the resulting anxiety felt by patrons of "artistic dance" (476).

António Ferro shared the modernists' orientation. Since his early public activities, he conceived art as a transfiguring element of life itself. In a 1917 lecture, for instance, Ferro praised silent movies above all as a "school of good taste" that greatly improved viewers' aesthetic sense by teaching them "how to wear a tie" and how to "arrange a *bibelot*" (Rodrigues 1995, 23–24). Also in accordance with these ideas, he led daring cultural projects such as *Teatro Novo* (New Theater), a company created in 1925 and based at the Foyer of the Tivoli Palace, in Lisbon. It was in the New Theater that Francis Graça first collaborated with the SPN's future director (Roubaud 2003). The company staged Jules Romains and Pirandello, but this was ill received by critics and lasted for only a month. Despite such a short-lived existence, the New Theater exemplifies how, in Ferro's projects, the politics of culture was always associated with aspirations to aesthetic and cultural refinement. The project included the theater room, a specialized library comprising documentation about contemporary theater, and a bar. A journalist at the time portrayed the interior decorations created by the modernist José Pacheko, as follows: "The Theater's décor is of an exuberant polychromy which even reaches the doormen, all dressed in red and gold [. . .]. The locker room is a poster shaped by red teeth and a counter also in red. We even feel bad for wearing black" (Rodrigues 1995, 113).

This enfolding aestheticism explains why António Ferro thought that the Portuguese nation should affirm itself through art. For the SPN's director, it would not be enough for a country to project its distinctive old "folk traditions" as a way of asserting the exclusivity of its culture. If art was above everything else, the country's prestige depended as well upon the demonstration of national "high artistic" production. This was true when Ferro first conceived the formation of a Portuguese dance company, in 1921, and would continue to guide his action as the SPN's director, namely regarding its folkloristic initiatives and the creation of the Verde Gaio. A 1946 Secretariat brochure promoting the VG stresses this conception quite clearly:

> Despite its freshness, originality or tradition, folk art, be it music, movement or even plastic performances, is not enough to achieve the quintessential quality of Art [...]. It is necessary that a superior spirit grasps the music, the choreography, the poetry of the people, and finds their fullness in order to allow them to overcome the hard and tall barriers of the simple ethnographic curiosity or archeological remnant [...]." (SNI 1946, 83–84)

It is in this sense that, for António Ferro, the Verde Gaio was the medium *par excellence* to present Portuguese folk culture. It was through the ballet and its music that folk materials could be exhibited as a reflection of the national essence and, at the same time, be transformed into sophisticated artistic items for consumption, effectively separated from popular cultural manifestations. On account of their proximity to commercialized and urban mass cultural practices, the regional groups of folk dance, on the contrary, lacked cultural prestige, thus threatening the SPN's plan. The mere existence of folk dance formations was seen as a threat to the company's reputation. In a 1940 speech, Ferro expressed this fear, saying he was conscious that the name Verde Gaio—the designation of a traditional rural dance—could promote the idea that the company was a kind of regional dance group, thus disqualifying it. Nine years later, when the company performed in Paris, he made a point to stress again the distinction between Verde Gaio and popular folk dance formations: "Verde Gaio is not a poor little folk group, but [...] an authentic ballet" (Ferro 1950, 57).

Celebrating the Folk without the Folk

By presenting the Verde Gaio as the prime vehicle to present "authentic" Portuguese folk culture, while simultaneously contesting regional dance groups as tasteless distortions of peasant traditions, the SPN also avoided incorporating the "folk" themselves in the Secretariat's events. In fact, despite praising the alleged beauty and harmony of the rural way of life—the "well-coordinated ballet" evoked by Fernanda de Castro—Ferro and his collaborators were quite disturbed by what they perceived as the harshness of folk manners and habits. As the archive shows, the participants in live demonstrations of folk culture organized by the Secretariat did not always behave according to a middle-class sensibility. In 1942, for instance, the SPN arranged in Lisbon a small exhibition of embroideries from the central eastern city of Castelo Branco, staging

3. Portuguese Rural Traditions as Cultural Exports

five women embroiderers from the region for public view. Three of them were dressed as village farmers and the other two as a noble ancient maiden and her servant, thus composing an idyllic picture of the rural way of life. However, the scenery masked the real social conditions of the embroiderers, who were poor working girls employed as apprentices at the Castelo Branco Embroideries School, where they made handicraft articles for the urban middle classes (Alves 2013, 147–50). The SPN's fantasy was not fully attained, as the craftswomen's conduct in the exhibition room did not meet the rules of good behavior expected by urban elite visitors. This we know through a letter Francisco Lage wrote to a Castelo Branco collaborator, complaining about their "bad manners" during the event (Alves 2013, 150).

I am unaware of any further documentation on similar situations regarding the presence of folk dance groups in the SPN's events. Nonetheless, in the 1950s, an exchange in correspondence between Francisco Lage and two Portuguese state agents abroad clearly reveals that the attitudes, behaviors, and appearance of dance group members were quite upsetting to the middle class and elite circles. In 1956 the representative of the Portuguese House in London sent the Secretariat a letter describing the "deplorable condition" of a Portuguese folk dance group (the *Rancho do Douro Litoral*) that had participated in a folklore festival and which he saw waiting for the train at Paddington station. According to his depiction, "the men had several days of beard, tangled hair, and wore dirty and patched blue overalls [. . .], and the girls also had a filthy look, with a kind of peroxide hair and badly dressed [. . .]. Seated on the platform's floor, surrounded by old large bottles of red wine and dirty, tasteless packages, the group's members offered a truly shameful display" (Alves 2013, 143). Shortly after, in response to the Portuguese consul in Dublin, who wanted the same northern *rancho* to participate in a festival organized by the Irish Folk Dance and Song Society, Francisco Lage stated that the group had to be overseen and disciplined by a responsible person, also adding that "people may dress modestly, but should take care of themselves in order to show they have civilized habits instead of behaving as if they were on their way to some village festivity" (143).

This paradox was far from exclusive to the SPN's ethnographic campaign. In fact, António Ferro's intervention relied on two centuries of nationalist uses of folk culture that were also intrinsically contradictory. In an essay from the late 1980s, Alan Dundes alluded to "feelings of ambivalence towards the folk and folklore" among intellectuals and scholars since the end of the eighteenth century: "On the one hand, the folk are all too common, the *vulgus in populo*. In Hume's words, the folk is rude. The folk is a backward, illiterate segment of the population of which elitist intellectuals are ashamed. On the other hand, the

78 VERA MARQUES ALVES

folk represents the glorified, romanticized remnants of a national patrimony which is something for zealous intellectuals to celebrate [. . .]. Intellectuals were both embarrassed by and proud of their folk and folklore" (1989, 48).

Given this paradox, Dundes argues that folklorists frequently embellished, modified, and suppressed elements of the traditions they collected and presented: at issue was the need to "elevate" the image of the nation supposedly represented by its folk culture. At the beginning of the nineteenth century, for instance, the Grimm brothers rewrote the tales they collected, changing their form and content in order to transform them into a German national treasure (Dundes 1989, 44–45). Dundes does not address examples of reinvention of folksongs and folk dances or other forms of folk life demonstrations, but, as expected, these were also the focus of recurrent nationalistic transfigurations, raising particular problems for the national elites interested in their celebration. Contrary to what happened in published tale collections or in folk art exhibitions, in live demonstrations the folk were themselves part of the ultimate display, hence rendering more visible the elite's ambiguities towards the folk and folk culture. Therefore, while the regional dance folk groups generated feelings of discomfort and anxiety, the Verde Gaio offered SPN the possibility to create a perfectly controlled image of the nation through the aesthetic manipulation of its ethnographic materials.

Notes

1. Between 1580 and 1640, Portugal was united with Spain, under the Spanish crown.

2. On the ideological orientation of Salazar and the Estado Novo, see for example Rosas (1996a and 1996b).

3. This and all following translations are by the author.

4. In 1935, the SPN invited several foreign intellectuals—major writers and journalists—to visit Portugal, in order to show them selected staged sceneries of Portugal, hoping that later they would publish laudatory stories about the country and the New State. Among the prestigious guests, besides Vuillermoz, were French authors Jules Romain, Fernand Gregh, François Mauriac, George Duhamel, the Spanish essayist and novelist Miguel Unamuno, Maurice Maeterlinck (winner of the Nobel Prize for Literature in 1911), and the Chilean poet Gabriela Mistral. For more about this intellectual trip, see Medina (1977) and Alves (2013, 43–46).

5. The House of Portugal in Paris was created in 1931 with the purpose of promoting the country abroad.

6. *Adufe* is a square frame drum, often adorned with colored ribbons, played in the Beira Baixa region of central eastern Portugal.

7. In September 1935, the Portuguese government organized a cultural fortnight at the League of Nations' capital, aimed at international political, diplomatic, and intellectual circles in Geneva. Besides the Portuguese folk art exhibition, the fortnight included several conferences and lectures.

References

Alves, Vera Marques. 2003. "O SNI e os ranchos folclóricos." In *Vozes do povo. A folclorização em Portugal*, edited by Salwa El-Shawan Castelo-Branco and Jorge Freitas Branco, 190–206. Oeiras, PT: Celta Editora.

———. 2013. *Arte popular e nação no Estado Novo: A política folclorista do Secretariado da Propaganda Nacional*. Lisboa: Imprensa de Ciências Sociais.

Barbosa, Carlos Alberto Sampaio. 2018. "Cornucópia visual mexicana: As fotografias do livro México seus recursos naturais, sua situação atual, 1922." *Estudos Ibero-Americanos* 44, no.1: 93–104. https://doi.org/10.15448/1980-864X.2018.1.27695.

Barthes, Roland. 1991. *Mythologies*. New York: Noonday Press, Farrar, Strauss, and Giroux.

Carvalho, Rita Almeida de, and António da Costa Pinto. 2018. "The 'Everyman' of the Portuguese New State during the Fascist Era." In *The "New Man" in Radical Right Ideology, 1919–45*, edited by Jorge Dagnino, Matthew Feldman, and Paul Stocker, 131–48. London: Bloomsbury.

Castelo-Branco, Salwa El-Shawan, and Jorge Freitas Branco. 2003. "Folclorização em Portugal: Uma perspectiva." In *Vozes do povo. A folclorização em Portugal*, edited by Salwa El-Shawan Castelo-Branco and Jorge Freitas Branco, 1–21. Oeiras, PT: Celta Editora.

Castro, Fernanda de. 1986. *Ao fim da memória: Memórias (1906–1939)*. Lisboa: Editorial Verbo.

Clayton, Michelle. 2014. "Modernism's Moving Bodies." *Modernist Cultures* 9, no. 1: 27–45.

Combat, June 15, 1949.

Corkill, David, and José Carlos Pina Almeida. 2009. "Commemoration and Propaganda in Salazar's Portugal: The Mundo Português Exposition of 1940." *Journal of Contemporary History* 44, no. 3: 381–99.

Dundes, Alan. 1989. *Folklore Matters*. Knoxville: The University of Tennessee Press.

Eksteins, Modris. 1990. *Rites of Spring: The Great War and the Birth of the Modern Age*. New York: Anchor Books.

Ferro, António. 1929. "Portugal em Barcelona." *Diário de Notícias*, June 4, 1929.

———. 1937. "Defendamos o nosso folclore!" *Diário de Notícias*, November 8, 1937.

———. 1948. *Museu de Arte Popular*. Lisboa: SNI.

———. 1950. *Bailados Portugueses "Verde Gaio" (1940–1950)*. Lisboa: SNI.

Franc-Tireur, June 11, 1949.

Gelbart, Matthew. 2007. *The Invention of "Folk Music" and "Art Music": Emerging Categories from Ossian to Wagner*. Cambridge: Cambridge University Press.

Homem que passa. 1921. "A Ilustração Portuguesa entrevista a Ilustração Portuguesa." *Ilustração Portuguesa*, October 8, 1921: 232–34

Le Parisien Liberé, June 11, 1949.

Les Lettres Françaises, June 16, 1949.

Llano, Samuel. 2013. *Whose Spain? Negotiating "Spanish Music" in Paris, 1908–1929*. Oxford: Oxford University Press.

Löfgren, Orvar. 1989. "The Nationalization of Culture." *Ethnologia Europaea*, 19: 5–24.

Lopéz, Rick A. 2010. *Crafting Mexico: Intellectuals, Artisans, and the State after the Revolution*. Durham, NC: Duke University Press.

Medina, João. 1977. *Salazar em França*. Lisboa: Ática.

Rodrigues, António. 1995. *António Ferro na Idade do Jazz-Band*. Lisboa: Livros Horizonte.

Rosas, Fernando. 1996a. "Salazar, António de Oliveira." In *Dicionário de história do Estado Novo*. Vol. 2. Edited by Fernando Rosas and J. M. Brandão de Brito, 861–76. Lisboa: Círculo de Leitores.

———. 1996b. "Constituição política de 1933." In *Dicionário de história do Estado Novo*. Vol. 1. Edited by Fernando Rosas and J. M. Brandão de Brito, 198–205. Lisboa: Círculo de Leitores.

Roubaud, Maria Luísa. 2003. "O Verde Gaio: Uma política do corpo no Estado Novo." In *Vozes do Povo: A folclorização em Portugal*, edited by Salwa El-Shawan Castelo-Branco and Jorge Freitas Branco, 337–53. Oeiras, PT: Celta Editora.

Santos, Mariana Pinto dos. 2017. "A Way of Being Modern." In *José de Almada Negreiros: A Way of Being Modern*, edited by Mariana Pinto dos Santos, 9–22. Lisbon: Fundação Calouste Gulbenkian.

Santos, Vítor Pavão dos. 1999. *Verde Gaio: Uma companhia portuguesa de bailado (1940–1950)*. Lisboa: Museu Nacional do Teatro.

Sardo, Susana. 2009. "Música Popular e diferenças regionais." In *Multiculturalidade: Raízes e estruturas*, 408–76. Lisboa: Universidade Católica Portuguesa.

SNI. 1946. *A cultura portuguesa e o estado*. Lisboa: Edições SNI.

Tenorio-Trillo, Mauricio. 1996. *Mexico at the World's Fairs: Crafting a Modern Nation*. Berkeley: University of California Press.

Tregulova, Zelfira. 2009. "The Diaghilev Project." In *A Feast of Wonders: Sergei Diaghilev and the Ballets Russes*, edited by John E. Bowlt, Zelfira Tregulova, and Nathalie Rosticher Giordano, 45–49. Milan: Skira Editore.

Veroli, Patrizia. 2013. "Le Mythe des Ballets Russes." In *I Ballets Russes di Diaghilev tra storia e mito*, edited by P. Veroli and G. Vinay, 473–86. Roma: Accademia Nazionale di Santa Cecilia.

Viñuales, Rodrigo Gutiérrez. 2003. "Roberto Montenegro y los artistas americanos en Mallorca (1914–1919)." *Anales del Instituto de Investigaciones Estéticas* 82: 93–121.

PART II

Sound Technologies and the Nation

4

Recording *zarzuela grande* in Spain in the Early Days of the Phonograph and Gramophone

EVA MOREDA RODRÍGUEZ

The first recordings ever made in Spain—from the arrival of commercial phonography in the mid-1890s to the invention of electrical recording in 1925—have received increased attention over the last twenty years, particularly at the hands of collectors and enthusiasts[1] and archives that have digitized part of their holdings.[2] While these initiatives have made invaluable contributions in terms of uncovering, cataloging, and dating recordings and providing some contextualization, critical approaches to this wealth of material that contextualize it within the growing body of research on early recording technologies are scant.[3] This chapter outlines one such critical approach by focusing on recordings of *zarzuela grande*. Even though *zarzuela grande* was by no means the most recorded genre (as I will explain later), its recordings offer important insights into how early recordings were integrated. The recordings likewise reveal, to an extent, the ways in which they influenced existing debates around music and national identity and around technology and national regeneration, the latter, in particular, integrated within broader discourses circulating transnationally. I say "to an extent" because we must bear in mind that the privilege of owning a phonograph was accessible only to the middle and upper classes at first.[4] At the same time, the international reach of some of these recordings allows us to gain more nuanced insights into how the early recording industry allowed repertoires, even vernacular ones,

84   EVA MOREDA RODRÍGUEZ

to circulate beyond their place of origin, remaking our "musical ear" (Denning 2015, 5–6). In fact, even though Denning aptly demonstrates that such changes only materialized on a large scale after the invention of electrical recording in 1924, examples like *zarzuela grande* suggest that some repertoires relied on circulation networks and understandings of recordings that were already in place from the very early years of the industry.

In this chapter, I first offer an overview of *zarzuela grande* before the invention of phonography, exploring the tensions between the *zarzuuela grande*, Spanish opera, and *género chico* in relation to debates around Spanish musical nationalism in the second half of the nineteenth century. I also briefly contextualize the two *zarzuelas* I focus on, namely, Emilio Arrieta's *Marina* and Ruperto Chapí's *La tempestad*. Finally, I analyze two bodies of recordings: those made by *gabinetes fonográficos* (phonographic offices) on wax cylinder format between 1896 and 1905 and those made in Spain on disc by Gramophone from 1899 onwards. My aim is not just to document who recorded *zarzuela grande* and when but also to discuss how recording and distribution decisions were partly informed by national identity concerns on two fronts: perceptions of what constituted national music and discourses that connected technology (including recording technologies) to national regeneration.

Zarzuela grande Before Recording Technologies

Modern *zarzuela* developed from the 1840s and soon adopted the standard, three-act format that would then be known as *zarzuela grande,* with spoken dialogue instead of operatic recitative.[5] Although the genre soon became popular among bourgeois urban audiences, from its beginnings it existed in a complicated relationship with opera, and this, as I will argue subsequently, impacted on the different practices followed by the *gabinetes* in the recording of both genres. Like their counterparts from around Europe, many Spanish composers of the nineteenth century aspired to found and develop a tradition of national opera. Seen as the highest, most prestigious form of musical theater, and also the most exportable one, national opera should speak to universal audiences while still portraying national identity in an "authentic" way (Young 2013, 117–18). Nevertheless, even though several operas were indeed composed and premiered in Spain at this time, the national opera project failed to materialize. Institutional support was scarce and Madrid's Teatro Real, which could have been the obvious stalwart, left most programming decisions in the hands of its Italian singers and companies. Because these decisions rarely favored Spanish operas

4. *Recording* zarzuela grande *in Spain*   85

and, when they did, they typically gave these limited rehearsal time, a repertoire of Spanish opera never consolidated (Young 2013, 121–23).

Most composers of Spanish operas at this time also wrote *zarzuela grande* and did not see the genres as incompatible. Some, like Antonio Peña y Goñi, envisaged a dual tradition of serious and comic opera as it existed in other European countries (particularly in France), with *zarzuela grande* occupying the latter space. The serious alternative, however, failed to develop, and some took to blaming the more commercially successful *zarzuela*, since composers devoted most of their efforts to this genre rather than to opera in order to pursue financial gains (Young 2013, 136). Italian opera—then the most successful form of musical theater in Spain—was seen as a threat to both Spanish opera and *zarzuela*, with critics claiming that the Italians teaching at the Real Conservatorio de Madrid and privately did not teach Spanish singers to sing in Spanish (Cotarelo y Mori 2001, 538–9; Peña y Goñi 2003, 103). It must be noted, though, that not even the most enthusiastic supporters of Spanish opera and *zarzuela grande* advocated for a completely indigenous style, with no foreign influences whatsoever: composer Francisco Asenjo Barbieri imported several innovations from French *opéra comique* and advised young composers to study Italian *bel canto* to learn how to write for the voice;[6] and Peña y Goñi did not necessarily disapprove of Spanish composers following Italian models, but criticized that composers did not add anything original and "national" to these (2003, 279). Similarly, while many *zarzuelas grandes* were set in recognizably Spanish locales, others were not. Therefore, while musical style or plot played a role in determining whether specific *zarzuelas* or the genre as a whole were sufficiently national, these were not the only factors. Generally speaking, the popularity of *zarzuela grande* with audiences was seen as a sign that Spaniards—or at least some of them—saw themselves reflected in the genre.

In the 1880s, the situation was complicated with the development of the *género chico*. Plays were shortened to one hour, and as a result theaters could program four different plays in one evening, maximizing profits and attracting audiences from a range of social classes. To adapt to this fast-paced industry, the new genre drew heavily on traditional and popular music rather than Italianate operatic writing. It typically featured lighter, contemporary subjects, and relied heavily on standardization.[7] Beyond the theater houses, *género chico* was alive in the streets, with organ grinders and street singers performing numbers from recent successful plays (Deleito y Piñuela 1949, 14; Llano 2018, 20). At the same time, Italian opera maintained its popularity (and prestige) with bourgeois audiences, but *zarzuela grande* started to decline (Mejías García 2014, 24). By the time commercial recordings were introduced in Spain, new *zarzuelas grandes* were regularly still being written and premiered, but much of the performance activity centered around tried-and-tested works, including the two this chapter focuses on: Emilio Arrieta's *Marina* and Ruperto Chapí's *La tempestad*.

Emilio Arrieta's *Marina*, set to a libretto by Miguel Ramos Carrión, exemplifies some of the tensions between Spanish opera and *zarzuela grande*. It first premiered in 1855 and, although not hugely successful initially, it then became more consolidated within the *zarzuela grande* repertoire thanks to frequent performances in the provinces (Encina Cortizo 1998, 226). In 1871, at the suggestion of tenor Enrico Tamberlick, Arrieta turned it into an opera, setting the spoken dialogues to recitative, writing additional numbers to transform the original two acts into three, and expanding the orchestration (423). *Marina* was premiered at the Teatro Real to considerable success and even made the theater slightly more receptive to Spanish operas (Young 2013, 120–21). However, Arrieta's strategy to transform his own *zarzuela* into an opera was never seriously considered as a viable option that other composers could follow to build a school of national opera, probably because institutional and audience support for the latter was weak anyway (Young 2013, 136–37).[8]

La tempestad was premiered in 1882, and its composer, Ruperto Chapí, was similarly affected by the tensions between opera and *zarzuela*. During his composition studies in Rome in from 1873 to 1878, he dedicated most of his efforts to writing operas, of which *Roger de Flor* (1878) was performed at the Teatro Real. Back in Spain, Chapí defected to *zarzuela grande*, with *La tempestad*, *La bruja* (1887), and *El rey que rabió* (1891) quickly establishing his reputation in the genre. From the early 1890s, he moved into the more lucrative *género chico*, and, whereas his *zarzuela grande Curro Vargas* (1898) was well received, it still could not compete in popularity or financial success with *El tambor de granaderos* (1894) and, especially, *La revoltosa* (1897).

Both *Marina* and *La tempestad* remained among the *zarzuelas grandes* performed most often, even during the heyday of *género chico*: between 1890 and 1905, there was not a single year that did not see at least one run of performances of each, either in Madrid, Barcelona, or the regions.[9] Both works were key to the *zarzuela grande* revival launched by Madrid's Teatro Circo de Parish during 1897 to 1898. *La tempestad* opened the season to great acclaim and *Marina* was performed shortly thereafter, attaining even greater success than the former.[10] The Parish opened its next season with *Marina* again, with newspaper *El Globo* claiming that "the much-desired rebirth of Spanish lyrical art has turned from dream into reality."[11] *Marina* stayed in the Parish repertoire for a decade, and it was also prominently featured in other theaters in Madrid that, encouraged by

4. *Recording* zarzuela grande *in Spain* 87

the successes at the Parish, organized their own *zarzuela grande* seasons, such as Teatro Lírico. *Marina's* operatic version was also programmed at opera venues. *La tempestad*, while not so prominent, was also performed several times at the Parish and elsewhere during these years, allegedly to great success each time.

Zarzuela grande, Take 1: *Gabinetes fonográficos*

From its invention in 1878, the phonograph was known in Spain through public or semi-public phonograph demonstrations led by entertainers and scientists.[12] However, commercial recordings for domestic consumption were only introduced in Spain in the years 1896 to 1898, after the launch of the Spring Motor, Home, and Standard Edison phonographs. These new devices were less cumbersome, easier to operate, and relatively cheaper than previous models. Small businesses, particularly those connected to applied science, healthcare, and technology (pharmacies, opticians, drugstores, manufacturers of scientific equipment, etc.), as well as newly opened establishments all over Spain, started to sell phonographs and other imported equipment and to make their own recordings on wax cylinder, employing local and visiting musicians. These establishments were known as *gabinetes fonográficos*. Evidence from press advertisements, press accounts, and surviving cylinders (see below) suggests that about forty *gabinetes* were active in the period between 1896 and 1905, with more than half in Madrid and Barcelona and many staying open for one or two years only. The *gabinetes* model was relatively unique in the international recording landscape at that time: in more industrialized countries, the market tended to be dominated by large companies such as Edison's and Pathé. *Gabinetes* were fatally impacted by the arrival of the gramophone, with some becoming Gramophone resellers from 1903 and the last standing *gabinete*, Hugens y Acosta, liquidating its assets in late 1905.

Over a thousand commercial recordings made by the *gabinetes* have survived in Spanish archives,[13] mostly consisting of two-minute cylinders.[14] Whenever I use the word "recording" in this context, I refer to recordings of single movements, arias or romanzas, and not full multi-movement works, operas, or *zarzuelas*. It is difficult to ascertain the extent to which the surviving cylinders might be representative of the *gabinetes'* output, and this, as I will illustrate later, complicates the conclusions we can reach about recordings of *zarzuela grande* (and other genres). Since cylinders could not be reliably duplicated, it is likely that most or all of these surviving cylinders were sole copies.[15] Singers would often make several recordings of the same number during a recording session,[16] but catalogs merely listed the titles of recordings they had available at the time of print, with no indication of how many were available. The little quantitative evidence that exists is not always reliable but suggests that surviving cylinders represent much less than 1% of those produced.[17] Singers were initially lukewarm to phonograph recordings, and a significant percentage of the *gabinetes'* output was recorded by working musicians who were not particularly well-known. There are no accounts or interviews with singers that can conclusively establish the reasons, but these are likely to include the laboriousness of the process, the relatively poor quality of the final product, and the fact that the recording industry was still in the process of establishing its prestige and reputation.[18]

The connections that *gabinetes* established between *zarzuela grande* recordings and discourses of national identity were expressed in two ways. Firstly, the *gabinetes* sought to align their products (in all genres) with broader social discourses around national identity, science, and technology. Secondly, their decisions on whether to record *zarzuela grande* versus opera and *género chico* were also informed, to a certain extent, by the discourses around national music described above. Key to understanding the first of these issues is the broader movement of *regeneracionismo* (regenerationism), which posited that Spain was in the midst of a deep crisis and solutions needed to be implemented at an economic, political, cultural, scientific, and even existential level (Harrison 2000, 55). *Regeneracionismo* originated in the 1870s but peaked after the 1898 *Desastre* (in the early years of the *gabinetes'* development), with Spain having lost its colonies and therefore feeling displaced in the international colonialist context (Andrés-Gallego 1998, 253; Salavert and Suárez Cortina 2007, 22). The movement was never centrally organized or directed; rather, it grouped individuals from different backgrounds (in terms of social class, political ideology, and institutional allegiances), often working within their own area of interest or expertise, although not all sectors of Spanish society equally took part or benefitted from *regeneracionismo*.

Gabinete owners, as middle-class professionals, would have been particularly aware of these discourses, and they positioned themselves within them in ways that would have likely resonated with their middle- and upper-class customer base, focusing on how their activities contributed to the economic development and modernization of Spain. They emphasized the scientific, research-based nature of what they did,[19] conveyed an impression of practical and pragmatic (rather than extravagant) luxury,[20] and underlined the contribution that the *gabinetes* made to the domestic economy through their national[21] and international trade networks.[22] They also occasionally voiced concerns about the alleged lack of institutional support for their activities,[23] in line with other *regeneracionistas* (Salavert and Suárez Cortina 2007, 11). These discourses and concerns

4. *Recording* zarzuela grande *in Spain*

were often disseminated through the magazine *El Cardo*, a lifestyle periodical which between 1900 and 1901 included a regular supplement on recorded music.

While *gabinete* owners would have been reasonably familiar with *regeneracionismo*, it is unlikely that they were equally so with the debates about *zarzuela grande*, *género chico*, and Spanish opera outlined above since none of them were musicians or are known to have had significant contacts with key figures in music debates. Their recording decisions are consonant in some respects with the differences in status of the genres as outlined above, but not in others. For example, it is not surprising that *zarzuela grande* was recorded to a smaller extent than other genres, with sixty-seven surviving recordings, given that *zarzuela grande* tended to attract smaller audiences on stage. The number of recordings is not insignificant, but it is certainly well below opera (259 recordings),[24] *género chico* (175), and flamenco (88).[25] On the other hand, the fact that opera was recorded more often than *género chico* and flamenco merits explanation: the latter did attract greater audiences in absolute terms, but opera audiences would typically have greater purchasing power, and opera also had a prestige that *gabinetes* were keen to capitalize on. *Zarzuela grande*, on the other hand, did not have the aura of opera nor the popularity of the *género chico*.

Beyond sheer numbers, the surviving recordings also reveal different strategies and attitudes towards each genre. Recordings of *La tempestad* (11) and especially *Marina* (26) clearly outnumber any other *zarzuela grande*, which count no more than four. In opera and *género chico*, recordings are spread more evenly. There are no less than nine operas of which ten or more cylinders have survived, and the most numerous, *La Bohème*, totals 19 cylinders—consonant with its popularity in Spain after its premiere at the Teatre del Liceu in April 1898. In *género chico* there is a clear winner too: *Gigantes y cabezudos* (14 cylinders), which became an instant hit in November 1898 for its relatable portrayal of Spaniards' sufferings in the home front during the Spanish-American war. Nevertheless, recordings of *Gigantes y cabezudos* represent a much smaller percentage of the total surviving number of recordings of *género chico* than *Marina* does for *zarzuela grande*.

What unites *La Bohème*, *Gigantes y cabezudos*, and *Marina* is that all three were being performed to great success during the years when the *gabinetes* were active. Cylinders are not dated, meaning that we cannot confirm how promptly *gabinetes* responded to stage successes; however, generally speaking, what this suggests is that *gabinetes*, while being sensitive to issues of prestige and popularity as discussed above, decided which specific works to record on the basis of what was popular on stage. With few contemporary *zarzuelas grandes* attaining the success of *La tempestad* and *Marina*, and the *zarzuela grande* scene being generally smaller and less active than opera and *género chico,* this would explain too why *gabinetes* focused their efforts mostly on these two works, as opposed to diversifying their catalogs with a range of materials.

The focus on recent stage successes as well as the quasi-artisanal recording processes described above (with each cylinder being a unique or quasi-unique exemplar) suggest that these early recordings were still intrinsically connected to the audiences' and performers' experiences of live music, still far from the notion of recording as commodified sound that developed later on.[26] In providing customers with the opportunity to recreate some of their live music experiences at home, *gabinetes* were following already existing ways of consuming and disseminating music. This is most obvious in *género chico,* where a range of practices contributed to making sure that the experience of seeing a particular play did not finish after the curtain fell. Organ grinders and street singers, as mentioned earlier, performed popular numbers on the streets, and individual plays would often reference each other under the form of sequels, prequels, contrafacta, and parodies that borrowed the plot, music, or characters from other successful plays (Bentivegna 2000, 1–15). *Zarzuela grande,* while more modestly represented on the streets, also featured parodies. Both Gerónimo Giménez's *La noche de la tempestad* (1900) and Guillermo Palacios's *El trueno gordo* (1903) were parodies of *La tempestad,* composed at a time in which the original was receiving renewed attention.

Further insights about the connection between *gabinetes* and live performance are provided by the locations of the former in Madrid. A number of *gabinetes* were located next to *zarzuela* and opera theaters,[27] suggesting that recordings could have been initially intended as mementos of a specific performance or series of performances for keen concertgoers. Another piece of evidence in this respect comes from the selection of singers who recorded *Marina.* Prominently represented among surviving recordings are tenors Manuel Figuerola and Rafael Bezares,[28] who both started their careers around this time and both sang *Marina* as a *zarzuela* on stage to considerable success. This is not to say, however, that the connection between recordings and live music was always straightforward. Some of the most successful singers to sing *Marina* on stage around these years never recorded it,[29] while some recordings of *Marina* and *La tempestad* feature singers who never sang *zarzuela grande* on stage[30] or who were admittedly amateur.[31] Therefore, while it is likely that some of the *gabinetes* tried to further the connection between live music and recordings by employing performers who had attained success on stage with *zarzuela grande,* they had to work within the limitations imposed by the reluctance of singers to record, as discussed above.

4. Recording zarzuela grande in Spain

Finally, whereas the *gabinetes'* recording practices are to a great extent consonant with the popularity enjoyed by *zarzuela grande* among Spanish audiences, there is less evidence that *gabinete* owners were willing to take a stance in the debates around Spanish opera, *género chico*, and *zarzuela grande*. The *gabinetes'* *regeneracionista* strategy involved the dissemination and normalization of domestic phonography in the belief that this would stimulate both international and domestic trade and contribute to raise the scientific and cultural capital of Spaniards.[32] Nevertheless, the *gabinetes* typically associated these values with the fact of merely owning and knowing how to operate a phonograph and not so much with the consumption of specific repertoires. There is, however, some evidence from their published writings that some *gabinete* owners were aware of the opera/*zarzuela* debates and wished to intervene in these, albeit in an unorthodox way, not consonant with the opinions of music critics and composers like Peña y Goñi and Asenjo Barbieri.[33] Indeed, these *gabinetes* regarded Italian, German, and French opera as more suitable to their civilizing, patriotic mission than *zarzuela*, because opera recordings allowed Spaniards to acquaint themselves with higher, superior art forms, even if these were not national. The magazine *El Cardo* repeatedly complained that *gabinetes* were forced to produce cylinders of *zarzuela* (instead of dedicating themselves exclusively to opera) because of the alleged ignorance of Spanish audiences, who voraciously consumed *zarzuela*, and because *zarzuela* recordings were consistently sold at lower prices than opera (but still higher than flamenco and wind bands).

Zarzuela grande, Take 2: Gramophone

From 1899, *gabinetes* had a competitor in the Gramophone company, which had started both to sell gramophones[34] and to make recordings in Spain.[35] While *gabinete* owners and customers initially despised the gramophone for its poor technical and artistic quality,[36] the new technology had several advantages over the phonograph: discs could be easily duplicated, so they could be sold at lower prices relative to phonograph cylinders, and a broader range of repertoires was on offer, as Gramophone engineers were being sent on recording trips all over the world. *Regeneracionista* traces were still present in Gramophone's publicity strategy, as the new device not only allowed customers to access music in the privacy of their own homes but also to enjoy the latest global technological developments in fidelity. Since the gramophone used at this stage 10-inch and 12-inch discs, containing three and four to five minutes of music respectively, the recordings I am referring to here still contain only individual music numbers rather than full *zarzuelas* or operas.

Gramophone started to record *zarzuela* not much later than the *gabinetes* did, with sound engineers from the company's London office first visiting Madrid in August 1899 and sending back 157 matrix recordings to the company's headquarters in Germany, of which 39 were rejected (Torrent i Marqués 2005, 9). Successive visits took place in 1900, 1902, and 1903, involving, in all cases, both Madrid and Barcelona. After the company opened an office in Barcelona later in 1903, recording sessions continued taking place regularly, with engineers occasionally venturing into the provinces to record local musicians. These visits caused some friction with the *gabinetes,* with *El Cardo* claiming that British engineers were not qualified to appropriately assess flamenco and *zarzuela* performers and that they hired many mediocre ones.[37] This claim, however, must be understood in a context of commercial rivalry. As has been discussed above, *gabinetes* often recorded mediocre singers too, and there were significant overlaps between the singers who recorded for the *gabinetes* between 1899 and 1903 and those who did so for Gramophone (for example, with Bezares, Figuerola, and Blanquer). Because of the lack of dates on the *gabinetes'* cylinders, we do not know whether singers tended to record for these first and then for Gramophone or vice-versa, but we can presume that some singers might have actively pursued or developed a reputation for being good at making recordings. Even though the phonograph and gramophone recording processes were different at this stage, they were both rather laborious, and both the Gramophone recording engineers and the musical directors of the *gabinetes* might have appreciated being able to rely on singers who could sing confidently in front of a recording device and follow the instructions imparted to them (Trezise 2009, 190). Nevertheless, as the gramophone consolidated both technologically and commercially, well-known stage singers did warm up to the idea of recording in the studio, presumably because of the development possibilities it offered to their careers in Spain and abroad, as is the case with famed *género chico tiple* Lucrecia Arana, who recorded more than twenty numbers in 1904 for Gramophone (Kelly 2006). In the realm of *zarzuela grande*, husband-and-wife duo Emilio Sagi-Barba and Luisa Vela and baritone Inocencio Navarro often took up the sorts of recording opportunities that in the earlier years would have gone to lesser-known performers. This helped to concentrate *zarzuela grande* repertoire in the hands of a few singers with solid stage experience and reputation—contrary to what was the case in the *gabinete* years, where less experienced and even amateur singers were often heard in cylinders.

Another key difference was that Gramophone, having a network of offices and representatives across Europe, was not constrained to the local market but operated globally. When recording in Spain, Gramophone focused on *zarzuela* (both

4. *Recording* zarzuela grande *in Spain*   93

zarzuela grande and *género chico*), flamenco, Spanish brass band music, and some traditional music (*jota,* choral societies). Unlike the *gabinetes,* Gramophone did not normally record Italian, German, or French opera in Spain: such jobs were now increasingly given to singers with international careers and reputations.[38] This is consonant with Gramophone's operations elsewhere, which have been extensively documented by scholars and collectors: recordings made locally of vernacular or "ethnic" repertoires[39] to cater to local markets that would not have warmed up to American brass band music or music hall. Some of those "ethnic" recordings, though, were also included in some of the company's US or international catalogs, therefore becoming an early example of the global circulation and relative uniformization of consumption habits that the recording industry would favor in successive decades.

This concern with speaking to markets outside Spain might be one of the reasons why, contrary to what *gabinetes* did, Gramophone recorded both *zarzuela grande* and *género chico* almost in equal measure and included the former in its international catalogs to a greater extent than the latter, with Sagi-Barba and Vela being regular names from the late 1900s and throughout the 1910s. One further reason for this is simply that the fortunes of *zarzuela grande* and *género chico* were reversed during these years: the latter started to decline after 1900, eventually morphing into the cabaret-style *géneros frívolos* (Salaün 2005, 136–37), whereas *zarzuela grande* underwent a revival thanks to composers such as Pablo Luna, Amadeu Vives, and Francisco Alonso. Gramophone indeed recorded numbers from some of these recent successes, but it also kept recording *Marina* and *La tempestad* to a greater extent than any other work in the repertoire. It is also likely, however, that Gramophone's strategy was informed by a belief that *zarzuela grande* traveled better than *género chico*. Having been written predominantly in an Italianate style and borrowing numerous themes and stereotypes from French and Italian opera (and operetta in the case of later works), *zarzuela grande* was deemed to be more successful in speaking to non-Spanish audiences than the very place- and circumstance-specific *género chico*.

This, however, does not mean that *zarzuela grande* composers and advocates felt vindicated regarding the international reach of the genre vis-à-vis opera. Debates around Spanish opera reappeared in the mid-1910s, particularly in the journal *Revista musical hispano-americana*. Composers and critics still lamented that Spanish opera had failed to develop and generally regarded *género chico* (particularly in its last years) as a degeneration of *zarzuela*, whereas *zarzuela grande* itself enjoyed some renewed consideration as an example of "arte nacional."[40] Recordings, however, rarely featured in such discussions, so we should not conclude that the international circulation of *zarzuela grande* recordings contributed significantly to this new stage in the debate in one way or another: it is more likely that the renewed appreciation for recordings of *zarzuela grande* was due to the recent revival of the genre on stage. Nevertheless, the early circulation of *zarzuela grande* recordings brought about two important changes that would then become more pressing in the coming decades, as the genre declined on stage but thrived in recordings that were often marketed outside Spain. First, such recordings suggest that consumers no longer expected recordings to simply replicate their live music experiences, as was the case in the *gabinetes* era. Second, they also suggest that *zarzuela grande* demonstrated that it could receive a modicum of interest outside Spain and travel beyond what its composers thought was possible.

Conclusion

Experimentation in the early years of commercial recording did not simply affect technologies and commercial models. The new listening practices and ways of thinking about music, sound, and repertoires stimulated by the phonograph and gramophone were equally significant. Moreover, it is often vernacular repertoires such as *zarzuela* and relatively small national or local scenes such as the Spanish one that allow the most fruitful opportunities to disentangle these complex processes. Technology and listening habits often changed very rapidly and might not have always left extensive or reliable sources that make it possible to track when and where they took place and developed. The above case study on *zarzuela grande* allows us to draw a few conclusions relevant to both the early history of recording technologies and the history and reception of *zarzuela*. In which concerns the former, it calls attention to the changing definitions and discourses surrounding live and recorded music and to the ways in which these discourses were informed by place-specific practices and debates that have only recently started to be studied and compared in a considered way (Roy 2021), such as, in this case, the theatrical culture surrounding *género chico* and *zarzuela grande*. In which concerns the latter, this case study suggests that the introduction of commercial recordings, which complicated the relationship between live and recorded music, added an extra layer to debates concerning the role of *zarzuela grande* in national identity-building processes both in Spain and abroad. New opportunities seemingly opened for the genre, most notably thanks to its ability to reach broader audiences beyond national borders. Yet, at the same time, an increasing distance emerged between recordings of the genre and its live performance—a chasm that would only become more pronounced in the decades to come, as *zarzuela* started to decline as a living music genre.

Notes

1. The only existing book-length study of the early recording industry in Spain is by Gómez-Montejano (2005). Barreiro (2007) is a CD release of early recordings with a short booklet, and Kelly (2006) is a catalog of Gramophone recordings made in Spain and Portugal. Numerous contributions that appeared between 2002 and 2010 in *Girant a 78 rpm*, the newsletter of the Associació per a la Salvaguarda del Patrimoni Enregistrat (a Catalonia-based association for the conservation of recordings), and on collector Carlos Martín Ballester's website (www.carlosmb.com), also offer considerable amounts of information.

2. Examples include: Biblioteca Nacional de España through Biblioteca Digital Hispánica (bdh.bne.es), Eresbil Archivo de la Música Vasca (www.eresbil.com), and Biblioteca de Catalunya through Memòria Digital de Catalunya (mdc1.csuc.cat).

3. Exceptions include my own work: Moreda Rodríguez (2017, 2019).

4. It was only from the early years of the twentieth century that the gramophone began to democratize access to recorded music, although the great spread of record consumption worldwide did not come until after electrical recording (Maisonneuve 2007, 52–56).

5. As opposed to Baroque *zarzuela*, which developed in the second half of the seventeenth century.

6. Francisco Asenjo Barbieri, "Carta a un joven compositor de música." *El imparcial*, February 18, 1878, 11. All further references to newspaper articles will appear in endnotes.

7. Present-day accounts of *teatro por horas* and *género chico* include Membrez (1987), Del Moral Ruiz (2004), and Young (2016).

8. The only other noteworthy example is Gerónimo Giménez's *género chico* piece *La Tempranica* (1900). His student Federico Moreno Torroba transformed it into an opera in 1930 (*María la Tempranica*), which was not very successful.

9. Press reviews suggest that *Marina*, although most often performed as a *zarzuela*, was sometimes performed as an opera. This, however, is difficult to establish with certainty, as the press sometimes used the terms "opera" and "*zarzuela*" rather loosely.

10. R. Blasco [first name unknown], "Parish." *La correspondencia de España*, October 3, 1897.

11. "Gacetillas teatrales." *El Globo*, October 2, 1898.

12. Demonstrations were held at a multiplicity of venues (e.g., theaters, cafés, inns, casinos, *ateneos*, clubs, schools, churches, civil halls), some for free and some requiring payment or membership of a club or society. See Moreda Rodríguez (2019, 246).

13. More than half of these are held at Eresbil (Archivo de la Música Vasca), with others at the Biblioteca Nacional de España, Museu Vicente Miralles Segarra in Valencia, Museu de la Mùsica in Barcelona, Biblioteca de Catalunya, and Centro de Documentación Musical de Andalucía.

14. This does not necessarily mean that all recordings were exactly two minutes in length, as the duration of these cylinders could be extended by forty or fifty seconds by reducing the playing speed.

15. One way of "duplicating" recordings consisted in recording the performance with two or more phonographs at the same time. Still, this would not have resulted in more than a few copies of each recording.

16. "Un gran adelanto." *Boletín fonográfico* 16 (1901): 16–20.

17. For example, *gabinete* Hugens y Acosta claimed in a magazine article in early 1901 to have sold 30,000 cylinders in the previous two years ("Industria fonográfica." *El cardo*, January 22, 1901, 14–15). If we assume that the figure was accurate and constant throughout their eight years of operation (even if such an assumption is problematic), this would yield a total of 120,000 cylinders. Of these, 162 have survived in public collections—a survival rate of one for every 741 cylinders.

18. On the other hand, with a minority of the Spanish population having access to recordings, it seems unlikely that singers were deterred by the possibility of losing live audiences, as was the case later.

19. "Madrid Artístico. Sociedad Fonográfica Española—Hugens y Acosta." *El Liberal* (Madrid), October 3, 1899.

20. "Nuevo establecimiento." *El correo militar* (Madrid), July 19, 1897.

21. Garcifernández, "Política europea." *Crónica meridional* (Almería), January 26, 1900.

22. "Exposición madrileña de pequeñas industrias." *El Siglo futuro* (Madrid), June 10, 1901.

23. Garcifernández, "Política europea." *La región extremeña* (Badajoz), February 8, 1900; Garcifernández, "Política europea." *La región extremeña* (Badajoz), March 1, 1900.

24. This includes Italian, French, German, and Spanish opera. Spanish opera recordings, however, are limited to a few cylinders of Tomás Bretón's *La Dolores*.

25. Flamenco was prominently recorded outside Andalusia, given that at the time flamenco was already popular outside its place of origin thanks to the *cafés cantantes* (cafés, mostly in large cities, which put on flamenco shows for their patrons).

26. For a discussion of the relationship between live and recorded music in these early recordings, see also Moreda Rodríguez (2020, 464, 468, 476–77).

27. No fewer than three *gabinetes* stood in the Calle del Príncipe a few yards from the Teatro de la Comedia, with a further two within a hundred yards. There was one *gabinete* within the same block as the Teatro de la Zarzuela and a further one within a hundred yards. Hugens y Acosta was located by the exit door of the well-attended Teatro Apolo. With the center of Madrid being rather compact at that time, only the Teatro Real and Teatro Novedades did not have a *gabinete* within a hundred yards of their premises.

28. Three recordings of *Marina* numbers by Figuerola have survived as well as five by Bezares.

29. Particularly tenor Eduardo García Bergés, widely regarded in the late nineteenth century as the best performer of the role of Jorge.

30. For example, tenor Bernardino Blanquer, whose stage engagements were limited to opera chorus and liturgical music.

31. Such as Valencian teenage soprano Amparo Cardenal, who recorded for Puerto y Novella.

32. "Nuevo establecimiento." *El Correo Militar,* July 19, 1897.

33. "Aquí y fuera de aquí." *El Cardo*, November 15, 1900; "Fonograma." *El Cardo*, February 28, 1901; Cilindrique, "Cosas fonográficas." *El Cardo*, April 22, 1901; Cilindrique, "De fonografía." *El Cardo*, September 8, 1901. Cilindrique is most likely a pseudonym for the Marqués de Alta-Villa.

4. Recording zarzuela grande in Spain

34. "Gacetillas." *El bien público* (Palma de Mallorca), December 13, 1899.

35. Details from recording sessions, as well as the musicians recorded in each session, can be gathered from Kelly (2006).

36. "El mercado fonográfico." *Boletín fonográfico* 25, (1901), 14.

37. Cilindrique, "De fonografía."

38. Exceptions include Josefina Huguet and Andrés Perelló de Segurola, who recorded opera extensively for Gramophone in Barcelona between 1902 and 1905. Both, however, had established international careers and reputations by that point. After 1905, they both moved on to record in Milan.

39. The term "ethnic" was used by recording companies from the very early years of gramophone disc production. It referred, in the first instance, to non-English language records "directed at both the cosmopolitan and foreign-born customers" (Spottswood 1990, xv). Many of the ethnic records marketed globally were in languages spoken by emigrant communities in the US (German, Hebrew, Yiddish, French, Spanish, Czech, Danish, Russian, Swedish, Polish, and Hungarian). Apart from language, global spread and perceived universalism also determined whether a record was considered ethnic or not: Italian opera and classical music were not considered ethnic, while English-language Irish and West Indian music were (Spottswood 1990, xvii).

40. Examples include: Conrado del Campo, "Sobre la situación actual de la música española." *Revista musical hispano-americana*, 1 (1914), 2–4; Juan Borrás de Palau, "Sobre la ópera nacional." *Revista musical hispano-americana*, 9 (1914), 4–5; Eduardo López Chavarri, "Teatro y música nacional." *Revista musical hispano-americana,* 16 (1915), 3; Rogelio Villar, "Divagaciones sobre el nacionalismo musical y los compositores españoles." *Revista musical hispano-americana*, 20 (1915), 2–5.

References

Andrés-Gallego, José. 1998. *Un 98 distinto: Regeneración, desastre, regeneracionismo.* Madrid: Ediciones Encuentro.

Barreiro, Javier. 2007. *Primeras grabaciones fonográficas en Aragón: 1898–1903 una colección de cilindros de cera.* Zaragoza, ES: Coda Out.

Bentivegna, Patricia. 2000. *Parody in the Género Chico.* New Orleans: University Press of the South.

Bolig, John R. 2004. *The Victor Red Seal Discography. Vol. I. Single-Sided Series (1903–1925).* Denver: Mainspring Press.

Cotarelo y Mori, Emilio. 2001. *Historia de la zarzuela o sea el drama lírico en España, desde su origen a fines del siglo XIX.* Madrid: Instituto Complutense de Ciencias Musicales.

Deleito y Piñuela, José. 1949. *Origen y apogeo del género chico.* Madrid: Revista de Occidente

Denning, Michael. 2015. *Noise Uprising: The Audiopolitics of a World Musical Revolution.* New York: Verso.

Encina Cortizo, María. 1998. *Emilio Arrieta: De la ópera a la zarzuela.* Madrid: Instituto Complutense de Ciencias Musicales.

Gómez-Montejano, Mariano. 2005. *El fonógrafo en España: Cilindros españoles.* Madrid: Self-published.

Harrison, Joseph. 2000. "Tackling National Decadence: Economic Regenerationism in Spain after the Colonial Debacle." In *Spain's 1898 Crisis: Regenerationism, Modernism, Post-colonialism*, edited by Joseph Harrison and Alan Hoyle, 55–67. Manchester: Manchester University Press.

Kelly, Alan. 2006. *The Gramophone Company Limited, The Spanish Catalogue: Including Portuguese Recordings*. N.p.: Self-published.

Llano, Samuel. 2018. *Discordant Notes: Marginality and Social Disorder in Madrid, 1850–1930*. New York: Oxford University Press.

Maisonneuve, Sophie. 2007. "La Voix de son Maître: Entre corps et technique, l'avènement d'une écoute musicale nouvelle au XXe siècle." In *Communications* 81, 47–59.

Mejías García, Enrique. 2014. "Cuestión de géneros: La zarzuela española frente al desafío historiográfico." In *Dimensiones y desafíos de la zarzuela*, edited by Tobias Brandenberger, 21–43. Berlin: Lit Verlag.

Membrez, Nancy J. 1987. "The *teatro por horas*: History, Dynamics and Comprehensive Bibliography of a Madrid Industry, 1867–1922 (Género chico, Género ínfimo and Early Cinema." PhD diss., University of California, Santa Barbara.

Moral Ruiz, Carmen del. 2004. *El género chico*. Madrid: Alianza.

Moreda Rodríguez, Eva. 2017. "Prefiguring the Spanish Recording Diva: How Gabinetes fonográficos (Phonography Studios) Changed Listening Practices, 1898–1905." In *Listening to Music: People, Practices and Experiences*, edited by Helen Barlow and David Rowland. Milton Keynes: The Open University. https://ledbooks.org/proceedings2017/#sec_192_h1.

———. 2019. "Travelling Phonographs in fin de siècle Spain: Recording Technologies and National Regeneration in Ruperto Chapí's *El fonógrafo ambulante*." In *Spanish Sound Studies*, special issue of the *Journal of Spanish Cultural Studies*, edited by Samuel Llano and Tom Whittaker, 20, no. 3: 241–55.

———. 2020. "Reconstructing *Zarzuela* Performance Practices ca. 1900: Wax Cylinder and Gramophone Disc Recordings of *Gigantes y cabezudos*." *Journal of Musicology* 37, no. 4, 459–87.

Peña y Goñi, Antonio. 2003. *La ópera española y la música dramática en el siglo XIX. Apuntes históricos*. Madrid: Instituto Complutense de Ciencias Musicales.

Roy, Élodie A. 2021. "Introduction: Entangled Phonographies." In *Phonographic Encounters: Mapping Transnational Cultures of Sound, 1890–1945*, edited by Élodie A. Roy and Eva Moreda Rodriguez, 1–13. Abingdon, UK: Routledge.

Salaün, Serge. 2005. "Cuplé y variedades (1890–1915)." In *La escena española en la encrucijada (1890–1910)*, edited by Serge Salaün, Evelyne Ricci, and Marie Salgues, 125–51. Madrid: Espiral Hispanoamericana.

Salavert, Vicente, and Manuel Suárez Cortina. 2007. "Introducción." In *El regeneracionismo en España: Política, educación, ciencia y sociedad*, edited by Vicente Salavert and Manuel Suárez Cortina, 9–19. Valencia: Universitat de Valencia.

Spottswood, Richard K. 1990. *Ethnic Music on Records: A Discography of Ethnic Recordings Produced in the United States, 1893–1942*. Urbana: University of Illinois Press.

Torrent i Marqués, Antoni. 2005. "Una recerca interessant (1° part)." *Girant a 78 rpm* 8: 9–11.

Trezise, Simon. 2009. "The Recorded Document: Interpretation and Discography." In *The Cambridge Companion to Recorded Music*, edited by Nicholas Cook, Erik Clarke, Daniel Leech-Wilkinson, and John Rink, 186–209. Cambridge: University of Cambridge.

Young, Clinton D. 2013. "Why Did Spain Fail to Develop Nationalist Opera?" *Bulletin for Spanish and Portuguese Historical Studies* 38, no. 1: 117–37.

———. 2016. *Music Theater and Popular Nationalism in Spain, 1880–1930*. Baton Rouge: Louisiana State University Press.

5

The Invisible Voices
of the Early Recording
Market in Portugal

LEONOR LOSA

The emergence and formal establishment of a phonographic market[1] in Portugal took place between the last decade of the nineteenth century and the second decade of the twentieth century as a predominantly urban phenomenon that was boosted by traders and shopkeepers. During this period, Portugal underwent various transformations related to both international and national politics, the economic and financial landscape, social movements, as well as the reconfiguration of the social and political fabric that progressively shaped the country. At the turn of the twentieth century, the Portuguese monarchy became gradually more socially and politically discredited,[2] which eventually led to a change of regime and the declaration of a republic on October 5, 1910. In this chapter, I argue that the emergence and establishment of the recording industry in Portugal, along with the commercialization and consumption of recorded music, were intricately bound up with social and political transformations in the country.

At the turn of the twentieth century, Portugal was predominantly rural. In 1910, only 15 percent of the total population lived in cities, distributed between the main urban centers of Lisbon (the capital) and Porto (Pereira 2010). Over half of the population worked in agricultural labor and industry accounted for 21 percent of the working population in 1911, against six percent for professional

5. Invisible Voices of the Early Recording Market in Portugal   101

trade-related activities and 1.6 percent in the liberal professions (2010). It was the latter group that would serve as the core driver of the phonographic market. Beyond national demographics, the last decade of the nineteenth century was also the scene of a "global crisis" (Rollo 2010). An international economic crisis, as well as national political and financial crises affected virtually every economic sector. Correspondingly in 1892, as a result of the increase in taxes and tariffs and the reduction in consumption, 400 stores in Lisbon were forced to close (Alves 2010). This negative economic climate had a significant impact on many commercial sectors, including the phonographic industry that forms the basis for this chapter.

The early twentieth century, on the other hand, was a period of recovery, marked by a counter-reaction to "the decadent pessimism of the previous generation" (Rollo 2010, 27). Concomitantly with growth in the industrial sector, plus the emergence of new industries, the spread of electricity, the establishment of a telephone network and major developments in transport (particularly the train service linking the country with Europe but also the impact of trams on the increasingly bustling urban life), the phonographic market began to be established in the country. As a result, recorded music became progressively integrated into the consumption habits of the urban middle classes.

An analysis of the early record market in Portugal is marked by two somewhat contradictory facts. On the one hand, the absence of discourse about recorded music in written sources would seem to indicate that Portuguese society did not integrate this sound technology into its social and consumer practices and that this new market did not take root locally. On the other hand, however, the large number of early commercial 78 rpm records in public and private collections,[3] the significant number of retail stores selling records in the first two decades of the twentieth century,[4] and the identification of commercial records of Portuguese phonographic brands, reveal that phonography was an intense social and economic activity. The historical interpretation presented in this chapter is an attempt to better understand the basis of this discrepancy between "weak" discourses and intense practices around recorded music in early twentieth-century Portugal.

Ethnomusicological research on the historical development of the economic relations generated by recorded music demonstrates the need to frame different local contexts while taking into account the economic and cultural relations between consumers and the companies that had a monopoly over the record industry (Wallis and Malm 1992; Manuel 2001; Gronow and Saunio 1998). Scholars differentiate between countries that had their own record companies and where production infrastructure (factories) existed, and other countries that depended on foreign factories and external infrastructures for developing businesses around recorded music and where international companies established local markets encouraging local consumption. Such local contexts have been described as "small countries" (Wallis and Malm 1984), "peripheral countries" (Gronow and Saunio 1998), or "non-western countries" (Manuel 2001). The use of these terms demonstrates the need to frame local contexts within the music industry according to the dynamics of economic and cultural relations with the companies that had a monopoly on the record industry. However, this kind of analysis implies a conception of modernity as a linear historical course and a teleological paradigm of development based on the binomial technology—capitalism. This dominant narrative of modernity, which Couze Venn (2000) conceptualizes as "occidentalism," ignores the relevance of alternative trajectories in different contexts and the ways in which such trajectories are also part of modernity. This is the case with Portugal, a country that does not fit these analytical categories, and thus challenges its position within modernity.

Based on a close analysis of the "modernization of sound" (Taylor, Katz, and Grajeda 2012) in Portugal, I argue that the local reality challenges standard scholarly narratives of modernity, not only because of the ways in which technology and capitalism were manifested, but above all, due to the affective and subjective relationship that Portuguese society developed with the commodities and structures of modernity. This analysis focuses on the particularities of the relationship between Portuguese society and the advent of recorded music. I argue that the study of local markets and of the local development of a consumer society reveals modes of existence that reach beyond economic relations as they are embedded in cultural and social practices.

This study's challenge to the prevalent narratives of modernity exposes the "zones of invisibility" of the Portuguese recording market to which the title of the chapter alludes. Throughout the chapter other social processes and historical facts that remain, more or less, metaphorically invisible will be explored. First, the chapter situates recording technologies and commodities within the development of a Western consumer society. Then, it analyzes the arrival of the main recording companies in Portugal as well as the ways in which Portuguese society reacted to their arrival. At the same time, it examines the dynamics of growth of the international industry in the local market. Finally, the chapter focuses on the role traders and shopkeepers played in the construction of a national market, focused on sound technologies and in the configuration of a national repertoire, and sketches out the social place of recorded sound technologies at the margins of the dominant culture.

The Early Impact of the Phonograph
and the Gramophone in Portugal

On April 15, 1878, the "Scientific News" section of the Portuguese newspaper *O Occidente* described in detail the functioning of Thomas Alva Edison's (1847–1931) "Phonographo Fallante," ("Talking Phonograph") in what appears to have been the first mention of his invention from the previous year. The article emphasized that "[t]he most unique thing about the phonograph is that the reproduction of sounds can occur at any time, and therefore much later after, and in a different place than that in which the spokesman's vibrations are inscribed on the instrument" (O Occidente 1878). This physical and temporal "detachment," which society had already experienced through other modern inventions such as photography, revolutionized the forms of perceiving the "real" and, in the case of sound, the forms of *listening* to music.

However, as Timothy Taylor, Mark Katz, and Toby Grajeda argue, aside from its technological features, sound recording is an intrinsic part of modernity because it emerges as a result of the transition to a consumer society and is thus part of "the processes by which music evolved from something that people primarily made for themselves or heard live to a commodity and object of consumption" (2012, 3). This process of commodification began with forms of musical consumption mediated by mechanical instruments and by the invention of sound recording technology, and it accelerated following the developments Émile Berliner (1851–1929) made to sound recording technology. Aimed at the mass production of musical recordings (Gronow and Saunio 1998), Berliner patented the gramophone, a new technology that enabled sound to be reproduced on flat discs. This new format acquired an expanded commercial scale as, unlike phonograph cylinders, it was relatively simple to make a press matrix from the original recording from which many discs might then be mass produced and thereby reach a large number of people across distinct geographical spaces.

Toward the end of the nineteenth century, some Portuguese shopkeepers began selling cylinders and phonographs, albeit on a small scale. During the first decade of the twentieth century, when demographic growth triggered a general rise in product sales and in the number of stores per inhabitant (Alves 2010), retailers in Lisbon and Porto (and to a lesser extent in other small urban centers around the country) began to invest in the retail sale of wax cylinders, shellac records, phonographs, and gramophones. Alongside the rising confidence of local storekeepers, the penetration of international record companies in the Portuguese market determined the success of these new commodities and their progressive integration into existing forms of consumption. As such, it is possible to trace the growth of an economy generated and mediated by sound recording, encompassing a chain of relationships between various agents, products, and patterns of consumption that configured a market structure.

In line with similar processes in the rest of Europe and the United States of America, as well as in countries under colonial structures of economic exploitation, such as Egypt or India, the establishment of this market in Portugal was guided by the individual strategies of foreign companies: from a more traditionalist market, based on the progressive introduction of new products alongside established forms of consumption, to more "aggressive" and modern capitalist interventions, such as the opening up of new market sectors, and the creation of new commodities and, consequently, new consumption habits.

"Gifting a Gramophone Is Chic": The Arrival of the First Record Companies in Portugal

In the late nineteenth and early twentieth centuries, the international phonographic market was dominated by large companies that controlled global recording, production, and distribution (Gronow 1983). The Gramophone Company, Edison Phonograph Company, Victor Talking Machine, International Talking Machine GmbH, Columbia Phonograph, and Lindström AG, held a joint monopoly over the recording industry, agreeing on the territories they each covered (1983). The companies that had the greatest impact in Portugal were the British Gramophone Company and the brands that from 1908 onwards were progressively integrated in the German group Lindström AG (such as Beka, Homokord, Odeon, Dahlia Records, among others) and the French company Pathé.

Although they entered the Portuguese market with the common goal of expanding their own markets, these different companies adopted distinct commercial strategies. The Gramophone Company and France's Pathé implemented a similar strategy by establishing stores under their company's own names (Losa 2013). However, labels such as Odeon, Beka, and Homokord were distributed through networks of "agents" who were, in effect, already established retailers with commercial experience in other markets (2013). Indeed, over the first two decades of the twentieth century, the relationship between the development of the local market and the transnational recording industry seems to have been based on the progressive adjustment and definition of both the commercial contours of the local market and the consumption patterns of Portuguese society.

Similar to other European and non-European territories, the first local recordings were made by international technicians who worked for the companies that held the phonographic monopoly and sought to spread the range of their commercial operations over wide geographic areas (Gronow 1983). Concomitant to the establishment of networks of commercial agents or large stores, the recording of local repertoires was crucial to the establishment of the recording market, as Frederick Gaisberg, the main sound engineer from Gramophone Company and whose work defined the early development of the commercial recording industry, shows in his autobiography (Gaisberg 1942). As Gronow and Englund (2007) argue, the expansion of the record industry encompasses the recording of new repertoire. Only by making available local and recognizable repertoire could the new commodities be the object of the curiosity and interest of potential local consumers. Recording technicians travelled around the world carrying their recording equipment, fleetingly stopping at different places and guessing which repertoires could catch the local public's attention. They stayed in each city only for a few days, recording as much repertoire as possible and often in makeshift spaces such as hotel rooms (Gaisberg 1942).

The first recording "expedition" of this sort in Portugal took place in the city of Porto in 1900 and was carried out by the recording technician Sinkler Darby on behalf of the Gramophone Company (then Gramophone & Typewriter Limited), the British partner of E. Berliner's Gramophone (Belchior 2013). However, it is unclear as to how many copies the Gramophone Company released into circulation in the still embryonic Portuguese recording market and when exactly this circulation happened. Furthermore, these early recordings covered a wide range of repertoires aligned with those that were fashionable at the time, such as compositions for military and civil wind bands, hymns, fado, and folk- or rural-inspired songs. Over the following years, many other recording sessions took place that widened the available repertoire, consolidated the Portuguese market, and confirmed the importance for local agents to rely on diverse foreign companies. The initial heterogeneity of recorded genres and musical styles progressively gave way to more restricted repertoires closer to the tastes of the Portuguese public. Oriented towards the more or less popular urban repertoires, these first recordings came to define the contours of Portuguese popular music (Losa 2013).

In addition to recording local repertoires, several record companies steadily increased their presence in the Portuguese commercial context by creating and investing in a new market sector (2013). The local integration of new technologies in each geographical context, and the cultural forms generated through this integration were in no way homogeneous. In Portugal, the creation of a new market around these technologies and the musical listening practices they generated developed through a complex process in which small-scale business agents played a crucial role. The peculiarities of the Portuguese context gave it an orientation different from Central European countries and determined which trade modalities prospered and which were condemned to failure (2013).

Different Implementation Strategies

Companies such as The Gramophone Company and Pathé based their commercial strategies on establishing autonomous market sectors, assuming, on the one hand, the unique and unprecedented nature of phonographic goods and, on the other hand, a framework for distinctive and luxury consumption. In 1904, through its French delegation Compagnie Française du Gramophone (CFG), The Gramophone Company opened a store in Lisbon, under the designation *Companhia Franceza do Gramophone*, while establishing a network of agents throughout the country's main cities. Between 1904 and 1905, CFG carried out a competitive advertising campaign running for about ten consecutive months in the *Illustração Portugueza*, a weekly magazine devoted to the themes of culture, politics, and arts that addressed an informed and higher social class public. The advertising slogan "Gifting a Gramophone, is chic, is elegant, it is 1905's most gracious gift" clearly demonstrates the desire to align the Gramophone brand and its products with the social aspirations and cultural tastes of Lisbon's elite. These graphically elaborate and appealing advertisements focused mainly on records from the "Celebrity Records" section of Gramophone Company's catalog, the recordings of classical instrumental and operatic repertoire of international leading performers, which were the most luxurious and expensive records. However, as in other European markets, the recordings of celebrated performers constituted a very small percentage of overall profits with most income accruing from recordings of military bands and popular music (Martland 1997, 63).

Similar to CFG, the French company Pathé was established in Porto, opening a store that occupied an entire building on the Rua de Cedofeita, one of the city's busiest streets. In 1906, in addition to the shop, the building also had a "recording room," a "phonograph repair shop," and a "warehouse" (Catálogo Pathé 1906). Pathé commercialized both cylinders and records and in its first year prioritized songs from the *teatro de revista*.[5] Pathé's catalog placed great emphasis on Portuguese recording "artists," reproducing their handwritten testimonials and praising the quality of Pathé's recordings (1906). In addition to these testimonials, the recordings featured photographs of the performers set against a graphically appealing ornamentation bearing characteristics of French art nouveau. The prominence attributed to the performers reflected the company's efforts to enhance the phonographic material and build a catalog of local celebrities. However, attempts to create autonomous market outlets

5. Invisible Voices of the Early Recording Market in Portugal 107

using an exclusively phonographic store and fostering "distinctive" patterns of consumption did not stand up to the competition of alternative, less specialized, and less elitist commercial modes. The Companhia Franceza do Gramophone store closed its doors at the end of 1906, and it is likely that the Pathé's store closed around the same time, although there is a lack of evidence to corroborate this claim.

At the same time as the arrival of the French Gramophone Company and Pathé, other small foreign companies such as Beka, Dacapo, Favorite, Fidelio Records, Dalia Records, Parlophone, Homokord, and Odeon[6] adopted a different strategy for their geographical expansion: they entered the Portuguese market by establishing commercial agreements with local traders already rooted in other retail and trade sectors, particularly bicycles, sewing machines, and other modern technological inventions.

The activities of tradesmen who welcomed the new sound-reproduction technologies were crucial to nurturing the necessary conditions for the development of a local market. By including new sound technologies into their traditional market sector, they enabled phonographic products to reach a broader swath of the population, fostered market competition by making products more affordable, and were active agents in diversifying recorded repertoires to appeal to broader audiences.

The surviving catalogs and records of the brands that followed this market strategy are more representative than those of the brands that established themselves based on international franchises such as Pathé and CFG, indicating that they were much more successful in local markets. Given that there was no rigid format, this business model also allowed local traders to establish their own record labels featuring Portuguese repertoires, which led to the formation of a locally motivated market throughout the first decade of the twentieth century. By the end of the 1910s, several stores were advertising phonography-related products with the main shopping thoroughfares of Lisbon and Porto containing at least one store selling modern phonographic materials (Losa 2013, 63). The record trade had now clearly taken root. Given the relatively high cost of gramophones and records, these products remained inaccessible to the majority of the population. However, the sheer number of stores reflects the rooting of this new market sector.[7] Although many of those stores were only partially dedicated to phonography, some cases emerged of small Portuguese entrepreneurs developing commercial structures that were exclusively dedicated to recorded music. In parallel to the onslaught of large foreign companies, traders such as José Castello Branco and Carlos Calderon in Lisbon, and Ricardo Lemos and Artur Barbedo in Porto, developed sophisticated and competitive business models.

Building a Locally Motivated Market Economy: The Role of Traders

The country's low level of industrialization meant that traders occupied the position of agents for international brands or dealers of imported products, resulting in their dependency on the economic systems imposed by international companies and a lack of autonomy. Throughout the twentieth century, this lack of autonomy on the part of local traders was quite evident in the recorded music sector that was driven by the expansionist agenda of a limited number of business groups acting according to the logics of modern capitalism. As a result, the phonographic market in Portugal became dependent on international structures and policies. While consumption practices around recorded commodities may well have developed across the country, production structures remained underdeveloped leading to an unbalanced pattern of development typical of semi-peripheral societies that may be characterized by an "articulated lack of coincidence between relations of capitalist production and relations of social reproduction" (Santos 1985, 872).

These unbalanced patterns of development would lead to the emergence of alternative forms of commercial organization to fill gaps in production. Established in Lisbon, the bicycle trader José Castello Branco included phonography-related products in his stores around 1905 and devised ways of circumventing the lack of commercial autonomy by creating his own exclusive brand: "Discos Simplex CB," registered in the *Industrial Property Bulletin* in 1906. The businessman combined the commercialization of foreign products, in particular Odeon for which he was a commercial agent, with the sale of his own products in his store located on Rua de Santo Antão in downtown Lisbon. Taking advantage of their recording expeditions, Castello Branco seems to have hired the services of recording technicians, coming to Portugal at the service of foreign companies, so they could record the repertoire that was then published by his brand. Similarly, Simplex records were also printed and manufactured in the same factories (usually in Germany) as those sold by international brands such as Beka or Homokord. For this reason, the catalog numbers that appear on Simplex disc labels correspond to the numerical series of different foreign brands, depending on the years in which they were recorded (Losa and Belchior 2010).

José Castello Branco's pioneering approach led to the founding of the first Portuguese recording label, which was one of the few Portuguese labels for several decades to come. In the 1908 "Simplex Records Catalogue," José Castello Branco published a large list of the store's stock that included Simplex-

5. Invisible Voices of the Early Recording Market in Portugal   109

branded gramophones, needles, and records alongside recordings on Gramophone's Odeon and Companhia Franceza labels. Castello Branco's success in the national market is quite evident: the merchant often advertised his store and its products, and in today's historical record collections there are a significant number of Simplex records as well as the German Beka and Homokord labels. Targeting more affordable products than those of competing brands, as the 1908 catalog makes clear, the brand became well known among consumers of recorded music.

In the mid-1910s, José Castello Branco's stores were omitted from the advertisement sections of the main periodicals due to the economic and social fallout arising from World War I. The merchant's silence in the years surrounding the war had a knock-on effect for other establishments marketing phonograms, which no longer appeared in advertisements. However, Castello Branco's own activities survived the economically and socially troubled period following the war. In the 1921 *Trade Almanac*, the trader appears in the "talking machines" commercial sector and now at a new address (Almanaque do Comercio de 1921). From 1926, however, technological changes and the new competitive and organizational strategies implemented by multinational companies exerted considerable pressure on businesses in a shifting local market. Simplex was no exception, and the company did not survive the technological modernization of, and ongoing changes to, the music market.

Despite the decline of Simplex, José Castello Branco developed an entrepreneurial and emancipatory attitude in the face of a difficult commercial context, an attitude that was characterized by the republican ideals of modernity and progress and the development of national markets that were closely aligned with the international economy and markets. José Castello Branco's launching of the Discos Simplex brand was fundamental for establishing a market economy with local roots around phonographic goods, bringing the Portuguese reality closer to the commercial models prevalent in countries with stronger industries.

Another example of creative commercial strategies that led to the development of solid phonographic market dynamics can be seen with the company Sociedade Phonographica Portugueza, a company owned by the trader and composer Carlos Calderon. As José Castello Branco's chief competitor, Carlos Calderon implemented a distinct commercial strategy in Lisbon. Carlos Maria Ferreira Calderon (1867–1945) is recognized for his work as a composer of *teatro de revista* and operetta, from 1895 and lasting until the 1930s (Rebello 2010). However, parallel to his activity as a composer, Carlos Calderon was a key actor in the phonographic industry in Portugal, both as a visionary and as an entrepreneur who sought to embrace every area of the music market (most notably musical theater, sheet music, and phonographic publishing).

According to the theater historian Luiz Francisco Rebello (2010), it was after 1908 that Carlos Calderon's activities as a composer became more regularly focused on the *teatro de revista*. Yet Calderon had already envisioned a potential business in phonographic publishing and from around 1904 began to run the Sociedade Phonographica Portugueza (SPP),[8] which combined both sheet music and recorded music publishing and trade. He first approached the music market in 1904 when he was a CFG agent, at the time when this brand was investing heavily in the country as discussed above. In 1906, he joined the Porto-based merchant Artur Barbedo, the leading CFG agent in the city, and together registered the "Ideal" brand (Boletim de Propriedade Industrial 1906, 20). Unlike Simplex, the data from written sources and the phonograms themselves suggest that the "Ideal" brand was designed for the co-production of phonograms between Carlos Calderon and the German company Beka. In April 1905, the German company's recording technicians held sessions for recording Portuguese repertoire. These sessions resulted in commercial albums being published on the Beka label that were intended for distribution by the various Portuguese retailers selling this brand. However, the same recording sessions resulted in commercial albums also being published on the "Ideal" Grande-Beka Records label, with evidence suggesting that these phonograms were the exclusive responsibility of Carlos Calderon and Artur Barbedo who also took charge of commercial distribution. As a result, these entrepreneurs guaranteed their leading role in local markets and their own commercial autonomy vis-à-vis the German company alongside a fair and shared distribution of profits. Moreover, within a few years, Calderon further expanded his commercial operation by establishing facilities for recording music in the store's basement (Losa 2013). In doing so, he removed his dependence on recording technicians from foreign companies or the cost of sending performers to record abroad.

In the 1920s, the SPP also went under the name of "Casa Odeon." At this time, Carlos Calderon was appointed as the local representative of Odeon, a brand that belonged to the German company Lindström. His commercial responsibilities subsequently increased as he also played the role of national agent for the Transoceanic Trading Company, a commercial mediator importing and exporting Lindström records, which was in business between 1919 and 1931 (Gronow and Saunio 1998). As the Transoceanic Trading Company agent, Carlos Calderon was responsible for negotiating recording contracts between Odeon and the performers or their representatives.

Creating the Recorded Music Repertoire

If the initial repertoires of commercial recordings seem to be heterogeneous, embracing a large spectrum of possible tastes, the taste orientation of Portuguese society began to be redefined and circumscribed. Alongside the work of storekeepers and sound technicians, local agents such as Carlos Calderon and José Castello Branco helped to define the recorded repertoires that would eventually lead to the emergence of a Portuguese popular-music field. In fact, Calderon's proximity to the musical-theatrical context is paradigmatic of what became a local pattern of music-market development in Portugal (Losa and Belchior 2010). This proximity of the first recorded repertoires to the musical-theatrical context is concomitant with other phonogram markets in Europe. For example, Gronow and Englund (2007) explore the "invention" of the recorded repertoire in Scandinavia, where musical theater also played a central role, and Eva Moreda Rodríguez examines the importance of *zarzuela grande* in the first years of recorded repertoire in Spain (in this volume and 2021). Directed towards a space of production and cultural consumption that articulated the cultural values of different social groups, the recorded repertoire coming from the theatrical context could be defined as a middlebrow field of cultural production (Middleton 1990; Oliveira, Silva, and Losa 2008), that is the intermediary field between high and low culture, where popular music takes shape in close relation to its mediatization (Manuel 1993). Having already occupied the role of sheet music publisher and producer, Carlos Calderon devised a commercial model for music production based on the production of different commodity formats related to the same repertoire: musical compositions for live theater; sheet music publications targeting a musically literate audience with habits of domestic music making; and the recording of theatrical figures that often targeted another consumer sector of society whose cultural taste and practices were of more popular origins. By establishing different formats and cultural practices related to the same repertoire, Calderon created a model that would shape the production of popular music in Portugal for decades to come.

It seems that José Castello Branco also played an important role in the configuration of the local recording repertories. Alongside Castello Branco's media strategies, the modern configuration and geographical locations of his stores and their competitive pricing policy, the recordings also ensured success as they were firmly based on the recent repertoires of Lisbon's *teatro de revista*'s most successful musical numbers and *cançonetas*, a very dynamic comical and semi-dramatic genre that integrated music and spoken text, usually involving a single performer and sometimes two in dialogue, which was presented during theater intervals. The similarity between the repertoire and performers of Simplex CB recordings and those of Homokord and Beka may indicate that Castello Branco was an intermediary between the consumers' expectations and the foreign technicians who made the recordings. In 1910, following a strategy of progressive adaptation of the market to consumer demand, there was an increase in fado recordings appearing in the catalogs of brands such as Homokord. In fact, as in other international examples,[9] the history of the urban popular music genre fado developed in close relation with the history of recorded music, the music market, and industry in Portugal (Losa 2013).

The Invisibility of the Discs

Around 1910, there is evidence to suggest that the market economy surrounding phonographic commodities had already been established in Portuguese urban centers. In addition to the commercialization of phonographic goods, the attempt to set up a factory of records and gramophones by the industrialist Joaquim Duarte Ferreira (Boletim de Propriedade Industrial 1904, 34) at the end of the decade confirms that the market was consolidating and could represent a potentially lucrative sector. Even though the attempt was unsuccessful, it still illustrates how, at the beginning of the twentieth century, the Portuguese industrial classes were motivated to launch modern manufacturing industries.

Within a few years, phonography seemed to have carved out a place within social patterns of consumption and inaugurated a new labor context for publishers, traders, and performers. However, despite the commercial intensity surrounding phonography, the forms of agency carried out by shopkeepers and small industrialists, the volume of recorded repertoires and the considerable presence of foreign brands in the local market, the mediation of music by technological modernity in Portuguese society was all but silenced in the discursive domain: recorded music did not figure as an object of analysis or appreciation in periodicals at the time. Lengthy sections regarding spoken theater or public concerts omitted the existence of these repertoires as commercial recordings and therefore as domestic commodities. A fascination with great performers was reflected in biographical notes praising their artistic achievements on stage. But these notes never mentioned the repertoires recorded by these artists for various record companies alongside their theatrical activity. The records thus remained invisible and at the margins of the constellation of cultural products and practices of Lisbon's elite society.

5. Invisible Voices of the Early Recording Market in Portugal   113

Although absent from public discourse, records still occupied an important position in the consumption habits and modes of musical enjoyment of the social groups that energized the market. The economic investment necessary for purchasing phonographic products reflects how they targeted a market with buying power. Although they remained on the margins of social discourse, and were excluded from the "dominant culture," records found an audience among middle-class consumers with some economic power but weakened cultural capital, such as the socio-professional classes of merchants and service workers. The spread of phonographic recordings shows that they tended to correspond to criteria of popular taste, detached from the distinctive and elitist consumption patterns of the Portuguese aristocracy in the period preceding the Declaration of the Republic.

However, this positioning of recorded music in the social practices of the middle classes cannot be interpreted simply through the binary of art/popular. An analysis of the recordings that circulated in the Portuguese commercial market in the early twentieth century shows transversal patterns of social consumption, since the genres recorded were enjoyed across social and musical spectrums (such as folk songs, hymns, fado, operetta and *teatro de revista* numbers, opera arias, instrumental pieces, waltzes, polkas, among other instrumental dances, and piano fantasies). The orchestral and operatic repertoires usually performed live occupied considerable space in the catalogs of the main local publishers. The impact of cultural practice on the formation of class distinctions did not arise so much from the repertoires consumed as from their format or contexts of presentation. Genres traditionally defined as popular, such as fado, occupied the evenings of the aristocracy (Nery 2004), both through the circulation of sheet music for domestic use and the hiring of *fadistas* to animate their halls (2004). Similarly, the repertoires traditionally characterized as distinctive, such as opera or the instrumental music of the Western classical tradition, featured in the houses of the petty bourgeoisie and were played on gramophones. Until the late 1920s, different repertoires remained accessible to the different social groups. However, the actual forms of mediation were differentiated, and technologically mediated music seems to have failed to gain access to the range of social practices that constituted the lifestyles of the elite.

Conclusion

This chapter has adopted two lines of analysis. On the one hand, it has described the processes through which Portuguese society encountered "sound modernization" and the ways in which the phonographic market emerged in the country. On the other hand, it has considered the particularities of this process, situating the development of the recording industry in Portugal in the wider context of the country's approach to "modernity." In this second line of analysis, modernity describes not only technological development and new forms of relationship with reality—of which sound recording is a model example—but can also be understood as a dominant narrative and epistemology of history based on the "genealogy of the present" and "the triumphalism of modernity" (Venn 2000, 8). In taking this understanding of modernity as a starting point, I have sought to demonstrate how social approaches to the modernization of sound were defined by localized modes sometimes contrary to the linear and homogeneous narrative of modernity. Moreover, by focusing on the role played by the agents of small commerce in Portuguese cities, I have privileged a historiographical narrative based more on the agency of the subjects than on large historical markers, an exercise that, I hope, brings a more nuanced and multidimensional understanding of historical processes.

Notes

This chapter is derived from the author's book *"Machinas Fallantes": A música gravada em Portugal no início do século XX.* The research emerged from the project "The Phonographic Industry in Twentieth Century Portugal," carried out by an interdisciplinary team at the Institute of Ethnomusicology, Center for Music and Dance of the NOVA University of Lisbon, coordinated by Salwa El-Shawan Castelo-Branco and supported by the National Foundation for Scientific Research (PTDC/HAH/70991/2006).

1. Although in the English-speaking literature the term most commonly used to refer to the industry and market generated around recorded music is "recording industry," throughout this text I also make recourse to the terms *phonography*, *phonographic industry*, and *phonographic market*, which best describe these phenomena in the Portuguese language. *Phonography* includes the extended relationships generated around recorded music expressed in the production, commercialization, social practices of listening and consumption, discursive production, and the modes of symbolization of recorded sound. By *phonographic industry* and *phonographic market*, I refer to the more circumscribed universe of economic relations of production and the consumption of records and goods associated with recorded music.

2. The British Ultimatum in 1890 that forced the Portuguese military to retreat from areas in southern Africa claimed by the British government, followed by the financial crisis of 1890–91, the spread of socialist ideals from northern Europe, the failure of the liberal model, and the call for economic protectionism, were determining factors for the social unrest that emerged among predominantly urban populations who questioned the oligarchy embodied by the Portuguese monarchy (Rosas 2010).

3. The main record collections analyzed in this chapter are archived at the Museu Nacional do Teatro (National Museum of Theatre), the Museu do Fado (Fado Museum),

5. Invisible Voices of the Early Recording Market in Portugal   115

as well as from the private collections of Luís Cangueiro, Francisco Siqueira, Anjos de Carvalho, and João Pedro Mendes dos Santos.

4. The mapping of the stores that commercialized records and phonographic commodities has been mainly carried out through an analysis of the advertisement sections of the period's newspapers and stamps glued in records and sheet music.

5. *Teatro de revista* is a genre of musical theater characterized by a sequence of spoken and sung "numbers" constituting a partially narrative structure that comments on current political and social events in a comic and satirical style. The music was usually accompanied by an orchestra. In addition to actors and singers, the *teatro de revista* also featured dancers.

6. From 1908, all these small brands were steadily integrated into the German company Lindström AG following a trend to acquire several small companies to build up large conglomerates. As the century progressed, this trend intensified and generated major transformations in the early patterns of development. In the mid-1920s, Lindström AG, initially a factory, was competing with the largest companies that globally dominated record production, such as The Gramophone Company, Columbia Graphophone, and Victor Talking Machine.

7. Although it is not an exhaustive survey, I identified about two dozen stores in Lisbon and Porto on the basis of advertisements in periodicals (Losa 2013, 63).

8. Portuguese Phonographic Society, a company registered by Madureira & C^a in 1901 (Boletim da Propriedade Industrial 1901, 171).

9. For the impact of mediatization on other musical genres, see Manuel (1993) and Racy (1978).

References

Almanaque do Comercio de 1921.

Alves, Daniel. 2010. "A república atrás do balcão—os lojistas de Lisboa na fase final da monarquia (1870–1910)." PhD diss., NOVA University of Lisbon.

Belchior, Susana. 2013. "Sinkler Darby's 1900 Expedition for the Gramophone Company in Portugal." In *The Lindström Project—Contributions to the History of the Record Industry—Beiträge zur Geschichte der Schallplattenindustrie*. Vol. 3. Edited by Pekka Gronow and Christiane Hofer, 50–55. Vienna: Gesellschaft fur Historische Tonträger.

Boletim da Propriedade Industrial, January 1901.

Boletim da Propriedade Industrial, January 1904.

Boletim da Propriedade Industrial, January 1906.

Gaisberg, F. W. 1942. *The Music Goes Round*. New York: The Macmillan Company.

Gronow, Pekka. 1983. "The Record Industry: The Growth of a Mass Medium." *Popular Music* 3: 53–75.

Gronow, Pekka, and Björn Englund. 2007. "Inventing Recorded Music: The Recorded Repertoire in Scandinavia, 1899–1925." *Popular Music* 26, no. 2: 281–304.

Gronow, Pekka, and Ilpo Saunio. 1998. *An International History of the Recording Industry*. London: Cassel.

Losa, Leonor. 2013. *"Machinas Fallantes": A música gravada em Portugal no início do século XX*. Lisbon: Tinta-da-China.

Losa, Leonor, and Susana Belchior. 2010. "The Introduction of Phonogram Market in

Portugal: Lindström Labels and Local Traders (1879–1925)." In *The Lindström Project—Contributions to the History of the Record Industry*. Vol. 2. Edited by Pekka Gronow and Christian Hofer, 67–71. Vienna: Gesellschaft fur Historische Tonträger.

Manuel, Peter. 1993. *Cassette Culture: Popular Music and Technology in North India*. Chicago: The University of Chicago Press.

———. 2001. "Popular Music (ii) World Popular Music." In *The New Grove Dictionary of Music and Musicians*, edited by Stanley Sadie and John Tyrrell. London: MacMillan Press.

Martland, Peter. 1997. *Since Records Began: EMI, The First 100 Years*. London: Batsford.

Middleton, Richard. 1990. *Studying Popular Music*. Milton Keynes, UK: Open University Press.

Moreda Rodríguez, Eva. 2021. *Inventing the Recording: The Phonograph and National Culture in Spain, 1877–1914*. Oxford: Oxford University Press.

Nery, Rui Vieira. 2004. *Para uma história do fado*. Maia, PT: Público, Comunicação Social.

Novo catalogo e repertorio portuguez Pathé. 1906. Fac-similed reproduction nº0031. Phonogalerie, Paris, 2006

Oliveira, Gonçalo Antunes de, João Silva, and Leonor Losa. 2008. "A edição de música impressa e a mediatização do fado: o caso do fado do 31." *Etno-Folk—Revista Galega de Música* 12: 55–68.

O Occidente, nº8, April 1878:64.

Pereira, David. 2010. "A sociedade." In *História da primeira República Portuguesa*, edited by Fernando Rosas and Maria Fernanda Rollo, 79–92. Lisbon: Tinta-da-china.

Racy. 1978. "Arabian Music and the Effects of Commercial Recording." *The World of Music* 20, no. 1: 47–55.

Rebello, Luiz Francisco. 2010. "Calderon, Carlos Maria Ferreira." In *Enciclopédia da música em Portugal no século XX*, edited by Salwa Castelo-Branco, 203–4. Lisbon: Círculo de Leitores.

Rollo, Maria Fernanda. 2010. "Da insustentabilidade do modelo à crise do sistema" In *História da primeira República Portuguesa*, edited by Fernando Rosas and Maria Fernanda Rollo, 27–42. Lisbon: Tinta-da-china.

Rosas, Fernando. 2010. "A crise do liberalismo oligárquico em Portugal." In *História da primeira República Portuguesa*, edited by Fernando Rosas and Maria Fernanda Rollo, 15–26. Lisbon: Tinta-da-china.

Santos, Boaventura de Sousa. 1985. "Estado e sociedade na semiperifieria do sistema mundial: O caso português." *Análise Social* 21, nos. 87, 88, 89: 869–901.

Taylor, Timothy, Mark Katz, and Toby Grajeda. 2012. *Music, Sound, and Technology in America: A Documentary History of Early Phonograph, Cinema, and Radio*. Durham, NC: Duke University Press.

Venn, Couze. 2000. *Occidentalism: Modernity and Subjectivity*. London: Sage.

Wallis, Roger, and Krister Malm. 1984. *Big Sounds from Small Peoples: The Music Industry in Small Countries*. New York: Pendragon.

———. 1992. *Media Policy and Music Activity*. London: Routledge.

5. Invisible Voices of the Early Recording Market in Portugal 117

Additional References

Katz, Mark. 2004. *Capturing Sound: How Technology Has Changed Music*. Berkeley: University of California Press.

Middleton, Richard. 2001. "Popular Music." In *The New Grove Dictionary of Music and Musicians*, edited by Stanley Sadie and John Tyrrell. London: MacMillan Press.

Rebello, Luiz Francisco. 2010b. "Opereta." In *Enciclopédia da música em Portugal no século XX*, edited by Salwa Castelo-Branco, 935–38. Lisbon: Círculo de Leitores.

———. 2010c. "Teatro de revista." In *Enciclopédia da música em Portugal no século XX*, edited by Salwa Castelo-Branco, 1248–53. Lisbon: Círculo de Leitores.

Rollo, Maria Fernanda. 1996. "Indústria/Industrialização." In *Dicionário de história do Estado Novo*. Vol. 1. Edited by Fernando Rosas and J.M. Brandão de Brito, 460–80. Venda Nova, PT: Bertrand Editora.

———. 2010b. "Paradigmas frustrados: perseguição e fuga da modernidade e do progresso." In *História da primeira República Portuguesa*, edited by Fernando Rosas and Maria Fernanda Rollo, 229–44. Lisbon: Tinta-da-china.

———. 2010c. "Economia e inovação: derivações em cenário de crise." In *História da primeira República Portuguesa*, edited by Fernando Rosas and Maria Fernanda Rollo, 523–34. Lisbon: Tinta-da-china.

Taylor, Timothy. 2007. "The Commodification of Music at the Dawn of the Era of 'Mechanical Music.'" *Ethnomusicology* 51, no. 2: 281–305.

6

Radio, Popular Music, and Nationalism in Portugal in the 1940s

PEDRO MOREIRA

In 1941, António Ferro was the then-new director of the National Radio (Emissora Nacional, henceforth NR) and simultaneously the head of the National Propaganda Secretariat (Secretariado da Propaganda Nacional—SPN), a post he held since 1933. He decided that the general programming, and especially music broadcasts on the NR, should sound more "Portuguese" and converge with the values and nationalist propaganda of the Portuguese authoritarian regime (Ferro 1950, 15–30). One of his strategies was to design a policy that aimed at "Portuguesefying" (*aportuguesamento*) the popular music (*música ligeira*)[1] broadcast on the NR and "shielding" audiences from the impact of foreign musical genres that were then popular such as jazz, tango, samba, and French song (Moreira 2012; Roxo and Castelo-Branco 2016). However, rather than forbidding these genres, they were recontextualized at a discursive level. The institutionalization of Portuguese popular music in the National Radio music production resulted in repertoires (mostly popular songs) that mixed local musical genres and styles, mainly drawing on rural musics, with selected foreign music styles such as those mentioned above. In order to implement this seemingly paradoxical strategy, a music production system was set up within the NR in the 1940s that paved the way for the creation of Portuguese music styles and repertoires that became popular locally but that also gained some international visibility.

6. Radio, Popular Music, and Nationalism in Portugal

This chapter examines the creation and institutionalization of Portuguese popular music within the NR during the 1940s, a period corresponding to António Ferro's administration. It will consider national discourses against the backdrop of the wider international context, highlighting how nationalist music mixed local and transnational musical styles and performance models. It will also examine how national and transnational repertoires contributed to the configuration of radio music production in the context of the Portuguese National Radio. Based on the assumption that national radio structures were formed through transnational processes and by drawing on a case study of the vocal group Irmãs Meireles, I interrogate how the tension between the local and the cosmopolitan (Turino 2013) informed the NR's nationalist ideological project and its strategy of "Portuguesifying" popular music.

I draw on a growing body of work that focuses on Portugal (Moreira 2012; Ribeiro 2005, 2007; Santos 2005; Silva 2005, 2010) and other countries (Birdsall 2012; Currid 2006; Hayes 2000; Hilmes 2012; Pinho and Mendívil 2019), which analyzes the use of radio by authoritarian regimes to inculcate nationalist ideologies, often instrumentalizing popular music. As Hilmes argues, nation-states used radio "as national circulatory systems, delivering the signs and symbols of the national imaginary across geographical space into individual homes and minds" (2012, 2). He also affirms that "The continuing presence of the transnational [. . .] shaped core values, aesthetics, and practices within each national tradition, whether in opposition, resistance, adaptation, exchange or emulation, or some combination of all of those" (3). Thus it is relevant to contextualize radio nationalism at a transnational level (Western 2018, 258), given that "national structures of radio were formed in transnational processes" (Badenoch and Föllmer 2018, 11) affecting, as we shall see, the National Radio's music policies and production.

The Estado Novo and National Radio

> "If this device does not fail, which seems to tremble at the slightest vibrations of my voice, I will be speaking at this moment to the largest audience that has ever gathered in Portugal to listen to someone's word." (António de Oliveira Salazar's Speech, Broadcast by the NR, *Diário de Lisboa*, December 9, 1934)[2]

The Portuguese authoritarian regime, dubbed Estado Novo (New State), was officially established in 1933 by António de Oliveira Salazar (1889–1970) and lasted until the April 25, 1974, revolution. It was anchored on the ideological cornerstones of nationalism, Catholicism, authority, ruralism, and traditionalism. As with other authoritarian regimes, such as those in Italy or Spain, a network of institutions exerted state control over all sectors of society, allowing for the transformation and resurgence of a country modeled by its dictator's ideology. In Portugal, cultural production operated within or was affected by several institutions, particularly the Secretariat of National Propaganda that designed cultural policy and sponsored, regulated, and promoted all cultural activities (Roxo and Castelo-Branco 2016, 213); the National Foundation for Joy at Work (Fundação Nacional para a Alegria no Trabalho—FNAT), which was in charge of workers' leisure time and popular culture (Valente 1999); and the Censorship Services that had a major impact on the media and all cultural activities.

The National Radio was officially founded in August 1935, after one and a half years of experimental activity, quickly becoming a key vehicle for disseminating the regime's ideology and political propaganda. Prior to the NR's foundation, there was much debate around the political and artistic role of radio. The First National Conference of Radiotelephony (I Congresso Nacional de Radiotelefonia), held in 1932 and organized by the newspaper *O Século*, served as the basis for the creation of the 1933 decree-law that regulated the NR and private radio stations that had been operating for almost a decade.[3] During the conference, the modernist composer Luís de Freitas Branco (1890–1955) called for the cooperation between engineers and musicians and proposed the introduction of a course on radio broadcasting at the National Conservatory in Lisbon, where he taught (Silva 2010, 1081). He was hopeful that the NR could help resolve the unemployment crisis faced by musicians since the end of the 1920s, a crisis that was provoked by the increasing dissemination of sound recordings, radio broadcasts, and sound cinema, and that led to a decrease in the number of orchestras and small ensembles during that period (Silva 2010, 1081), similar to what happened with the BBC (Doctor 1999, 16). His proposal that the NR should found a symphony orchestra that could employ musicians was implemented in 1934 under the direction of his brother, the conductor Pedro de Freitas Branco (1896–1963). The musical milieu was also hopeful that the NR would have the capacity to stimulate and to centralize musical production that was adrift (*O Século*, November 26, 1931).

The 1932 conference also provided a platform for debate around radio's political mission and how it could serve as a medium for the regime's propaganda, although the role that radio could play was not always clear. A parallel is found here in the Italian regime, where initially Mussolini did not "realize its [radio] potential as a vehicle for propaganda" (Ragnedda 2014, 201). In Portugal, up to the 1940s, the radio as a propaganda tool was a controversial issue that led to disputes among politicians about who should head the National Radio. During the first two radio administrations (1934–1940), the NR was the responsibility of the General Administration of Posts, Telegraphs, and Telephones (Administração Geral dos Correios, Telefones e Telégrafos—AGCTT), resisting the SPN's authority and António Ferro's ambition. Politically, Salazar understood that the NR could be a propaganda tool, but he was ambivalent about delivering all propaganda issues to the SPN and especially to António Ferro, trying to please other figures of the regime, mainly Couto dos Santos, Director of the AGCTT, and Duarte Pacheco, Minister of Public Works and Communications. In 1934, this led several figures of the regime to question the existence of the NR as a political project and to rising tensions between the NR and Ferro's SPN, which even threatened to broadcast political propaganda on a private radio station (Ribeiro 2007, 180).

National Radio's Administrations, Programming, and Their Nationalist Orientations

Radio broadcasting depended not only on the national political framework and transnational factors (Birdsall and Walewska-Choptiany 2019; Western 2018; Hilmes 2012) but also on the agency, and personal, intellectual, and artistic profiles of the radio administrators in defining the NR's policy and programming. Political and artistic concerns were, in different ways, the main policy priorities for the NR's first three administrations led by António Joyce (1934–1935), Henrique Galvão (1935–1940), and António Ferro (1941–1949).

The NR's first director, António Joyce (1888–1964), was a well-known composer and choir conductor. His main concern was to create a structure for music production, which meant that he lacked a political strategy for the NR. Joyce was influenced by international models for organizing radio orchestras and applying these to the Portuguese case. In particular he was inspired by the BBC's model,[4] which led him to found several orchestras in an effort to respond to the musicians' employment crisis during a period marked by the appearance of several radio orchestras across Europe and the US (Lawson 2003, 277–78).[5] The NR orchestra model included a "Symphony Orchestra; a Music-Hall Orchestra; a String Orchestra; a Sextet with harmonium, and chamber music ensembles[. . .]" (O Século, April 7, 1934). According to Joyce, the "renaissance of Portuguese Music" was dependent on radio orchestras, since "we currently have no orchestra formed in Portugal [and] our musicians are unemployed" (Rádio Jornal, July 22, 1934). Following the BBC's model where radio was considered the center of music production (Doctor 1999, 17),[6] Joyce spent a considerable part of his budget on the Music Department, configuring the NR as an almost exclusively artistic project (Moreira 2012, 127–28). He was also responsible for founding the Portuguese Music Section (Secção Musical Portuguesa) and hired

122 PEDRO MOREIRA

Ruy Coelho (1889–1986), the regime's "semi-official" composer, to run it. His goal was to support Portuguese art music composition and the collection of rural musics that could serve as the basis for the creation of a nationalist repertoire (Moreira 2012, 50).

Budgetary problems and the lack of a political strategy for the NR were problematic issues for Salazar and other figures of the regime. In March 1935, the government appointed Fernando Homem Christo (1900–1995), a former student of Salazar at the University of Coimbra and a member of the National Union (União Nacional), the regime's official political party, with the mission of reporting on the NR's activities and establishing a political plan. Christo revealed what he considered to be the almost nonexistence of supporters of the regime among the staff, which led him to call for urgent change in programming and personnel.[7] This meant the end of Joyce's administration. However, for Salazar and his staff, Christo's radical political vision, connected to the regime's ultra-extreme-right wing ideology, disqualified him from running the NR's political program. Ferro was not under consideration either. In 1935, Henrique Galvão was appointed as the new director for the NR. He was an important military member of the regime well known for his rigor, his ideological loyalty, and his links to colonial affairs due to his positions as Portuguese representative at the Colonial Congress of Paris in 1931, director of the Colonial Fairs of Luanda (Angola) and Lourenço Marques (Mozambique) in 1932, and director of the First Colonial Exhibition in Porto in 1934. As a high-ranking military officer, Galvão had the important mission of making the NR a "respectable" Estado Novo institution as well as rescuing it from the difficult financial situation inherited from the previous administration. The NR was to serve as "another enlisted soldier, a force at the service of the Estado Novo," as stated at the official inauguration in August 1935 (*Boletim da Emissora Nacional*, no. 1, August, 1935).

Unlike his predecessor, Galvão brought to the NR a strongly nationalist ideological project that intended to transform it into the "voice" of the Estado Novo. He implemented reformist measures that included financial rigor and the reorganization of the music department that had consumed a significant part of the budget, reducing the number of orchestras to three: a Symphony Orchestra, a Portuguese Orchestra, and a Music-Hall Orchestra (Moreira 2012, 128).

During a period characterized by access to several foreign radio stations in Portugal, mainly the BBC but also German and Italian stations that broadcasted in Portuguese, Galvão launched a plan to increase the NR's coverage on medium and shortwave stations aimed at rural Portugal, the Portuguese colonies, and emigrant communities.[8] Shortwave radio stations, at a transnational level,

6. Radio, Popular Music, and Nationalism in Portugal   123

"intensified existing competition over available frequencies and the attention of listening audiences" (Birdsall and Walewska-Choptiany 2019, 440), and had considerable impact during the war time in what has been called a "war of the waves" (Gagliarducci, Onorato, Sobbrio, and Tabellini 2020). For Galvão, Portugal needed to mark its political position in the international (Lusophone) domain, broadcasting the regime's propaganda on selected radio programs and affirming its popular culture and national identity.

Galvão's plan to transform the NR into an institution that could contribute to the building of a national identity that aligned with Salazar's vision overlapped with António Ferro's and the SPN's approach, especially when he announced several radio programs and live events that celebrated folklore and popular culture like the Folkloric and Ethnographic Parade (Cortejo Folclórico e Etnográfico), which took place in Lisbon in 1937 with all regions represented (Ribeiro 2012, 177).[9] In January 1938, Galvão and Ferro argued in newspaper articles over who should organize events exhibiting folklore and popular culture, revealing their different positions (177–78). The dispute continued until 1940, when, on the occasion of the Exhibition of the Portuguese World (Exposição do Mundo Português), the largest propaganda event of Salazar's regime held in Lisbon to celebrate the double centenary of the foundation of Portugal (1140) and the restoration of its independence from the Spanish crown (1640), Galvão gained control over the Parade of the Portuguese World (Cortejo do Mundo Português), leaving out António Ferro and the SPN. Following a dispute with the minister Duarte Pacheco, Galvão was removed from his position as the NR's director and Ferro was appointed as its new director in 1941.

António Ferro's "Politics of the Spirit" and the "Portuguesification" of Popular Music (1941–1949)

World War II had a considerable impact on Portuguese national institutions, which had to reframe and adapt their activities. In the political domain, Salazar understood that radio and propaganda should go hand in hand, accepting Ferro's own vision that had been influenced by international authoritarian models. In 1939, a governmental decree limited private radios to broadcast only a few hours a day from the same transmitter, forbid publicity as a way of revenue, and implemented a government employee to supervise broadcastings. Rádio Clube Português, a pro-regime private radio station that had an important propaganda role during the Spanish Civil War (Pena Rodríguez 2011), and Rádio Renscença, the Catholic radio station, continued their broadcasts with some restrictions (Santos 2005). By 1941, Ferro had absolute control over the NR but also a "disguised" monopoly system that allowed him to implement his vision of the Estado Novo's ideology.

António Ferro took office as the NR's director in 1941, combining this position with the SPN directorship. He started his career as a journalist and writer. In the interwar period, he interviewed major political and intellectual figures such as Gabriele d'Annunzio, Jean Cocteau, Mussolini, Primo de Rivera, and Salazar, and traveled to the US and several European countries. As an intellectual, he was influenced by the modernist and cosmopolitan avant-garde, a perspective that did not always align with Salazar's traditionalist and provincial outlook. Nevertheless, Ferro, considered the "inventor of Salazarism" (Raimundo 2015), was important in defining the regime's propaganda strategy until 1949, when he was removed from office. He reorganized the cultural field, reinventing Portugal and its traditions (Castelo-Branco and Branco 2003).

Taking up the position as the NR's director also meant that Ferro needed to align the radio's programming policy with the Estado Novo's main ideological pillars and priorities and with the SPN's cultural policy dubbed as the "Politics of the Spirit" (*Política do Espírito*), which undergirded cultural production in the 1930s and 1940s. The Politics of the Spirit "was intended to create a modern cultural configuration for Portugal, in which the nation was imagined according to the regime's imperialist ideals" (Roxo and Castelo-Branco 2016, 213), instrumentalizing expressive culture as political propaganda with the aim of creating an official aesthetics of the regime. This involved, among other aspects, promoting stylized and modernized representations of the rural world (Alves 2013), a strategy that was applied to the NR's musical production (Moreira 2012). For António Ferro, control over public radio was essential to affirm the nation's vitality during war time; it was a way of emphasizing Portuguese "neutrality" and "peace" granted by Salazar's leadership in contrast to the war-time propaganda encountered in Germany or France (Fagot 2014). Ferro knew the international scenario and the importance of radio broadcasting. As he stated: "We are going through a moment in which listening to the radio is to feel the heartbeat of the nations, to know the state of their soul" (Ferro 1950, 24). Thus, he considered that his mission as the new director of the NR was vital to the country, arguing that "To the National Radio, the most powerful instrument of direct propaganda that exists in our country, it largely belongs the heavy responsibility for the civic, moral, and artistic education of our people" (19). Anchored to the Politics of the Spirit, Ferro's strategy was to "Portuguesify" the NR's programming and, in particular, popular music. This was also the basis of several of the SPN's initiatives (Alves, 2013).

6. Radio, Popular Music, and Nationalism in Portugal 125

In the case of the NR, Ferro aimed to mix elements of Portuguese popular culture with international models—in what he considered to be the "mixture of Portugal with the world and with our era" (Ferro 1950, 40)—in a stylized modernization of presumably traditional elements. In Ferro's opinion, this strategy provided a solution to the problem of excessive exposure to foreign popular music and the scarcity of Portuguese popular music (37–41). The strategy was based on the notion that so-called "rural" music was an "authentic" element of Portuguese culture and was underpinned by a nationalist agenda in which music could be in the "service" of the state (Bohlman 2004, 119). As part of the SPN's folkloristic initiatives, the use of popular culture served to integrate people across the nation as part of an imagined community (Anderson 1983), but it also served as a living portrait of a culturally rich nation where "traditional" expressive culture was to be introduced to the modern world for entertainment and leisure (Alves 2013).

Central to the NR's strategy of Portuguesifying music was the collection of rural musics that were harmonized and arranged, or used as the basis for the creation of art and popular music compositions, as a way of counteracting the influence of American, French, Spanish, and Brazilian musics.[10] In a broadcast speech from 1942, the NR's director stated that light or popular programs should be taken very seriously, never forgetting their main function as entertainment (Ferro 1950, 37), an idea that was central to Ferro's vision for popular music production. In his words, he indicated what should be done: "Replace that frenetic music by Portuguese popular music, which has the same seductive power? Replace it by our own melodies, which are not limited to being regionalist [and] folkloric [. . .], but that can be listened to with pleasure in Lisbon, as well as in Paris, Berlin, Rome, London, or New York?" (39).

Ferro's Portuguesifying project had several opponents in the musical milieu, particularly the art music composer Fernando Lopes-Graça (1906–1994) who fought against the regime's ideology and strategy for culture, including the folklorization of rural musics. He was very critical about the use of the label "Portuguese music" to refer to music remotely based on traditional genres, which he believed could be "very 'nationalist' but [not] national, in the sense that the national identifies with the capabilities or translates the capacities of a people to create universal or universalizing values" (Lopes-Graça 1989, 61–62). However, Ferro's intention was to promote the creation of hybrid styles, mixing musics collected in rural areas with internationally popular musical styles and genres. In order to achieve this goal, he mobilized composers, arrangers, singers, conductors, and orchestras to compose and to perform this repertoire on radio programs.

Institutionalizing the "Portuguesification" of Popular Music

The institutionalization of the "Portuguesification" of popular music was an important political move by António Ferro's administration, affecting all music production, including art and popular musics. He invited the composer Pedro do Prado[11] (1908–1990) to take office as Director of the NR's Music Department with the aim of implementing the "Portuguesification" policy. In 1942, Prado and Ferro founded the Musical Studies Bureau (Gabinete de Estudos Musicais—MSB), a department that provided support for the creation of a repertoire of both popular and art music grounded in rural musics (*Rádio Nacional*, March 22, 1942). The MSB was structured into four sections dedicated to the harmonization of rural melodies by art music composers; the composition of art music inspired by national historical events and figures, using stylized rural melodies; the arrangement of popular songs for voice, sometimes with orchestral accompaniment, based on rural musics; and the recording and editing of music produced within the framework of the MSB (*Rádio Nacional*, March 22, 1942). The strategy developed by the MSB was meant to compensate for the scarcity of Portuguese popular music considered adequate for broadcasting by the NR. As Ferro questioned: "But where is, actually, that music? It is not enough to fill the NR's light dance programs [. . .]. Regarding traditional music [*música típica*] there are not many records that are appropriate for broadcast" (1950, 39). And he continues, affirming that "[. . .] nothing will be able to destroy, for now, the nonexistence of Portuguese popular music [*música ligeira portuguesa*]" (41), considering that the NR should have an important role in solving this problem.

The NR's popular music was intended to entertain the audience with national musical references but also to include what António Ferro referred to as the "*international* imagination" (40), by which he meant popular song and dance genres and styles such as one-step, fox-trot, swing, but also French popular songs, Brazilian samba, and Argentinian tango. This illustrates that the regime's attitude towards the inclusion of genres such as jazz or tango in radio broadcasting were sometimes contradictory as was the case with other European contexts such as Italy (Ragnedda 2014, 204–6). For this purpose, Ferro commissioned composers to create songs that combined national "popular rhythms" finding a "desirable formula" that resulted in the "mixture of Portugal with the world and with our era" (Ferro 1950, 40). The "desirable formula" also meant the establishment of the NR's own music production system. This included: hiring composers, arrangers and conductors, and founding different orchestras that could perform the new repertoire, most notably the *Orquestra Ligeira* (Popular Music Orchestra) conducted by Armando Tavares Belo (1911–1993) and inspired by American big bands and the *Orquestra Típica Portuguesa* (Portuguese Typical Orchestra), consisting of traditional chordophones and wind instruments, conducted by José Belo Marques (1898–1986).[12] The above-mentioned composers were almost entirely devoted to composing and arranging new repertoire for the NR's orchestras and vocal groups.

The following step was to find and to coach appropriate voices for singing the repertoire composed by the NR's composers, mainly vocal quartets, trios and duets, but also soloists. In 1943, the NR launched singing competitions with the goal of finding new voices and rewarding some of its famous voices (Moreira 2012, 237). In 1947, as it was still difficult to find new singers, António Ferro and Mota Pereira, a former opera singer, launched the Centro de Preparação de Artistas (Center for Preparing Artists), a center for training the NR's singers in vocal techniques and to sing with orchestral accompaniment.

Several vocal groups were formed within the NR and became the main attraction of popular radio broadcasts, such as variety shows and, particularly, the Evenings for Workers (Serões para trabalhadores) organized with FNAT (the National Foundation for Joy at Work) since 1941. Mainly trained and rehearsed by radio orchestra conductors, they emulated international popular singers and film stars. The American Andrews Sisters and Boswell Sisters were the models for several vocal duos and trios founded and promoted by the NR, namely the Irmãs Santos, Irmãs Meireles, and the Irmãs Remartinez. The Americanization of vocal styles and performance models during this period had parallels in other dictatorships, for example the Trio Lescano in Italy (Forgacs and Gundle 2007, 184)[13] and the Hermanas Arveu and Hermanas Russell in Spain (Iglesias 2013, 8), groups that were linked to the swing era and were usually formed by and rehearsed with well-known jazz orchestra conductors.[14] As Iglesias argues regarding swing in Spain, the success of "sister" vocal groups in dictatorial regimes during the late 1930s and 1940s was based on the fact that swing was mainly a form of "physical entertainment" (dance) and not of "aesthetic contemplation" (2013, 7). It created an interest in jazz production and consumption both in Portugal (Roxo and Castelo-Branco 2016) and Spain (Iglesias 2013). In Portugal, other factors contributed to the popularity of the "sister" groups, mainly the modernist ideas of António Ferro, the influence of international phonographic labels and Hollywood films, and the centrality and strength of the NR's music production system.

Nationalism and the "International Imagination": The Irmãs Meireles

Radio singers, especially in popular music genres, had great popularity in the 1930s and 1940s, becoming well-known stars in their own countries but also internationally. The NR's singers became very popular, bringing to people's homes and through live performance the results of a programming policy and musical production system oriented towards the creation and promotion of a nationalist repertoire that would be mixed with international music genres. The Irmãs Meireles (Meireles Sisters) was one of the most popular vocal groups in Portugal during the 1940s but also had a prominent international career. Also known as Trio Meireles, this vocal group consisted of three sisters from Porto and was modelled on the Andrews Sisters (Moreira 2012).[15] In 1943, António Ferro and his wife, the writer Fernanda de Castro, invited the Meireles sisters to form a vocal ensemble. For Ferro, the idea of creating a group that could be the "voice of the nationalist" regime, but that evoked an "international imagination" at the same time, was fundamental (Ferro 1950, 40). He provided the conditions within the NR for training and promoting the Irmãs Meireles.

Soon after the formation of the Irmãs Meireles, the composer and conductor Tavares Belo, who conducted a jazz orchestra at Casino Estoril, was hired by the NR. He trained the group in vocal techniques and composed and made arrangements of repertoire, both with orchestra and *a capella*, which was adequate for their voices. They rehearsed this repertoire with the NR's Popular Music Orchestra that Belo also conducted. In 1943, the group began performing the new repertoire, alongside major international hits, on several radio programs. In 1945, they were invited to perform in Barcelona, Spain, at the Cine-Olimpia and Salon Rigat, also recording their first phonograms for His Masters Voice (*Diário de Lisboa*, October 10, 1972).

The discourse surrounding the Irmãs Meireles was in tune with António Ferro's own ideas, as it emphasized their mission to bring attention to Portuguese rural and traditional music and to well-known international songs. As one of the sisters, Cidália, stated: "The government helped us in our 'crusade,' paying for our studies. We can say they hired the maestro Tavares Belo almost exclusively to teach and train us. We then toured over all of Portugal, disseminating and elevating national music. In Minho, [a region in the northwest of Portugal] people did not know music from the south, and vice-versa. That was our mission: to unveil to every corner of the country the music from all the other corners" (*Álbum da canção* no. 41, July 1, 1966).

6. Radio, Popular Music, and Nationalism in Portugal   129

Following World War II, the Portuguese regime changed its cultural policy, which affected António Ferro's strategy of using some singers to project Portugal's image abroad. The Irmãs Meireles were the products of his effort to "Portuguesify" popular music by creating a formula that presumably reconciled "authenticity" with the "international imagination" (Ferro 1950, 40). In 1947, the Irmãs Meireles went to Brazil with the mission to promote Portuguese music on Brazilian National Radio and in local concert halls. Their success in Rio de Janeiro and other Brazilian cities was considerable, as highlighted in several newspaper articles. According to Cidália Meireles: "[...] our name crossed the borders of Brazil and our presence was demanded in other countries in Latin America. We performed in Argentina, Chile—we went for a month and stayed eight—Uruguay. Then we returned to Brazil, where we made a new artistic tour" (*Álbum da canção* no. 41, July 1, 1966). During their tour in Brazil, they recorded for major commercial labels such as Sinter, Capitol, and Continental.

The repertoire they performed in several theaters across Brazil was the same that they sang in Portugal, composed for them by Belo Marques, Tavares Belo, Silva Marques, and other NR composers. The shows followed a tripartite structure, mixing "Portuguese folklore" with "international music" and "popular melodies." The program presented at the Municipal Theater of São Paulo on October 13, 1947, illustrates the show model, which alternated between solo and trio numbers and repertoire by the NR's composers. The program was divided into three parts: the first was dedicated to "Portuguese folklore"; the second to "international music," from Franz Schubert to Hekel Tavares and London Ronald; and the third to "popular melodies" by George Gershwin, Ary Barroso, and Tavares Belo (Borges 2016, 107–9).

Between 1948 and 1950, the Irmãs Meireles toured in Argentina, Chile, Peru, and Colombia, where they also performed with local artists (Borges 2016). In 1949, after almost two years on tour, they returned to Portugal where they were received like national heroes, as documented by local newspapers: "The artistic tour of the Irmãs Meireles was not only a commercial success, [but] a victory for the Portuguese Radio. It was [. . .] a consoling and happy moment for all Portuguese that, in other countries, show the dignity, effort, and the qualities of a race spread throughout the world, with their soul rooted in our patriotic land" (*Rádio Nacional*, April 2, 1949). In 1949, the year António Ferro's administration as the head of the SPN and the NR came to an end, the Meireles sisters returned to Brazil and ended their career as a trio two years later.

Final Observations

The politics of nationalism played out on the Portuguese National Radio reflect different perspectives on the role of radio in propaganda, as illustrated by its three administrations. The pressures of civil society and the musicians' employment crisis played major roles in defining the NR's strategy during its first year, namely to give priority to "artistic" projects influenced by the BBC's orchestra model. The replacement of its director in 1935 signaled the fact that the NR was of capital importance in promoting the Portuguese nationalist project and affirming its position among the most important Estado Novo institutions. However, the nationalist approach adopted by the NR was different from that of the SPN directed by António Ferro. In 1941, when he took office as the NR's director, his project of reconciling Portuguese and "international" influences was extended to the NR, where he founded a music production system with the goal of creating a music repertoire, orchestras, and vocal ensembles to perform it.

I contend that the Irmãs Meireles were promoters of António Ferro's program of "Portuguesifying" popular music, embodying its contradictory nature. If, according to Ferro, the presumably authentic rural melodies constituted the basis for his project and its mark of "authenticity," the NR's sound was imagined through the models disseminated by the transnational music industry, including orchestral arrangements of local melodies and the American "sisters" performance model. As several scholars have shown, radio promoted a dynamic conception of nationalism, its power being played between different worlds: on the one hand, the ideology of nationalism based on ideas about authenticity and uniqueness, and on the other hand, the impact of the transnational circulation of new formats and performance models by the music industry. In the Portuguese case, like most countries during this period, it was the State that produced the necessary discourse and created the framework for institutionalizing transnational performance models. For Ferro, this was "the mixture of Portugal with the world and with our era" (1950, 40).

Notes

This chapter draws on research I carried out for my doctoral dissertation on the politics of radio programming and the production of popular music by the three administrations that directed the NR from 1934 to 1949 (Moreira 2012), funded by a scholarship from FCT (2004–2008) and under the supervision of Professor Salwa El-Shawan Castelo-Branco. I conducted archival research at the Historical Radio Archives (RDP), at the National Archives (Torre do Tombo), the National Library (Biblioteca Nacional), and the Hemeroteca Municipal de Lisboa (Municipal Library of Portuguese Periodical Press). I also interviewed radio musicians and employees who were active during the period under research.

6. Radio, Popular Music, and Nationalism in Portugal   131

1. "*Música ligeira* (literally, light music) is a generic term that was first used in Portugal in the late nineteenth century to designate music produced within the framework of the music media as well as of new forms of urban entertainment, especially the *revista* (revue) theater, commercial recordings, and radio [. . .]. Approximating to the English term "popular music," *música ligeira* encompasses a variety of musical styles and genres, most importantly the *canção ligeira* (light song), a strophic song, with or without a refrain characterized by a simple melody and a simple harmonic accompaniment" (Moreira, Cidra, and Castelo-Branco 2017, 503).

2. All translations from Portuguese are the author's.

3. Unlike other authoritarian regimes, the Estado Novo allowed public and private radio broadcasting to coexist (Silva 2005, 2010; Moreira 2012).

4. The BBC's "Comprehensive Orchestral Organization" (Kenyon 1981, 35) was based on a symphony orchestra that was then subdivided into smaller orchestras that performed classical and popular music.

5. Several radio orchestras where founded in the 1920s and 1930s by European radio organizations, such as Swedish Radio Orchestra (1923); Rundfunks Sinfonie Orchester, Berlin; MDR Symphony Orchestra, Leipzig (1924); Danish Radio Symphony Orchestra (1925); Prague Radio Symphony Orchestra (1926); Finnish Radio Symphony Orchestra (1927); Radio Symphony Orchestra, Frankfurt; Slovak Radio Symphony Orchestra (1929); BBC Symphony Orchestra, UK; Tchaikovsky Symphony Orchestra of Moscow Radio (1930); BBC Northern Orchestra (1933); Orchestre Nationale de France (1934); Flemish Radio Orchestra (1935); Symphony Orchestra of the RAI, Rome (1936); and Orchestre Phillarmonique de Radio France (1937) (Lawson 2003, 277–78). In Spain, due to the Civil War (1936–1939) the radio orchestra debate took place in the early 1940s, resulting in the foundation of the National Radio Chamber Orchestra (Orquestra de Cámara de Radio Nacional) in 1945 and the National Radio Symphonic Orchestra (Orquestra Sinfónica de Radio Nacional) in 1947. For further details, see García Estefanía (1999, 215–27).

6. According to Doctor, the BBC "was an intrinsic player in the new music industry, setting new standards and developing new trends as a powerful employer of musicians, as a commissioning body for new compositions, as a disseminator of music repertoires— inevitably shaping new audiences—and as a leading distributor of music-related funds" (1999, 17).

7. Christo's report, deposited at the Torre do Tombo National Archive (AOS/CO/OP- 7/ subdivision 2), provides a general political analysis of the NR, describing its daily activity and the personal and political profiles of its most important staff.

8. Radio Broadcasts to Angola, Mozambique, Europe, Brazil, and the United States began in 1936, on short wave, from a 5-kW transmitter built by the NR's employees.

9. For the Estado Novo's policy toward folklore and folklorization, see Castelo-Branco and Branco (2003).

10. In his speeches, Ferro lightly mentions fado that was also broadcasted by the NR (Ferro 1950, 20). If in the 1930s there was an intense debate whether the NR should broadcast fado as "national song," during the 1940s it became a part of several NR shows. For the regime's ambivalence towards fado, see Nery (2012, 305–9).

11. Pedro de Oliveira Leitão do Prado (1908–90) was responsible for the NR's popular and art music departments between 1942 and 1974. Together with António Ferro, he

was one of the most influential figures in the organization of a music production system for the NR in the 1940s. He was responsible for the founding of the Music Studies Bureau (1942), a symphony concert series at the São Carlos and Tivoli theaters in Lisbon (Caseirão 2010, 1063).

12. For more information on these composers and orchestras, see the relevant entries in Castelo-Branco (2010).

13. According to Forgacs and Gundle, "The Trio Lescano were one of the few acts to suffer as a result of the Nazi occupation. Banned from the radio on account of their mother's Jewish background, they continued to perform live until they were arrested in Milan in late 1943 and imprisoned" (2007, 184).

14. As Iván Iglesias states: "Both trios were created, inspired, and directed by two prominent Spanish jazz musicians and composers whose fame had survived the Civil War: the Arveu, by the pianist Sigfredo Ribera, and the Russell, by the multi-instrumentalist Sebastián Albalat" (2013, 8).

15. The Irmãs Meireles was composed of Cidália Meireles (1925–1972), Rosária Meireles (1926–2022), and "Milita" (Emília) Meireles (1928–2021).

References

Alves, Vera Marques. 2013. *Arte popular e nação no Estado Novo: A política folclorista do Secretariado da Propaganda Nacional*. Lisboa: ICS.

Anderson, Benedict. 1983. *Imagined Communities: Reflections on the Origin and Spread of Nationalism*. London: Verso.

Badenoch, Alexander, and Golo Föllmer. 2018. "Transnationalizing Radio Research: New Encounters with an Old Medium." In *Transnationalizing Radio Research: New Approaches to an Old Medium*, edited by Alexander Badenoch and Golo Föllmer, 11–30. Bielefeld, DE: Transcript Verlag. https://doi.org/10.14361/9783839439135-001.

Birdsall, Carolyn. 2012. *Nazi Soundscapes: Sound, Technology and Urban Space in Germany, 1933–1945*. Amsterdam: Amsterdam University Press.

Birdsall, Carolyn, and Joanna Walewska-Choptiany. 2019. "Reconstructing Media Culture: Transnational Perspectives on Radio in Silesia, 1924–1948." *Historical Journal of Film, Radio and Television* 39, no. 3: 439–78. https://doi.org/10.1080/01439685.2019.1643096.

Bohlman, Philip V. 2004. *The Music of European Nationalism: Cultural Identity and Modern History*. Santa Barbara: ABC-CLIO.

Borges, Paulo. 2016. *Irmãs Meireles: Os rouxinóis de Portugal*. Lisboa: Chiado Editora.

Caseirão, Bruno. 2010. "Pedro Do Prado." In *Enciclopédia da música em Portugal no século XX*. Vol. L-P. Edited by Salwa Castelo-Branco, 1063. Lisboa: Círculo de Leitores/Temas e Debates.

Castelo-Branco, Salwa, ed. 2010. *Enciclopédia da música em Portugal no século XX*. 4 Vols. Lisboa: Círculo de Leitores/Temas e Debates.

Castelo-Branco, Salwa El-Shawan, and Jorge Freitas Branco. 2003. *Vozes do povo: A folclorização em Portugal*. Oeiras, PT: Celta Editora. https://books.openedition.org/etnograficapress/537.

Currid, Brian. 2006. *A National Acoustics: Music and Mass Publicity in Weimar and Nazi Germany*. Minneapolis: University of Minnesota Press.

6. Radio, Popular Music, and Nationalism in Portugal

Doctor, Jennifer. 1999. *The BBC and Ultra-Modern Music, 1922–1936: Shaping a Nation's Tastes*. Cambridge: Cambridge University Press.

Ferro, António. 1950. *Problemas da rádio: 1941–1950*. Lisboa: Edições SNI.

Fagot, Maude. 2014. "Radio Propaganda in France and in Germany during the Phoney War." *Revue Historique* 671, no. 3: 629–54. https://doi.org/10.3917/rhis.143.0629.

Forgacs, David, and Stephen Gundle. 2007. *Mass Culture and Italian Society from Fascism to the Cold War*. Bloomington: Indiana University Press.

García Estefanía, Álvaro. 1999. "Pioneros musicales de Radio Nacional de España: Ataúlfo Argenta y La Orquesta de Cámara de Radio Nacional." *Cuadernos de Música Iberoamericana* 7: 215–33. https://revistas.ucm.es/index.php/CMIB/article/view/61234.

Gagliarducci, Stefano, Massimiliano Gaetano Onorato, Francesco Sobbrio, and Guido Tabellini. 2020. "War of the Waves: Radio and Resistance during World War II." *American Economic Journal: Applied Economics* 12, no. 4: 1–38. https://doi.org/10.1257/APP.20190410.

Hayes, Joy Elizabeth. 2000. *Radio Nation: Communication, Popular Culture, and Nationalism in Mexico, 1920–1950*. Tucson: University of Arizona Press.

Hilmes, Michele. 2012. *Network Nations: A Transnational History of British and American Broadcasting*. New York: Routledge.

Iglesias, Iván. 2013. "Hechicero de las pasiones del alma: El jazz y la subversión de la biopolítica franquista (1939–1959)." *TRANS-Revista Transcultural de Música/Transcultural Music Review* 17: 1–23. https://www.sibetrans.com/trans/public/docs/trans-17-10.pdf.

Kenyon, Nicholas. 1981. *The BBC Symphony Orchestra: The First Fifty Years, 1930–1980*. London: British Broadcasting Corporation.

Lawson, Colin. 2003. *The Cambridge Companion to the Orchestra*. Cambridge: Cambridge University Press.

Lopes-Graça, Fernando. 1989. *A música portuguesa e os seus problemas I*. Lisboa: Caminho.

Moreira, Pedro. 2012. "'Cantando Espalharei por toda a parte': Programação, produção musical e o 'aportuguesamento' da 'música ligeira' na Emissora Nacional de Radiodifusão (1934–1949)." PhD diss., Universidade Nova de Lisboa-Faculdade de Ciências Sociais e Humanas.

Moreira, Pedro, Rui Cidra, and Salwa El-Shawan Castelo-Branco. 2017. "Música Ligeira." In *Bloomsbury Encyclopedia of Popular Music of the World*. Vol. XI. Edited by Paolo Prato and David Horn, 503–4. London: Bloomsbury Academic.

Nery, Rui Vieira. 2012. *A History of Portuguese Fado*. Lisboa: Imprensa Nacional Casa da Moeda.

Pena Rodríguez, Alberto. 2011. "La 'Guerra del Éter.'" *Diacronie* 7, no. 3. https://doi.org/10.4000/diacronie.3266.

Pinho, Márcio, and Julio Mendívil. 2019. "Broadcasting the New Nation: Radio and the Invention of National Genres in Latin America." In *Music Radio: Building Communities, Mediating Genres*, edited by Morten Michelsen, Mads Krogh, Steen Kaargaard Nielsen, and Iben Have, 101–19. London: Bloomsbury.

Ragnedda, Massimo. 2014. "Radio Broadcasting in Fascist Italy: Between Censorship, Total Control, Jazz and Futurism." In *Broadcasting in the Modernist Era*, edited by Matthew Feldman, Erik Tonning, and Henry Mead, 195–211. London: Bloomsbury Academic.

Raimundo, Orlando. 2015. *António Ferro: O inventor do Salazarismo*. Lisboa: Dom Quixote.

Ribeiro, Carla Patrícia Silva. 2012. "Cultura popular em Portugal: de Almeida Garrett a António Ferro." *População e Sociedade* 20: 167–83. https://www.cepese.pt/portal./pt/populacao-e-sociedade/edicoes/populacao-e-sociedade-n-0-20/cultura-popular-em-portugal-de-almeida-garrett-a-antonio-ferro/cultura-popular-em-portugal-de-almeida-garrett-a-antonio-ferro/@@display-file/file/Cultura%20popular%20em%20Portugal.pdf.

Ribeiro, Nelson. 2005. *A Emissora nacional nos primeiros anos do Estado Novo (1933–1945)*. Lisboa: Quimera.

———. 2007. "A Emissora Nacional: Das emissões experimentais à oficialização (1933–1936)." *Comunicação & Cultura* 3: 175–99. https://doi.org/10.34632/comunicacaoecultura.2007.446.

Roxo, Pedro, and Salwa El-Shawan Castelo-Branco. 2016. "Jazz, Race and Politics in Colonial Portugal: Discourses and Representations (1924–1971)." In *Jazz Worlds/World Jazz*, edited by Philip Bohlman and Goffredo Plastino, 200–235. Chicago: University of Chicago Press.

Santos, Rogério. 2005. *As Vozes da Rádio (1924–1939)*. Lisboa: Caminho.

Silva, Manuel Deniz. 2005. "'La musique a besoin d'une dictature': Musique et politique dans les premières années de l'Etat Nouveau (1926–1945)." PhD diss., Université de Paris.

———. 2010. "Rádio." In *Enciclopédia da música em Portugal no eéculo XX*. Vol. P-Z. Edited by Salwa Castelo-Branco, 1080–87. Lisboa: Círculo de Leitores/Temas e Debates.

Turino, Thomas. 2013. "Nationalism and Latin American Music: Selected Case Studies and Theoretical Considerations." *Latin American Music Review/Revista de Música Latinoamericana* 24, no. 2: 169–209. http://www.jstor.org/stable/3598738.

Valente, José Carlos. 1999. *Estado Novo e Alegria no Trabalho: Uma história política da FNAT (1935–1958)*. Lisboa: Edições Colibri.

Western, Tom. 2018. "Introduction: Ethnomusicologies of Radio." *Ethnomusicology Forum* 27, no. 3: 255–64. https://doi.org/10.1080/17411912.2018.1550943.

7

Protest Song and Recording in the Final Stages of the Estado Novo in Portugal (1960–1974)

HUGO CASTRO

This chapter focuses on the Portuguese protest song movement in the 1960s and 1970s, which emerged in the academic, cultural, and political milieus of Lisbon, Coimbra, and Porto, as well as in France, where several exiled musicians were active. The movement was embedded in the political and social contexts of opposition against the authoritarian regime dubbed the Estado Novo (New State). The commitment of protest singers to social and political intervention, and their defiance towards the policies of the dictator António de Oliveira Salazar (ruled 1933–1968) and his successor Marcello Caetano (ruled 1968–1974), led to them being labelled by the media as *cantores de intervenção* (intervention singers).[1] Today, the main figures and repertoires of the Portuguese protest song movement are powerfully embedded in Portugal's collective memory as central to the struggle against the dictatorship.

I argue that the Portuguese protest song movement was a crucial vehicle for resistance to the totalitarian regime and played a central role in raising political and social awareness. In addition, members of the movement proposed to reconfigure socially and artistically Portuguese "*música popular*."[2] This reconfiguration involved the development of new music practices, styles, and methods of phonographic production that had a significant impact on the recording industry, arousing the interest of the media in protest singers and their repertoires. These changes were fundamental to the establishment of protest song as a means of cultural and political expression against the regime. Such opposition is poignantly exemplified by the use of the song "Grândola, Vila Morena" ("Grândola, Brown/Tanned Town"), composed and perfomed by José Afonso (1929–1987), as a signal broadcast on the radio for the Portuguese armed forces to launch the military coup of April 25, 1974, that ended the Estado Novo regime. Since then, this song has continued to be performed in official celebrations of the 1974 revolution and at moments of crisis, for the vindication of social and economic rights, and to seek political change.

Protest song has become an important focal point for musicological scholarship, which considers the relationship between musical practice and political activity. As discussed by James Garratt (2018), the intersection between music and politics often implies multiple interactions and functions that change over time and across cultures. In the 1960s, Portuguese protest song followed the developments of several protest song movements around the globe, which shaped the perception of music as a medium for political expression. According to Eyerman and Jamison (1998), the social and political awareness inherent in protest song enabled protest singers to play a central role in the cognitive practices of the activist movements in which they were involved. These movements capitalized on the intersections between the aesthetic and ideological dimensions (Nooshin 2009, 6), reinscribing the style and thematic content of popular song with consequences that went beyond their original contexts (Garratt 2018, xii–xiii). Protest song movements in Europe and the Americas were effective in using song to affirm a political cultural identity. Notable examples include: the North American folk revival of the 1950s and early 1960s; the Nueva Canción of Chile, Argentina, and Uruguay; Cuba's Nueva Trova; Brazil's Tropicalismo; Galicia's Voces Ceibes; and Catalonia's Nova Cançó, as well as the repertoire of French singer-songwriters, most notably Georges Brassens, Jean Ferrat, and Collete Magny (Tumas-Serna 1992; Eyerman and Jamison 1998; Lebrun 2009; Ayats and Salicrú-Maltas 2013). The parallels between the protest song movement in Portugal and in other countries are notable, especially the protest song movements in Spain, particularly in the way they galvanized collective performances of resistance against Franco's dictatorship (Pérez-Villalba 2007). In this sense, as David McDonald (2013) argues, "resistance music" and "protest song" should be seen not only as categories based on stylistic attributes but should also be read in conjunction with the musical-political processes that characterize projects of extensive social change.

In Portugal, there is a growing body of ethnomusicological research on the country's protest song movement. Maria de São José Côrte-Real (2010) offers a systematic analysis of the practices and musical production of several key figures, contextualizing their trajectories within the authoritarian regime and the revolutionary period that followed. The *Enciclopédia da música em Portugal no século XX* (Castelo-Branco 2010) includes over seventy entries on protest song, its main figures (singer-songwriters and poets), and its genres. My master's thesis (Castro 2012) focuses on the phonographic production of Portuguese protest song, and my doctoral dissertation provides an in-depth analysis of the reconfiguration of its practices and styles in the post-revolutionary period (Castro 2022). Other scholars deal with musicians' biographies (Pimentel and Vieira 2009; Raposo 2005; Silva 2000) and compare the censorship practices of politically engaged song during the dictatorships of Brazil and Portugal (Fiúza 2006). Several publications by journalists and promoters provide firsthand testimonies and biographies of musicians (Correia 1984; Salvador 2014; Teles 2009). This chapter draws primarily on research I conducted over eight years, involving an in-depth analysis of written documentation, sound recordings, and interviews with musicians, publishers, and other agents.

The Emergence of Portuguese Protest Song

Fernando Lopes-Graça

Following World War II, Lopes-Graça composed a set of songs which became known as *canções heróicas* (Heroic Songs), that were regularly performed by the Coro da Academia de Amadores da Música, which he conducted. Set to politically engaged poetry, they were intended to nurture an aesthetic and ideological movement that was aimed at "stimulating action by linking poetry and song" and to raise awareness of the importance of music in the transformation of Portuguese society (Lopes-Graça 1946, 5). Forbidden to be sung live, the *canções heróicas* would be replaced by a new set of songs, which Lopes-Graça called *canções regionais portuguesas* (Portuguese Regional Songs). Many of these songs were arrangements of rural songs from different regions of Portugal, or melodies inspired therein. Lopes-Graça's efforts in the documentation and renewal of traditional music were intended to counteract the then-hegemonic conception of Portuguese "popular" music and culture as promoted and instrumentalized by the institutions of the Estado Novo.[3] By reflecting "a collective reality" recognized by the "people" or the "folk," these songs represented the "authentic" roots of Portuguese music, corresponding to the "transformation and deepening" of the "meaning, aesthetics, and social essence" of traditional Portuguese music (Côrte-Real 2010, 224–26).

Lopes-Graça used the terms "folk song" and "regional or rustic song" to emphasize the criteria of "orality" and "authenticity" as opposed to what he called "counterfeit folklore," a reference to the folkloric representations of rural musics promoted by the Estado Novo, which he considered to be both "musically and poetically poor" (Castelo-Branco and Cidra 2010, 876). The recordings made by Michel Giacometti (a Corsican collector based in Portugal) in several rural areas and transcribed by Lopes-Graça are examples of the renewed interest in exploring traditional music, which Lopes-Graça considered to be the "basis for the creation of a Portuguese musical idiom and a means of artistic education and ideological combat" (877). Throughout the 1960s and 1970s, these recordings inspired other composers and poets to create a politically engaged urban popular music repertoire, which instrumentalized rural musics for political action and cultural transformation (Castelo-Branco 2013; Côrte-Real 2010; Correia 1984).

José Afonso and Adriano Correia de Oliveira

In the early 1960s, a profound economic crisis contributed to worsening living conditions for most of the population, inciting general discontent and the politicization of various working-class sectors who joined opposition groups to the dictatorship (Rosas 2015). Consequently, the government intensified its repressive measures and the persecution of political organizations and its members, in particular those connected to the Portuguese Communist Party. In addition, the outbreak of the Colonial War in Africa in 1961, which lasted for thirteen years, had a negative economic and social impact. Thousands of young men were recruited to military service. This resulted in general dissatisfaction, massive emigration, and the exile of musicians, intellectuals, and politicians who opposed the regime (2015).

Politically engaged students at the Universities of Porto, Lisbon, and Coimbra represented one of the most combative sectors of resistance during the years that followed (Bebiano 2006). In 1962 and 1969, the "academic crisis"[4] led to various initiatives of Coimbra's left-leaning academic organizations involving students in political decisions, demanding freedom of expression, and the improvement of conditions in universities (Rosas 2015). In this context, as I will discuss below, expressive culture, especially music, was mobilized in the opposition to the totalitarian regime.

Adriano Correia de Oliveira (1942–1982) and José Afonso, both members of the University of Coimbra's student opposition movements, were prominent singers within the Coimbra Song Tradition (*Canção de Coimbra*) and played a central role in its stylistic revitalization.[5] In the early 1950s and throughout the 1960s, these singers were committed to breaking with the musical style and thematic content that characterized the *Canção de Coimbra*. For José Afonso,

7. Protest Song and Recording in the Estado Novo 139

the social environment surrounding this genre at the time constituted what he called an "artificial scenario of an elite folklore," distant from the social relevance that he aimed for in his songs (Afonso 1970).

José Afonso and Adriano Correia de Oliveira configured a new and politically engaged repertoire that broke with the "romanticism" and "lyricism" associated with Coimbra's songs and which incorporated elements from different musical traditions. This repertoire, which they designated *trovas* and *baladas*, was characterized by the centrality of the text, simple melodies adapted from or inspired by traditional songs, and a simple harmonic accompaniment by an acoustic guitar (e.g., alternating I-V-I). This new style is exemplified by songs such as "Charamba" (a traditional dance song from the Azores) and "Canção da Beira-Baixa" ("Song from Beira-Baixa"), performed by Adriano Correia de Oliveira, and "Ronda dos Paisanos" ("Round of Countrymen") or "Os Bravos" ("The Brave Ones"), performed by José Afonso.

During the first half of the 1960s, most of the repertoire performed by José Afonso and Adriano Correia de Oliveira was published on EP, containing songs freed from the "rashes of Coimbra's sounds" (Pimentel and Vieira 2009, 64) and that transmitted messages of discontent. In 1963 and 1964, both singers recorded socially and politically engaged songs, namely "Os Vampiros" ("The Vampires") and "Menino do Bairro Negro" ("Boy from the Black Neighborhood") by José Afonso and "Trova do Vento que Passa" ("Song of the Passing Wind"), a poem by Manuel Alegre, a former student at the University of Coimbra and a well-known poet and political activist against the regime, performed by Adriano Correia de Oliveira. In a letter addressed to his brother, José Afonso designates these songs as *canções de replica*, that is "songs of response," which he defined as a new type of song that could "resonate in the public's spirit, raising their conscience instead of distracting them" (Pimentel and Vieira 2009, 64). These songs were sung recurrently in public, especially in student meetings, social gatherings, and political assemblies, which were often clandestine or the target of police intervention. Their significance lies in the fact that they represented the stylistic rupture of the *Canção de Coimbra*, as well as the use of music and poetry to articulate social protest inscribed in metaphorical lyrics that alluded to the country's social and political situation. The reference to the "vampires that eat everything and leave nothing" in José Afonso's song, or the ambivalence between repression and resistance inscribed in Alegre's verses in the song "Trova do Vento que Passa,"[6] led to the use of these songs as icons of the student movement and of resistance to the authoritarian regime.

The above-mentioned songs of José Afonso were recorded in an old convent on the outskirts of Coimbra with scarce technical resources (a simple mono-recorder). Due to the lyrics' open opposition to the regime, the circulation and distribution of the EPs containing these songs was prohibited in 1965 by the State General Security Directorate.[7] Following the prohibition of the lyrics, the record publisher Discos Rapsódia published new instrumental versions of José Afonso's songs "Os Vampiros" and "Menino do Bairro Negro," which were authorized for commercial distribution, reinforcing the impact of the meaning of the original song lyrics. These songs by José Afonso and Adriano Correia de Oliveira had very little media projection and were not broadcast on radio, thus their social impact was limited to small opposition groups of intellectuals and students.

Portuguese Protest Singers in Paris

In Paris, exiled musicians Luís Cília (b. 1943) and José Mário Branco (1942–2019) consolidated their musical activity through contact with the cultural and political milieus of various left-wing organizations. At the time, such organizations proliferated in France as a consequence of the Sino-Soviet conflict. Moreover, they stimulated stylistic changes in the protest song repertoire that some organizations produced, enabling the publication of exiled singers' debut albums. Freed from the regime's persecution and inspired by the new styles of the *trovas* and *baladas*, as well as musicians residing in Paris, Cília and Branco created a politically engaged repertoire that denounced the regime and the Colonial War that it waged in the former African colonies.

Luís Cília, exiled in Paris in 1963, developed personal and artistic relationships with Collete Magny, George Brassens, and Paco Ibañez, among other politically engaged musicians, which facilitated his contacts with French record publishers such as Le Chant du Monde (associated with the French Communist Party) and Moshe Naim, labels that were interested in recording political repertoire from different countries (Luís Cília, personal communication, 2018). Cília published the LPs *Portugal-Angola: Chants de Lutte* (*Portugal-Angola: Songs of Struggle*) in 1964; the EP *Portugal Resiste* (*Portugal Resists*) in 1965; and the trilogy *La Poesie Portugaise de nos jours et des toujours* (*Portuguese Poetry Today and Forever*) in 1967, 1969, and 1971. The songs recorded on these albums were set to the poetry of prominent Portuguese poets (Luís de Camões and Fernando Pessoa) and the politically engaged poetry of some of the major figures of Portuguese neorealist literature, such as Manuel Alegre, José Saramago, Carlos Oliveira, and José Gomes Ferreira.[8] These songs were characterized by simple melodic contours and harmonic accompaniment on the acoustic guitar, highlighting the poems, usually sung in a low register, emphasizing the melancholy and gloom expressed in the lyrics. Being a member of the Portuguese Communist Party and having published his albums on French labels known for politically engaged songs, Cília's recordings were subject to censorship in Portugal. Nonetheless, he became one of the most prominent representatives of Portuguese politically engaged song, particularly in the international context, participating in several events, such as the Encuentro Internacional de la Canción Protesta de Casa de las Américas (International Meeting of the Protest Song) in Cuba, in 1967.

José Mário Branco, a former member of the Portuguese Communist Party, was exiled in Paris from 1963 until the 1974 revolution for refusing to comply with compulsory military service. He was involved in cultural and political organizations with a Maoist orientation and consolidated his musical activities in Paris during the political turmoil of May 1968. Alongside Luís Cília, Sérgio Godinho, and other prominent musicians at the time, Branco performed his own songs (in Portuguese and French) as well as protest songs from Italy, France, and Spain in factories occupied by striking workers and associations of Portuguese immigrants (José Mário Branco, personal communication, 2017). His proximity to the ideas of Lopes-Graça had an impact on both his conception of music as "an idiom of its own" (2017) and his appreciation for Portuguese traditional music, which became central in his compositions (Castro and Andrade 2020). These aspects were reflected in the first EP he published, which includes musical settings of the lyrics of Iberian medieval songs in the Galician-Portuguese language (thirteenth century "Cantigas de Amigo" from the Cancioneiro da Vaticana), published in 1969 by the label Arquivos Sonoros Portugueses. These songs were promoted in the liner notes as a "new current and a catalytic force in Portuguese popular song" (Arquivos Sonoros Portugueses). José Mário Branco's political posture was clear in the author's edition of a single, published in 1970 with the intention of clandestine distribution in Portugal, including the political songs "Ronda do Soldadinho" ("Soldier's Round") and "Mãos ao Ar!" ("Hands Up!"), which explicitly denounced the political situation in Portugal and the illegitimacy of colonial occupation (José Mário Branco, personal communication, 2012).

The Mediatization of Protest Song at the End of the 1960s

The repertoire that mixed traditional music and politically engaged poetry published by José Afonso and Adriano Correia de Oliveira in Portugal, and Luís Cília and José Mário Branco in Paris, constituted a highly influential aesthetic formulation and political expression of resistance to the dictatorship. José Afonso's and Adriano Correia de Oliveira's *trovas* and *baladas* expressed marked social discontent in ways that inspired a new generation of musicians and poets who became politically engaged during the second half of the 1960s, including

Francisco Fanhais, Manuel Freire, Vieira da Silva, and José Jorge Letria, among others. For Fanhais, a priest who belonged to a faction of progressive Catholic critics of the regime, these songs represented "something new, inaudible until then, in terms of music and poetry" (Francisco Fanhais, personal communication, 2018). These musicians adopted a musical style similar to that introduced by José Afonso and Adriano Correia de Oliveira and shared their social and political engagement. Political expression was notoriously channeled through the joint participation of these musicians in multiple live performances, many of which were protest events against the regime that were carried out clandestinely or under police surveillance.

As was the case with protest song movements in Spain (Ayats and Salicrú-Maltas 2013), the movement in Portugal was restricted to a small group of young people from petty-bourgeois origins, coming from the intellectual and student sectors of urban centers and universities. Without formal musical training, the vast majority of the musicians who promoted the protest song movement in Portugal were inspired by the international protest song movements mentioned above. These songs were characterized by the performance model of a singer accompanied by an acoustic guitar, performing poems that alluded to the social and political problems of the country and that were set to simple and easy-to-memorize melodies. As stated by singer-songwriter José Jorge Letria, who was also a student and journalist at the time, it was the context in which these songs emerged that made them a source of inspiration for the development of a movement of cultural resistance, which influenced other forms of artistic expression such as literature, the visual arts, theater, and amateur cinema (José Jorge Letria, personal communication, 2012). New performers and repertoires increasingly gained recognition through different media (Raposo 2005), recognition that was directly related to changes in the regime that occurred towards the end of the decade.

Music Periodicals, Radio, and Television

In 1968, Marcello Caetano replaced the weakened prime minister Salazar. He initiated the revision of the constitution and introduced liberal measures and reforms in the political, economic, and social spheres. This period (1968–1970), known as "Marcelista Spring," created, for a brief period, an expectation regarding the "openness" of the regime. However, there were no major changes in the repressive and authoritarian policies, neither was the course of the Colonial War altered. The political prisons and the persecution of oppositionists were maintained, which in turn strengthened resistance to the government (Rosas

7. Protest Song and Recording in the Estado Novo   143

2015, 11). However, there was a slight slowdown in censorship, renamed Prior Examination.[9] Nevertheless, periodicals, radio, and television broadcasts were monitored, which implied that, in some cases, media agents had to negotiate with the authorities or use metaphorical language and other means to ensure publication (Fiúza 2006). As for the recording industry, until 1972 there was no law that mandated preliminary "prior examination" of the materials to be published. In any case, as censorship was applied to all other media, if the records of protest singers were not being seized by the police, most of the time they were not allowed to be broadcast on radio or television (2006).

The role of some journalists, radio, and television programmers, as well as record publishers, was to introduce new performers and repertoires representing new values and musical styles that appealed to younger audiences. *Mundo da Canção (World of Song)*, launched in 1969, was a periodical entirely dedicated to popular music. As repeatedly mentioned in the editorials, the objectives were to promote music with content that was considered significant for Portuguese youth, the periodical's target audience (Anon. 1969). Until 1974, it was one of the few periodicals that repeatedly disseminated musical styles that were considered by some journalists, critics, and musicians to represent an alternative to the musical genres and styles that dominated most of the media, such as *canção ligeira* (light song) and fado, whose recordings represented a substantial portion of record sales in Portugal (Castro 2012). Although the periodical included articles on diverse musical genres including folk, jazz, and pop-rock, it also highlighted national and international protest music. Through opinion articles, interviews, biographies, song lyrics, and record advertisements, the periodical promoted reflection on the renewal of Portuguese popular music, with particular emphasis on musicians associated with the protest song movement such as José Afonso, Adriano Correia de Oliveira, José Mário Branco, Sérgio Godinho, José Jorge Letria, Manuel Freire, and Francisco Fanhais, among others (Castro 2017).

Some radio programs, such as *Página Um* (broadcast on Rádio Renascença, a Catholic radio station) became known for broadcasting songs by new protest singers, especially *trovas* and *baladas*. The participation of some of these musicians on live television shows such as *Zip-Zip* (a popular talk-show broadcast on Portuguese State Television—RTP—for nine months in 1969) is noteworthy. Although there was no particular connection between the producers of this talk show and opposition movements, it brought attention to the young performers associated with the innovative *baladas* (Lopes 2012, 165–66). Even if *Zip-Zip* did not express a clear political stance against the regime, and despite the prohibition of some performers such as José Afonso, the participation in the program of several prominent protest singers such as Francisco Fanhais, Manuel Freire, and José Barata Moura helped to disseminate protest song to a wider public, eventually leading to the program's suspension.

The participation of protest singers on radio and TV shows created opportunities for some artists to publish their first records on labels launched following the success of individual shows. For example, after the suspension of the television show, *Zip-Zip* created its own label and radio program, publishing and broadcasting several records (Lopes 2012) such as the first album of Francisco Fanhais, *Canções da Cidade Nova* (*Songs from the New City*) and Manuel Freire's EP that included a song set to the poem "Pedra Filosofal" ("Philosopher's Stone"), a song that became very popular following its broadcast on television.

Record Publishers

The beginning of the 1960s marked a turning point in the establishment of new methods of phonographic production that favored the emergence of small record publishers, such as Orfeu and Sassetti. These publishers looked for a diversity of genres, repertoires, and performers that had not been recorded but that could offer an alternative to the musical genres and aesthetics that were hitherto dominant in the media (Losa 2010, 639). In particular, Orfeu and Sassetti took an interest in the repertoire of the then-emerging protest singers and published records featuring most of them.

The record company Orfeu was founded in 1953 in Porto by Arnaldo Trindade, a businessman and an enthusiast for new trends in music and poetry. He published records based on his personal taste and preference for selected musical genres, especially Coimbra's songs, as well as a wide diversity of performers and genres, ranging from regional ensembles and folklore groups (mostly from the north of Portugal, especially areas that are close to Porto), recited poetry, and pop-rock groups. Starting in the early 1960s, Orfeu published recordings of several singers of Coimbra's songs, among them Adriano Correia de Oliveira, who had an exclusive contract with Orfeu between 1960 and 1982. Similarly, in 1968, José Afonso sought to publish his new album with several record labels, and his friendship with Adriano Correia de Oliveira facilitated his introduction to Arnaldo Trindade, who was an admirer of José Afonso's music. Afonso was under police surveillance and had several of his records seized. Although this made it difficult for him to publish new albums, Arnaldo Trindade offered him a contract, more or less under the same terms of the preexisting contract with Oliveira. The contract made it possible for Afonso to dedicate himself professionally to musical activity, guaranteeing a monthly salary in return for publishing an album each year and for recommending new performers to the publisher.

7. Protest Song and Recording in the Estado Novo

Thanks to the mediation of the two artists, Orfeu was able to record several protest singers throughout the 1970s, including Francisco Fanhais, Samuel Quedas, Fausto Bordalo Dias, Luís Cília, and José Jorge Letria. The repertoire recorded by these artists was categorized by Arnaldo Trindade as "text song" or "theme song" (Arnaldo Trindade, personal communication, 2016). The integration of these musicians in the label's catalog established Orfeu as a pivotal publisher of politically engaged popular music (Castro 2012).

Following Orfeu's lead (Losa 2010, 640), at the beginning of the 1970s, the newly founded label Sassetti started a comprehensive record-publishing project exploring different musical genres and investing in new trends of Portuguese popular song. This investment eventually resulted in their merging with the record label Zip-Zip in 1972, which considerably enriched their catalog with protest song repertoire. José Afonso advised Sassetti to publish some of the exiled musicians in France, thus enabling the recording of the first albums of José Mário Branco and Sérgio Godinho (José Mário Branco, personal communication, 2017). Most significantly, the network of politically engaged musicians residing in Portugal and France enabled José Mário Branco, who had working experience in Parisian recording studios, to produce the albums of politically engaged musicians, including himself, and to introduce myriad innovations in the instrumental arrangements and technical quality of the recordings (Castro and Andrade 2020).

Record Production and the Renewal of Portuguese Protest Song

Until 1970, José Afonso's and Adriano Correia de Oliveira's albums, published by Orfeu, resulted from a simple recording procedure of capturing a solo voice accompanied by an acoustic guitar. A pivotal moment occurred in Paris when José Mário Branco was enlisted as a composer, singer, producer, and arranger. Branco was influenced by the trends and approaches used in the phonographic recording of emerging Anglo-American pop-rock styles at the time. The exploitation of resources such as multitrack recording and new forms of sound processing allowed for the configuration of new musical sounds that went beyond the mere recording of a musician or an ensemble (Castro and Andrade 2020). These conditions grounded the production of Branco's first LPs: *Mudam-se os Tempos, Mudam-se as Vontades*, and *Margem de Certa Maneira*, both recorded in the Château d'Hérouville studios outside Paris in 1971 and 1972 respectively. Branco was chosen by José Afonso to produce and author the arrangements of his landmark albums *Cantigas do Maio* (1971) and *Venham Mais Cinco* (1973). Branco was also responsible for the production of the debut albums of Sérgio Godinho and José Jorge Letria, *Os Sobreviventes (The Survivors)* and *Até ao Pescoço (Up to the Neck)* respectively, both published by Sassetti in 1972.

These new albums marked a change toward a more "modern" phonographic conception. They were based on the construction of a musical sound that could only result from the technical capabilities of a recording studio equipped with a multitrack recorder (2020). As stated by Branco, they were conceived not as mere representations of a live musical performance but as phonographic works, or what he designated as "sound stagings" (José Mário Branco, personal communication, 2017). These records are characterized by stylistic diversity in the arrangements of each track. The album *Cantigas do Maio* ranges from songs for five or six instruments and choirs, as in the song "Maio Maduro Maio" ("May Mature May"), to arrangements without any instrumental support such as the remarkable "Grândola, Vila Morena," whose accompaniment consists exclusively of a four-voice choir and sound effects produced by rhythmically walking on gravel. Thus, Branco's "sound staging," drawing on Portuguese traditional music, urban popular music styles such as the *chanson française*,[10] and rock, amplified the meaning of the sung text and in the process articulated aesthetics and political ideologies (2020). These landmark albums also stimulated discussions about the communicative effectiveness of the repertoire of other singers identified with the protest song movement. For José Mário Branco, the poor aesthetic quality of some repertoire configured by the usual singing of "subversive" poetry accompanied by the acoustic guitar had the opposite effect of the one intended. As Branco wrote, these albums represented a stance on "surpassing the characteristic sound of the *baladeiros*"[11] (2008, 150). The use of a diversity of sounds and instruments, original and engaged lyrics, no longer "clinging" to opposition poets (2008), distinguished Branco's production from the previous model in which singers were accompanied by an acoustic guitar. For José Afonso, this was a welcome move away from being connoted as a *baladeiro* (Afonso 1971).

As suggested by McDonald (2013), the dynamic relationship between the role of music and the social and political awareness of audiences is, in part, developed by the musicians who seek experimentation and innovation in their practices. The new set of songs featured on these albums marked a significant transition in the ways that protest song was understood by some media outlets, publishers, and musicians. Several periodicals regarded these songs as milestones of musical change, thus consolidating protest song as a representative model for the renewal of Portuguese popular music more broadly. In 1972, the magazine *Flama* referred to José Mário Branco as "the voice of change," (Branco 1972) while *Mundo da Canção* published an editorial entitled "Renovation," dedicated

7. Protest Song and Recording in the Estado Novo

entirely to these albums and singers, characterizing them as a "breath of fresh air" and stating that 1971 "was crucial for the New Portuguese Music, to which one really should listen and spread" (Anon. 1972).

The reception of these records in the public domain illustrated the disruptive dimension that was often attributed to these repertoires, where they were often viewed as alternatives to the mainstream aesthetic conventions that characterized the industry and carried innocuous social and political meaning. The publication of these protest songs across several records highlights the ability these musicians had to represent simultaneously the artistic and the political potential of popular music inspired by traditional Portuguese elements as well as the innovative approaches used by these musicians in the recording process and in the introduction of sounds and lyrics with significant social and political content.

On the other hand, the impact of this renewal process on Portuguese popular music led to an unusual reaction by the government, which sought to contain the disruptive potential of protest singers. According to journalist João Paulo Guerra, Marcello Caetano referred to the need to suppress these singers and songwriters and to ban them from the media, who in his opinion "brazenly [made] a frontal attack against the social order" (Raposo 2005, 9). In 1972, the General Director of Information, Geraldes Cardoso, issued a letter determining the type of songs that should be banned, sending this instruction to the publishers (Moutinho 1975). The enactment of the Prior Examination Act targeted songs that included ridicule, threatened the established power, referred to the Colonial War, expressed shock, or exalted public contestation. It also prohibited the "publication or broadcasting of songs or other musical forms which, through their content and purpose, or because of the circumstances in which they are composed, jeopardize legally protected interests" (Prior Examination Act 1972).

According to Arnaldo Trindade, despite the prohibition of some songs, the publishers adopted strategies to circumvent the law and were willing to put these albums in circulation, combining commercial interests with ideological and aesthetic values. The composer and poet José Niza, who was also a producer and media agent working for Orfeu, played an important role in managing the relationship with the censorship agency and in negotiating the recording of politically engaged lyrics. He stated:

> I realized that there was some room for maneuver and that we had to take advantage of it. I give you an example: in 1972, when Zeca [José] Afonso and I were preparing the recording of the album *Eu Vou Ser Como a Toupeira* (*I Will be Like the Mole*), I asked him to give me not only the poems he intended to sing, but also more vio-

lent and explicit ones. These surplus poems would serve as a provocative bait for the wrath of the censors' blue pencil,[12] and were to be cut. I knew—or thought I knew—that the regime didn't want to totally silence Zeca, but just to control him, as with [the television program] *Zip-Zip*. Silencing Zeca, Adriano, Manuel Freire, Fanhais, and others would provoke a boomerang effect that would turn against the regime and reverse the cost–benefit logic. The trick worked: when the lyrics were returned [by the censors], from the songs we wanted to record, only "A morte saíu à rua" ("Death Went Out on the Street") was prohibited. Even so, I didn't conform. I called Dr. Pedro Feytor Pinto, then Director General of Information, whom I had known since the days of Coimbra and the Academic Tuna [a string ensemble or *rondalla* composed of students at the University of Coimbra], where he had been a contemporary of Zeca. We had lunch. He knew that the song described the murder by PIDE of the Communist painter Dias Coelho, although the name was not mentioned in Zeca's poem. And I told him: "But who knows who Dias Coelho was? Where is the problem?" When we got out of the cafe, "A morte saíu à rua" was authorized! (Niza 2007, 11–12)

On March 29, 1974, protest singers were the central feature of the First Portuguese Song Meeting, held at the Coliseu dos Recreios, one of the largest performance venues in Lisbon, with the aim of distributing the 1972 Press Awards. For the first time, several musicians such as José Afonso, José Jorge Letria, Adriano Correia de Oliveira, Manuel Freire, Fausto, José Barata Moura, Carlos Paredes, Vitorino, Fernando Tordo, and Ary dos Santos, among others, performed on the same stage. Although surrounded by police and censors who wanted to postpone the beginning of the show and ban some songs, the event took place and was described as unprecedented by several newspapers. The prizes awarded revealed the role of the show in affirming the "new Portuguese song," with awards given to musicians Sérgio Godinho, the production team of the record *Os Sobreviventes* (including José Mário Branco), and José Afonso, but also to radio shows featuring protest singers such as *Tempo Zip* and *Página Um*.

The end of the show was the high point of the evening: "Grândola, Vila Morena," by José Afonso, was sung in chorus by almost everyone present, foreseeing the coup d'état that would take place just three weeks later, ending the totalitarian regime and starting a new process that marked the transition to Portuguese democracy. By then, the Portuguese protest song was consolidated as a movement that had played an essential role in the social and cultural transformation of Portuguese popular music. The popularization and media impact of politically engaged musicians and repertoires, as well as the reconfiguration of practices and meanings attributed to protest song, were essential in raising social awareness against the regime. As in Spain, where political singers played

7. Protest Song and Recording in the Estado Novo 149

a central role before and during the political transition from the dictatorship to democracy (Pérez-Villalba 2007), throughout the revolutionary period in Portugal, the protest song movement served as a public expression in support of democracy and freedom.

Notes

Research leading to this chapter was supported by the project "Orfeu (1956-1983): políticas e estéticas da produção e consumo de popular music no Portugal moderno" (PCTDC/ART-OUT/32320/2017 funded by the Fundação para a Ciência e a Tecnologia).

1. In Portugal the term "protest song," although quite widespread, was used in alternation with the designation "intervention song," which became connected with the revolutionary period (from 1974 onward) and is still used today to refer to the protest singers of the 1960s and 1970s. During these decades, the terms were discussed by both musicians and the media and more recently by academics (Côrte-Real 2010; Castro 2012).

2. Throughout the nineteenth and twentieth centuries, the notion of *música popular* acquired several meanings that are distinct from its literal translation as "popular music." During the 1960s and 1970s, *música popular* was used in academic and journalistic discourse to refer both to music in rural areas as well as to urban popular musics that were partly inspired by rural musical styles (Castelo-Branco 2013, 665).

3. During the Estado Novo, the concept of "popular" (referring to music and culture, as in *música popular* and *cultura popular*) was re-signified and used as a symbol of Portuguese nationalism, embodying the ideological strategy known as "politics of the spirit," the regime's cultural policy. In this context, *cultura popular* was a broad notion that designated the most widespread modes of rural and urban expressive culture anchored in the notion of *povo* (folk). The term was especially associated with supposedly traditional and conservative expressive culture from rural regions, which was considered a foundational element of national identity to be protected from the threats of modernity (Castelo-Branco 2013, 667).

4. "Academic crisis" is an expression used by the media and students in relation to the conflicts of 1962 and 1969 between Portuguese university students and the Estado Novo regime, during which the government responded violently to the various forms of student protest.

5. *Canção de Coimbra* is a generic term that designates "a diverse set of musical genres and practices associated mainly with the academic sociability traditions of the University of Coimbra," (Equipa redactorial EMPXX 2010, 216–17) including the so-called *Fado de Coimbra* (Coimbra's Fado), a musical tradition that emerged from Lisbon's fado, between the end of the nineteenth and the beginning of the twentieth centuries. *Canção de Coimbra* was reconfigured in the 1920s and 1930s, introducing stylized versions of regional musical traditions and popular songs, then in the 1940s and 1950s it became characterized by sentimental and nostalgic lyrics and vocal style and a simple harmonic accompaniment by the Portuguese guitar.

6. Here is an excerpt of part of the lyrics: "Mesmo na noite mais triste / Em tempo de servidão / Há sempre alguém que resiste / Há sempre alguém que diz não" ("Even in

the saddest night / in a time of servitude / there is always someone who resists / there is always someone who says no").

7. Apprehension warrant by the Portuguese State Police, January 12, 1966, Torre do Tombo Archives, Lisbon.

8. In 1967, Luis Cília was invited by the Portuguese Communist Party to compose the music and lyrics of a song to be broadcast on clandestine radio stations. He composed "Avante Camarada!" which has been used as the unofficial hymn of the Communist Party up to the present.

9. The practice of censorship existed since the constitution of the Estado Novo in 1933. In 1972, the Directorate of Censorship Services was transformed into a General Directorate of Information and "censorship" received the designation of "prior examination."

10. *Chanson Française* is a generic term that denotes a song repertoire and style, highlighting French language and poetry. It was popularized in the 1950s and 1960s by singer-songwriters such as Georges Brassens, Jacques Brel, and Léo Ferré, among others.

11. *Baladeiros* is a term that was used by the media and musicians to denote the singers of *trovas* and *baladas*. In particular, it was used during a *Zip-Zip* show in an ironic plot, presented by the comedian Raúl Solnado, about the profile of the new performers who appeared on the program solely accompanied by the acoustic guitar, hence a certain pejorative connotation that is associated with the term.

12. "Blue pencil" is a reference to the act of censorship, since a blue pencil was frequently used to mark censored items.

References

Anon. 1969. "Editorial." *Mundo da Canção* no. 1, December 1969.

Anon. 1972. "Editorial: Renovação." *Mundo da Canção* no. 25, January 1972.

Afonso, José. 1970. "José Afonso em *Cena 7.*" *A Capital*, December 1970.

———. 1971. "José Afonso: Não quero ser vedeta." *Flama* no. 1240, December 1971.

Ayats, Jaume, and Maria Salicrú-Maltas. 2013. "The Nova Cançó." In *Made in Spain: Studies in Popular Music*, edited by Sílvia Martínez and Héctor Fouce, 28–41. New York: Routledge.

Bebiano, Rui. 2006. *Anos inquietos. Vozes do movimento estudantil em Coimbra (1961–1974)*. Porto: Afrontamento.

Branco, José Mário. 1972. "José Mário Branco: A voz da mudança." *Flama* no. 1244, January 1972.

———. 2008 "As canções de protesto e o fim da ditadura." In *Os Anos de Salazar*. Vol. 30. Edited by António Simões do Paço, 145–53. Lisbon: Centro Editor CDA.

Castelo-Branco, Salwa ed. 2010. *Enciclopédia da música em Portugal no século XX*. Lisbon: Círculo de Leitores/Temas e Debates.

Castelo-Branco, Salwa El-Shawan. 2013. "The Politics of Music Categorization in Portugal." In *The Cambridge History of World Music*, edited by Philip Bohlman, 661–77. Cambridge: Cambridge University Press.

Castelo-Branco, Salwa, and Rui Cidra. 2010. "Música Popular." In *Enciclopédia da música em Portugal no século XX*, edited by Salwa Castelo-Branco, 875–78. Lisbon: Círculo de Leitores/Temas e Debates.

7. Protest Song and Recording in the Estado Novo   151

Castro, José Hugo Pires. 2012. "Discos na Luta: A produção fonográfica na canção de protesto em Portugal nas décadas de 1960 e 1970." MA thesis, New University of Lisbon.

———. 2017. "Música e política na revista Mundo da Canção no período revolucionário português (1974–1976)." *Cuadernos de Etnomusicología* 10, 241–67.

———. 2022. "'A Cantiga só é arma quando a luta acompanhar!': Canção e política na Revolução dos Cravos em Portugal." PhD diss., New University of Lisbon.

Castro, Hugo, and Ricardo Andrade. 2020. "José Mário Branco: Algumas notas." *Cena's* no. 16, February 2020.

Correia, Mário. 1984. *Música popular portuguesa: Um ponto de partida*. Coimbra, PT: Centelha/Mundo da Canção.

Côrte-Real, Maria de S. José. 2010. "Canção de Intervenção." In *Enciclopédia da música em Portugal no século XX*, edited by Salwa Castelo-Branco, 220–28. Lisbon: Círculo de Leitores/Temas e Debates.

Equipa Redactorial EMPXX. 2010. "Canção de Coimbra." In *Enciclopédia da música em Portugal no século XX*, edited by Salwa Castelo-Branco, 215–20. Lisbon: Círculo de Leitores/Temas e Debates.

Eyerman, Ron, and Andrew Jamison. 1998. *Music and Social Movements: Mobilizing Traditions in the Twentieth Century*. Cambridge: Cambridge University Press.

Fiuza, Alexandre Felipe. 2006. "Entre um samba e um fado: A censura e a repressão aos músicos no Brasil e em Portugal nas décadas de 1960 e 1970." PhD diss., Universidade Estadual Paulista.

Garratt, James. 2018. *Music and Politics: A Critical Introduction*. Cambridge: Cambridge University Press.

Lebrun, Barbara. 2009. *Protest Music in France: Production, Identity and Audiences*. Farnham, UK: Ashgate.

Lopes, Sofia. 2012. "'Duas horas vivas numa TV morta': Zip-Zip, música e televisão no preâmbulo da democracia em Portugal." MA thesis, New University of Lisbon.

Lopes-Graça, Fernando. 1946. *Marchas, danças e canções: Próprias para grupos vocais ou instrumentos populares*. Lisbon: Seara Nova.

Losa, Leonor. 2010. "Indústria fonográfica." In *Enciclopédia da música em Portugal no século XX*, edited by Salwa Castelo-Branco, 632–43. Lisbon: Círculo de Leitores/Temas e Debates.

McDonald, David. 2013. *My Voice Is My Weapon: Music, Nationalism, and the Poetics of Palestinian Resistance*. Durham, NC: Duke University Press.

Moutinho, José Viale. 1975. *Memória do canto livre em Portugal*. Lisbon: Editorial Futura.

Niza, José. 2007. *Adriano Correia de Oliveira: Obra completa*. Lisbon: Público Comunicação Social, S.A.

Nooshin, Laudan. 2009. *Music and the Play of Power in the Middle East, North Africa, and Central Asia*. Farnham, UK: Ashgate.

Perez-Villalba, Esther. 2007. *How Political Singers Facilitated the Spanish Transition to Democracy, 1960–1982: The Cultural Construction of a New Identity*. New York: Edwin Mellen Press.

Pimentel, Irene, and Joaquim Vieira. 2009. *Fotobiografias do séc. XX: José Afonso*. Casais de Mem Martins, PT: Círculo de Leitores.

Raposo, Eduardo. 2005. *Canto de Intervenção: 1960–1974*. Lisbon: Público Comunicação Social, SA.

Rosas, Fernando. 2015. "A transição falhada." In *O dia da liberdade, 25 de Abril de 1974*, edited by Pedro Lauret, 6–18. Aveleda, PT: Verso da História.

Salvador, José. 2014. *Zeca Afonso: Livra-te do medo*. Porto: Porto Editora.

Silva, Octávio Fonseca. 2000. *José Mário Branco. O Canto da Inquietação*. Porto: Mundo da Canção.

Teles, Viriato. 2009. *As voltas de um andarilho: Fragmentos da vida e obra de José Afonso*. Lisbon: Assírio & Alvim.

Tumas-Serna, Jane. 1992. "The 'Nueva Canción' Movement and Its Mass-Mediated Performance." *Latin American Music Review* 13, no. 2, 139–57.

PART III

Negotiating the State, Nation, and Region

8

Towards a Critical Approach to Flamenco Hybridity in Post-Franco Spain

Rock Music, Nation, and Heritage in Andalusia

DIEGO GARCÍA-PEINAZO

In 1962, the Spanish music magazine *Discóbolo* published an article that states, "flamenco and modern rhythms fight each other for the preferences of juke-box customers" ("Música en los bares" 1962, 25). One year later, the same magazine featured an interview with Pablito Rodrigo, a ten-year-old child who had extraordinary musical skills for the new rhythms of popular song. Pablito showed his preference for contemporary popular music styles, saying, "Flamenco NO, Twist SÍ" ("Pablito Rodrigo, intérprete de ritmos modernos" 1963, 15). Yet despite these clear distinctions between flamenco and "modern popular music," flamenco cannot be understood without its historical links with modernity (Steingress 2002; Romero 2016). The mixing of flamenco and other genres of popular music has been a constant since at least the second half of the nineteenth century: from *zarzuela*, jazz, *cuplé*, rock and roll, beat, or progressive rock, to world music, heavy metal, hip-hop, EDM, or trap, among others. However, even when it is common to find narratives that celebrate flamenco hybridity and the genre's encounters with other musics, the nature of these relations has not always been stable and indisputable.

156   DIEGO GARCÍA-PEINAZO

This chapter examines some of the conflicting dynamics surrounding flamenco hybridity through a case study of rock music in Andalusia during the Spanish Transition to Democracy (ca. 1975–1982), a period when regional identities, political claims against centralization, and the resignification of cultural discourses and practices (re)emerged.[1] On the one hand, this chapter focuses on so-called *rock andaluz* bands (from now on referred to as RA), a hybrid musical phenomenon mixing progressive rock and flamenco that reached its peak in the 1970s. On the other hand, I consider other rock music bands in Andalusia during the period that did not use flamenco music in their recorded songs.[2] Drawing on press sources, oral interviews, and recorded songs, I analyze how flamenco evocations became an aesthetic and ideological requirement for rock bands to be considered as genuinely "Andalusian" during the second half of the 1970s. Moreover, such evocations became a symbolic imperative in order to create, during the Spanish transition to democracy, a "genuine" and "authentic" rock expression that could articulate an identity distinct from that of the Anglo-American canon of progressive rock. In Andalusia today, the RA movement has become progressively canonized as one of the most important stages in the history of Andalusian popular music. These two main ways of understanding rock—that is, bands that included "authoctonous" musical references such as flamenco and bands that shunned these aesthetic devices in the construction of their identity and image—coexisted during the transition to democracy. However, recent heritagization processes of the history of Andalusian popular music of the second half of the twentieth century primarily reinforce the centrality of a flamenco hybridity in the construction of narratives about the "real roots" of rock in Southern Spain.

Popular Music, Flamenco, and Identities in Spain: The Case of *Rock Andaluz*

As Samuel Llano points out, the formation and categorization of "Spanish music" is "a dynamic historical and cultural process that precisely encompasses a set of individual and collective experiences, as well as the personal and institutional agents engaged in their practice" (2013, 237). Throughout the twentieth century, popular music has often included elements that reinforce the idea of a "local/national color," and in this context flamenco has definitely played a central role in the formation of an "imagined community" around what it means to be Spanish. In this sense, even when flamenco might be understood more broadly as a popular music expression, in this chapter I often adopt the definition of flamenco as "traditional music," because this is how several rock bands in An-

8. Towards a Critical Approach to Flamenco Hybridity   157

dalusia view the genre. In so doing, they set up discursive, contrasting relations between metaphors of modernities, tradition, and the Other in popular music.

Interactions between flamenco and the emergent rock and roll can be found since the late 1950s in popular music for dance orchestras with labels such as "flamenco rock" or "flamenco rock and roll" (García-Peinazo 2017, 86–90), with such interactions being developed further during the 1960s, especially in relation to the beat movement (Alonso González 2005; 2010a). Nonetheless, in the late 1960s there was an initial lack of significant interest in flamenco music among numerous rock musicians from Andalusia, since at this time flamenco represented, for them, an anti-modern and even a Francoist manifestation.[3] However, in the late Francoist period, flamenco carved out spaces of symbolic contestation and political subversion, such as the so-called "flamenco protesta" movement in the late 1960s (Ordóñez Eslava 2013). In the mid-1970s, as the Franco regime came to an end, popular musicians in Andalusia stopped ignoring flamenco and began to integrate it in the musical discourse of rock.

Rock andaluz arose in tandem with regional claims in southern Spain that re-emerged at the end of the Franco era (1975) and was one of the most famous popular music expressions in Andalusia until the consolidation of democracy in Spain around 1982. This musical phenomenon merged common styles performed by Anglo-American progressive and hard rock bands with references to traditional musics from Andalusia. This musical strategy also occurred in other peripheral sub-state nations in Spain such as the Basque Country, Asturias, Catalonia, and Galicia, among others (García Salueña 2017). During the 1970s, this tendency was characterized as "rock con raíces" (rock with roots) and was promoted by the label Gong-Movieplay and its producer Gonzalo García Pelayo (García-Peinazo 2019). Flamenco music was the privileged intertextual genre performed by RA bands such as Triana, Alameda, or Medina Azahara in their resignification of tradition in Andalusia, although other musics, from *copla* to evocations of Arab music and Andalusí traditional musics, was also included.[4] In addition to the mostly exclusive use of lyrics in the Spanish language, RA also utilized the Andalusian "accent" as a means of expression.

RA can also be understood as a process through which the construction of rock as a global practice in peripheral countries dialogued with the rock canon articulated by US and UK bands during the 1970s. In accordance with the conventional periods of pop-rock history outlined by Motti Regev (2013), countries peripheral to the canon of popular music transition from mimesis of the canon to the use of local elements to evidence the differences between "national" rock styles—vernacular languages rather than English, use of melodic, harmonic, and rhythmic structures of traditional musics, etc.—but also to combine with other "international" common styles. Regev describes this process as "expressive isomorphism" and "aesthetic cosmopolitanism" (2013). On the other hand, during the Spanish transition to democracy, flamenco was resignified by a generation of young Andalusian rock musicians, who were able to transform a music that supposedly represented Francoist values into a transgressive, distinctive music from Andalusia. In the search for these "roots," flamenco was relocated as the clearest example of an "authentic" expression of Andalusian music. One of the members of Triana—the most emblematic RA band—argues that his group embodied the idea of "Andalusia without its [negative] stereotypes" (Rodriguez Rodway-Triana, personal communication, June 2, 2015).[5]

According to Cruces Roldán, after *mairenismo*,[6] between 1970 and 1990, there was a proliferation of festivals and competitions in Andalusia and other locations in Spain as well as the (re)emergence of flamenco *peñismo* (the gathering of flamenco *aficionados*, especially at emblematic venues for flamenco performance called *peñas*) and the "articulation of flamenco audiences around cult discography" (2017, 336). In this context, flamenco music was paradoxically understood by RA bands of the late 1970s according to the categories of "purity" and "authenticity" in a way that might be curiously reminiscent of *mairenismo* but in a popular music setting (García-Peinazo 2017, 333). In this sense, in his study of flamenco jazz during Franco's regime, Iván Iglesias points out that albums such as Pedro Iturralde's *Flamenco Jazz* (1967) constitute, through the use of flamenco, an expression of ideas about flamenco purity promulgated by *mairenismo* as well as an implicit recognition of the poet García Lorca as a leftwing intellectual: "What Iturralde combined with jazz in his Hispavox albums, consciously or unconsciously, was the matter of gitanismo[7] and mairenismo, an aesthetic that many Spanish young people and intellectuals identified at that time with 'true' flamenco art and with the political opposition to the Franco regime" (Iglesias 2017, 331).[8]

At this point it should be emphasized that the relationship between popular music and national/regional identity was articulated during the 1970s according to complex and often contradictory readings of what Andalusia represented to RA bands. In contrast to the idea of Andalusian identity as a homogeneous expression, several authors have pointed out that fragmentation and localism complicate Andalusian identity due to factors such as feelings of marginalization in some parts of the region due to the alleged process of recentralization in Seville, the capital of Andalusia. Indeed, this has led to fragmentation around what constitutes the Andalusian territory, especially the division between west Andalusia and east Andalusia. González Alcantud (2004) examines this fragmentation between two symbolic cores, around west and east, and the presence

8. Towards a Critical Approach to Flamenco Hybridity 159

of localisms across the Andalusian region. In this sense, flamenco can also be observed under the umbrella of these two cores in Andalusia in their relationship with political geography, as Machin-Autenrieth (2017) has demonstrated (see especially the chapter "Flamenco, Something of Ours?"). If most RA bands were from west Andalusia, several practices around rock in Andalusia articulated this discursive tendency to polarize into "two Andalusias" (García-Peinazo 2013a; 2017). Furthermore, Andalusian identity as performed by RA bands was also articulated through essentialist discourses in several Spanish rock magazines, which discussed the lack of authenticity and racial roots of bands from other locations outside of Spain. These bands hybridized flamenco with rock, such as the Californian group Carmen, and their work was covered by UK music magazines such as *Melody Maker*, which branded Carmen as "The World's First Flamenco Rock Band" (García-Peinazo 2020b).

"Rock for Andalusia" and Its Others

The narratives about the history of rock in Andalusia often highlight RA as a turning point in popular music. However, these narratives sometimes minimize the fact that even when it was common for bands in Andalusia during the 1970s to assume the aesthetics and ideology of *rock con raíces*, that is, the inclusion of flamenco as a central element in their music, other rock bands from Andalusia did not include any of these evocations. In this context, it is important to explore the complex dynamics surrounding the inclusion and non-inclusion of these musical practices. In what follows, I present some examples that illustrate the main arguments of other rock bands in Andalusia that were against the RA movement.

The symbolic association of flamenco and *copla* with Francoism[9] was a crucial factor in the decision taken by Los Solos (a rock band from Jerez de la Frontera in Cádiz) to relegate these genres to the background. Their bass player, Tito Gil, remembers that during the rise of RA (the second half of the 1970s), it was more difficult to arrange live performances for his band. Gil points out that during the transition to democracy, "rock andaluz sounded to us like copla, as a pro-Franco past, even when this movement reached its peak after Franco's death" (Tito Gil, personal interview, March 15, 2013). Dofus, another rock band from Granada that published its debut and only studio album *Suite Azul Rock* (1979), did not feel any sort of aesthetic or stylistic interest in the RA movement, not even its flamenco evocations: "We never wanted to mix our music with copla or flamenco. Never. It was foreign to us [. . .]. The musical training and education, no matter who may disagree, was completely Anglo-American" (Jolís Gualda, personal communication, March 21, 2013).

The hegemony of Andalusia's capital, Seville, in terms of the music industry when compared to other cities, and the supposedly lesser presence of flamenco in East Andalusia, were other arguments used against RA. For example, Dofus's vocalist, guitarist, and band leader Jolís Gualda suggests that the RA scene was mainly related to Seville, Córdoba, and Cádiz, arguing that there was no popular flamenco scene in Granada at the time (Jolís Gualda, personal interview, March 21, 2013). Similarly, Nono Cruz, guitarist for La Banda de los Hermanos Cruz, a band from Granada, stated in 1977 in the Spanish rock magazine *Popular 1*: "There has been a sort of fashion for roots [. . .]. These roots are artificial [. . .]. While a lot of musicians create unreal roots, we suffer the plundering of our own music [. . .]. The idea of roots is harmful for our band, since RA bands appropriate flamenco music, and because they associate flamenco with Andalusia." Here, Cruz expressed his critique towards centralization processes in the music industry, and the secondary place occupied by cities such as Granada: "apart from Madrid and Barcelona, in Andalusia it seems that only Seville exists, and the rest are marginalized" (Esteban 1977, 66).

The tendency to focus on local identities (i.e., related to particular cities or neighborhoods inside Andalusia) instead of an homogeneous Andalusian identity was another way to discuss the RA movement. Tabletom, a rock band from Málaga that published its first album, *Mezclalina*, in 1979—a key year in the success of groups such as Medina Azahara, Alameda, and Triana—rejected the RA phenomenon. "In the Spanish transition to democracy, we did not like flamenco music, until we started afterwards listening to Camarón [de la Isla], Paco de Lucía, etc. But at that time we had never listened to flamenco. In our family there was no place for flamenco music [In reference to RA bands]. However, we also felt very Andalusian and felt that our music—and the things we said and sang—defended a lot of aspects of what we liked about Andalusia [. . .]. We did not play RA, we played 'rock étnico-malagueño [ethnic rock from Malaga]'" (Perico Ramírez, guitarist, *Tabletom*, personal communication, April 5, 2013).[10] In spite of the testimonies above, the West Andalusian origins of RA bands cannot be understood as the exclusive reason for the tendency to oppose flamenco evocations in other rock bands. There were also other rock bands in Seville that did not follow the RA tendency to include flamenco references, like The Storm, a band that was completely opposed to the idea and aesthetic premises of RA.

The Storm: Flamenco as Anxiety of Influence

The Sevillian band The Storm gained recognition around 1974. That year, they represented Spain in the BBC Radio 2 Contest *European Pop Jury* ("Storm repre-

8. Towards a Critical Approach to Flamenco Hybridity   161

sentan a España" 1974, 15). The Storm were also the support band at a concert by British rock band Queen in Barcelona in 1974. However, and despite this initial success, in the second half of the 1970s, with the emergence of RA, The Storm was described in several rock magazines of the period in terms of their "lack of originality," "lack of authenticity," and "lack of independence" from Anglo-American rock.

All these values were considered "negative" and in opposition to the development of a particular expression of rock with "home" roots. For example, such sentiment was expressed in the words of music critics such as Jesús Ordovás, who published an article on the band in 1978 with the telling title "The Storm: Dependent Language," in *Disco Exprés*, which was probably the most influential rock music magazine in Spain during the 1970s: "Why do you not create songs in Andalusian, man? You are Andalusians, aren't you?" (Ordovás 1978, 14). The emergence of RA meant that The Storm was seen as an "out of fashion" band in the new musical context of rock in Andalusia. Ordovás finished his article by lauding the originality, and unique and indigenous character of the RA bands that hybridized flamenco and Andalusian music with rock, like Triana, Imán, and Guadalquivir. At the same time, he suggested that The Storm had to change their musical style and must go the same way as RA bands in order to overcome "their limitations and Anglo-American subordinations and build their own style" (14). The Storm was, then, undervalued in rock magazines due to their stylistic decision. The main consequence was a necessity for The Storm to demonstrate that they had flamenco roots and flamenco "blood." As a result, members of the band tried to prove their flamenco lineage or ancestry stating "we have flamenco blood but we belong to the rock generation and so we do rock" (Serra I Fabra 1975, 6).

However, in their two studio albums (LP *Storm*, 1974; LP *El día de la tormenta*, 1979) there was no trace of elements potentially connotative of flamenco or Andalusian-based music such as evocations of the flamenco guitar, Andalusian cadences, *ayeos* and *jaleos*,[11] or the so-called *compases de doce*.[12] In terms of melodic and harmonic structures, the music of The Storm is mainly based on the Aeolian and the Dorian modes, often used in hard rock bands such as Deep Purple, the main musical stylistic reference for The Storm. It should be noted that Deep Purple often employed the harmonic minor scale in their songs, e.g., in "Highway Star" and "Child in Time" (1972), a scale that uses the augmented second, an element that became a signature of their electric guitar and Hammond organ solos. The influence of Deep Purple guitarist Richie Blackmore and his solos—with a strong influence of Baroque repertoires (Walser 1992, 268)—on The Storm is also remarkable, with structures such as the *Bachian* scale, which allows the presence of chords close to the Dorian mode.

It is interesting that the interval of the augmented second, a melodic structure frequent in the music of Deep Purple, was not included in The Storm's melodic constructions. From the point of view of musical meaning, it is significant that in spite of the influence of Deep Purple on the musical style of The Storm, we can perceive a sort of "selective listening" of the well-known British band. The network of significations is even more complex because not only is this kind of musical structure often used by Deep Purple, but it is also a common musical stereotype to evoke flamenco music and Spanish sounds, alongside the importance of timbre in the construction of cultural and social meaning in harmonic and melodic patterns (Tagg 2013, 305–42). The matter of non-inclusion of the augmented second in the music of The Storm, in order to avoid the possibility of an evocation of the "Spanish sound," exemplifies how musical style operates as a toolkit in which some elements are included and others excluded according to cultural and social meanings and contexts.

Here, Ann Swidler's notion of culture as a "toolkit" implies the existence of a series of skills, habits, and conceptions of the world that individuals use differently according to the context through differing "strategies of action" (1996). Building these strategies implies selecting and choosing particular elements of culture that articulate concrete meanings in specific circumstances (Swidler 1996, 148). Furthermore, in their approach to cultural appropriation and otherness in different musics, Born and Hesmondhalgh argue that it is important to explore "the nature of hybrids resulting from their musical borrowings, and how certain musics are constituted through the purposive or ambivalent absenting or mastery of other musics and cultures" (2000, 3). Musical style is, then, a matter of choice and representation. If, following musicologist Allan F. Moore (2012, 8), stylistic analysis of popular music is crucial in order to clarify what is normative and what is not in a defined style, then The Storm's exclusion of augmented seconds—a normative compositional device in Deep Purple's music—can be interpreted as a strategy in order to avoid RA's association with flamenco sonorities.

The Storm were questioned in relation to this stylistic choice, since according to rock magazines such as *Disco Exprés* they did not create an "original mix between rock, flamenco, and pop" (Ordovás 1978, 15). In this sense, it is not only possible to appreciate the symbolic exclusion of bands that did not use flamenco music during the rise of *rock con raíces* but also a discourse of resistance based on the ideals of authenticity around hard rock music. The Storm tried to validate their musical style in terms of a sort of authenticity around rock.[13] This point is expressed by Diego Ruiz, drummer of The Storm, who considers that the band "resisted" RA and the inclusion of flamenco during its successful period in the

8. *Towards a Critical Approach to Flamenco Hybridity* 163

late 1970s: "I am Sevillian! From San Jerónimo! It was a time in which we (The Storm) thought about the possibility of playing RA music, but we said 'we could, but we will not do it!'" (Diego Ruiz, personal communication, December 18, 2014). In relation to the international image of The Storm as a Spanish or Andalusian band, Ruiz suggests that it was easier for bands such as "Triana, Guadalquivir, Alameda, Medina Azahara" [RA bands] to forge a national or regional image than it was for a hard rock group—The Storm—from Spain, since RA bands were identified with "Andalusia and the image of [the] Spanish product" (2014). The reception and vicissitudes of the Sevillian band The Storm during the emergence of the RA movement entailed, therefore, a process of symbolic marginalization due to hegemonic narratives about ethnicity and purity in Andalusian popular music history based on a presupposed greater degree of authenticity of some roots when compared to others. In this sense, it could be argued that flamenco was regarded as a form of oppression in terms of musical style.

Rock Andaluz as Heritage in Andalusia: From Covers to PDO Wines

Today, new processes around the production of RA as cultural heritage are being enacted by institutions, cultural industries, the media, and fan clubs that continue to remember the "legacy" of the musical practices of the 1970s. Cultural associations like Arabian Rock (Jerez de la Frontera, Cádiz) describe RA bands from that decade in terms of "our wine cellar" and "certificate of origin" and highlight the need to "safeguard" this music as "heritage." Furthermore, the Andalusian Educational System of the Junta de Andalucía (the regional government) has recently legitimized RA's status as "heritage" by including it in its official syllabus for secondary schools in the region, stating that this is a movement that is "part of our Andalusian cultural heritage" (Orden de 14 de junio de 2016, 291). This move aligns with recent efforts within regional policy to institutionalize several Andalusian cultural practices, most notably since UNESCO's inscription of flamenco on the Representative List of the Intangible Cultural Heritage of Humanity (Machin-Autenrieth 2020). Ultimately, all these processes might be linked with the so-called "second wave of decentralization" (Keating and Wilson 2009, 549), which has occurred across different autonomous communities such as Andalusia since the early twenty-first century.

The practice of covering is also a space for the construction of heritage narratives. A cover implies the resignification of previous musical texts such as "reference cover versions" (López-Cano 2012), from parody to satire, pastiche, or "devotional" tribute. In the same way, cover or tribute bands that perform in

Andalusia today try to revive the sound, lyrics, and topics of RA from the 1970s. As is common in selective readings of the history of popular music, particular bands are viewed as representative models for the process of revival. Examples such as the tribute band Zaguán show the cultural impact of the RA band Triana as the icon of popular music history in Andalusia (García-Peinazo 2014b).

Serge Lacasse has pointed out that "transphonography" and its typologies—such as interphonography or hyperphonography—are more precise terms than transtextuality in refering to the processes of textuality in recorded popular song (2018). According to Lacasse, the cover is a type of "hyperphonography" that can articulate different models, since it depends on a degree of transformation of the musical text (19). In this sense, it is also possible to find bands that include allusions to RA "phonographic heritage," and that even when they cannot be considered as tribute bands, these allusions often tend to mix different perspectives of covering. The Sevillian bands Derby Motoreta's Burrito Kachimba, and Quentin Gas & Los Zíngaros are two interesting examples of these hybrid strategies in which RA has become popular heritage in Andalusia.

Derby Motoreta's Burrito Kachimba recorded its self-titled debut album in 2019. They are defined in the press as "a 'kinki' revision of RA with psychedelic evocations" (Tocino 2019) and as a legacy of RA of the 1970s in which the band "goes around causing trouble with those sounds" (Mendoza Arriaga 2019). In fact, the band uses several timbres that are reminiscent of progressive rock of the 1970s, such as analog synthesizers like the Mini Moog. Other stylistic devices close to RA, such as the distorted Phrygian I-bII-bIII-bII-I harmonic pattern in the electric guitar or the use of *ayeos* and vocal expressions in this mode are also common in the music of Derby Motoreta's Burrito Kachimba.

"Grecas," a track from their debut album, *Derby Motoreta's Burrito Kachimba* (2019), comprises all these aspects. After a hard rock/funk rock–based intro (00:00–00:11)—homophonic structures with two electric guitars playing a riff in octaves—a prototypical Andalusian (Phrygian) cadence is played by the electric guitar with overdrive, combining power chords and palm muting (00:12–00:18). The voice of the singer appears in the first repetition of this harmonic pattern with clear vocal resonances of Jesús de la Rosa, singer of the band Triana, and probably the most important icon in the history of RA. Apart from the fact that the title of the song, "Grecas," operates as an intertextual reference to the Gypsy rock band of the 1970s called Las Grecas, the lyrics of the song incorporate allusions to Lole y Manuel, another iconic duo closely related to the RA of the 1970s. The verse "el aire huele a pan nuevo" ("the air smells like freshly baked bread"), written by the poet Flores Talavera as part of the lyrics of Lole y Manuel's song

8. Towards a Critical Approach to Flamenco Hybridity 165

"Nuevo Día" (album *Nuevo Día*, 1975), can be heard in "Grecas" (around 01:19) but with a different harmonic structure.

Quentin Gas & Los Zíngaros, another recent band from Seville, honor the RA phenomenon in their three recent albums (*Big Sur*, 2016; *Caravana*, 2017; *Sinfonía Universal Cap. 02*, 2018). *Caravana* is probably the album with the most musical references to bands such as Triana, something that can be heard in the constant presence of the Phrygian harmonic patterns played on the Hammond. This stylistic device, characteristic of the music of Triana in emblematic songs such as "Recuerdos de una noche" (1975), is the main compositional strategy in Quentin Gas & Los Zíngaros' album *Caravana*. In the popular music magazine *Mondo Sonoro* it is described as an "electric storm of riffs, *quejíos*,[14] and omnipresent keyboard" (Pérez 2017). The augmented second is also used in the Hammond organ solo of the song "Caravana" (01:33–01:58). In their latest album, *Sinfonía Universal Cap. 02* (2018), the treatment of timbre through music production coexists with these tributes to RA. Quentin Gas & Los Zíngaros's track titled "IO" introduces an allusion to the emblematic verse "todo es de color" (performed by bands from the 1970s such as Triana, Goma, and Lole y Manuel). In this song, however, instead of the expected "todo es de color" ("everything is in colour"), they sing "todo no es de color" ("not everything is in color"), using a vocal line with *quejíos* in the Phrygian mode (around 02:05).

The examples mentioned above are related to the revival and canonization of RA through practices of covering, tribute bands and musical allusions, and through the use of heritagization discourses by fans and audiences. In all these narratives, RA bands of the 1970s are described and understood in terms of Protected Designation of Origin (PDO), that is, a "popular music heritage" from a differential, particular geographical location (Andalusia) that must be preserved. Ultimately, these efforts evidence that the history of RA, then, has become the entire—selective—history of rock in Andalusia.

Epliogue: How Equal Is Flamenco Hybridity?

Gerhard Steingress describes flamenco hybridity in terms of the tension between the discourses of "purity" and "experimentation" as well as in terms of its relationships with modernity (2002). He accounts for four main "steps" or stages of hybridity in flamenco's history (177–88). In the fourth and last step (from 1955 to 1990), Steingress includes hybrid forms such as jazz, rock, pop, as well as the so-called *Nuevo Flamenco* (New Flamenco) of the 1980s. (For a detailed study of *Nuevo Flamenco*, see Cruces Roldán 2017, 369–404.) Similarly, a significant example of the importance of hybridity as a core element of flamenco history can be found in the books written by the journalist and flamenco expert Luis Clemente, even when this author often uses the term "fusion" instead of "hybridity" (Clemente 1995; 2002). In his works, flamenco hybridity is often understood as a celebratory practice that always contributes to the evolution of the genre: a history of wondrous fusions, which reflects positive encounters between different cultural expressions.

Despite the rise of interest in hybridity in flamenco, not enough attention has been devoted in academic literature to the ways in which flamenco has become intertwined with discourses and tensions relevant to other contemporary popular musical practices that, even if they may not use any direct references to flamenco music, coexist within the discursive construction of "Andalusian music" and, by extension, Andalusian identity. The complex and at times conflicting relationship between flamenco and popular music styles is often minimized or ignored in both flamenco studies and popular music studies. This oversight is due to a tendency to observe hybridity in flamenco as a "celebration" of intercultural exchanges between diverse musics rather than as a critical approach that understands hybridity as a space where the hegemony of some music styles is constructed at the expense of others. A critical approach that focuses on power relationships around flamenco music is missing from current scholarship.[15]

In his critical study about hybridity, Pieterse points out that "hybridity skips over questions of power and inequality," since "hybridity is not parity" (2001, 224). In the same way, Alabarces (2012) suggests that even though hybridity has become a frequent practice in the twentieth century, this fact does not hide power relationships, since hybridity discourses in academia have sometimes operated as a form of fetishism articulated by researchers (18). In his critical revision of García Canclini's work, Alabarces underlines that power issues have been relegated to the background in studies about hybridity, since there is less consideration of what is inside the mix and the power relationships that emerge (17). Alabarces exposes the necessity to analyze "who speaks, who represents. What is said and what is represented. And, more important, who manages, authorizes, and spreads this representation and this voice" (31).

Describing the popular music context in Spain during the 1970s, music journalist Diego Manrique pointed out that "the matter of roots" has carried with it "an attitude close to xenophobia" (1976, 20). After studying the case of RA in this chapter, I argue that the hybridization of rock music and flamenco—and in a broader sense, the notion of "Andalusian music" and "Spanish music"—functioned as a sort of aesthetic imposition in that context. It was used to create a form of local/regional rock that was in opposition to other rock bands

8. Towards a Critical Approach to Flamenco Hybridity   167

in Andalusia that were negatively characterized as "mimetic bands." However, this situation was only a fragment of the complex socio-political context of post-Franco Spain. While RA was relatively hegemonic in the second half of the 1970s, it was partly forgotten in the 1980s. As with audiences today, flamenco hybridity is celebrated by some citizens but criticized by others. Overall, what is key here is to understand that musical style in recorded popular song constituted a space for inclusions and exclusions, a fact that contributes to the rhizomatic nature of cultural identities.

Notes

1. The complex relation between music and politics during the transition to democracy has been examined across several scenes and music styles. Regarding Western art music, see Medina (2010) and Solís Marquínez (2020); for songwriters in Spain, see Martínez (2016); for music and left-wing political campaigning, see García-Peinazo (2014a); for popular music, politics, and (unofficial) national anthems, see García-Peinazo (2020a); for an overview of rock music and politics during the transition to democracy, see Val (2017). An overview of the Spanish transition to democracy can be found in Tusell (2007). Regarding culture, politics, and national identity during that period, see Balfour and Quiroga (2007).

2. Works by Moore (2001), Everett (2009), and Covach and Flory (2012), among others, constitute important overall approaches to rock history and musical structures. For rock music and place in local and global contexts, see Regev (2020) and Stahl (2020).

3. See also the avoidance of flamenco by Nova Cançó songwriters in Catalunya due to its perceived Francoist connotations (Ayats and Salicrú-Maltas 2013).

4. For evocations of Andalusí traditional music, I mean here both the musical practices during the Al-Andalus period in the Iberian Peninsula (ca. ss. 711–1492) and contemporary Andalusí orchestras as musical practices in North Africa. For the study of different fusion between flamenco and Arab-Andalusian musics, see Steingress (2002); Cruces Roldán (2003); Paetzold (2009); García-Peinazo (2013b); Shannon (2015); Machin-Autenrieth (2019). The fusions between both musics are also one of the core research areas of the European Research Council-founded project "Past and Present Musical Encounters Across the Strait of Gibraltar" (MESG, 2018–2023).

5. It should be noted that images and meanings about an exotic Andalusia had been constructed in Andalusia, Spain, and other countries since the late eighteenth century. An approximation about some of these stereotypes, with a consideration of their musical manifestations, can be found in Alonso (2010b).

6. *Mairenismo* is understood as a cultural ideology that started in the 1950s through the writings and ideas of the *cantaor* (flamenco singer) Antonio Mairena about the necessity of the "rebirth" of the presumed purity and roots of real Andalusian gypsy *cante* in contrast to the "degeneration" and mass popularization of flamenco practices such as the so-called *ópera flamenca*.

7. The term "gitanismo" refers to the narratives that emphasize the predominance of Gypsy (Gitano) people in the history and roots of flamenco.

8. "Lo que Iturralde combinó con el jazz en sus discos de Hispavox, consciente o inconscientemente, fue gitanismo o mairenismo, estética que muchos jóvenes e intelectuales españoles identificaban entonces con el 'verdadero' arte flamenco y con la oposición política al régimen de Franco" (translation by the author).

9. It should be noted that even though *copla* has often been linked to Francoism, this perspective is reductionist, since it only considers one of multiple significations of this musical practice. For example, see Stephanie Sieburth (2016) for an analysis of *copla* as a space for political dissidence through the case study of Conchita Piquer.

10. "El rock andaluz es para mí, simplemente que si eres andaluz y haces rock, ya lo puedes llamar rock andaluz; ahora, si hablamos de lo que se ha etiquetado como el estilo musical que se ha denominado rock andaluz, lo respeto como cualquier otro estilo, pero Tabletom nunca nos hemos identicado con esa manera de hacer. Nuestra música no la consideramos rock andaluz, lo que pasa es que si eres andaluz y haces rock pues entramos dentro del rock andaluz, pero no en el estilo musical [. . .] nuestra música, más que rock andaluz, yo la llamaría 'rock étnico malagueño.'" Original text of the interview in Spanish, cited in García-Peinazo (2013a, 306).

11. In flamenco music, *ayeos* and *jaleos* refer to, respectively, vocal melismata and shouted out/spoken vocal expressions during performances.

12. *Compases de doce*—twelve-beat patterns—are rhythmic and metric structures that constitute the core of *palos* such as *siguiriyas*, *bulerías*, *alegrías*, and *soleares*, among others.

13. For authenticities in rock music, see Keightley (2001); for the concept of "multiple authenticities" in RA, see García-Peinazo (2017).

14. In flamenco, *quejíos* are paralinguistic musical expressions related to an extreme, dramatized use of sung voice.

15. An exception related to this issue can be found in Samuel Llano's study about flamenco as a palimpsest (2020).

References

Alabarces, Pablo. 2012. "Transculturas populares: El retorno de las culturas populares en las ciencias sociales latinoamericanas." *Cultura y Representaciones Sociales* 7, no. 13: 7–39.

Alonso González, Celsa. 2005. "El beat español: entre la frivolidad, la modernidad y la subversión." *Cuadernos de Música Iberoamericana* 10: 225–53.

———. 2010a. "Símbolos y estereotipos nacionales en la música popular de los años sesenta: Entre la representación y la negociación." In *Creación musical, cultura popular y construcción nacional en la España contemporánea*, edited by Celsa Alonso González, Julio Arce, and Teresa Fraile Preito, 205–31. Madrid: ICCMU.

———. 2010b. "En el espejo de 'los otros': Andalucismo, exotismo e hispanismo." In *Creación musical, cultura popular y construcción nacional en la España contemporánea*, edited by Celsa Alonso González, Julio Arce, and Teresa Fraile Preito, 83–104. Madrid: ICCMU.

Ayats, Jaume, and María Salicrú-Maltas. 2013. "Singing Against the Dictatorship (1959–1975): The Nova Cançó." In *Made in Spain: Studies in Popular Music*, edited by Sílvia Martínez and Héctor Fouce, 28–41. London: Routledge.

Balfour, Sebastián, and Alejandro Quiroga. 2007. *The Reinvention of Spain: Nation and Identity Since Democracy*. Oxford: Oxford University Press.

Born, Georgina, and David Hesmondhalgh. 2000. "Introduction: On Difference, Representation, and Appropriation in Music." In *Western Music and Its Others: Difference,*

8. Towards a Critical Approach to Flamenco Hybridity   169

Representation, and Appropriation in Music, edited by Georgina Born and David Hesmondhalgh, 1–58. Berkeley: University of California Press.

Celemente, Luis. 1995. *Filigranas: Una historia de las fusiones flamencas*. Valencia: La Máscara.

———. 2002. *Flamenco! de evolución*. Sevilla: Lapislázuli.

Covach, John, and Andrew Flory. 2012. *What's That Sound? An Introduction to Rock and Its History*. New York: W. W. Norton.

Cruces Roldán, Cristina. 2002. *El flamenco y la música andalusí: Argumentos para un encuentro*. Barcelona: Carena.

———. 2017. *Flamenco. Negro sobre blanco: Investigación, patrimonio, cine y neoflamenco*. Sevilla: Universidad de Sevilla.

Esteban, José María. 1977. "Patilleros, revivales y sinfónicos hispánicos." *Popular 1* 54, December 1977, 66.

Everett, Walter. 2009. *The Foundations of Rock: From "Blue Suede Shoes" to "Suite: Judy Blue Eyes."* New York: Oxford University Press.

García Salueña, Eduardo. 2017. *Música para la libertad: Nuevas tecnologías, experimentación y procesos de fusión en el rock progresivo de la España de la Transición: La zona norte*. Gijón, ES: Norte Sur.

García-Peinazo, Diego. 2013a. "El Ideal del Rock Andaluz: Lógica y conflicto en la construcción musical de una identidad andaluza." *Musiker: Cuadernos de música* 20: 299–325.

———. 2013b. "Rock andaluz, orientalismos e identidad en la Andalucía de la transición (1975–1982)." In *Musicología Global, Musicología Local*, edited by Javier Marín López, Germán Gan Quesada, Elena Torres Clemente, and Pilar Ramos López, 759–78. Madrid: Sociedad Española de Musicología.

———. 2014a. "Música, prensa y argumentaciones políticas de la transición española en los órganos de expresión del PCE y el PSOE (1977–1982)." *Ensayos: Revista de la Facultad de Educación de Albacete* 29: 95–113.

———. 2014b. "Prácticas culturales en torno al rock andaluz: Entre el imaginario y la nostalgia de Andalucía." In *Andalucía en la música: Expresión de comunidad, construcción de identidad*, edited by Francisco J. García Gallardo and Herminia Arredondo Pérez, 151–71. Seville: Centro de Estudios Andaluces.

———. 2017. *Rock andaluz: Significación musical, identidades e ideología en la España del tardofranquismo y la Transición (1969–1982)*. Madrid: Sociedad Española de Musicología.

———. 2019. "¿Es 'nuestra música'? Rock con raíces e identidades nacionales en España." *ANDULI: Revista Andaluza de Ciencias Sociales* 18: 73–92.

———. 2020a. "'Libertad sin ira,' indignación en (la) Transición: Reapropiaciones políticas y relatos sonoros de un himno para la España democrática (1976–2017)." *Historia y Política* 43: 361–85.

———. 2020b. "'The World's First Flamenco Rock Band'? Anglo-American Progressive Rock, Politics and National Identity in Spain around Carmen's *Fandangos in Space* (1973)." *Rock Music Studies* 7, no. 1: 1–20.

González Alcantud, José Antonio. 2004. *Deseo y negación de Andalucía: Lo local y la contraposición Oriente/Occidente en la realidad andaluza*. Granada: Universidad de Granada.

Iglesias, Iván. 2017. *La modernidad elusiva: Jazz, baile y política en la Guerra Civil española y el Franquismo (1936–1968)*. Madrid: CSIC.

Keating, Michael, and Alex Wilson. 2009. "Renegotiating the State of Autonomies: Statute Reform and Multi-level politics in Spain." *West European Politics* 32, no. 3: 536–58.

Keightley, Keir. 2001. "Reconsidering Rock." In *The Cambridge Companion to Pop and Rock*, edited by Simon Frith, Will Straw, and John Street, 109–42. Cambridge: Cambridge University Press.

Lacasse, Serge. 2018. "Toward a Model of Transphonography." In *The Pop Palimpsest: Intertextuality in Recorded Popular Song*, edited by Lori Burns and Serge Lacasse, 9–60. Ann Arbor: University of Michigan Press.

Llano, Samuel. 2013. *Whose Spain? Negotiating "Spanish Music" in Paris, 1909–1929*. Oxford: Oxford University Press.

———. 2020. "Flamenco as Palimpsest: Reading Through Hybridity." In *Transnational Spanish Studies*, edited by Catherine Davies and Rory O'Bryen, 161–75. Liverpool: Liverpool University Press.

López-Cano, Rubén. 2012. "Lo original es la versión: Covers, versiones y originales en la música popular urbana." *ArtCultura: Uberlândia* 14, no. 24: 81–98.

Machin-Autenrieth, Matthew. 2017. *Flamenco, Regionalism and Musical Heritage in Southern Spain*. Farnham, UK: Routledge.

———. 2019. "Spanish Musical Responses to Moroccan Immigration and the Cultural Memory of al-Andalus." *Twentieth-Century Music* 16, no. 2: 259–87.

———. 2020. "Flamenco for Andalusia, Flamenco for Humanity: Regionalisation and Intangible Cultural Heritage in Spain." In *Cultural Mapping and Musical Diversity*, edited by Britta Sweers and Sarah M. Ross, 256–78. Sheffield, UK: Equinox.

Manrique, Diego A. 1976. "Rock, ¿Qué rock? Cómo usar los kilovatios y la saliva." *Star* 26: 20.

Martínez, Sílvia. 2016. "Judges, Guitars, Freedom and the Mainstream: Problematizing the Early Cantautor in Spain." In *The Singer-Songwriter in Europe: Paradigms, Politics and Place*, edited by Isabelle Marc and Stuart Green, 123–35. New York: Routledge.

Medina, Ángel. 2010. "Acotaciones musicales a la transición democrática en España." In *Creación musical, cultura popular y construcción nacional en la España Contemporánea*, edited by Celsa Alonso, 267–82. Madrid: Instituto Complutense de Ciencias Musicales.

Mendoza Arriaga, Alejandro. 2019. "Derby Motoreta's Burrito Kachimba, un delirio de psicodelia y flamenco." *El País*, February 9, 2019. https://elpais.com/cultura/2019/02/09/actualidad/1549669838_455114.html.

Moore, Allan F. 2001. *Rock: The Primary Text. Developing a Musicology of Rock*. Aldershot, UK: Ashgate.

———. 2012. *Song Means: Analysing and Interpreting Recorded Popular Song*. Surrey, UK: Ashgate.

"Música en los bares." 1962. *Discóbolo* 4, May 10, 1962: 25.

"Orden de 14 de junio de 2016, por la que se desarrolla en currículo de educación secundaria obligatoria en Andalucía." 2016. *Boletín Oficial de la Junta de Andalucía*, 144, July 28, 2016. https://www.juntadeandalucia.es/boja/2016/144/18.

Ordóñez Eslava, Pedro. 2013. "Qualities of Flamenco in the Francoism: Between the Renaissance and the Concience of Protest." In *Music and Francoism*, edited by Gemma Pérez Zalduondo and Germán Gan Quesada, 265–83. Turnhout, BE: Brepols.

Ordovás, Jesús. 1978. "Triana y la nueva avalancha andaluza por la cara." *Disco Exprés* 467, March 3, 1978.

8. Towards a Critical Approach to Flamenco Hybridity 171

"Pablito Rodrigo, intérprete de ritmos modernos." *Discóbolo* 24, March 15, 1963: 15.

Paetzold, Christopher. 2009. "Singing beneath the Alhambra: The North African and Arabic Past and Present in Contemporary Andalusian Music." *Journal of Spanish Cultural Studies* 10, no. 2: 207–23.

Pérez, David. 2017. "Quentin Gas & Los Zíngaros: Caravana." *Mondo Sonoro*, February 16, 2017. https://www.mondosonoro.com/criticas/discos-musica/quentin-gas-caravana.

Pieterse, Jan N. 2001. "Hybridity, So What? The Anti-Hybridity Backlash and the Riddles of Recognition." *Theory Culture and Society* 18, no. 2–3: 219–45.

Regev, Motti. 2013. *Pop-Rock Music: Aesthetic Cosmopolitanism in Late Modernity*. Cambridge: Polity.

———. 2020. "In the World: Beyond the English-Speaking West." In *The Bloomsbury Handbook of Rock Music Research*, edited by Allan Moore and Paul Carr, 459–68. New York: Bloomsbury Academic.

Romero, Pedro G. 2016. *El ojo partido: Flamenco, cultura de masas y vanguardias. Tientos y materiales para una corrección óptica de la historia del flamenco*. Seville: Athenaica.

Serra i Fabra, Jordi. 1975. "I. 15 H Burgos 1975." *Popular 1*, October 22, 1975: 6.

Shannon, Jonathan Holt. 2015. *Performing Al-Andalus: Music and Nostalgia Across the Mediterranean*. Bloomington: Indiana University Press.

Sieburth, Stephanie. 2016. *Coplas para sobrevivir: Conchita Piquer, los vencidos y la represión franquista*. Madrid: Cátedra.

Solís Marquínez, Ana Toya. 2020. "Creación musical académica en la transición democrática española (1975–1982): Políticas, debates y realizaciones." PhD diss., Universidad de Oviedo. https://digibuo.uniovi.es/dspace/handle/10651/57074.

Stahl, Geoff. 2020. "Rock Music and Place." In *The Bloomsbury Handbook of Rock Music Research*, edited by Allan Moore and Paul Carr, 487–96. New York: Bloomsbury Academic.

Steingress, Gerhard. 2002. "Flamenco Fusion and New Flamenco as Postmodern Phenomena: An Essay on Creative Ambiguity in Popular Music." In *Songs of the Minotaur: Hybridity and Popular Music in the Era of Globalization*, edited by Gerhard Steingress, 169–216. Münster: Liv Verlag.

Swidler, Ann. 1996. "La cultura en acción: Símbolos y estrategias." *Zona Abierta* 77/78: 127–62.

Tagg, Philip. 2013. *Music's Meanings: A Modern Musicology for Non-Musos*. New York: The Mass Media Music Scholars' Press.

Tocino, Pablo. 2019. "Derby Motoreta's Burrito Kachimba." *MondoSonoro*, March 3, 2019. https://www.mondosonoro.com/artistas-musica/derby-motoretas-burrito-kachimba.

Tusell, Javier. 2007. *La Transición a la democracia: España (1975–1982)*. Madrid: Espasa Calpe.

Val, Fernán del. 2017. *Rockeros insurgentes, modernos complacientes: Un análisis sociológico del rock en la Transición (1975–1985)*. Madrid: Fundación de la Sociedad General de Autores y Editores.

Walser, Robert. 1992. "Eruptions: Heavy Metal Appropriations of Classical Virtuosity." *Popular Music* 11, no. 3: 263–308.

9

Portuguese Rock or
Rock in Portuguese?

*Controversies Concerning the
"Portugueseness" of Rock Music Made
in Portugal in the Early 1980s*

RICARDO ANDRADE

Introduction

1980 was a turning point for rock music in Portugal. The commercial success of two songs released that year—"Chico Fininho" ("Thin Chico") by Rui Veloso and "Cavalos de Corrida" ("Racing Horses") by the band UHF[1]—triggered what the media referred to as the "boom of Portuguese rock." This phenomenon was characterized by the sudden rise in the recording, publication, and dissemination of Portuguese rock groups and repertoire. Up until this point, record labels were generally disinterested in recording original repertoire by local rock groups. The use of Portuguese was also often characterized by several musicians in the local press as being difficult to match with the sonic specificities of rock music.

The success of Rui Veloso (b. 1957) and UHF (founded in 1978) triggered a new demand for "Portuguese rock" by record labels, which was accompanied by intense media promotion of rock made in Portugal, the development of artistic management and live sound businesses, and a greater acceptance of rock music sung in the Portuguese language, in tune with the need for "direct" and "unmediated" expressions popularized by the new punk and new wave styles. The unprecedented success of Portuguese rock groups in the early 1980s

9. Portuguese Rock or Rock in Portuguese?

stimulated debates among musicians, record industry agents, and journalists about the creation and promotion of "Portuguese rock" and the possibility of contemplating rock music as "Portuguese." There were several controversies around issues such as the presumed "origins" of the genre and its geographical location (that is, rock music as a "universal expression" or as an "imported practice"); the use of the native language as a defining characteristic of the "Portugueseness" of rock; the suitability of rock music for articulating Portuguese phonetics; and the commercial interests inherent in the constitution of the category of "Portuguese rock."

This chapter focuses on the "boom" of Portuguese rock in the 1980s. Following a brief political and socio-cultural contextualization, I address the discursive constructions of "Portuguese rock" (*rock português*) articulated by musicians, journalists, and other agents, the controversies regarding the use of the Portuguese language in rock lyrics, and the relationship between these processes and the musical, socio-cultural, and political changes in the country.

The Setting

The 1970s was a decade of profound political and social transformation in Portugal. The country was ruled by an authoritarian right-wing regime (*Estado Novo*) from 1933[2] up until the *coup d'état* on April 25, 1974, which led to the formation of a democratic regime and the end of colonial rule. The final years of the authoritarian regime were marked by widespread poverty and illiteracy, intense emigration, and a war in Portugal's African colonies that had begun in 1961. A revolutionary process followed the 1974 *coup d'état*, leading to the gradual democratization of political and social life through the institution of free elections and the end of state censorship. This was followed by the consolidation of a multi-party regime of parliamentary representation and the institutionalization of the social state. This period was also strongly marked by deep social changes that included the increase of migratory flows from the countryside to the city, the tertiarization of society, the increasing professionalization of women, and an increase in the education levels of the population.

The opening of the Portuguese economy to European and American markets during this period facilitated access to foreign cultural goods, including sound recordings and films, parallel to an increase in the purchase power of the emerging middle class. An increasingly cosmopolitan Portuguese society aspired to reproduce lifestyles regarded as "modern" and to acquire cultural capital through new consumer habits and expressive modes such as music and an emerging audiovisual culture (Trindade 2015). At the same time, the younger generation became increasingly "depoliticized," especially when compared to the involvement of the youth in opposition to the regime in the 1960s and early 1970s and during the revolutionary process in the mid-1970s (2015). This decrease in youth engagement with politics was substituted by the development of an imaginary "modernity" in the discourse of musicians and listeners, in which rock music played a central role. These changes were seen as an approximation to the values and lifestyles found in Western Europe and the United States that were regarded as more "developed" and "modern."

Rock in Portuguese

During the final decades of the authoritarian regime, several musicians considered rock music to be a viable aesthetic alternative to the hegemonic genres and styles promoted by the Portuguese media, in particular fado and *música ligeira*[3] (literally, "light music"). This hegemony was commonly referred to as *nacional-cançonetismo* ("national-songerism," a play on national-socialism), an expression that denoted repertoires of popular music usually associated with the production systems of state radio (Emissora Nacional) and the televised Rádio e Televisão de Portugal (RTP) Song Festival.[4] The 1960s and 1970s were marked by a slow process of change in which several rock musicians in Portugal sought to assimilate or emulate what they understood to be the main characteristics of the rock universe of the "distant" Anglo-American world. The international dissemination of rock and roll's "modern rhythms" throughout the 1950s and 1960s, the subsequent construction of rock music as an "art form" from the late 1960s, and the popularization of the rock concert as a model of performance, inspired the configuration of new groups (*conjuntos*). During the 1960s and 1970s, the repertoire of Portuguese rock groups consisted mostly of covers of international pop-rock hits,[5] rarely including original compositions. Most rock bands considered the performance of original songs unfeasible because of the audiences' unfamiliarity with this repertoire, which was because Portuguese record labels and radio stations had little interest in recording Portuguese rock groups, usually justified by the availability of recordings of British and American bands.

The involvement of musicians and audiences in rock music in the 1970s was inseparable from their interest in cultural and political modernization. Portuguese rock musicians strove to create music that was clearly distinguished from fado and *nacional cançonetismo* and from the emphasis of these genres on themes such as loss, longing, religiosity, and patriotic sentiment, underlying values that many associated with the authoritarian regime. While a few records included

9. Portuguese Rock or Rock in Portuguese?

original repertoire sung in Portuguese, most rock groups chose to sing in English, which they considered to be a distinctive characteristic of rock. During the last years of the dictatorship, there was a prominent shift from French to Anglo-American external cultural influences, and this change further contributed to an increase in rock lyrics being written in English.

For rock musicians at the time, the notion of "Portuguese music" was closely linked to fado and other Portuguese-language musical genres regularly broadcast on the radio during their early youth. This was one of the motivations that led to the general rejection of the use of Portuguese in rock lyrics. In an interview published in January 1981, António Manuel Ribeiro, UHF's lead singer, stated that during his adolescence his conception of "Portuguese music" was limited to "decadent fado[6] and *songerism*" (Macedo 1981). Rock guitarist Jorge Trindade associated these two genres with "banal lyrics" and characterized fado as the "son of a minor god."[7] Tozé Brito, member of the rock groups Pop Five Music Incorporated and Quarteto 1111, states that during his adolescence in the northern city of Porto, "you didn't sing in Portuguese" in rock bands and "whoever did it had bad taste and was considered corny" (Castel-Branco 1981).

The rejection of native languages in pop-rock lyrics was common in other non-English speaking countries, even those that had not experienced dictatorships. In an article on the first decades of rock music in Japan, Katsuya Minamida explores debates in the press at the turn of the 1960s to the 1970s about the validity of the use of Japanese within rock music and the concept of "Japanese rock," a debate that finds a parallel within the context of the Portuguese boom (2014). According to sociologist Michael Spanu, musicians in France regarded the use of English in pop-rock music as a way of distinguishing from "mainstream music" in French and conferred to rock a certain sense of desired otherness (2015, 519). As the ethnomusicologist Harris Berger points out, the choice of a certain foreign language over the local one, or the belief that the foreign language holds higher status, may constitute ways of performing a distinct social identity (2003, xv-xvi). In the Portuguese case, these choices helped construct an imagined identity of what it is to be a rock musician in North America and Britain, an identity that was of pivotal importance in Portugal during the late 1970s and early 1980s for marking a generational rupture with both the Estado Novo and the revolutionary period.

Throughout the 1970s, the supposed "corniness" or inadequacy of Portuguese for rock lyrics was also justified on the grounds of an alleged lack of articulation between the phonetics of the Portuguese language and rock music. According to António Garcez, lead singer of the 1970s and 1980s rock groups Pentágono, Psico, Arte & Ofício, and Roxigénio:

[People ask me in the USA]: how do you say "I love you" in Portuguese"? "It's horrible, man: *amo-te!*" [. . .] But then I say: "Brazilian is very beautiful." "How is it?" "*Te amo*" [. . .] Brazilian Portuguese has musicality, like Italian. [. . .] [Portuguese from Portugal has] many consonants, it is a very hard language, not flexible.[8]

The preference for English was also sometimes justified by downgrading the importance of the communicative function of lyrical content. For António Garcez, what was essential was the specific "musicality" of the English language:

I don't care about the lyrics! [. . .] A guy listens to lyrics of super-famous songs where the lyrics are nothing. [. . .] Even in the Beatles. [. . .] I was interested in the sound of the voice! [. . .] My English was not very good, but I would take the microphone and just scream—no one had my voice, man![9]

For several Portuguese rock musicians, English was considered a kind of *lingua franca* of rock that was linked to its very genesis. Some musicians frequently compared the use of Portuguese lyrics in rock music and the hypothetical use of English in musical genres considered typically "Portuguese" such as fado. António Garcez argued the following:

I insist, rock is an English word, it does not exist in our dictionary. So it doesn't make sense for me to sing rock music in Portuguese. It is just like someone who wants to sing fado in English. It loses its interest. (Dias 1981)

Finally, the use of English was also seen by some rock groups such as Arte & Ofício and Tantra as offering the potential for developing an international career, which was never fully realized.

Protest Music

Despite the general rejection of rock being sung in Portuguese, there were contexts in which the language was actively embraced by some musicians. The creation of a protest-song repertoire by new singer-songwriters during the 1960s and 1970s[10] led to a greater acceptance of the Portuguese language by rock musicians in the early 1980s. The early records by José Afonso and Adriano Correia de Oliveira, published in the first half of the 1960s, inaugurated the protest song movement. By the late 1960s, this movement had some media coverage in the press and on television, namely through the TV show *Zip-Zip*, one of the main promotional stages for protest singers. Within this musical movement, the first LPs by José Mário Branco and Sérgio Godinho—recorded in 1971 at the Château d' Hérouville studios near Paris (famous for several recordings by major British pop-rock artists)—were considered by musicians and the press as remarkable examples of the creative ways in which the Portuguese language could be set to music influenced by new Anglo-American musical styles. José Mário Branco's first LP, *Mudam-se os Tempos, Mudam-se as Vontades*, and Sérgio Godinho's first EP, *Romance de Um Dia na Estrada*, were both published in the same year.

According to some of the protagonists of the "boom of Portuguese rock" in the early 1980s, these records exemplified the possibility of creating new musical styles with Portuguese lyrics. Although the press did not characterize Branco's and Godinho's songs as "rock" music per se, several rock musicians were inspired by the metaphorical and jovial language of Godinho's Portuguese lyrics, which denounced the political and social situation in Portugal. They also drew inspiration from the new musical sounds derived from the technological capabilities of multitrack recording and the use of drums, electric guitars, and organs. In the words of journalist and rock musician, António Duarte:

> [T]he great master of singing in Portuguese was Sérgio Godinho. [. . .] He was the bridge between [politically] interventive music [. . .] rock music, and pop music. [. . .] José Mário Branco [was also responsible for this].[11]

The change in political regime had a direct impact on the content of the lyrics. During the dictatorship, the intended meanings of lyrics were veiled by metaphors and other figures of speech in order to escape censorship. However, during the revolutionary process of 1974–1975, the identification of protest singers with different political parties motivated new thematic content directly expressing their alignment with the party lines of new political organizations (Castro 2019). During the revolutionary years, political song was omnipresent in the media. For rock musician António Manuel Ribeiro (member of the group UHF), despite the social and political importance of protest singers, their ubiquity brought "a huge qualitative lowering" in the musical landscape of the revolutionary period,[12] given the general simplicity of the songs and the agitprop quality of the lyrics. Although Rui Veloso had claimed to have enjoyed Sérgio Godinho's and José Mário Branco's pre-1974 LPs, he made a similar critique:

> [F]ollowing April 25, 1974, due to the concern with more direct lyrics, musicians became less concerned with musical quality and therefore the panorama declined a lot (Cabrita 1980).

However, the more straightforward lyrical content of some of the repertoire written in Portuguese during the second half of the 1970s reflected a broader valorization of directly exposing the vicissitudes of marginalized social groups that was characteristic of new rock styles such as punk. During a period in which rock sung in Portuguese was not generally accepted, the main precursors of punk in Portugal—the groups Os Faíscas, Aqui d'el-Rock, UHF, and Minas & Armadilhas—made the point of singing in their native language for greater effectiveness in communicating their message. Their lyrics differed greatly from the mystical and "fantastical" inclination of the repertoire of groups such as Tantra, which were inspired by English progressive rock groups such as Yes, Emerson, Lake & Palmer, and Genesis. In the view of Paulo Borges, lead singer of the punk group Minas & Armadilhas, the contrast between punk and progressive rock was also based on the opposition between greater social and political awareness and an "alienated" stance towards negative aspects of society:

> It was a breath of fresh air in the midst of a population that consumed music, in a way that seemed a bit too much like a numbing of consciousness. [. . .] Most of my friends were like that. Freaks, hippies. A lot of progressive rock. [. . .] But suddenly it [punk] sounded to me as something new, different, and it corresponded to my revolutionary impulse, a bit nihilistic [. . .] with a bit of social commitment.[13]

According to Borges, this commitment involved the need for "direct" communication, unmediated by a foreign language, in order to portray the specifics of the "real." This idea of "realism" in Portugal's punk in the late 1970s was often associated with the vicissitudes of "disgruntled and marginal" residents in increasingly industrialized areas and with issues such as prostitution, delinquency, police brutality, labor exploitation, and social alienation, which, according to UHF's António Manuel Ribeiro, constituted the "natural product of urban societies" (Macedo 1981). The expression of this realism by early punk musicians and fans, and the possibility of "having a voice" through music, was also linked to their desire to discard the complexity and technical ostentation that they saw as characteristic of progressive rock and that could only be afforded by those musicians with greater financial capacity. According to Paulo Borges, these social concerns were reflected both in the musical materials—the aggressive simplicity of his group's sound—and the use of the vernacular.

Ar de Rock

The latter years of the 1970s in Portugal were marked by a political, cultural, and economic turn towards the rest of Western Europe that was often compared in the press with the values of modernity and democracy. This new momentum had repercussions for the production and publication policies of the main Portuguese record labels. In 1978, Rui Valentim de Carvalho was administrator of one of the largest and most active record labels in the country, Valentim de Carvalho. He hired Nuno Rodrigues and António Pinho, members of the Banda do Casaco,[14] as producers and subsequently A&R (Artists and Repertoire), in response to

9. Portuguese Rock or Rock in Portuguese?

the widespread belief that the company's staff and catalog were unattuned to new currents in popular music.[15] The company also hired Carvalho's nephews Francisco Vasconcelos and David Ferreira, both of whom played an important role in signing new Portuguese rock groups. Rock groups were also promoted by radio presenters dedicated to rock music such as António Sérgio and Luís Filipe Barros and by new periodicals such as *Rock Week*, *Música & Som*, and, most important, the weekly *Se7e*. The above-mentioned record publishers contended that their interest in recording rock sung in Portuguese was a way of differentiating "national" from "international" records on the local market and a means of avoiding poorly written and sung English lyrics. Here, António Pinho is categorical:

> For me, even today it makes no sense to record in another language if I am recording in Portugal. And it is not a matter of patriotism, it is a matter of principle. [. . .] We are usually bad in writing [lyrics] in another language. [. . .] And the market was needing this kind of music to be sung in Portuguese.[16]

António Pinho demanded that singer Rui Veloso and lyricist Carlos Tê write lyrics in Portuguese and discard their English texts. Tê wrote lyrics that Veloso set to new music featuring urban and rural characters and social realities in language often qualified by the press as "youthful" and as being filled with new urban jargon. The resulting album, *Ar de Rock* (1980), was promoted by Valentim de Carvalho as an example of the artistic success of rock music sung in Portuguese and in an attempt to counteract the then-popular opinion that the use of Portuguese was corny. Although the musical characteristics of the song "Chico Fininho" (the main single from the LP) are distinct from the then-recent trends of punk and new wave—the song took melodic and harmonic influence from blues—its direct, jovial, and irreverent language, dealing with the vicissitudes of a drug addict in Porto, contributed to the song's great commercial and media success. For David Ferreira, Carlos Tê's texts had a lyrical quality that was aligned with the "direct" character of the new punk and new wave styles, which contributed to the popularity of the album *Ar de Rock*:

> Rui himself, without being a punk artist . . . there is a direct communication there that has nothing to do with what existed before, such as what happened with Tantra. [. . .] *Ar de Rock* is an immediate album. It is an album that . . . despite being a blues album, it has a new wave feel to it in its simple message.[17]

When Francisco Vasconcelos, David Ferreira's editorial partner, first contacted Porto's rock group GNR, he also put as a condition for recording their music that the group replace its English lyrics with Portuguese ones. Vasconcelos associated Portuguese language with an idea of "hardness," which "had something to do with punk," "an edge similar to the other edges that were also out there" in new rock styles.[18] The need expressed by punk bands to communicate directly with the public meant that the use of the Portuguese language, and its respective explicitness when compared to English, was understood by some musicians and publishers as a novelty.

The publication of Rui Veloso's landmark album *Ar de Rock* was widely regarded by musicians and the press as a pivotal moment for the widespread acceptance of the use of Portuguese in rock music and for engaging in themes that reflected the experiences and social concerns of musicians. Weeks after the album's release, radio and television presenter Julio Isidro consecrated Veloso's and Tê's efforts as an example of "a new idiom" of "healthy extroversion" that "dusted off" the idea that rock music "could only be sung in English" (1980). One year following its publication, the newspaper *Se7e* published the following description:

> This Portuguese-speaking Rock begins to have common denominators. Through it, situations are denounced and hopes are expressed. You can argue for integration in the EEC (European Economic Community) or you can say that TV sucks. All this is expressed in words that everyone now understands, speaking of things that everyone knows, that everyone feels. [. . .] This is the great revolution. ("Rock Português," 1981)

The success of songs such as "Chico Fininho" and "Cavalos de Corrida" was followed by an intense investment by record labels in rock music sung in Portuguese. However, some musicians regarded composing in Portuguese as an added difficulty, because they considered the language to be "less musical." For example, Luís Ventura, lead singer of the rock group Street Kids, stated that if the use of the English language "limits understanding," singing in Portuguese "greatly limits the framing of the music" (Dias 1981). A general lack of habit in listening to rock music sung in Portuguese motivated several discussions about the difficulties of writing lyrics in this language. A point that was often made was that the frequency of sibilant phonemes and consonants in European Portuguese, in contrast to the supposed more regular use of vowels in English (and Brazilian Portuguese), constituted an obstacle to setting Portuguese lyrics to rock music. Even Rui Veloso, the main protagonist of the "boom" of Portuguese rock, seemed to agree with this point, arguing that the record label's imposition of singing in Portuguese ended up influencing the repertoire's musical style, which became closer to the music sung in Portuguese that he was used to listening to:

> [C]omposing in English is a lot easier. The English language has much softer sounds. The Portuguese language has hard sounds. The "rr," the "â," the very open "aas." It

9. Portuguese Rock or Rock in Portuguese?

is sometimes difficult to get them into music. [. . .] I always end up writing ballads, man! (Cabrita 1980)

The unprecedented investment in rock music sung in Portuguese was also seen by some musicians—especially those who were active before the "boom"—as an opportunistic approach by record labels that started investing heavily in rock music after the success of Valentim de Carvalho and by those groups that converted (or even translated) their lyrics. Drummer Flash Gordon (Emanuel Ramalho) of the group Street Kids referred to the pressure that musicians felt: "This story of singing in Portuguese was almost a weapon aimed at musicians. Most bands have cowered, others not. We sing in English and go on" (Dias 1981).

Another important factor was the parliamentary approval of a law stipulating that 50 percent of music broadcast on radio and television must be by Portuguese authors and sung in Portuguese, a regulation that reinforced the promotion of Portuguese rock groups (*Diário da República*, no. 165, 1981). Despite a general lack of compliance with this law, its approval led some radio broadcasters to air more music sung in Portuguese, influencing new groups to abandon English lyrics. This also led some influential radio broadcasters like Luís Filipe Barros to encourage record labels to record rock sung in Portuguese, given the necessity of having Portuguese vocal repertoire on his radio show.

Portuguese Rock

The legitimacy of the term "Portuguese rock" was intensely debated in the press during the rock "boom" of the early 1980s. The main issue was whether there could be a Portuguese rock music or whether such a label constituted a misconception. As discussed below, for some musicians and journalists, given its Anglo-American origin, rock could never be qualified as "Portuguese" but only as a music sung in Portuguese. Some musicians understood the popularity of the category "Portuguese rock" as a commercial ploy engineered by record labels and the media as a way of enhancing the commercial viability of the recordings of new rock groups. This concern even extended to the music of bands that, in the opinion of some musicians, were not "authentic" because they started out accompanying dance parties before turning into rock bands (as was the case with Grupo de Baile and CTT). The argument used by the majority of those who defended the nonexistence of "Portuguese rock" was based on the musical and linguistic aspects seen as structural elements of the genre. This argument is clearly expressed by rock musician Aníbal Miranda:

> I think that there isn't any "Portuguese rock" but just rock sung in Portuguese. I think rock music is essentially English. [. . .] In fact, I very much doubt that English people would ever sing "Chico Fininho" in Portuguese. (Marques 1981)

Those who thought that rock music could also be "Portuguese" based their argument on the supposed "universality" of the genre as well as it being internationally used to portray modern societies, of which they considered Portugal to be one. The widely spread idea that rock is "universal" was also connected to the rise of the youth as a distinct social category in the 1950s (particularly in the US). The articulation of rock music, clothing, and lifestyles by the youth was internationally disseminated through movies, magazines, and other media (Bennett 2001, 16–17; Longhurst and Bogdanović 2014; Shuker 2008). The influence of rock music and associated lifestyles was also materialized in the constitution of local "scenes" and "movements" around the world. The very adoption of national languages other than English by these movements and scenes was a significant change that allowed for greater communication between musicians and audiences and attracted investments from various industries (Wallis and Malm 1984, 302–11). In Portugal, the acceptance of the "universality" of rock also reflected the social and economic aspirations of musicians toward what they understood to be the cultural practices of western "modernity"; it was aligned as well with the idea that the individual and social concerns of the "youth" were internationally shared and articulated through their musical practices. Finally, in Portugal the supposed universality of rock was also based on a presumed evolutionary genealogy of the practice as multi-situated and not merely North American and British. According to the members of the group Rocktrote:

> [R]ock was not born in England as many claim. Rock was born in America and Africa in the clubs, where it was sung by workers and exported to England where it gained greater acceptance, namely through The Beatles. But that does not mean that rock is English, it can now be considered universal. (Lopes 1981)

Musicians and critics who argued that it was inconsistent to label much of the rock music made in Portugal as "Portuguese" based their judgment on the idea that "Portugueseness" in rock could only result from the close relationship between the structural elements of rock and those of the repertoires understood to be typically Portuguese, particularly traditional music. Trabalhadores do Comércio was one of the groups particularly concerned with this issue. For Sérgio Castro, the group's founder, the use of the Portuguese language in "rock music with strictly Anglo-American characteristics" is a "mistake" (Dias 1982). In order to articulate a humorous critique of the concept of "Portuguese rock," the Trab-

9. Portuguese Rock or Rock in Portuguese? 183

alhadores do Comércio exaggerated elements associated with Portugueseness in their music, using the distinct northern Portuguese accent, emphasizing their regional identity, and occasionally including references to Portuguese traditional music. The emphasis on the northern accent was anchored on Castro's idea that this accent is closer to the Portuguese presumably spoken in the nation-state's cradle (northern Portugal) and, therefore, is more "authentically" Portuguese (Castro 2011, 151–52).

During the 1980s, Heróis do Mar was one of the most popular examples of asserting "Portugueseness" in pop-rock music. Their name derives from the first verse of the national anthem. The group's ideology, militaristic attire, and lyrics were inspired by Portugal's history, especially the maritime expansion of the fifteenth and sixteenth centuries. The emergence of the group was a source of huge controversy in the press, given the strong association established by some journalists between the symbols adopted by the group and the glorification of Portugal's "heroic" past promoted by the recently ended authoritarian regimes of Salazar and Caetano. Although the group emerged in 1981 during the height of "Portuguese rock," it refused to be included in this category. In doing so, it distanced itself from the other groups that became popular in this period, whose repertoire was closer to hard rock and heavy metal styles. However, the group claimed that their music was "truly Portuguese," despite also being influenced by British groups such as Spandau Ballet and the Human League. According to Pedro Ayres Magalhães, the group's bassist and main ideologue, the group created "musical structures that could be spoken in Portuguese," adding that "the Portuguese language has a certain musicality, a certain articulation."[19] The notion of a "Portuguese musicality" intersected with an image of Portugal—more specifically of Lisbon—as a "mulatto" and "multicultural" city. This idea resonated with the controversial romanticization of the colonial past as one that had facilitated the encounter between different cultures during the maritime expansion. In Heróis do Mar's first album, this idea was musically materialized in songs such as "Salmo" and "Bailai," characterized by Magalhães' inspiration from "African" rhythms.

The debate over the "Portugueseness" of rock music culminated in a sequence of articles published in the music journal *Se7e* toward the end of 1982. This was a moment when the decline in the number of "Portuguese rock" groups and the economic crisis of Portuguese record labels, which paralleled the country's financial crisis, were frequently debated in the press. In the article that inaugurated this debate, António Duarte argued that rock music could be considered Portuguese, given that even musical genres usually regarded as being "typically" Portuguese, such as fado, had remote and diverse origins:

It is rock. It is made by Portuguese: Portuguese Rock. Don't come to me saying that rock can't be "Portuguese." [. . .] And also do not come to me saying that Portuguese music is just fado or folk music . . . Because, fado has remote origins in the Cape Verdean *mornas*; Portuguese folk music is more Celtic than Portuguese, and it also branches on northeastern Brazil's *modas*. [. . .] And Rock 'n' Roll comes from the Rhythm 'n' Blues, which is black; and the Rhythm 'n' Blues comes from the blues of African slaves. (Duarte 1982)

Such statements triggered an intense debate between musicians and journalists that dragged on in this periodical for months. In particular, this debate involved António Duarte and Miguel Esteves Cardoso, an emerging pop-rock critic and one of the main promoters of new British pop groups in Portugal such as Joy Division, New Order, and The Durutti Column. In response to Duarte, Cardoso reiterated that "Portuguese Rock is no different from Anglo-American Rock. Not only is it not different, it cannot also be equal: it is worse!" (Esteves Cardoso 1982). However, he emphasized that Heróis do Mar were a representative case of "Portugueseness" within pop music, not so much because they evoked specific musical characteristics, but because they framed them within the "Portuguese poetic tradition" (1982). This argument was also connected to Cardoso's ideological identification with the group, given his conservative and even monarchist inclinations. Despite some confusion and conceptual divergence, the exchange of comments between Duarte and Cardoso motivated a "shower of letters" ("Há ou não há Rock Português?" 1982) addressed to *Se7e*, by fans and musicians representing the opposing positions of the two journalists. This intense correspondence culminated with the newspaper pleading readers not to communicate further on the subject:

Se7e and its readers contributed to reduce the army of unemployed people in this country [. . .] the CTT [Mail, Telephone, and Telegraph Company] [. . .] had to hire staff in order to handle the avalanche of letters and postcards that arrived at our [. . .] newsroom [. . .]. Do not send further contributions to the discussion: we would not know what to do with them. ("No fim do debate" 1982)

Conclusion

The changes triggered by the "boom of Portuguese rock" were fundamental for the long-term consolidation of pop-rock practices in Portugal. The music and debates that constituted the "boom" helped to solidify the practice of singing rock music in Portuguese and to turn it into both an important commercial factor and a pivotal identifying element in locally produced rock music, in line with other musical genres. If before 1980 the use of the Portuguese language in rock music was uncommon, years later the use of the English language became a cause of media frenzy, exemplified by the debate during the 1990s concerning the huge success of some rock groups that sang almost exclusively in English.

In the early 1980s, "Portuguese rock" contributed notably to the consolidation of a "modern" cosmopolitan youth identity. However, although the use of the Portuguese language allowed for more direct communication between rock bands and their audiences, this was also considered an opportunistic move, even by some of the record labels that needed to promote rock sung in Portuguese. In short, the "boom of Portuguese rock" was marked by several debates concerning the (supposed) contradiction inherent in the promotion of rock's perceived "subversiveness" through the national record industry. Above all, "Portuguese rock" in the early 1980s constituted different ways of reimagining the country and what it meant to be "Portuguese" and "modern."

Notes

This chapter is the outcome of research I carried out for my doctoral dissertation on the "boom of Portuguese rock" in the early 1980s (Andrade 2020), in which I examined the dynamics of creating and performing this repertoire in Portugal, considering the social, institutional, and technical specificities and constraints of that period. This research was based on field and archival work, including over 50 interviews with musicians and other agents, and content analysis of relevant periodicals published between 1976 and 1985. It draws on the pioneering work on popular music in Portugal carried out within the framework of the Instituto de Etnomusicologia—Centro de Estudos em Música e Dança of the NOVA University of Lisbon during the past 25 years. Some of the results of this research were published in the *Enciclopédia da música em Portugal no século XX* (Castelo-Branco 2010).

1. "UHF" stands for Ultra High Frequency. However, the group only uses the acronym as their designation.

2. After seven years of military dictatorship, which would end the first Portuguese Republic after the coup of May 28, 1926.

3. The songs usually identified with this genre were promoted by the National Radio (Emissora Nacional) and regularly performed by formally trained singers, often with orchestral accompaniment (Moreira, Cidra, and Castelo-Branco 2010). The lyrics were characterized by their detractors as being futile, superficial, and reminiscent of values promoted by the authoritarian regime such as romantic love, patriotism, and religious devotion (César 2010). The uses of *música ligeira* in Portugal are similar to those of *musica leggera* in Italy, as explained by Fabbri and Plastino (2014, 2).

4. The RTP Song Festival is an annual competition initiated in 1964. Every year the winner represents Portugal in the Eurovision Song Contest (César, Tilly, and Cidra 2010).

5. Some rock lyrics of original compositions in the Portuguese language that addressed political issues were subject to state censorship. However, as I discuss, censorship was not the major motivation prompting musicians to sing in English.

6. According to extant research, up to the end of World War II, the dictatorship held

an ambivalent and sometimes hostile stance towards fado. However, from the 1950s up to its fall in 1974, realizing its potential for creating a populist image and promoting tourism, this regime promoted fado as the "national song" in Portugal and abroad (Castelo-Branco and Moreno Fernández 2019, 83; Nery 2012, 333).

7. Interview with the author, October 14, 2015.

8. Interview with the author, July 25, 2015.

9. Interview with the author, July 25, 2015.

10. For more on protest song in Portugal, see the chapter by Hugo Castro in this volume.

11. Interview with the author, September 27, 2015.

12. Interview with the author, September 27, 2015.

13. Interview with the author, May 18, 2018.

14. Formed in 1973, the Banda do Casaco was pivotal in combining pop music with local traditional repertoires, promoting a somewhat "experimental" trend within popular music in Portugal (Tilly 2010).

15. Rodrigues and Pinho became responsible for hiring and selecting artists for composing, arranging, and recording new repertoire.

16. Interview with the author and Miguel Almeida, June 26, 2014.

17. Interview with the author and Miguel Almeida, January 20, 2015.

18. Interview with the author, Miguel Almeida, and António Tilly, February 2, 2015.

19. Interview with the author, February 7, 2016.

References

Andrade, Ricardo. 2020. "*Ar de Rock*: O boom do rock em Portugal de inícios da década de 1980." PhD diss., Universidade Nova de Lisboa.

Andreia, Eunice. 1981. "Trabalhadores do Comércio: Sindicato do Rock é liderado." *Musicalíssimo*, January [15–31], 1981.

Bennett, Andy. 2001. *Cultures of Popular Music*. Buckingham, UK: Open University Press.

Berger, Harris H. 2003. "Introduction: Politics and Aesthetics of Language Choice and Dialect in Popular Music." In *Global Pop, Local Language*, edited by Harris Berger and Michael Thomas Carroll, ix–xxvi. Jackson: University Press of Mississippi.

Cabrita, Aníbal. 1980. "Rui Veloso: Quem o Agarra?" *Musicalíssimo*, September [1–14], 1980.

Castel-Branco, João. 1981. "Questão dos 50% de Música Portuguesa: Depõem Tó Zé Brito e António Pinho pela Polygram." *Musicalíssimo*, February 24-March 2, 1981.

Castelo-Branco, Salwa, ed. 2010. *Enciclopédia da música em Portugal no século XX*. Lisboa: Círculo de Leitores.

Castelo-Branco, Salwa El-Shawan, and Susana Moreno Fernández. 2019. *Music in Portugal and Spain*. New York: Oxford University Press.

Castro, Hugo. 2019. "A cantiga só é arma quando a luta acompanhar: Canção e política na revolução dos cravos (1974–76)." PhD diss., Universidade Nova de Lisboa.

Castro, Sérgio. 2011. *Das Turmêntas hà Boua Isperansa: Trabalhadores do Comércio*. iPlay / Tigres de Bengala.

César, António João. 2010. "Nacional-cançonetismo." In *Enciclopédia da música em Portugal no século XX*. Vol. 3. Edited by Salwa Castelo-Branco, 901. Lisbon: Círculo de Leitores.

9. Portuguese Rock or Rock in Portuguese? 187

César, António João, António Tilly, and Rui Cidra. 2010. "Festival RTP da Canção." In *Enciclopédia da música em Portugal no século XX*. Vol. 2. Edited by Salwa Castelo-Branco, 501–4. Lisboa: Círculo de Leitores.

Dias, Manuel. 1981. "Roxigénio abre polémica: Estamos adiantados vinte anos em relação ao Rui Veloso." *Se7e*, January 7, 1981.

———. 1982. "Sérgio Castro entre Arte & Ofício e Os Trabalhadores do Comércio: 'Cantar Rock em português é um profundo equívoco.'" *Se7e*, February 23, 1982.

Dias, Mário. 1981. "Street Kids: Trabalhamos com simplicidade, outras bandas querem apenas o poder. . . ." *Musicalíssimo*, May 13–19, 1981.

Duarte, António. 1982. "Um problema nacional finalmente resolvido: Rock português— vive e deixa viver." *Se7e*, November 17, 1982.

Esteves Cardoso, Miguel. 1982. "Miguel Esteves Cardoso responde a António Duarte: Rock português não morre—deixa-se morrer." *Se7e*, November 24, 1982.

Fabbri, Franco, and Goffredo Plastino. 2014. "Introduction: An Egg of Columbus: How Can Italian Popular Music Studies Stand on Their Own?" In *Made in Italy: Studies in Popular Music*, edited by Franco Fabbri and Goffredo Plastino, 2–12. Abingdon, UK: Routledge.

"Há ou não há Rock Português? Cartas de leitores baralham e tornam a dar." 1982. *Se7e*, December 15, 1982.

Isidro, Júlio. 1980. "Página Ideal: Da autoria de Júlio Isidro, realizador do programa Grafonola Ideal." *Musicalíssimo*, August [15–31], 1980.

Longhurst, Brian, and Danijela Bogdanović. 2014. *Popular Music & Society*, 3rd ed. Cambridge: Polity Press.

Lopes, Teixeira. 1981. "Rocktrote: Porque a sociedade é louca nasceu mundo louco." *Musicalíssimo*, September 16–22, 1981.

Macedo, António. 1981. "UHF: "O nosso Rock é a voz dos descontentes." *Se7e*, January 14, 1981.

Marques, Pedro. 1981. "Aníbal Miranda: Rock Tripeiro." *Musicalíssimo*, April 1–7, 1981.

Minamida, Katsuya. 2014. "The Development of Japanese Rock: A Bourdieuan Analysis." In *Made in Japan: Studies in Popular Music*, edited by Tōru Mitsui, 120–38. Abingdon, UK: Routledge.

Moreira, Pedro, Rui Cidra, and Salwa Castelo-Branco. 2010. "Música Ligeira." In *Enciclopédia da música em Portugal no século XX*. Vol. 3. Edited by Salwa Castelo-Branco, 872–75. Lisboa: Círculo de Leitores.

Nery, Rui. 2012. *A History of Portuguese Fado*. Lisboa: Imprensa Nacional Casa da Moeda.

"No fim do debate a questão mantém-se: Há ou não há rock português?" 1982. *Se7e*, December 22, 1982.

"Rock Português." 1981. *Se7e*, June 24, 1981.

Shuker, Roy. 2008. *Understanding Popular Music Culture*, 3rd ed. London: Routledge.

Spanu, Michael. 2015. "Sing it Yourself! Uses and Representations of the English Language in French Popular and Underground Music." In *Keep it Simple, Make it Fast! An Approach to Underground Music Scenes*, edited by Paula Guerra and Tânia Moreira, 513–23. Porto: University of Porto.

Tilly, António. 2010. "Banda do Casaco." In *Enciclopédia da música em Portugal no século XX*. Vol. 1. Edited by Salwa Castelo-Branco, 106–7. Lisbon: Círculo de Leitores.

Trindade, Luís. 2015. "O 'Gosto' Do *Se7e*: Uma História Cultural Do Semanário *Se7e*." *Ler História* 67: 45–61.

Wallis, Roger, and Krister Malm. 1984. *Big Sounds from Small Peoples: The Music Industry in Small Countries*. London: Constable.

Discography

1971. José Mário Branco. *Mudam-se os Tempos, Mudam-se as Vontades* (LP; Guilda da Música/Sassetti)

1971. Sérgio Godinho. *Romance de um Dia Na Estrada* (EP; Guilda da Música/Sassetti)

1972. Sérgio Godinho. *Os Sobreviventes* (EP; Guilda da Música/Sassetti)

1977. Tantra. *Mistérios & Maravilhas* (LP; EMI-Valentim de Carvalho)

1979. Arte & Ofício. *Faces* (LP; Orfeu / Arnaldo Trindade)

1980. Rui Veloso. *Ar de Rock* (LP; EMI-Valentim de Carvalho)

1980. UHF. *Cavalos de Corrida / Palavras* (7" single; EMI-Valentim de Carvalho)

1980. Roxigénio. *Roxigénio* (LP; GAF)

1981. Tantra. *Humanoid Flesh* (LP; EMI-Valentim de Carvalho)

1981. GNR. *Portugal na CEE / Espelho Meu* (7" single; EMI-Valentim de Carvalho)

1981. Heróis do Mar. *Heróis do Mar* (LP; Polygram)

1981. Trabalhadores do Comércio. *Trip's À Moda Do Pôrto* (LP; Polydor)

1981. Taxi. *Taxi* (LP; Polydor)

1981. UHF. *À Flor da Pele* (LP; EMI-Valentim de Carvalho)

1981. Grupo de Baile. *Patchouly* (7" single; EMI-Valentim de Carvalho)

1982. GNR. *Independança* (LP- EMI-Valentim de Carvalho)

10

Indie Music as a Controversial Space on Spanish Identity

Class, Youth, and Discontent

HÉCTOR FOUCE AND FERNÁN DEL VAL

The End of the Long Summer Festival

In the days following May 15, 2011, many Spanish city squares were occupied by protesters calling for changes to the political system and electoral law and particularly for the end of the two-party system and its control by economic powers. This movement arose in 2010 in the wake of the Arab Spring and was followed by similar street protests around the world. Since 2008, following the international credit crunch, Spain has suffered the effects of a deep economic crisis that has particularly affected the housing market and the banking sector. After years of easy credit and household indebtedness, banks began to take possession of the properties of borrowers defaulting on their mortgages against a backdrop of rising unemployment and cuts in social policies.

The crowds that occupied the streets in Spain to express their outrage were mainly middle-class young people. University students, graduates, and civil servants chanted slogans such as "Lo llaman democracia y no lo es" ("They call it democracy, but it isn't"). Unlike previous social movements of the 1980s, such as those led by miners, steelworkers, and shipbuilding workers who fought against industrial reconversion, these middle-class citizens were not characterized by a politicized class culture but by political apathy. For many, the anti-austerity movement (also referred to as the 15-M Movement, the *Indignados* Movement, and Take the Square) was their first experience of collective political action (Sanz and Mateos 2011).

This outpouring of political activism emerged in a country that had experienced a very long cycle of economic growth and prosperity, leading to the establishment of a culture of hedonistic consumption (López and Rodríguez 2010) as well as the abandonment of classical political identities (based on ideological divisions between left and right) and the collective action associated with them. During this period of prosperity, social movements were barely present in the public sphere while the political experience of most Spaniards was reduced simply to voting on election days.

The contrast between the abundance of studies and reflections on the 1980s and the lack of interest in analyzing the following decades is striking. The 15-M Movement rejects the idealization of the Spanish Transition,[1] criticizing the co-option of the political discussion by political elites. In turn, the movement opened a new line of thinking on how to reconnect Spanish culture with political debates in the public domain (Labrador 2014; Lenore 2014; Martínez 2012; Maura 2018). In this chapter, we attempt to examine these changes from the perspective of popular music studies.

The "soundtrack"[2] for the post-transition years (1990–2011) was dominated by indie, a music genre that originated in the United States of America and the United Kingdom. Characterized by the sound of electric guitars, certain intellectual depth and introspective themes, indie music celebrated creative independence and promoted alternative management models, often at odds with artists' everyday practices (Hesmondhalgh 1999). In the early 1990s in Spain, this style became consolidated in the underground scene and by the early 2000s it was featured in summer festivals across the country. All towns touted the wonders of organizing a festival, very often with public contributions, to attract young people willing to spend their holiday money over three or four days of music, dancing, and partying.

The trajectory of the indie rock band Los Planetas is a good example of the evolution of the indie scene that ran in parallel with the political evolution of the middle classes in Spain. Undoubtedly, Los Planetas emerged as the main exponent of Spanish indie, replicating the transition of this music scene from alternative to mainstream markets. It launched its first album (*Super 8*) in 1994 with the major label RCA and then headlined major festivals, combining its guitar rock with flamenco and experimental contributions. The title of their record *La leyenda del espacio* (*The Legend of Space*), released in 2007, refers to the revolu-

10. Indie Music as a Controversial Space on Spanish Identity   191

tionary flamenco album *La leyenda del tiempo* (*The Legend of Time*) by Camarón de la Isla. Along with the collaboration of the well-known flamenco singer Enrique Morente, the album sought to "adapt traditional flamenco *palos* (rhythmic patterns) without *palmas* (clapping) or Spanish guitars" (Águila 2007).[3]

The turn of the band toward the political sphere is symptomatic of the politization of the Spanish middle classes. In 1996 they released the song "Vuelve la canción protesta" ("The Protest Song Returns"), which refers dismissively to how political songs are meant to change the world. However, in 2012 the band's vocalist and songwriter, Jota, released the song "La nueva reconquista de Graná" ("The New Reconquest of Granada," with "Graná" depicting the characteristic Andalusian accent from southern Spain) with his other band, *Grupo de expertos Solynieve* (Expert Group Sun-and-snow). The song established a parallelism between the Catholic reconquest in 1492 and the citizens who shouted in the streets, "We are not goods in the hands of politicians and bankers." Los Planetas titled its 2017 album *Zona temporalmente autónoma* (*Temporary Autonomous Zone*), echoing the ideas of American anarchist thinker Hakim Bey, who describes the socio-political tactic of creating spaces that temporarily elude formal structures of social control.

The stylistic journey of Los Planetas condenses the ideological, social, and thematic evolution of indie: from introspection and political apathy to awareness, from alternative to mainstream culture, from the Anglo-Saxon heritage to embracing national culture (as many groups began singing in English and then switched to Spanish). And over the fifteen years that acted as a bridge between the two centuries, indie bands such as Los Planetas were caught up with the wider political evolution of the middle classes in Spain, from consumerism and discontent to outrage. In this chapter, we connect the pathway that the Spanish middle classes have traversed between 1990 and 2011 with transformations in the attitudes and lyrics of indie music in Spain during the same period. We argue that the political protest that emerged in 2011 as a response to austerity politics had been reflected earlier in the feeling of discontent that some indie bands expressed in their song lyrics prior to the 15-M movement.

The rebuttal of the Spanish Transition has reignited the debate around definitions of Spanish national identity by introducing new political parameters into an environment of controversy traditionally defined by binary oppositions such as modernity/tradition, left/right, and nationalism/cosmopolitanism. This process has involved looking back in search of the reconstruction of the immediate past and the memory of Spanish democracy but from less celebratory and more critical perspectives.

Music, Politics, and Social Class
in Democratic Spain

During the 1960s, the dominant idea of modernity in Spain was linked with "Francoist political engineering," which led to the emergence of middle classes through industrialization, rural-urban migration, strengthening of the civil service, and urban transformation (Labrador 2014). Modernity was one of the elements of "the change" ("el cambio") that the Socialist Party (PSOE) offered as the motto of its first government in 1982: to be modern was to be European and to reject the autarky that characterized Franco's policy for many years. But Spain's accession to the EEC (European Economic Union) in 1986 also meant that the Spanish economy was fully integrated into a neoliberal framework. During the first democratic years, to be modern was also to be cosmopolitan (so, European) and also entailed the rejection of the Marxist heritage that had characterized the Francoist opposition (Fouce 2006; Maura 2018). As Vilarós (1998) points out, when Franco died, anti-Francoism died too.

The perception of popular music as an element of cultural modernization was especially striking in the 1980s when the Spanish Transition and the Madrid Scene (*La movida madrileña*) converged (Fouce 2006). The hegemonic discourse portrayed the 1980s as a decade when a young democracy, undergoing a full institutional and social transformation, wiped the slate clean and, inspired by the immediacy of punk and new wave, set out to create a cosmopolitan and contemporary cultural movement (*La movida*), led mainly by young people coming from the new middle classes (Val 2017). The price to be paid, on the one hand, was the harboring of contempt for all previous national styles and, on the other, the radical rejection of the political commitment that marked the politically engaged music of the singer-songwriters (*cantautores*) during the last decades of the dictatorship, since it was felt that music had stopped functioning as a space of resistance once the democratic regime and the right of free expression had been re-established.

Some scholars (Subirats 2002; Martínez 2012) consider that the abandonment of the political dimension during the creation of a modern national identity was a tribute to the new neoliberal sensibilities that the Socialist Party introduced in Spain. The Socialist Party's support of *La movida madrileña* was personified by Madrid's mayor Enrique Tierno Galván, whose cultural policy promoted free concerts and nightlife (Wheeler 2018). Some analysts see this policy as a way to integrate a generation marked by disenchantment (Fouce 2006). For most analysts, however, it was a deft maneuver to depoliticize the youth in parallel to the co-option of the combative neighborhood organizations of the new districts in the city.[4] The cosmopolitan discourse of the bands that were part of *La movida* celebrated makeup and masks, sexuality, consumption, and nightlife. It was the perfect soundtrack for this type of modernity, for a movement that sought to dissociate itself from party politics despite the subversive nature of its practices: the occupation of public space and the free enjoyment of non-normative sexualities became part of the legacy of *La movida*.

Even though *La movida* became part of the Spanish imaginary as the soundtrack of the 1980s, political songs and scenes still had an enormous impact during those years. Movements linked to the working classes through the musicians' social origin or the symbolic universes they were related to—including heavy metal, urban rock, Basque radical rock,[5] punk, hardcore, and to a lesser extent rap—addressed social issues in their lyrics, and musicians shouted political slogans in their concerts, articulating very vibrant local scenes (Val 2017). However, these music scenes had a limited scope and often functioned as smaller niches of production and consumption that were distanced from mainstream audiences. That is, songs with political content were left out of what some authors have called the "Transition Culture" (Martínez 2012), understood as a set of rules, codes, and guidelines of conduct about which topics and perspectives on Spanish culture are likely to be addressed. In this sense, political and social criticism was left out of popular music.

By the late 1980s, the groups of *La movida* had already become mainstream and their discourse had become exhausted. As Wheeler notes, "La movida became a showcase for the country's (post-)modernity and new democratic credential both at home and abroad" (2018, 144). During the 1980s, new wave paved the road for the emergence of mainstream pop all around the world. But at the end of the decade, alternative music became popular once again in the United States and England. For many Spaniards, it was the inspiration they needed to create a discourse that appealed to a new generation that was coming of age (Cruz 2015).

Economic Expansion and Youth Discontent

The middle classes have been a fundamental backbone of Spanish democracy, both sociologically and ideologically, and a key element in the modernization of Spanish democracy and culture. As the historian Pablo Sánchez León (2014) points out, since the late 1950s, politicians, philosophers, and scholars promoted the idea that the middle classes were fundamental to overcome social conflicts in Spain. This idea was accompanied by the expansion of this social class during the 1960s. This change in the Spanish social structure was also understood as a change in the values of Spanish people more broadly (Tezanos 1975, 38). Sánchez León (2014) argues that the emergence of the middle classes in the 1960s reflected attempts to reduce social inequalities in Spain and to increase social mobility, based on improvements in education and imported new forms of consumption and leisure (Carr and Fusi 1979, 106). The promises of modernity and social mobility inherited from Francoism were a central element of the Spanish democratic discourse both during the Transition and the coming years.

This narrative blows up when the financial crisis erupted in 2008. The cycle of economic growth that took place between 1995 and 2007 was based on consumption growth, not on wage growth: the purchasing power of families was maintained with easy credit, which was in turn supported by an immense housing bubble. Real estate was the asset that guaranteed families' borrowing capacity, so when banks needed to increase their capital base in 2008, they began to take possession of the secured properties of borrowers defaulting on their mortgages. High structural unemployment rates, reduced social mobility, and growing job precariousness (especially among young people) were the dark side of a country in the midst of a surprisingly long upward cycle, sustained by the massive inflow of foreign capital to finance construction (López and Rodríguez 2010).

It is important to remember that the period of growth that began in 1995 was preceded by a global crisis. The Barcelona 1992 Summer Olympics and the Universal Exposition of Seville (Expo '92) were presented as proof of the success of the Spanish transition to democracy and as hallmarks through which Spaniards could show off their renewed pride to the world (Maura 2018). The investments associated with these celebrations delayed the arrival of the crisis in Spain, but in 1993 unemployment reached an all-time high and the value of the national currency (*peseta*) was depreciated three times to try to maintain export capacity.

The Spanish Socialist Workers' Party (PSOE) lost its absolute majority in Parliament in 1993. The front pages of Spanish newspapers were filled with financial scandals (such as the Banesto case[6]) as well as political scandals (such as the escape of the former chief of Spain's Civil Guard, Luis Roldán, and the prosecution of former interior minister José Barrionuevo for his "dirty war" against ETA). Increased migration into Spanish cities during the 1990s and the transformation of urban social demographics led to racial conflicts that culminated in the murder of the Dominican immigrant Lucrecia Pérez on the outskirts of Madrid in 1992. The early 1990s saw instances of political conflict and violence on the streets: news coverage of urban tribes, especially skinheads, were common during that period. The media acquired a new centrality thanks to private television channels, which began broadcasting in 1989. Competi-

10. Indie Music as a Controversial Space on Spanish Identity   195

tion between television networks gave way to the proliferation of infotainment programming. The morbid coverage of the disappearance and murder of three teenage girls from the Valencian town of Alcásser in 1992 exposed a new way of understanding public space and contrasted the Spain that celebrated the Fifth Centenary of the discovery of America with a country where ignorance, brutality, and incompetence lived on (Maura 2018).[7]

The overcoming of the crisis and the expansion cycle coincided with the emergence of the Internet. The middle-class youth, which is the social base for indie music, fits the profile of the creative classes that gave way to the emergence of the "hipster" in the 2010s (Florida 2014). The Internet made it easy and cheap for users to access cultural resources. The means of cultural production became cheaper as they became digital: a large contingent of young people learned to create web pages, design brochures and magazines, and edit video and sound on their laptops, which opened up a world of creative opportunities at a lower cost.

However, the optimism associated with the early years of the Internet, a technology that the media presented as a "land of opportunity" for adventurers and entrepreneurs, contrasted with the reality of young people who were unable to consolidate their adult life due to low-paying and precarious jobs, a work model based on short-term projects rather than long-term contracts, and a housing market that made it difficult for them to leave their parents' home (Cruces 2012; Rowan 2010). This is a generation that enjoys a cultural wealth thanks to the digital revolution and the emergence of low-cost consumption but that, in contrast, lacks economic resources. This tension between a symbolic world full of opportunities and promises, and the reality of a precarious job market became a breeding ground for the discontent that followed the years of economic expansion and erupted with the 2008 crisis.

Journalist Esteban Hernández (2014) points out that the 2008 crisis marked the end of the middle classes not only in Spain but throughout the Western world. This alleged end of the middle classes mainly affected young people who were educated according to a middle-class ideology, which is based on compliance with norms, trust in social institutions, faith in effort as a form of promotion, and confidence in progress. Middle-class parents were confident that their children would live in better conditions than they did. The scepticism generated towards institutions by the crisis and corruption, the massification of higher education, and the flexibility of employment contracts are elements that have broken the covenant of trust on which the middle class is based, as well as the political framework that had been built since the Transition.

Most governments invoked austerity politics in order to solve the crisis. The anti-austerity movement was a response by the children of these middle classes and the claim that the crisis was not only economic but also ideological and cultural. A series of demonstrations against spending cuts and the economic crisis occupied emblematic squares in cities such as Madrid (Puerta del Sol) and Barcelona (Plaza Catalunya). Neighborhood assemblies sprang up and camped out for almost a month. The *Indignados* movement took inspiration from the Arab Spring and was imitated in several countries under the Occupy motto.[8] The members of these assemblies critiqued the electoral system, the political parties, the education system, and the economy, defining themselves in opposition to an elite generated by the confluence of interests of politicians and bankers (Romanos 2017).

For some authors (Labrador 2014; Martínez 2012), the anti-austerity movement also implies the end of a way of seeing the Spanish Transition to Democracy, since the movement calls for the rewriting of the Constitution and the end of the two-party system, which had generated political stability and created strong governments at the price of commodifying democracy. As Romanos points out, the goal of this movement was to end the commodification of individuals—one of the mottos was "We are not goods in the hands of politicians and bankers"—and hold the political and economic elites accountable for the crisis (2017, 143).

Research on this movement, compiled by Romanos (2017, 147), has provided some data on its sociological composition: a balanced presence of men and women; an average age close to 30 years; a high educational level (university students and graduates); a large presence of civil servants, health workers and other professionals; and a striking under-representation of the working classes. In light of this, it is possible to regard the anti-austerity movement as a social movement mainly led by the middle classes. In addition, it is important to note that some spaces linked to art and culture, such as *La Tabacalera* Social Center in Madrid, functioned as incubators of the ideas and dynamics that led to the emergence of the movement.

The defence of democracy had united Spaniards under the flagship of national identity since Franco's death. According to the dominant discourse, from 1978 to 2011, to discuss some aspects of the Constitution was equal to attacking Spanish democracy and was tantamount to being a "bad Spaniard" ("mal español"), referring here to the title of a song from the indie band Love of Lesbian that ironizes about the corruption of the political parties that defend the Constitution and a centralist view of Spain. However, the 15-M proposed that this pact should be revised around civic and political values (Rendueles 2013; Moreno-Caballud 2014). It was possible to be Spanish and, at the same time, to want to amend the democratic public space and create new rules.

As Sampedro and Llobera have pointed out, the 15-M was a "consensual dissent": most Spaniards shared a "generalized dissent to the way the economic crisis is being handled while also demanding a regeneration of democracy beyond the limits established along the transition" (2014, 64). Their analysis of the data from sociological surveys reveals "cross-sectional support for the 15-M [. . .] coming from people of different age groups, genders, employment status and levels of urbanization" (64). Three out of every four citizens sympathized with the 15-M's arguments, and one out of every two agreed with its protest strategies (75). Interestingly, the autonomy claims of territories such as Cataluña, País Vasco, or Galicia have no space in the 15-M discussions. The "consensual dissent" was established while at the same time rejecting wider debates around autonomy and definitions of Spanish identity. The 15-M used the same slogans and sought the same changes in the different Spanish territories, and as such the movement was able to unify people around Spain under the proposal of a new country. But its impact was not to last. On June 15, 2011, activists protested in front of the Parliament of Catalonia and forced President Artur Mas to leave by helicopter. In October 2017, some of these activists supported Catalonia's declaration of independence after agreeing with the parties that had approved the most aggressive austerity policies in the entire Spanish state.

Indie in Spain: From Individual Discontent to Collective Actions

The indie scene emerged in Spain in the late 1980s and early 1990s[9] in various epicenters: Madrid, Barcelona, Asturias, Andalusia, and Castile and León (Barrera 2014). According to Cruz (2015), the young people involved came mainly from the middle classes and were the children of engineers, public authorities, executives, and high-ranking military officials. Thanks to their families, who held sufficient cultural and economic capital to allow them to study English and to travel, these young people became aware of foreign music record releases through magazines and fanzines. In this sense, the class composition was not very different from that of the seminal groups that created *La movida* (Val 2017).

From a political perspective, indie music was characterized by its refusal to take a political stand in its lyrics, a focus on more intimate aspects, and a preference for English lyrics. Teresa Iturrioz, bassist of Le Mans, observed the following: "Aventuras de Kirlian and Le Mans had a more aesthetic than activist conception of music. There was no social message. Music was the message. It also coincided in time with Basque Radical Rock and so I thought why not make more beautiful music?" (Cruz 2015, 219). As mentioned above, a song released by

Los Planetas in 1996, "Vuelve la canción protesta" ("The Protest Song Returns"), derogated a new generation of singer-songwriters who emerged in those years and reclaimed the protest song. It is an example of the attitude that indie bands had during the 1990s about the political claims of other musicians. Los Planetas' song states:

> These are the new prophets of the new revolution.
> We are going to change the world with this song.
> Politicians and bankers tremble,
> the protest song returns.

The lyrics ironize about the power of political songs to frighten politicians and bankers. Interestingly, politicians and bankers were the ones blamed for the crisis almost twenty years later during the anti-austerity movement.

From 2011 until the present, the debate around how music and musicians should be linked with politics has been revived in the Spanish public domain. An example of this is the book on indie and hipster culture by journalist Víctor Lenore, *Indies, hipsters y gafapastas* (2014), which notes that this culture is eminently elitist and that its discourse has been absorbed by the capitalist system. According to Lenore, the apoliticism of the indie scene, focused on talking about its inner world and without taking into account social problems, has helped the scene to be co-opted by major labels and the mainstream.[10] On the other hand, the works of Peris Llorca (2015; 2018) try to challenge this vision: Spanish indie is a genre in which we can observe traces of the discontent generated by the false promise of young middle-class culture. According to Peris Llorca, that trace is to be found in songs that capture "a certain middle-class discontent that has to do with the frustration over the expectations about modernisation [. . .] the opposite of the euphoria caused by the exercise of modernity that characterised *La movida* of the 1980s" (2015, 137).

This is the discontent of a generation that is suffering the bitter side of neoliberalism: minimum wages, temporary contracts, mortgages, and the contradiction between the good life promised by their parents and their real life. This discontent emerges in the songs of indie bands through different themes: in the case of Surfin Bichos, it emerges through sordid references to a dark, crazy, foolish Spain that has been excluded and is falling behind (Peris Llorca 2018, 137). Los Planetas allude to discontent by articulating a view of drugs as "a response to that radical dissatisfaction, to that lack of something that cannot be named" (138). La Habitación Roja (The Red Room) problematize discontent and its exploration of individualism, failure, and the use of love as a lifesaver in storms (Peris Llorca 2015).

10. Indie Music as a Controversial Space on Spanish Identity   199

In previous work (Val and Fouce 2016), we have already explored the ways in which some social movements, such as the demonstrations against the Iraq War in 2003 and the protests outside the headquarters of the conservative People's Party following the Madrid train bombings (known as the 11-M) in 2004, questioned the covenant on which the Transition Culture was based: politics doesn't get into culture and culture doesn't get into politics (Martínez 2012). In the early 2000s, some bands began to introduce political themes in their songs. La Habitación Roja, for example, introduced some accounts of the life of the minimum-wage earner ("Van a por nosotros"/"They're after us," 2005) and scathing and direct criticism of former Prime Minister José María Aznar for his involvement in the Iraq war ("Tened piedad del expresidente"/"Have mercy on the former President," 2007). Aznar was also the target of criticism in Iván Ferreiro's song "Ciudadano A" ("Citizen A," 2005).

However, it was after the anti-austerity movement that political content was explicitly introduced in Spanish indie. Several groups wrote songs that connected with the anti-austerity movement's criticism of bankers and, above all, the political class: Grupo de Expertos Solynieve ("La nueva Reconquista de Graná"/"The New Reconquest of Granada," 2012); Niños Mutantes ("Caerán los bancos"/"Banks Will Fall," 2012); Pony Bravo ("El político neoliberal"/"The Neoliberal Politician," 2013); Love of Lesbian ("Mal Español"/"Bad Spaniard," 2014); Amaral ("Ratonera"/"Mouse Trap," 2014); and Supersubmarina ("Hasta que sangren"/"Until They Bleed," 2014). In some cases, the critical attitude of these bands was temporary as they went back to previous themes in subsequent songs. In the case of other groups and solo artists, political issues were to stay. We can even talk about the emergence of groups like León Benavente, Maronda, Las Odio and Siete70, which emerged within the indie scene with a political dimension intrinsic to their lyrics.

The support of feminism is one of the discursive lines that characterized the political states of indie music from 2011. In recent years, feminism has been gaining visibility in Spain, thanks to the #MeToo movement, the general feminist strike of March 8, 2018, and the protests in Pamplona against the sentence given to the five men (la Manada, the Pack) accused of gang-raping a woman at the running of the bulls festival in Pamplona. (They were found guilty of sexual abuse rather than the more serious offence of rape.) For example, in "Hoy la bestia cena en casa" ("Today the Beast Has Dinner at Home," 2018), singer-songwriter Zahara criticizes the Spanish liberal parties that support surrogacy: "If you are so brave, lend me your belly. Sell me your sisters' newborns."

Two paradigmatic cases stand out within this politicization of the indie scene. The first one is Asturian musician Nacho Vegas, a former member of key bands in the emergence of the Spanish indie scene (Manta Ray and Eliminator Jr) who then began a career as an electric singer-songwriter. His records explore the personality of the damned and the addict with dark, tortuous texts. But from 2011 onward, his discourse began to change through songs such as "Cómo hacer crack" ("How to Make Crack"), a single in which he, metaphorically, addresses the social ruptures taking place in Spanish society. In 2014, Nacho Vegas released the album *Polvorado*, in which the political discourse becomes more explicit, connecting with the tradition of anti-Franco singer-songwriters. The album includes songs with labor-movement mottos and Marxist reminiscences. It was strongly criticized[11] on the basis that "he lost his lyricism to write pamphlets [. . .] and reject velvet melodies in order to create easy music" (Rodríguez Lenin 2014). This album also reflects a community feeling characteristic of the anti-austerity movement in phrases such as "they want us in solitude, they will have us together." His following work, an EP titled *Canciones populistas* (*Populist Songs*, 2015), delves into that theme through a cover of a Phil Ochs' song ("Love Me, I'm a Liberal"), which is adapted to the Spanish political context. The political attitude of this musician is not only reflected in his songs but also in his relationship with the record industry, since he produces his music himself. Moreover, in his concerts he criticized the banks that were evicting citizens and strongly supported the foreclosure association *Plataforma de Afectados por la Hipoteca* (PAH, Platform for People Affected by Mortgages), which was linked to the anti-austerity movement.[12]

From the point of view of the construction of a discourse that appeals to the "us" (the citizens) versus the "them" (the banks and politicians), the evolution of the band Vetusta Morla is also worthy of analysis. Morla's lyrics convey complaints and denounce social problems, but in a veiled manner, much in the same way as other indie bands did, according to Peris Llorca (2018). It is not until the band's third album, *La deriva* (*Adrift*, 2014), when the political discourse becomes crystal-clear.[13] An example of this is the title song for the album, whose lyrics refer to the lack of direction and the loss of points of reference in the context of social crisis. The narrative voice in this song evolves from the first-person to the third-person plural: "We will have to find a solution / May our fate not measure us up." On that same album, in the song "Golpe maestro" ("Masterstroke"), a clear reference to banks and politicians, Morla once again alludes to collective action as a form of hope in the context of crisis. The possibility of identifying and punishing the people responsible remains open after acts of corruption and larceny were committed: "It was a perfect robbery, except for this: we still have our throat, fists and feet left. It wasn't a masterstroke, they left a trail, they can run now. Thirst is back," concluded the song.

10. Indie Music as a Controversial Space on Spanish Identity   201

Their appeal to common and collective experience is an example of the political evolution of the indie scene and the middle classes in Spain. At the beginning of the indie scene, the media ridiculed the collective efforts of other music scenes to address political conflicts (Lenore, 2014). The indie musical discourse transmits a diffuse malaise lived individually and without considering its causes. However, in the anti-austerity movement the middle classes became aware of the real causes of their problems and realized that relief would only come from collective mobilizations and not from individual actions.

In this sense, the emergence of bands such as La Maravillosa Orquesta del Alcohol (La M.O.D.A.), which has become established in the indie scene in recent years and has reflected its evolution, is very important. The band formed in Burgos, in inland Spain, and is characterized by the fact that its lyrics condemn politicians' abandonment of rural areas. Its pessimistic songs address social problems, such as the exodus of Spanish youth, always from a community perspective. In fact, the aesthetic of the seven members of the band is reminiscent of construction workers. The band's songs are full of chants and call-and-response techniques in which all members collaborate. In turn, the band has been influenced by folk, rock, indie, punk, and has collaborated with rap and hip-hop groups, in an amalgam that overcomes the differences and resistances between the music scenes that characterized Spanish music of the 1990s. Such an eclectic band would not have been possible in Spain prior to the anti-austerity movement. This politicization of the scene has not been well received by music critics, nor by other music scenes, who believe that this shift is not authentic but rather an opportunistic attempt to be involved in a movement that for a time became "cool" (Rodríguez Lenin 2014).

Conclusion

In this chapter, we have sought to establish the connections between the life experiences of the middle-class youth in Spain and their musical expressions. Spanish national identity in the years following the Transition to Democracy has been related to the consolidation of the middle classes and urban life. This identity gravitates around the ideas of modernity and cosmopolitanism, which were related to the affluence from the 1980s onwards. The basis for this promise of affluence has been Spain's integration with Europe and the neoliberal economic policies centered around consumption. Cultural identity during the years of democracy has been constructed as a result of the "culture of transition" in which politics and culture should be separate realms.

The occupation of Puerta del Sol and other Spanish squares has confronted this "culture of transition," a consequence of the failure to uphold the promise of affluence due to austerity politics. 15-M's demands, heavily supported by Spaniards of all ages, occupations, music genres, and economic backgrounds, were temporarily an attempt to unify the nation under a "new deal" that sought to redefine the basis of national identity. Indie bands, whose members come mainly from middle classes, have turned their songs toward social and political issues in the wake of the politicization of Spanish society that followed the 2008 crisis and austerity policies. Indie songs already anticipated the unrest of a generation that in 2011 occupied city squares to propose a new identity around new values and new narratives of the past.

Notes

This research is supported by the project titled "Public Problems and Controversies: Diversity and Participation in the Media Sphere," which has been funded by the Spanish National Plan for Research, Development, and Innovation Oriented to the Challenges of Society, call 2017 (Ref: CSO2017–82109-R).

1. The Spanish Transition to Democracy (*la Transición*) refers to the period following the Franco regime in which Spain gradually moved towards the consolidation of a democratic, parliamentary system (1975–1982).

2. We use the term "soundtrack" to emphasize the connections between the social and political environment and the music that was perceived as being related to this historical moment, not just because of its "sound," but also because of the shared values expressed by the semiotics of genre (Fabbri 1981). The connections between indie music and the 1990s as a historical period are extensively explored by González Férriz (2020).

3. All translations from Spanish are by the authors.

4. During the Transition several social movements emerged in cities such as Madrid or Barcelona, which sought improvements to the social conditions of working-class neigborhoods (Pérez Quintana and Sánchez León 2008).

5. Basque Radical Rock (*Rock radikal vasco*) was a very successful movement inspired by punk bands such as The Clash and was linked with the left-wing nationalist parties of the Basque Country.

6. In 1993, the Spanish Central Bank dismissed the Board of Directors of Banesto bank because its risky practices made its clients unable to retrieve their money. Mario Conde, Banesto CEO, was the incarnation of the yuppie model in Spain until his incarceration.

7. The media coverage of the case and its impact on Spanish society is addressed extensively in the documentary *The Alcàsser Murders* (Bambú Producciones and Netflix 2019).

8. Castells (2015) provides a general overview of the different movements calling for democracy in the 2010s. See Graeber (2013) for insights on Occupy Wall Street.

9. For a chronological account of this scene, see Cruz (2015).

10. As David Hesmondhalgh (1999) has explained, the contradictions of the indie industry are enormous, and the Spanish scene is a good example of that.

10. Indie Music as a Controversial Space on Spanish Identity   203

11. See the review of the album and the interview published by *Rockdelux* 327.

12. See https://www.elconfidencial.com/cultura/2016–01–22/nacho-vegas-trolea-a -la-banca_1139764/.

13. For an audiovisual analysis of the band's music videos, see Fouce and Val (2017).

References

Aguila, Guillermo Z. del. 2007. "La Leyenda del Espacio." *Rockdelux* 251.

Barrera, Fernando. 2014. "Hibridación, globalización y tecnología: Flamenco y música indie en Andalucía (1977–2012)." PhD diss., Universidad de Granada.

Carr, Raymond, and Juan Pablo Fusi. 1979. *España, de la dictadura a la democracia*. Barcelona: Planeta.

Castells, Manuel. 2015. *Networks of Outrage and Hope*. Cambridge: Polity.

Cruces, Francisco. 2012. "Jóvenes y corrientes culturales emergentes." In *Jóvenes, culturas urbanas y redes digitales*, edited by Francisco Cruces and Néstor García Canclini. Madrid: Ariel, Fundación Telefónica.

Cruz, Nando. 2015. *Pequeño Circo: Historia oral del indie en España*. Barcelona: Contra.

Fabbri, Franco. 1981 "A Theory of Musical Genres: Two Applications." In *Popular Music Perspectives*, edited by David Horn and Phillip Tagg, 52–81. Göteborg, SE: IASPM.

Florida, Richard. 2014. *The Rise of the Creative Class*. New York: Basic Books.

Fouce, Héctor. 2006. *El futuro ya está aquí: Música pop y cambio cultural en España*. Madrid: Velecio.

———. 2009. "Un largo verano de festivales: Categorías de experiencia y culturas productivas en la industria musical española." *Revista Latina de Comunicación Social* 64. http://www.revistalatinacs.org/09/art/33_832_43_ULEPICC_12/Hector_Fource.html.

Fouce, Héctor, and Fernán del Val. 2013. "La movida: Popular Music as the Discourse of Modernity in Democratic Spain." In *Made in Spain: Studies in Popular Music*, edited by Silvia Martínez and Héctor Fouce, 125–34. New York: Routledge.

———. 2017. "Indignación y política en la música popular española: El imaginario de los videoclips independientes." *Signa* 26: 663–74.

González Férriz, Ramón. 2020. *La trampa del optimismo*. Barcelona: Debate.

Graeber, David. 2013. *The Democracy Project*. New York: Spiegel and Grau.

Hernández, Esteban. 2014. *El fin de la clase media*. Madrid: Clave Intelectual.

Hesmondhalgh, David. 1999. "Indie: the Institutional Politics and Aesthetics of a Popular Music Genre." *Cultural Studies* 13, no.1: 34–61.

Labrador, Germán. 2014. "¿Lo llamaban democracia? La crítica estética de la política en la Transición Española y el imaginario de la historia en el 15-M." *Kamchatka: Revista de Análisis Cultural* 4: 11–61.

Lenore, Víctor. 2014. *Indies, hipsters y gafapastas: Crónica de una dominación cultural*. Madrid: Capitán Swing.

———. 2018. *Espectros de la movida*. Madrid: Akal.

López, Isidro, and Emmanuel Rodríguez. 2010. *Fin de ciclo: Financierización, territorio, y sociedad en la onda larga del capitalismo hispano (1959–2010)*. Madrid: Traficantes de Sueños.

Martínez, Guillem, ed. 2012. *CT o la cultura de la transición: Crítica a 35 años de cultura española*. Barcelona: Debolsillo.

Martínez, Silvia, and Héctor Fouce, eds. 2013. *Made in Spain: Studies in Popular Music*. New York: Routledge.

Maura, Eduardo. 2018. *Los 90: Euforia y miedo en la modernidad democrática española*. Madrid: Akal.

Moreno-Caballud, Luis. 2014. "Cuando cualquiera escribe: Procesos democratizadores de la cultura escrita en crisis de la cultura de la transición española." *Journal of Spanish Cultural Studies* 15, nos. 1–2: 13–26.

Pérez Quintana, Vicente, and Pablo Sánchez León, eds. 2008. *Memoria ciudadana y movimiento vecinal: Madrid, 1968–2008*. Madrid: La Catarata.

Peris Llorca, Jesús. 2015. "Las canciones de 'La habitación roja' en el contexto del rock independiente español de los años 90: Nostalgia de la solidez en la cultura de masas." *Forma: Revista d'estudis Comparatius: Art, Literatura, Pensament* 11: 131–48.

———. 2018. "Las letras del rock independiente español: Huecos en la cultura de la transición." In *Cultura e imaginación política*, edited by Jaume Peris, 131–41. Mexico: Rilma.

Rendueles García, Cesar. 2013. *Sociofobia: El cambio político en la era de la utopía digital*. Madrid: Capitán Swing.

Rodríguez Lenin, Jesús. 2014. "Dándonos de Hostias (Dialécticas)." *Rockdelux* 327.

Romanos, Eduardo. 2017. "Late Neoliberalism and Its Indignados: Contention in Austerity Spain." In *Late Neoliberalism and Its Discontents in the Economic Crisis: Comparing Social Movements in the European Periphery*, edited by Donatella Della Porta, Massimiliano Andretta, Tiago Fernandes, Francis O'Connor, Eduardo Romanos, and Markos Vogiatzoglou, 131–67. Cham, CH: Palgrave Macmillan.

Rowan, Jaron. 2010. *Emprendizajes en cultura*. Madrid: Traficantes de Sueños.

Sampedro, Víctor, and Josep Lobera. 2014. "The Spanish 15-M Movement: A Consensual Dissent?" *Journal of Spanish Cultural Studies* 15, nos. 1–2: 61–80.

Sánchez León, Pablo. 2014. "Desclasamiento y desencanto: La representación de las clases medias como eje de una relectura generacional de la transición española." *Kamchatka* 4: 63–99.

Sanz, Jesús, and Oscar Mateos. 2011. "15-M: Apuntes para el análisis de un movimiento en construcción." *Revista de Fomento Social* 66: 517–44.

Subirats, Eduardo. 2002. *Intransiciones: Crítica de la cultura española*. Madrid: Biblioteca Nueva.

Tezanos, José Félix. 1975. *Estructura de clases en la españa actual*. Madrid: Cuadernos para el diálogo.

Val, Fernán del. 2017. *Rockeros insurgentes, modernos complacientes: Un análisis sociológico del rock en la transición (1975–1985)*. Madrid: Fundación Autor.

Val, Fernán del, and Héctor Fouce. 2016. "De la apatía a la indignación: Narrativas del rock independiente español en época de crisis." *Methaodos, Revista de Ciencias Sociales* 4, no. 1: 58–72.

Vilarós, Teresa. 1998. *El mono del desencanto: Una crítica cultural de la transición española (1973–1993)*. Madrid: Siglo XXI.

Wheeler, Duncan. 2018. "You've Got to Fight for Your Right to Party? Spanish Punk Rockers and Democratic Values." *Popular Music and Society* 41, no. 2: 132–53.

11

Catalonia vs Spain

How Sonorous Is Nationalism?

JOSEP MARTÍ

Introduction

The importance of music in constructing social norms and structures is especially clear in the role that it plays in relation to three basic parameters of social logic: identity, social order, and the need for exchange (Martí 2018). Music is so important to us because it adapts to the dynamics of each of these three different parameters, regardless of the aesthetic values that we attach to it. Music contributes to generating and strengthening collective and individual identities, it marks social structures (gender, class, ethnicity), and thanks to the affects it triggers and the emotions it articulates, it can be considered as a first-order relational fact (Martí 2019a). Through music, "structures of feeling" (Eyerman and Jamison 1998, 161) are built that are important for the formation of identities that reinforce or challenge social orders. Some of these structures are directly related to nationalism. The motivations behind nationalist movements are always multiple and complex and cross political and cultural domains. In Catalonia, however, one of the aspects that undoubtedly explains the large mobilizations that have taken place in recent years is the strong emotional charge associated with the Catalan nationalist movement and its sonic expressions.

Interest in the emotional dimension of political conflicts and movements is quite recent in the social sciences. It was stimulated in part by the emergence of the so-called "affective turn" in the mid-1990s (Clough and Halley 2007), a reaction to what was considered to be an excess of attention towards language and discourse. Affect theory takes a further step toward overcoming the Cartesian dualism inherent in the traditional separation between reason and emotion. Affects, feelings, and emotions play a crucial role in sociability. Affect is pre-personal since it is not subjected to the limitations of consciousness or of representation. Feelings are personal and biographical, and emotions are social (Massumi 1996). Although it is appropriate to distinguish between affects, feelings, and emotions, these are not ontologically discrete entities: they need to be understood as different states or moments of the same continuum of energy flows through which we relate to everything that surrounds us. Recent publications about nationalism, some of which are focused on music (Wood 2004), reflect this interest in the affective turn.[1] If we take into account the close relationship between music and emotions, and the fact that music triggers affects, then it should not be surprising that a prominent soundtrack emerged during the Catalan independence movement, in which intense emotions were involved.

This chapter is based on empirical data collected mainly from the autumn of 2017 until the spring of 2019. During this period, the international media reported on the social unrest in Spain triggered by the emergence of the Catalan sovereigntist movement. On October 1, 2017, the Catalan autonomous government called for a referendum on the independence of Catalonia, following previous attempts to reach an agreement with the Spanish government about a referendum. Although the Spanish government did not allow the consultation, the referendum did go ahead, following several weeks of tension exacerbated by the electoral victory of pro-independence candidates and a failed attempt to proclaim a Catalan Republic on October 27 of the same year. The State responded by increasing its interference in local politics, as well as through the use of police violence, and the imprisonment or exile of members of the Catalan government and leaders of civic societies. The Spanish government forced a new regional election in Catalonia in December 2017, but contrary to what was expected, the result yielded again a pro-independence parliamentary majority. These months of social upheaval witnessed the emergence of a wealth of sonic expressions that are explored in this chapter.

The Sounds of September 20

On the morning of September 20, 2017, a few days before the referendum, the Spanish police searched the offices of members of the Catalan government in Barcelona and arrested some workers with the aim of preventing the planned referendum. This action triggered citizen mobilizations throughout the entire day.[2] The culminating moment was a protest in front of the Department of Econ-

FIGURE 11.1. Barcelona protests on September 20, 2017. Photo: P. Tordera

omy, an event in which protesters were also subjected to searches and arrests. The protest began in the morning and lasted until early on the following day, peaking in the evening, when upwards of 40,000 people had gathered (Figure 11.1).[3] The urban space in which the protests took place was like a living being that breathed and grew as more people arrived, generating an all-encompassing, ever-expanding atmosphere. In situations like this, it is appropriate to speak of "affective atmospheres," that is, spatially discharged affective structures that are autonomous from the bodies from which they arise (Anderson 2009, 80) and powerfully contribute to provoking emotions.

The protests of September 20 are a good starting point to discuss the "soundtrack"[4] of this period of upheaval. The noises from police helicopters, the whistles they elicited among the protesters, the slogans, politicians' speeches, the songs of the crowds, the music emitted from loudspeakers and a few bands performing on small stages made up a very characteristic sonic magma, which is called "emotional style" (Gammerl 2012).[5] The idea of "magma" is used here as a metaphor, alluding to viscosity, fusion, energy, heat, and the heterogeneity of materials.

Judging from the highly charged nature of the protest, the most generalized feelings that appeared to flow from the crowd congregated before the Department of Economy appeared to be indignation, anger, and hope. The events that had taken place throughout the month of September, particularly the arrival in Catalonia of some thousand violence-prone Spanish police officers, provoked the rise of indignation. The rage that rose throughout September 20 in response to police occupations and arrests was expressed through protest slogans such as "Fora / les forces / d'ocu- / pa- / ció" (Occupation forces out), "Els carrers seran sempre nostres" (The streets will always be ours), and "No / tinc / por'" (I have no fear). Another feeling that stood out among independence supporters was the hope that Catalan sovereignty would be achieved. While people were congregating at the site of the demonstration, a large banner was displayed on one of the buildings with the words "Welcome to the Catalan Republic." Other slogans that could be heard prominently, besides the aforementioned, directly expressed a desire for independence: "Aquí / comença / la nostra independència" (Our independence begins here); "Ni un / pas / enrere" (Not one step back), "Vo- / ta- / rem!" (We shall vote); and "In- / indé- / independencià" (Independence).

Songs were broadcast from loudspeakers, many of them belonging to the old repertoire of the Catalan *Nova Cançó* (mainly Lluis Llach and Maria del Mar Bonet),[6] a repertoire associated with protest during the late Franco regime. People also sang hymns like the Catalan national anthem "Els Segadors" or the "Cant de la Senyera."[7] At certain moments, in what could count as proof of the transversal character of the sovereigntist movement, one could hear the "Viro-lai,"[8] a religious hymn used as a Catalan anthem during politically critical times in which other hymns had been prohibited (for example during the Spanish dictatorships of Primo de Rivera, 1923–1930, and of General Franco, 1936–1975). Some groups played *gralles*[9] and drums. The protesters directly addressed the Spanish police officers not only with their slogans but also through parodic songs. In addition, music groups spontaneously went on stage and contributed to the protest with their performances.

The leaders of the civic societies *Assemblea Nacional Catalana* (Catalan National Assembly) and *Òmnium Cultural* used megaphones to voice expressions of protest against the actions of the Spanish government and in favor of the right of Catalans to decide. Durkheim would have described these moments as a "collective effervescence." The crowd "boiled," and bodies gave themselves over to affective flows, releasing waves of pure energy that engendered contagious feelings and weaved a solid emotional dimension. It is appropriate to speak of "affective-discursive assemblages" (Wetherell et al., 2015, 57) that generated dense emotional atmospheres, creating proximity, affiliation, and inclusive relations (58). A Japanese woman, who was among the crowd out of curiosity, could not be rid of these emotional flows: "You're going to get independence," she

FIGURE 11.2. Barcelona protests on September 20, 2017. Photo: R. Vilallonga

told those who stood close to her. We already know that "affect is infectious" (Connolly 2002, 75).

The demonstrations of September 20 can be analyzed as an assemblage in the sense articulated by Deleuze. What really matters in assemblages is not what bodies, objects, or social institutions ontologically are but rather, as he observes, "the capacities for action, interaction, feeling and desire produced in bodies or groups of bodies by affective flows" (Fox and Alldred 2015, 401–2). The notion of "assemblage" implies the idea of movement and connectivity, of a processual agency, of relationality. Assemblages are heterogeneous because they establish connections between elements of the most diverse nature, such as organic beings, inorganic social entities, or ideas. When we associate the concept of assemblage to a specific space, for example the street where the protest takes place, we can also speak of "emplacement," a concept that refers to the close connection between body, mind, and environment (Howes 2005, 7). Sound flows as it travels through the assemblage where bodies are located, affecting them in the process. This set of sensations experienced by the participants is also related with the feeling of being with others who share their dreams, aims, and emotions, as well as confronting others through feelings of anger or protest. All this happens in an urban space that is disputed and serves as a metaphor for the confrontation between protestors and police. This slogan "els carrers seran sempre nostres" implies that the protesters claim the public space as their own. The occupation of the public space is, in itself, an act of protest.

Experiences such as those that occurred on September 20 produce deep effects and affective reactions by the people. These demonstrations had not been organized according to an established schedule but were rather spontaneous protests in response to immediate political events. In situations of this kind, in which sonic experiences intertwine with strong emotions, "affective capsules" are constituted. These are experiential moments which are lived with such intensity that they are stored in the body and may emerge at a later point when the appropriate situations demand them. The sonic magma that surrounded the people who congregated on September 20 conveyed in a completely entangled manner semiotic and affective elements (Wetherell et al., 2015, 59), such as, on the one hand, the proclamations, slogans, and song lyrics, and, on the other hand, feelings, emotions, and bodily experience.

The Sound on the Street

The protests of September 20 were very rich in sonic expressions. In addition to those already mentioned, one could add the noisy *caceroladas* ("Caceroladas" 2017)[10] that were heard in the evening in towns across Catalonia in protest against the aggression of the Spanish state. The sonic assemblages formed on that day are among the many that have contributed to the "emoscape" (Kenway and Fahey 2011) of the sovereigntist movement in Catalonia. This emotional landscape is constructed and maintained through multiple elements of both a visual nature—flags, banners, graffiti, yellow ribbons[11] (Figure 11.3)—and a sonic nature. The street is one of the main witnesses to the conflict, and it is not a silent one. Countless demonstrations took place from the autumn of 2017 to the early months of 2019, not only in the city of Barcelona but across Catalonia, in an emotional style similar to that described in the context of September 20. The sonic dimension of the slogans, beyond the messages that they convey, make up a very important part of the soundscape of these mobilizations.

In multitudinous demonstrations, slogans tend not to be uttered in unison. Rather, someone begins to voice a slogan and people join in progressively. Those who initiate a slogan usually go in groups, however, and their call is immediately supported by their companions, facilitating its spread. Little by little, the slogan weakens until it disappears in order for protesters to avoid clashing with other slogans. Within these sonic flows, a message is articulated and uttered through a well-defined rhythmic pattern, that is repeated *ad libitum*, marking the protest

FIGURE 11.3. Yellow ribbons used to protest the imprisonment of Catalan leaders. Photo: J. Martí

space and imbuing it with life through the ensemble of bodies chanting together. Sonic practices territorialize behavior as they combine physical vibrations with bodily sensations and culturally conditioned meanings (Eisenberg 2015, 199). In these affective atmospheres, the simultaneous shouting of the slogan, while rhythmically punctuating the syllables with hand clapping and whistles, reinforces community feelings and acts as a (materially) binding agent: "When music cements social identities, this is not talking metaphorically: sounds literally make bodies stick to each other and to particular places" (Saldanha 2009, 74). The effect is that of a single body formed by each of the protesters' bodies. Social actors not only perceive the energizing effects of these sonic flows but contribute to their creation.

The shouts of the slogans in the demonstrations are only one element of the soundscape of the protest. Revolution, protest, or turmoil are mostly "noise." In intense days like September 20, 2017, for example, the continued buzzing of the helicopters flying over Barcelona was impossible to ignore, leading some people to stay home. For others, however, this noise was a source of energy and outrage that prompted them to go out into the streets to join the protests against police detentions and searches. In fact, helicopters flew over the streets of Barcelona during many of the protests in the city. The deep, continuous noise they generate is not in itself unpleasant particularly when compared to the sirens of police cars, which are more strident and invasive. However, when people at home realize that the buzzing of the helicopters is linked to protests in

212 JOSEP MARTÍ

the street, it can become more irritating, or perhaps exciting, if one is heading to the protest. Noises were also generated in an organized manner. In recent years, for example, it has become usual at sporting events to greet the Spanish anthem with massive whistles. Noise also manifests in the form of *caceroladas* such as those that have been heard in Barcelona on numerous occasions, mainly in protest against the imprisonment of Catalan leaders or in opposition to the king in his rare visits to the city.[12]

Songs

The sonic magma of these events is formed by the noises of sirens and helicopter engines, slogans, and *caceroladas*, as well as by songs.[13] One of the key characteristics of the Catalan protest movement is the constant presence of music either through loudspeakers or live performance. The lyrics of the songs may be directly related to the protests, but this is not always the case. Very often the songs do not make explicit political claims: "It's not about content, it's about the energy," answered English musician MC Tempz to a journalist when asked about the reasons why people use his music during protests, in spite of the fact that it does not convey any political meanings (Hancox 2011, 265). Music has a strong binding power when performed in a group and plays an entertainment function in long-lasting gatherings. Music is in fact only an element within the whole assemblage, and its agentic capacity is always relative to the different elements that relate to it.

The Catalonian national anthem "Els Segadors," whether sung by the participants or on the megaphones, is one of the most ubiquitous songs in protests and, very often, has ritual value. It is sung at the closure of numerous acts, such as those that demand the freeing of political prisoners and the return of exiles. Another emblematic Catalan song, the "Cant dels Ocells" ("Song of the Birds"), was the most recurrent piece of music at protests together with "Els Segadors." Since the autumn of 2017, many of the citizen initiatives in support of imprisoned former members of the Catalan government and leaders of civic societies have made use of this song. "Cant del Ocells" had been formerly popularized by the well-known cellist Pau Casals (1876–1973), who was also in exile during the Franco regime. The "Cant dels Ocells" is an interesting case of semantic metamorphosis. Originally a Christmas song, it has become an emblematic song of Catalonia thanks to Pau Casals.[14] Furthermore, its continued use in current protests has increased its revindicative character.[15] In contrast, "L'Estaca" ("The Stake"), one of the songs most often heard in protests, has almost preserved the same spirit of protest it held at the time of its creation by the singer-songwriter

11. *Catalonia vs Spain*

Lluís Llach during the Franco dictatorship. This also explains why "L'Estaca" has been sung in the context of many different social movements beyond Catalonia (Dillane et al., 2018, 219–21).

The emotional circumstances lived during this period of revolt have also engendered parodic songs. These songs arise from very specific events, quickly reach a peak of popularity, and gradually disappear. "On estan les paperetes?" ("Where are the Ballots?"), one of the hits of the autumn of 2017, emerged as an improvised song following searches at a printing house in the city of Valls, in which the Spanish police was looking for referendum ballot papers. A large group of protesters gathered spontaneously in front of the establishment during the search and improvised this song to mock the police.[16] Thanks to its easy intonation and simple lyrics, "On estan les paperetes?" has been sung frequently at later demonstrations not connected to this incident. Other songs that make fun of the Spanish police include "El Cant dels Adéus" ("The Farewell Song")[17] and "Passi-ho bé" ("Goodbye"), a song very commonly used in Catalonia during the 1970s to close festive gatherings.[18]

Songs could also express homage to a political figure, such as the former premier of the Catalan government Carles Puigdemont, based on the German popular song "Es tanzt ein Bi Ba Butzemann" ("A Bi-Ba-Butzemann is Dancing"). Puigdemont fled Spain after a failed attempt to establish the Catalan Republic in October 2017 and has since then resided in exile in Belgium. In the spring of 2018, while travelling through Germany, he was arrested by the police following a request of extradition by the Spanish court. After some months, a German court of justice denied the extradition alleging nonconformity with the Spanish courts. The whole process gave rise to high emotional tensions in Catalonia, with people fearing that Puigdemont would be delivered to Spain. During this time, someone discovered the children's song "Es tanzt ein Bi Ba Butzemann," its refrain sounded to Catalan ears similar to "Viva Puigdemont" ("Long Live Puigdemont"). The video showing the original children's song went viral on social media in Catalonia, a fact echoed by the German press at the time ("Katalonienkonflikt" 2018). A parody of the original video with lyrics in Catalan was released on YouTube shortly after,[19] and people soon began to sing the beginning of this song during demonstrations, using Catalan words adapted to the political circumstances ("I ara, la versió del 'Viva Puigdemont,' en corals i caramelles" 2018) (see Figure 11.4).

The use of these song parodies points to a totally different affective dimension than that of the interpretation of musical pieces such as "Els Segadors," "El Cant dels Ocells," or "L'Estaca" discussed above. The implicit solemnity of these songs is nowhere in the parodies, which use humor and mockery as forms of protest

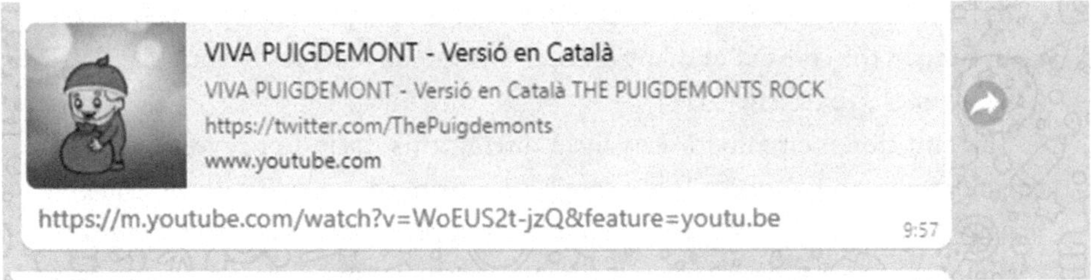

FIGURE 11.4. Following the good results achieved by Carles Puigdemont in the European polls on May 26, 2019, the song circulated again in social media.

against the establishment (Hart 2016, 201). Humor has been a constant presence in the emoscape of the Catalan sovereigntist struggle, as is evident in the overwhelming, constant circulation of textual, visual, and video memes through social network apps such as WhatsApp. Throughout this period, many musicians and bands have composed songs to support the Catalan protest movement. Their styles could not be more varied, ranging from the classic singer-songwriter song, to rock, fusion, reggae, ska, Latin rhythms, rap, hip-hop, pop-rock, folk, and electronic music (Martí 2019b).

The transversal aspect of the Catalan sovereignist movement is evident in the different types of musical domains in which it is enacted. Its political claims are not only expressed through new popular music but are also manifest in the field of folk or traditional music, for example in the *sardana* or *castells*,[20] as well as classical music contexts, such as concerts or choral singing performed during protests. Intellectuals such as Noam Chomsky have expressed solidarity with the Catalan political demands, as have musicians from the international scene. "The Reapers," a song by the American heavy metal band A Sound of Thunder, is a hybridized version of the Catalan national anthem "Els Segadors." The Icelandic singer Björk, artists such as Joan Báez, Peter Gabriel, Steven Patrick Morrissey, and the Irish band U2 have also shown their solidarity in one way or another (Martí 2019b, 90–91)

Yet, the proactive involvement of some musicians in the conflict has earned them negative criticism. Popular musicians such as Albert Pla, Cesk Freixas, and the early-music specialist Jordi Savall have been criticized and/or boycotted on the Spanish stages. On the other hand, singers such as Joan Manel Serrat and Raimon, who have been very influential in the Catalan music scene, have also received bitter criticism in Catalonia because of their position against independence.

FIGURE 11.5. Concert held in Barcelona, December 2, 2017, in support of political prisoners with around 50,000 attendees.

FIGURE 11.6. The widely attended concert held in Barcelona, December 3, 2017. An estimated 10,000 musicians and choir singers gathered in support of political prisoners.

Viva España

Spanish nationalists have also resorted to music within this tense atmosphere, but the levels of "musical mobilization"[21] they have achieved are not as apparent as those of the Catalan pro-independence movement. A well-known example is a version of the Spanish national anthem with lyrics by pop singer Marta Sánchez, which was made public in early 2018. Marta Sánchez's proposal was warmly welcomed by the Spanish right, who were eager to add lyrics to a wordless anthem (see Chapter 2 in this volume). In addition to the Spanish anthem, a repertoire of songs with a clear brand of Spanishness can be heard in acts in support of Spanish nationalism or against Catalan independence. The most frequently played tune is undoubtedly "Y Viva España," an old hit by Manolo Escobar, a very well-known performer of the Spanish *copla* genre. The hymn of the Spanish legion, "El novio de la Muerte," is commonly played in acts organized or attended by the extreme right, and *rumba catalana* songs by Peret and Los Manolos are often played during anti-secessionist demonstrations. *Rumba catalana*'s festival character, the fact that its lyrics make no direct or indirect reference to politics and, above all, it being sung in Spanish, make it well suited to construct a collective identity for the anti-secessionist movement.

The reuse of song repertoires for political aims may occasionally become controversial. This was the case with the appropriation of songs by the well-known singer Joan Manuel Serrat to counter Catalan independence. Serrat was one of the founders of the anti-Francoist *Nova Cançó* movement, but as the Spanish-Catalan conflict worsened, he took a stance against secession, leading to attempts to turn his celebrated hit "Mediterráneo" into an anti-independence anthem. In the autumn of 2017, prompted by the protest *caceroladas* organized

¿Estás en Cataluña y te molesta la cacerolada de las diez de la noche? Siempre puedes poner 'Mediterráneo', del gran J.M. Serrat.

♡ 1.607   20:40 - 22 sept. 2017

FIGURE 11.7. "Are you living in Catalonia, and is the *cacerolada* at ten o'clock at night bothering you? You can always put on 'Mediterráneo' by the great J.M. Serrat." —Tweet by a politician of the Spanish right. ("Una campaña" 2017)

in Barcelona and other Catalan locations, a call was circulated on social media proposing to use Serrat's "Mediterráneo" to counteract the *caceroladas* (Figure 11.7). Following this, the music could be heard coming out of loudspeakers and through open windows.

Attempts to use Serrat's repertoire politically, particularly his song "Mediterráneo," were met with Serrat's full opposition (Serrat 2017). In the Spanish context, musical performances criticizing or mocking the Catalan secessionists also circulated on social media, especially during moments of considerable tension. The witty Andalusian carnival *chirigotas* showed particular creativity in the use of humor and parody.[22] One does not find the same level of musical mobilization among the Spanish anti-secessionist Catalan population, however, than the one that characterized the sovereignist movement.

Conclusion

Recent electoral data from Catalonia clearly show that while half of the Catalan population stands for independence the other half is openly opposed or is indifferent.[23] It is noteworthy that the level of musical mobilization on the sovereignist side was much more prominent than among anti-independence groups. The creation of a new political reality in Catalonia based on republican values,[24] and not just around the notion of Catalan identity, mobilized more enthusiasm than the idea of preserving the status quo, even if the latter option may be the preferred one for many Catalans. We should also not forget that, according to some commentators, Spain, at the time of writing this text, is experiencing a regression in democratic values.[25] Not only is the separation of powers not

FIGURE 11.8. Message propagated through social network platforms in support of the rapper Valtonyc, who was convicted for insulting the Spanish monarchy and glorifying terrorism in the lyrics of his songs. He has been in exile since May 2018.

always respected, politicians and artists have been incarcerated or are in exile for political reasons ("Valtonyc, Hasel, La Insurgencia" 2018). Moreover, the widespread view that the anti-secessionist position is supported and guaranteed by the strength of the State plays down incentives for civic mobilization. Expressions in support of centralism have a reactive nature. Spanish flags are placed on those streets that were previously flooded with pro-independence Catalan flags, and demonstrations in support of Spain's unity have been organized where thousands of citizens have previously demonstrated in support of independence. Sovereignty generates enthusiasm, and enthusiasm triggers intense emotions.

The strong involvement of musical practices in the political events related to the Catalan sovereignty process testifies to music's political relevance. The soundtrack arising from these mobilizations is shaped by newly created musical compositions, appropriations, song parodies, hybrids (for example "The Reapers" by A Sound of Thunder and "Es tanzt ein Bi Ba Butzemann"). Pro-independence protests did not rely only on a well-defined musical genre such as "protest song" but instead mobilized a great diversity of styles.[26] This is a direct consequence of the social transversality of the sovereignist movement, of the massive involvement of the population, and the dense associative framework that characterizes Catalonia.[27] Social and political combativeness is expressed through diverse genres of popular and folk music and on the "art music" stages.

11. Catalonia vs Spain

The sequence of events that took place in Catalonia from 2017 to 2019 has powerfully contributed to the emergence of an emoscape that is equipped with its own affective and discursive canons and that will become part of Catalonia's "emotional archive" (Kenway and Fahey 2011, 190). In view of the sovereignist movement's firm commitment to music, it seems possible to speak of "musical mobilization" in this context and to recognize an entanglement of affects and discourses that have emerged through these mobilizations.

Notes

This research has been supported by the Spanish National R+D project FEM2016–77963-C2–1-P. An earlier version of this chapter was presented at the XV Congreso de la Sociedad de Etnomusicologia SIbE (Oviedo 2018).

1. See for instance Clarke, Hoggett, and Thompson (2006); Demertzis (2013); Thompson and Hoggett (2012); Wetherell et al., (2015).

2. See the documentary *20-S* directed by Lluís Arcarazo and Jaume Roures (2018). All the websites cited in this chapter were accessed in November 2022.

3. As is usual in political protests, social media has had a huge impact on mobilizations such as those in Catalonia. People launch campaigns and share calls for demonstrations and other forms of protest through social media, and share texts, images, and videos in the process.

4. I use "soundtrack" here in a metaphorical sense. In the same way that every film has its own soundtrack, the upheaval initiated in 2017 also had its particular soundscape in the form of music and/or other sonic expressions.

5. According to Gammerl, "emotional styles encompass the experience, fostering, and display of emotions, and oscillate between discursive patterns and embodied practices as well as between common scripts and specific appropriations" (2012, 163).

6. For more on *Nova Cançó* see Antoni Castells (2011).

7. The "Cant de la Senyera" ("Song of the Catalan Flag") was created in 1896 as the anthem of the *Orfeó Català*. It has also been used as a Catalan anthem, especially during the times in which "Els Segadors" was prohibited.

8. Since 1880, the Virolai has been the hymn of the Patron Saint of Catalonia, the Virgin of Montserrat. She is worshiped in the sanctuary of Montserrat, which has traditionally been considered an emblem of Catalan identity.

9. The *gralla* is a traditional double reed wind instrument.

10. This form of protest demonstration based on cadenced noise is a well-known practice in Europe. The so-called "charivari" is aimed at expressing negative critique through noise. It seems that the first *caceroladas* took place in France against the so-called July Monarchy in 1830 (Combis 2017). In this regard, see also Peñafiel (2015).

11. In the Spanish/Catalan conflict of 2017, yellow ribbons were used in public spaces to protest against the imprisonment of Catalan leaders.

12. For an example of *cacerolada* on September 20, 2017, in Barcelona see: https://www.youtube.com/watch?v=t4Sip1U_QmE.

13. On the role of songs in protests, see Dillane et al., (2018); Kutschke and Norton (2013); Lebrun (2009); Manabe (2016); and Martinelli (2017).

14. Following his exile from Francoist Spain in 1939, Casals began all of his concerts by playing this song. For several decades, the song has often been played in Catalonia, not only in concerts but also in ritual contexts where it is always associated with Catalan nationalism. On the concept of "emblematic song," see Martí (1995, 232–33); on the "Cant dels Ocells" as an emblematic song, see Martí (2000, 130–48).

15. At the end of a concert I attended in 2019, when "El Cant dels Ocells" was played, most of the auditorium stood up. I had never seen such a reaction to this song before. This demonstrates the relevance gained by this song during the course of the recent conflict.

16. The parody is based on "La moto," a popular festive song.

17. Based on the melody of "Auld Lang Syne" with lyrics by Robert Burns. The wide popularization of this song in Catalonia is due to the widespread Scout Movement, which traditionally uses this melody as a farewell song.

18. Freely translated the title as "Bye-bye," the song was composed in 1970 by the group *La Trinca*, one of the representatives of the *Nova Cançó* movement.

19. "Petits teutons" by Dani Gasulla. See https://www.youtube.com/watch?v=h4035x ETdpc.

20. In the Catalan festive tradition, the *castells*, which are recognized as Intangible Cultural Heritage of Humanity by UNESCO, are human towers that can reach a considerable height. Their performances are always accompanied by shawms (*gralles*) and drums (*tambors*).

21. The term "musical mobilization" refers to the idea of making all kinds of musical resources, including human resources (professional musicians or amateurs in the form of orchestras, choirs, bands, solo singers etc) and practices (for instance solidarity concerts, repertoire, new musical creations, etc.), work together at the service of a particular idea or ideology.

22. The *chirigotas* are humorous groups that perform satirical pieces, very often alluding to political issues. The Catalan secessionist movement was a recurring theme in the carnivals of 2018 and 2019. See for instance a *chirigota* at the Cádiz Carnival (2018) making fun of the former premier of the Catalan government Carles Puigdemont: https://www.youtube.com/watch?v=2S9nsA1ZRNc.

23. See Brew (2019).

24. In Spain the Republic is not only seen as a concrete form of state organization but also as a set of values. Among the "republican values" one could consider democracy, social equity, separation of powers, secularism, public goods, progress, and above all the abolition of the monarchy. Republicanism in Spain is commonly identified with the political left.

25. According to the World Economic Forum in its report of 2017, Spain is ranked 58 out of 137 countries for judicial independence, immediately after countries such as Kenya, Lithuania, and Botswana. See https://www3.weforum.org/docs/GCR2017–2018/05FullReport/TheGlobalCompetitivenessReport2017%E2%80%932018.pdf. According to Streck (2019), in response to the repression of pro-independence politicians in 2019, it is possible to say that "Spain is technically no longer a democracy."

26. "Protest song" is too limited a concept to characterize the use of music in protest. See Kutschke and Norton (2013, 125–26).

27. About associationism in Catalonia, see Giner (1984).

References

Anderson, Ben. 2009. "Affective Atmospheres." *Emotion, Space and Society* 2, no. 2: 77–81.

Arcarazo, Lluís and Jaume Roures, dirs. 2018. *20-S.* Barcelona: Mediapro. https://youtu.be/do5KQV5Qgow?t=5.

Brew, Joe. 2019. "The Demographic 'Tic Toc' and Catalonia's Independence." *Vilaweb*, May 17, 2019. https://english.vilaweb.cat/noticies/demographic-independence-joe-brew.

"Caceroladas en varias ciudades de Catalunya cierran una jornada de protesta contra la operación policial." 2017. *Público*, September 20, 2017. https://www.publico.es/politica/directo-catalunya-referendum-1o.html.

"Una campaña en las redes propone contrarrestar las caceroladas con el 'Mediterráneo' de Serrat." *Diario de León*, September 23, 2017. https://www.diariodeleon.es/noticias/espana/campana-redes-propone-contrarrestar-caceroladas-mediterraneo-serrat_1190108.html.

Castells, Antoni. 2011. "La Nova Cançó, Protest Song (Països Catalans)." In *Encyclopedia of Social Movement Media,* edited by John D. H. Downing, 293–95. Thousand Oaks, CA: Sage.

Clarke, Simon, Paul Hoggett, and Simon Thompson, eds. 2006. *Emotion, Politics, and Society.* New York: Palgrave Macmillan.

Clough, Patricia T., and Jean Halley, eds. 2007. *The Affective Turn: Theorizing the Social.* Durham, NC: Duke University Press.

Combis, Hélène. 2017. "De la Monarchie de juillet à François Fillon: Petite histoire de la casserole comme outil politique." *France Culture*, March 3, 2017. https://www.franceculture.fr/histoire/de-la-monarchie-de-juillet-francois-fillon-petite-histoire-de-la-casserole-comme-outil.

Connolly, William E. 2002. *Neuropolitics: Thinking, Culture, Speed.* Minneapolis: University of Minnesota Press.

Demertzis, Nicolas, ed. 2013. *Emotions in Politics: The Affect Dimension in Political Tension.* London: Palgrave Macmillan.

Dillane, Aileen, Martin Power, Eoin Devereux, and Amanda Haynes, eds. 2018. *Songs of Social Protest: International Perspectives.* London: Rowman & Littlefield.

Eisenberg, Andrew J. 2015. "Space." In *Keywords in Sound,* edited by David Novak and Matt Sakakeeny, 193–207. Durham, NC: Duke University Press.

Eyerman, Ron, and Andrew Jamison. 1998. *Music and Social Movements.* Cambridge: Cambridge University Press.

Fox, Nick J., and Pam Alldred. 2015. "New Materialist Social Inquiry: Designs, Methods and the Research-Assemblage." *International Journal of Social Research Methodology* 18, no. 4: 399–414.

Gammerl, Benno. 2012. "Emotional Styles: Concepts and Challenges." *Rethinking History* 16, no. 2: 161–75.

Giner, Salvador. 1984. *The Social Structure of Catalonia.* Sheffield, UK: The Anglo-Catalan Society.

Hancox, Dan, ed. 2011. *Fight Back! A Reader on the Winter of Protest.* London: Open Democracy.

Hart, Marjolein 't. 2016. "The Role of Humor in Protest Culture." In *Protest Cultures: A*

Companion, edited by Kathrin Fahlenbrach, Martin Klimke, and Joachim Scharloth, 198–200. New York: Berghahn Books.

Howes, David. 2005. "Introduction." In *Empire of the Senses: The Sensory Culture Reader*, edited by David Howes, 1–17. Oxford: Berg.

"I ara, la versió del 'Viva Puigdemont,' en corals i caramelles." 2018. *Nació/Digital*, April 15, 2018. https://www.naciodigital.cat/noticia/152795/video-ara-versio-viva-puigdemont -corals-caramelles.

"Katalonienkonflikt: Es tanzt ein Bi-Ba-Puigdemont." 2018. *Süddeutsche Zeitung*, April 13, 2018. https://www.sueddeutsche.de/panorama/katalonienkonflikt-es-tanzt-ein-bi -ba-puigdemont-1.3944332.

Kenway, Jane, and Johannah Fahey. 2011. "Getting Emotional about 'Brain Mobility.'" *Emotion, Space and Society* 4, no. 3: 187–94.

Kutschke, Beate, and Barley Norton, eds. 2013. *Music and Protest in 1968*. Cambridge: Cambridge University Press.

Lebrun, Barbara. 2009. *Protest Music in France: Production, Identity and Audiences*. Farnham, UK: Ashgate.

Manabe, Noriko. 2016. *The Revolution Will Not Be Televised: Protest Music After Fukushima*. Oxford: Oxford University Press.

Martí, Josep. 1995. "Ein emblematisches Lied aus l'Alguer (Sardinien)." In *Der Hahn im Korb. Allerneuesten Geschichten um Rolf W. Brednich*, edited by Gudrun Schwibbe and Ira Spieker, 229–34. Göttingen, DE: Schmerse.

———. 2000. *Más allá del arte: La música como generadora de realidades sociales*. Sant Cugat del Vallès, ES: Deriva.

———. 2018. "Not Without My Music: Music as a Social Fact." In *Making Music, Making Society*, edited by Josep Martí and Sara Revilla, 13–34. Newcastle, UK: Cambridge Scholars Publishing.

———. 2019a. "Beyond Representation: Relationality and Affect in Musical Practices." *Journal of Posthuman Studies* 3, no. 2: 159–80.

———. 2019b. "Sons i revolta a l'escenari polític català." *Quaderns de l'Institut Català d'Antropologia* 23, no. 2: 80–98.

Martinelli, Dario. 2017. *Give Peace a Chant: Popular Music, Politics and Social Protest*. Cham, CH: Springer.

Massumi, Brian. 1996. "The Autonomy of Affect." In *Deleuze: A Critical Reader*, edited by Paul Patton, 217–40. Oxford: Basil Blackwell.

Peñafiel, Ricardo. 2015. "Le sens des casseroles: Charivaris, cacerolazos et création d'espaces publics transgressifs dans et par le bruit." *Cahiers des imaginaires* 11: 9–28.

Saldanha, Arun. 2009. "Music is Force." *Massachusetts Review* 50, no. 1–2: 70–80.

Serrat, Joan Manuel. 2017. "Prefereixo passar por que vergonya." Interview by N. Martorell. *El Periódico*, September 26, 2017. https://www.elperiodico.cat/ca/oci-i-cultura/ 20170926/entrevista-joan-manuel-serrat-referendum-independencia-catalunya -6310863.

Streck, Ralf. 2019. "Spanien ist technisch gesehen keine Demokratie mehr." *Telepolis*, May 25, 2019. https://www.heise.de/tp/features/Spanien-ist-technisch-gesehen-keine -demokratie-mehr-4432063.html.

Thompson, Simon, and Paul Hoggett. 2012. *Politics and the Emotions: The Affective Turn in Contemporary Political Studies*. New York: Bloomsbury Academic.

"Valtonyc, Hasel, La Insurgencia, Strawberry y otra treintena de condenas por enaltecimiento desde 2016." *Público*, March 3, 2018. https://www.publico.es/sociedad/enaltecimiento-terrorismo-strawberry-valtonyc-hasel-insurgencia-treintena-condenas-enaltecimiento-2016.html.

Wetherell, Margaret, Tim McCreanor, Alex McConville, Helen Moewaka Barnes, and Jade le Grice. 2015. "Settling Space and Covering the Nation: Some Conceptual Considerations in Analysing Affect and Discourse." *Emotion, Space and Society* 16: 56–64.

Wood, Nichola. 2004. "Taking the Nation to Heart: A Musical Exploration of the Role and Significance of Emotional Geographies in the (Re)production of Scottish National Identities." PhD diss., University of Edinburgh.

PART IV

Musical Heritagization and the State

12

Intangible Cultural Heritage and State Regimes in Portugal and Spain

SALWA EL-SHAWAN CASTELO-BRANCO
AND CRISTINA SÁNCHEZ-CARRETERO

Introduction

Heritage is ubiquitous in the late-modern world. It is a product of modernity as well as one of the main producing factors of modernity (Harrison 2013; Santamarina Campos 2013). Existing heritage regimes illustrate a shift from political projects based on distinction and the creation of national identities to economic projects linked to transnational capital: from a nation-building project to national identities to be consumed (Comaroff and Comaroff 2009; Santamarina Campos and Mármol 2017, 365). In this chapter, we map UNESCO's Intangible Cultural Heritage (ICH) trajectories in Portugal and Spain using the concept of heritage regime(s) to understand these trajectories.

The idea of "heritage regime" is well established in studies on heritage (Bendix, Eggert, and Peselmann 2012; Coombe and Weiss 2015; De Cesari 2012; Geismar 2015; Hafstein 2012; Sánchez-Carretero 2012). Critical heritage scholars have mobilized the concept of "regime(s)" as an analytical tool for understanding the politics of heritage and the multiple ways in which heritage intersects with "government" in the broader sense of Foucauldian governmentality (Foucault 1979). Heritage politics are also closely linked to the framework of an "international heritage regime" promoted by UNESCO. The concepts, principles, norms, and procedures outlined in UNESCO's conventions have reshaped state heritage regimes throughout the world, affecting heritage policies and their implementation and creating "a strong de facto alliance between national and international actors" (De Cesari 2012, 400–401).

Understanding heritage as a regime places emphasis on the system of ordered procedures and bureaucracy (Sánchez-Carretero et al., 2019). The Foucauldian idea of a regime of truth can be applied to the heritage field, with the understanding that "each society has its truth regime, its 'general policy' of truth" (Foucault 1977, 14). This truth regime is constituted by the mechanisms, techniques, and procedures that maintain the political, economic, and institutional status of those who are charged with saying what counts as truth (13–14). In the last decade, analyses of heritage governmentality have focused on the tools that are used to register and regulate heritage regimes: inventories, files, and other technologies of heritage bureaucracy (Hafstein 2009; Tauschek 2015) as well as the mechanisms by which expert knowledge is legitimized (De Cesari 2012; Mármol and Santamarina Campos 2019; Kirshenblatt-Gimblett 2004).

Heritage praxis has been central in ethnomusicology through institutional work, community engagement, and critical reflection (Diamond and Castelo-Branco 2021, 8–13; Howard 2012; Norton and Matsumoto 2019). In the Iberian Peninsula as elsewhere, ethnomusicologists and anthropologists have documented, safeguarded, and disseminated music heritage, founded and managed sound and audiovisual archives, museums, and research centers, and engaged in repatriating sound recordings to communities of origin and advocating for their cultural rights. Many have contributed to shaping, implementing, and evaluating state and international heritage regimes and to heritagizing local music practices. Recent debates in ethnomusicology have focused on the sustainability of musical heritage and the ethics and politics of heritage praxis (Seeger and Schippers 2022; Schippers and Grant 2016). Drawing on a critical reading of the interdisciplinary literature on cultural heritage, in this chapter we discuss state and international heritage regimes in democratic Portugal and Spain as technologies of heritage bureaucracy prior to and following the implementation of UNESCO's ICH paradigm. In so doing, we illustrate how heritage regimes, and the act of safeguarding national music heritage, serve the goals of the State and, in the process, flatten out local musical diversity.

UNESCO's 2003 Convention for the Safeguarding of the Intangible Cultural Heritage

UNESCO was founded in 1945 in the aftermath of World War II with the mission of contributing to "peace and security by promoting collaboration among the

12. Intangible Cultural Heritage and State Regimes

nations through education, science and culture" (UNESCO 2020, 6). It furthers its goals through programs, projects, and conventions that forge and define concepts and set standards and procedures to which signatory states are legally bound. As the "key location of heritage politics today" (De Cesari 2012, 401), UNESCO's concepts, programs, and conventions have been influential in many member states, including Portugal and Spain, anchoring "authorized heritage discourse,"[1] national and regional cultural policies, and heritage governance.

UNESCO's 2003 Convention was partly modelled on the 1972 Convention Concerning the Protection of World Cultural and Natural Heritage (WCNH), which defined and promoted the idea of heritage as a universal concern. It charged "States-Parties" with the responsibility of identifying and preserving iconic natural and cultural properties of "outstanding universal value" and established a listing mechanism. The impetus for the 2003 Convention came from countries in the Global South that sought to "counterbalance the Eurocentric, monumentalist and materialist bias of the WCNH with an alternative conception of cultural heritage" (Hafstein 2018, 135). The 2003 Convention was catalyzed by its predecessor, the "Proclamation of the Masterpieces of the Oral and Intangible Heritage of Humanity" (2001, 2003, and 2005), a program that aimed to raise awareness of oral and intangible heritage (Aikawa-Faure 2009). Representing a major shift from "territorial definitions," materiality, and exceptionalism, the 2003 Convention positions ICH practices and expressions "in relation to communities rather than places" (Bortolloto 2017, 46). The Convention designates communities as the main authorities for the definition, safeguarding, and management of their practices: "intangible cultural heritage means the practices, representations, knowledge, skills—as well as the instruments, objects, artefacts and cultural spaces associated therewith—that communities, groups, and in some cases individuals recognize as part of their cultural heritage" (UNESCO 2022, Article 2). As pointed out by Valdimar Hafstein (2014, 50), the lack of a definition of communities "positioned squarely as collective subjects within states and subject to states" renders their empowerment problematic, and the participatory principle is often hampered by bureaucracy, by culture brokers, and by the paradox inherent in the Convention as an international treaty between UNESCO and state governments.

Certification as ICH is made through the approval of proposals for inscription on the Representative List of the Intangible Cultural Heritage of Humanity, or the List of Intangible Cultural Heritage in Need of Urgent Safeguarding. Additional recognition is given through the Register for Good Safeguarding Practices. The problems inherent in making lists and in their uses have been extensively discussed (Hafstein 2018, 53–89). To date, the 2003 Convention has been ratified by 175 "States-Parties" and is considered one of UNESCO's most successful programs. UNESCO's ICH paradigm and its impact on heritage discourse, cultural policies, state bureaucracies, and communities of practice has been diverse and is the focus of a multidisciplinary critical reflection that informs our analytical perspective.

Heritage Regimes in Democratic Portugal and Spain Prior to UNESCO's 2003 Convention

Spain

Spain ratified UNESCO's 2003 Convention in 2006 and, from that moment, the terminology of "intangible heritage" (*patrimonio inmaterial*) has been widely adopted in Spanish policy. Before 2006, the categories "ethnological" or "ethnographic" heritage were already included in the Spanish Historical Heritage Law of 1985 and the heritage laws of the autonomous governments and are terms that remain in use. The 1985 law was the first to implement the specific categories of "tradition" or "folklore" under the umbrella term "Ethnographic Heritage," per Law 16/1985, Title IV, Articles 46 and 47 (Ley 16/1985). However, the safeguarding of festivals started in 1931, during the Spanish Second Republic, when the *Misteri d'Elx* was declared a "National Monument"[2] (Carrera Díaz 2015, 138). In the legislative documents prior to the 1985 law, expressions such as "folkloric," "picturesque," or "typical" were employed.[3] The 1985 law established three levels of protection: 1) unregistered assets; 2) assets with medium level of protection; and 3) the highest level of protection to those elements or practices declared assets of cultural interest (or in Spanish, *bien de interés cultural*, BIC). This law granted to the central government the competence to declare BIC and established that "the assets that make up the Spanish Historical Heritage declared of cultural interest by ministry of this Law or by Royal Decree on an individual basis will enjoy singular protection and guardianship," per Law 16/1985, Article 9.1 (Ley 16/1985). Galicia, Catalonia, and the Basque Country presented appeals to the Spanish Constitutional Court, which in 1991 ruled against the central government and granted to each of the autonomous governments the ability to inscribe heritage assets as BIC (Carrera Díaz 2015; González Cambeiro 2016; Plata García 2017). Many competences have been transferred to the autonomies, which vary depending on the community, but which all follow the constitution and state laws. In relation to heritage legislation, all autonomous communities[4] follow the state law but also have their own laws approved by their autonomous ruling bodies. In addition to the protection categories mentioned above, some regional legislations include specific ICH measures. Andalusia has been a pioneer in these measures and instituted the

12. Intangible Cultural Heritage and State Regimes   231

policy instrument "Place of Ethnological Interest," which appears in the 1991 Andalusian Historic Heritage Law. Places of Ethnological Interest are defined as "places, spaces, constructions or installations linked to ways of life, culture, activities or modes of production related to the people of Andalusia and that deserve to be preserved because of its relevant ethnological value" (Ley 1/1991). According to anthropologist Gema Carrera Díaz (2015, 141–42), it is important to keep in mind the sometimes conflicting relationship between the state law and the laws of the autonomous communities. The first heritage law at the autonomous level was enacted by Castilla-La Mancha in Law 4/1990, May 30, of the Historic Heritage of Castilla-La Mancha (Ley 4/1990), and it is the only one that does not include any mention of ethnological or ethnographic heritage. Following the UNESCO Convention, however, the term ICH was included in its 2013 law (Ley 4/2013). The Basque Country, Andalusia, and the Balearic Islands followed a holistic approach in their regional laws, mentioning "tangible and intangible" assets. Catalonia, on the other hand, opted for two different laws: one dedicated to cultural heritage, Law 9/1993, September 30 (Ley 9/1993), and one dedicated to traditional culture, Law 2/1993, March 5 (Ley 2/1993). The first distinguishes between "tangible and intangible" assets, while the second focuses on "traditional and popular culture," defined as "manifestations of the life and collective memory of Catalonia, past and present" (Carrera Díaz 2015, 141).

Regarding musical heritage specifically, Article 49.1 of the 1985 Spanish Historical Heritage Law mentions "any other graphic, sound or image expression, collected on any type of material support" (Ley 16/1985). In addition, discs and audiovisual materials are also included in Article 50 (Gembero Ustárroz 2005, 146). The competences in terms of musical heritage are implemented according to the laws of the autonomous communities. In some cases, the concrete recordings were protected using the BIC category. For instance, in 1999 the sound recordings of the flamenco singer La Niña de los Peines were declared assets of cultural interest by the Andalusian Government.[5]

Portugal

Portugal ratified UNESCO's 2003 Convention for the Safeguarding of the Intangible Cultural Heritage in 2008. Since then, the letter and spirit of the Convention have been adapted to cultural heritage legislation. An administrative structure has been set up in central government to implement the convention's requirements, and ICH (*património cultural imaterial*) has become part of the local "authorized heritage discourse" (Smith 2006).

Prior to the implementation of UNESCO's "international heritage regime," a "state heritage regime" was configured by successive government administrations following the 1974 revolution that enabled the transition to democracy. This state regime prioritized safeguarding and valorizing cultural heritage as one of the pillars of national identity and created an administrative apparatus for its governance. At the same time, following the establishment of democracy, the grassroots associative movement expanded considerably, especially at the local level, and played an important role in the boom of heritage practices and other cultural activities (Castelo-Branco, Lima, and Neves 2003). According to a survey conducted in 1998 by a research team from the Ethnomusicology Institute of the NOVA University of Lisbon, more than 70 percent of traditional music and dance groups active in that year were founded following 1974 (2003).

The state heritage regime has been designed, implemented, and regulated through a three-tiered administrative structure: central government and its regional delegations, local municipalities, and the autonomous regions of the Azores and Madeira. The central government is the main governing body that enacts national legislation and sustains an institutional structure that ensures governance throughout the territory. The regulation of "cultural" activities, including heritage, at the national level is largely the responsibility of the Ministry of Culture or State Secretariat of Culture and its regional delegations. Local governance is exercised by municipalities that are responsible for development, education, culture, and the quality of life of their population. Since democracy, municipalities have played a crucial role in sustaining heritage practices by sponsoring voluntary associations that support folklore and choral groups, civil wind bands, and local festivities, among other activities. Since 1995, public spending on culture by municipal governments in continental Portugal exceeded that of central government (Santos et al., 1998, 94–100; 109–10), a tendency that continues to this day (Garcia et al., 2020, 52–56).[6] In many cases, municipalities spearheaded proposals to inscribe ICH practices on the national inventory or on one of UNESCO's lists (see below). Regional governments in Madeira and the Azores enjoy full autonomy in the exercise of legislative and executive powers in all domains, including heritage.

The 1976 constitution, the first in democratic Portugal, and its subsequent revisions consecrated the State's obligation to "preserve, defend and value the cultural heritage of the Portuguese people" (Articles 73 and 78). Moreover, the first constitutional government (1976–1977) set as one of its priorities "inventorying, classifying, conserving and defending cultural heritage" (Santos et al., 1998, 67). In 1975, a General Directorate for Cultural Heritage—GDCH (Direcção-Geral do Património Cultural)—was institutionalized in the State Secretariat for Culture (Decree-Law 409/75). It was succeeded by the Portuguese Institute of Cultural Heritage (Instituto Português do Património Cultural, IPPC) that

12. Intangible Cultural Heritage and State Regimes

functioned between 1980 and 1990 (Decree-Law 59/80). This was the first public institution dedicated to the study, classification, and preservation of cultural heritage. It included departments of musicology, and ethnology, museums, "movable heritage," and "intangible heritage" (Decree-Law 216/90). The Musicology Department, initially part of the GDCH, gathered dispersed manuscript collections of Portuguese music from the eighteenth to the twentieth centuries, sound recordings, and musical instruments. It also promoted the restoration of musical instruments and launched a publication series (Brissos 2010, 644). The National Institute for Worker's Leisure Time (Instituto Nacional para o Aproveitamento dos Tempos Livres dos Trabalhadores, INATEL), a governmental institution that succeeded the Estado Novo's National Foundation for Joy at Work (Fundação Nacional de Alegria no Trabalho, FNAT), was reconfigured in 1975. One of its activities has been the regulation of, and financial and technical support for, amateur folklore groups and civil wind bands. The INATEL is also one of four accredited Portuguese NGOs acting in an advisory capacity to UNESCO's Intergovernmental Committee for ICH, the other three being the Centro em Rede de Investigação em Antropologia (an inter-university research center in anthropology), the Cultural Cooperative Memória Imaterial, International Association of Paremiology, and the Portuguese Folklore Federation.

Central government enacted three "Basic Laws" for cultural heritage (Lei de Bases do Património Cultural 1985, 2001, and 2009) and created institutional structures for its governing. The first legal framework for regulating heritage was enacted in 1985 (Decree-Law 13/1985). It defined cultural heritage as consisting of "all tangible and intangible goods that, because of their acknowledged value, should be considered of relevant interest for the continuity and identity of Portuguese culture through time" (Article 1). Although intangible heritage (previously used as a label by the IPPC) is not defined in this legislation, Article 43 refers to the State's duty to protect the Portuguese language and its "cultural, ethnological, and ethnographic values"; to "revitalize and preserve popular cultural traditions that are threatened to disappear"; and to "promote the collection, preservation, and popular fruition of photographic, filmic, phonographic, and other domains of intangible cultural heritage" (Article 43). Despite their importance, the measures enunciated in the first legislative framework for ICH were not carried out as the decree laws were not regulated (Santos et al., 1998, 85; Marques 2018, 107).[7]

In the 1990s, the IPPC was replaced by several institutions with shared and overlapping responsibilities, focusing mostly on inventorying, classifying, and safeguarding monuments and artifacts. The Portuguese Institute of Museums (Instituto Português de Museus, IPM), founded in 1991, to which the government attributed the technical and administrative responsibility of all museums, included ICH in its administrative structure (Division of Inventory, Classification and Safeguarding of Movable and Immaterial Heritage—Divisão de Inventário, Classificação e Salvaguarda do Património Móvel e Imaterial). However, there were no reported activities in this domain nor reference to ICH until the founding of the Institute of Museums and Conservation (Instituto de Museus e Conservação, IMC) in 2007, a lacuna that is attributed to the lack of human resources and to the assumption that issues pertaining to ICH would be dealt with by the National Museum of Ethnology (Costa 2018, 37–38).

In 2001, a new "Basic Law" (107/2001) was published that established the policy and regime for the protection and valorization of cultural heritage: "Intangible goods constituting structuring segments of Portuguese identity and collective memory" integrate the definition of cultural heritage (Article 2.4). Published two years prior to UNESCO's 2003 Convention, this "Basic Law" did not consider the programs promoted by UNESCO such as the Masterpieces of Oral and Intangible Culture of Humanity nor the ICH legislation adopted in Brazil and some regions of Spain (Costa 2015, 184). Based on the 1985 law, only Articles 91 and 92 of the 2001 law define ICH as encompassing "orally transmitted culture and traditional modes of doing" of local communities and refer to the need to register, preserve, valorize, and certify ICH. Reference to the ICH of "ethnic minorities" in this law and its updated versions published in 2009 and 2015 is an innovative and significant step towards a diverse and inclusive perspective on heritage (2015). This law provided the legislative framework that enabled the inscription of the Cape Verdean ritual known as Kola San Jon (KSJ), practiced by Cape Verdean immigrants in the Cova da Moura neighborhood near Lisbon, on the National Inventory of ICH (NIICH), Matriz PCI, in 2013. The inscription contributed to the revitalization of what was seen as a rundown and problematic neighborhood, a geographic and human space that is intrinsic to KSJ, that the municipality had planned to demolish and to the "'reclassification' of Cape Verdean and Portuguese identities within a post-colonial context" (Miguel and Sardo 2014).[8]

Heritage Regimes following UNESCO's 2003 Convention: The ICH Paradigm

Spain

From 2008 to 2020, Spain obtained 20 inscriptions: 17 cultural practices and expressions of ICH inscribed on UNESCO's Representative List of the Intangible Cultural Heritage of Humanity (ICH List), and three on the Register of

12. Intangible Cultural Heritage and State Regimes 235

Good Safeguarding Practices (RGSP).[9] Globally, Spain has a strong record of inscriptions, holding the fifth position after China (35), France (22), Japan (22), and the Republic of Korea (21). Five of the ICH List inscriptions involve other countries: the Mediterranean diet; falconry; the art of dry-stone walling; summer solstice festivals in the Pyrenees; and the ceramics of Talavera in Puebla, Tlaxcala, Talavera de la Reina, and El Puente del Arzobispo.

Alongside these multinational inscriptions, Spain has a successful track record of single inscriptions, which are related to music in different ways: *tamborradas* (drum playing); the festivity of "la Mare de Déu"; the chant of the Sybil on the island of Majorca; flamenco; human towers; the whistled language of the island of La Gomera (Canary Islands); the Mystery Play of Elche; and the Patum de Berga. Others are also related to music, such as the patios of Cordoba ("the patios also host traditional singing, flamenco guitar playing, and dancing"[10]) and the Fallas in Valencia where marching bands parade the streets.[11] Only two of the individual inscriptions on the list, the irrigators' tribunals of the Spanish Mediterranean coast and the Wine Horses of Caravaca, are not in any way related to music. Following the 2003 Convention, the ICH paradigm has developed into a model that is framed by the 2015 national law of ICH (Law 10/2015 of Intangible Cultural Heritage Safeguarding). The ideas embedded in this law differ from the Convention's premises both from a legislative point of view and from the perspective of cultural diversity. From a legislative point of view, the category *patrimonio inmaterial* has been adopted in place of *patrimonio etnológico*. The adjective "ethnologic" continues to be applied to the type of heritage (in addition to archaeological heritage or industrial heritage), while *inmaterial* applies to specific safeguarding measures. From the point of view of cultural diversity, as anthropologist Gema Carrera Díaz explains, since the 2015 law there has been a shift to "supraterritoriality" (2015, 166–68). In other words, with this law the Spanish State Administration regained the competence to make declarations, which had been withdrawn in 1991.

In 2015, the legal tool "Representative Manifestations of ICH" (*Manifestación Representativa del Patrimonio Cultural Inmaterial*) was created. Through this tool, the "intangible" is understood as a lack of materiality, distinct from the notion of "intangible" as processual and holistic that is in the spirit of the Convention. The tool also moves away from the Convention regarding cultural diversity. While the Convention seeks to preserve diversity, the 2015 law seeks to promote a deterritorialization effect looking for common elements "in favor of a renewed Spanish nationalism" (166). Here, the term "deterritorialization drive" is useful as it refers to the move away from anchoring nominations in concrete practices and communities of practices. The logic that lies beneath the "deterritorialization drive" of the ICH nominations can be summarized as follows: if a "common ICH heritage" can be established in different territories of Spain (autonomous communities), a common "culture" can be demonstrated and, therefore, a common nation—instead of a single state with different nations—that transcends the division of autonomous communities. It is not a coincidence that the *Semana Santa* (Holy Week celebrations), for instance, was declared Spanish National ICH Representative Manifestation in 2017, during a time when the conservative government of Partido Popular (Popular Party) was seeking further re-centralization of the State. The deterritorialization drive can be easily exemplified by the *tamborrada* and the flamenco UNESCO ICH List inscriptions or the recently created Spanish national category of "Representative Manifestation of the ICH." For the first time, in April 2017, three cultural practices were regarded as part of the "common" Spanish culture during Mariano Rajoy's right-wing presidency. It was the first time that the 2015 ICH law applied this specific instrument. In 2017, the *Semana Santa* was declared as a national ICH (Real Decreto 384/2017, April 8, 2017) together with the *Trashumancia* (Real Decreto 385/2017), and Carnival (Real Decreto 383/2017).

These inscriptions created a lot of controversy in the media as well as in parliament. They were criticized as an attempt to homogenize Spanish culture without stressing cultural diversity. Moreover, these controversies emerged immediately following the creation of a specific law to protect bullfighting. Literally, the law was entitled "Law to regulate bullfighting as cultural heritage" (Law 18/2013, November 12),[12] in response to the Catalan prohibition of bullfighting in 2010. The instrumentalization of ICH as an ideological tool in this context is marked by the following key events: first, Catalan Act 28/2010 declared illegal bullfighting that ended in the death of the bulls; three years later, the Spanish Act 18/2013 for the protection of bullfighting as Cultural Heritage was created; and finally, the Constitutional Court Sentence (October 20, 2016) declared null and void Article 1 of the Catalan Act 28/2010. This sentence used the Spanish National Act 18/2013 and the 2015 Intangible Heritage Law as justification to declare the Catalan Act unconstitutional. The right-wing Partido Popular appealed Act 28/2010, which prohibited bullfights in Catalonia. Six years later, the Constitutional Court (Judgment 177/2016) upheld the appeal on the grounds of competence (Mulà 2018). Leaving aside implications in terms of animal rights and respect of so-called "universal values" (Bronner 2005; Kapchan 2014) that are embedded in the bullfighting/anti-bullfighting controversy, we want to stress the political implications in terms of state nationalism and heritagization.

In addition to the 2015 Spanish ICH law and the inscription processes, the post-2003 Convention paradigm is clearly exemplified in Spain in the "National

12. Intangible Cultural Heritage and State Regimes 237

Plan of Safeguarding of Intangible Cultural Heritage."[13] The Spanish National Institute of Cultural Heritage (IPCE) centralized its lines of action in different national plans. In 2015, a specific plan dedicated to ICH was implemented. This plan includes the main ideas of the 2003 UNESCO ICH Convention: the interconnection between the tangible and the intangible dimensions; the focus on ICH as a social process, its dynamic quality, and sensorial features; and the importance of safeguarding as opposed to "conservation" models to avoid fossilizing effects.

Portugal

Following Portugal's ratification of the 2003 Convention in 2008, a new heritage regime grounded on UNESCO's ICH paradigm was enacted, including legislation, bureaucracies, inventories, and other procedures.[14] In preparation for the ratification process, in 2007 an institutional structure for governing ICH was carved out in the Ministry of Culture, initially at the ICH Department of the Institute of Museums and Conservation (Instituto de Museus e Conservação, IMC) which replaced the Instituto Português de Museus (IPM). This department established the policy and course of action for ICH and for museums, filling the gap that followed the extinction of the IPPC in 1990 (Costa 2013, 93; Costa 2018, 23–24). Ethnographic museums, under the tutelage of the IMC, played an important role in safeguarding ICH. Most important, the National Museum of Ethnology, founded in 1965, houses significant collections of cultural and an audiovisual archive focusing on Portugal and its former colonies (Costa 2013, 4). Since 2012, the responsibility for ICH was transferred to the Division of Immovable, Movable, and Intangible Heritage (Divisão do Património Imóvel, Móvel e Imaterial) of the General Directorate of Heritage (Direcção Geral do Património Cultural), a complex State machine where ICH's visibility and activities became centered on the management of the National Inventory of ICH (NIICH), which was again transferred to the Ethnology Museum in 2015 (Costa 2018, 65–67, 79–80).

ICH legislation, norms, and procedures were enacted in articulation with the Basic Heritage Laws decreed since 2001 (Costa 2013, 93–94). Decree-Law 139/2009 updated in Decree-Law 149/2015 establishes the legal framework and safeguarding measures for ICH, defines its domains according to the terms of Article 2.2 of the 2003 Convention, and highlights its diversity and importance for the collective identity and memory of communities and groups. This legislation also institutionalized a publicly accessible National Inventory (NIICH)[15] launched in 2011 as the authorizing mechanism for the legal protection and safeguarding of ICH practices and as a prerequisite for applications for inscription on UNESCO's ICH lists. Similarly, the Regional Government of the Azores launched an ICH Regional Inventory in 2011. Since the establishment of the NIICH, there has been a rush to inscribe local cultural practices by municipalities and other stakeholders, especially those located in sparsely populated or economically debilitated areas that regard national and, more important, UNESCO's certification as a seal of quality that can increase visibility and attract tourism. Although the definition of ICH in the above-mentioned Portuguese legislation, based on UNESCO's 2003 Convention, is all-encompassing (including "oral expressions and traditions," "artistic expression and performance," as well as "social, ritual, and festive practices"), its application has been somewhat restrictive. Moreover, definitions of ICH seem to be predicated on ideologies of authenticity that informed the documentation and research of rural musics by folklorists, ethnographers, and collectors throughout a good part of the twentieth century. For example, representations by folklore groups of local practices of music and dance, widespread throughout Portugal, are not considered eligible for inclusion within the category of ICH and therefore do not qualify for inscription on the NIICH (Costa 2013, 100). Decree-Laws 139/2009 and 149/2015 acknowledge the significance of ICH for the "internationalization of Portuguese culture," a tacit recognition of its potential in the branding and tourist promotion of the country which, as we argue, has been one of the driving forces for the rush for inscriptions on the national inventory and on UNESCO's ICH lists. In addition to central government, the Regional Directorates for Culture (Direcções Regionais de Cultura) are responsible for implementing ICH legislation at the regional level, promoting the inventorying of ICH, and liaising with the central government. Municipalities also play a central role in supporting, valorizing, and safeguarding ICH and have spearheaded applications to the NIICH and UNESCO lists.

Finally, the Portuguese National Commission of UNESCO, based at the Ministry of Foreign Affairs, is another important actor in the governmentalized ICH arena. Its mission is to promote the implementation of UNESCO's goals and conventions in Portugal. In the domain of ICH, the Commission acts as a regulator and facilitator, providing technical assistance in the preparation of applications for inscription on UNESCO's lists and submitting validated applications to UNESCO on behalf of the Portuguese government. This work is carried out in collaboration with a working group of experts from the General Directorate for Cultural Heritage and three of the four Portuguese NGOs accredited by UNESCO's ICH Intergovernmental Committee (Costa 2018, 108). In Portugal, nine cultural practices were inscribed in the years leading up to 2021: six on the ICH List and two on the Urgent Safeguarding list. Out of the six included on the ICH List, two are related to music (fado and Cante Alentejano), two are

12. Intangible Cultural Heritage and State Regimes 239

transnational initiatives (Mediterranean diet and falconry), one is related to crafts (Estremoz clay figures), and three are festivities that include music and dance (winter festivities, Carnival of Podence, and the Community Festivities in Campo Maior). Those included on the Urgent Safeguarding list also deal with crafts (Bisalhães black pottery manufacturing process and manufacture of cowbells).

UNESCO's ICH paradigm, adopted by States Parties like Portugal, is implemented within a "highly politicized web of relations," which includes government institutions, research centers, museums, grassroots associations, the media, communities, tradition custodians, other stakeholders, and scholars (Santos and Muller 2011, 208). As De Cesari points out, "despite the participatory rhetoric, it is experts who are given the main role in UNESCO's policies and, therefore, have a lot of power in their implementation" (2012, 409). In Portugal, the regulation of ICH legislation specifies training in anthropology as a prerequisite for the study and documentation of ICH.[16] The elaboration of ICH legislation and the conception and management of the NIICH were entrusted to an anthropologist who has led the process since its inception.[17] The documentation, research, and safeguarding plan required for inscription on the NIICH or on UNESCO's ICH lists have been primarily carried out by anthropologists, ethnomusicologists, and other scholars in collaboration with communities of practice, who have become important players in the "chain of mediations" (Sandroni 2010, 386) that the implementation of UNESCO's ICH paradigm entails.[18] This work, carried out individually or by teams affiliated with research centers based at universities, has involved defining and sometimes labelling the object of heritagization; circumscribing and mobilizing communities of practice that, in some cases, are geographically dispersed and belong to different generations and social groups; conducting surveys and interviews with custodians of tradition (performance groups, individuals); locating and digitalizing extant audiovisual and written documentation; mediating between communities of practice, institutions, associations, and other stakeholders; and documenting and disseminating heritage practices in academic and non-academic circles, among many other activities.

The role of scholars in heritage making as researchers, advocates, and mediators poses epistemological, methodological, and ethical challenges. As recent publications have shown, each heritagization process has had its motivations, history, politics, institutional and individual actors, and challenges, often entailing both agreement and conflict (Abreu 2014; Castelo-Branco 2022 and in this volume; Costa 2015; Durand et al., 2018; Miguel and Sardo 2014; Miguel 2016; Patrix 2015; Pestana and Barriga 2019; Pestana and Oliveira 2017). The outcomes have also been very diverse and need to be systematically evaluated.

Conclusion

Since the 1970s, UNESCO has played a central role in forging and defining key concepts such as heritage and intangible cultural heritage, in promoting the idea of heritage as a universal concern, and in fostering safeguarding at national and international levels. UNESCO's concepts, programs, and conventions are influential in many member states, including Portugal and Spain, anchoring cultural policies and catalyzing safeguarding initiatives.

Both Iberian countries share similarities and differences regarding the implementation and management of the ICH paradigm and its repercussions. In both countries, as elsewhere, the adoption of the ICH paradigm has produced more governmentality, expanding the institutional dimension of the state, sometimes triggering friction and conflict (De Cesari 2012, 407). These effects go against the agency attributed to communities by the 2003 UNESCO Convention. While heritage legislation and management in Portugal is largely in the hands of central government, the Spanish State delegates much of this responsibility to the autonomous communities, each having its own laws and policies. In both Iberian countries, the label of ICH was adopted in academic and public discourse on expressive practices that were previously categorized as "folklore," "ethnographic," "popular," and "traditional." It includes under one label a diversity of local, regional, national, and transnational genres, expressive practices, and knowledge. An "ideologically grounded symbolic construct" (Castelo-Branco 2013, 661), ICH and, more broadly, heritage have been used as political instruments to emphasize unity or difference within and between communities and practices, to create new identifications and reinforce existing ones, to provide legal protection, and to certify local products with a seal of quality that increases their value as commodities in the global tourist and popular music markets (Jiménez-Esquinas and Sánchez-Carretero 2018). As a "body of ideas and practices," UNESCO's international heritage discourse is deeply entangled with the "logics of the nation-state," creating a tension that is highlighted by the notion of regime (De Cesari 2012, 400).

In Portugal and Spain, the expressive practices and traditional knowledge that have been certified as ICH are diverse, yet music is one of the common elements that defines many nominations in these countries, as exemplified with the cases of flamenco (see Chapter 14), fado, and Cante Alentejano (see Chapter 13), as well as other festivals and practices of which music is a part. Another common element between Portuguese and Spanish ICH regimes is the interlink between political and economic purposes. The policies, institutional structures, and funding allocated to heritage and to the culture sector more broadly have been con-

12. Intangible Cultural Heritage and State Regimes

ditioned by the ideologies and policies of the political parties in power and the priorities of decision makers. In general, the institutional structure that governs heritage has been unstable, understaffed, and underfunded, often undermining the implementation of cultural policies and the continuity of activities.

Finally, we would like to emphasize that state and international heritage regimes have left an indelible mark on the ideas—as well as the social, political, and economic relations—affecting the revitalization, reinterpretation, and sustainability of expressive practices embedded in the label "intangible cultural heritage." Maybe the safeguarding processes of the heritage regime(s) might indeed bring the destruction of the same cultural practices these regimes intend to protect. However, many domains of expressive practice in Portugal and Spain continue to mobilize memory embodied through poetry, music, dance, costume, ritual, and other expressive modes.

Notes

The contribution of Sánchez-Carretero to this publication is part of the project "HabitPAT. Los cuidados del patrimonio" (PID2020–118696RB-I00) funded by MCIN/AEI/ 10.13039/501100011033.

1. Coined by Australian heritage scholar Laurajane Smith, the term "authorized heritage discourse" refers to the "dominant Western discourse about heritage [. . .] that works to naturalize a range of assumptions about the nature and meaning of heritage" (2006, 6).

2. Spain's *Mystery Play of Elche*, a liturgical theatrical performance that harks back to the Middle Ages, was proclaimed by UNESCO as one of the Masterpieces of the Oral and Intangible Heritage of Humanity in 2001 and incorporated in the ICH representative list in 2008.

3. Gema Carrera Díaz's PhD dissertation (2015) offers a detailed overview of the Spanish national and regional context of the legislative bodies applied to intangible heritage, with a particular focus on Andalusian legislation. Sara González Cambeiro's doctoral dissertation (2016) is also dedicated to Spanish ICH legislation and management.

4. After Franco's death in 1975 and the end of the dictatorship, the Constitution of 1978 established the autonomous communities as the first-level political and administrative division. Spain is not a federal country. It has a central government and a territorial administration known as the "State of the Autonomies."

5. See https://www.boe.es/diario_boe/txt.php?id=BOE-A-1999–17359.

6. According to *Council of Europe/ERICarts, Compendium of Cultural Policies and Trends in Europe in 2013*, 73.2 percent of public expenditure in the cultural sector was made by local governments (Garcia et. al. 2020, 68).

7. See also http://www.matrizpci.dgpc.pt/MatrizPCI.Web/Pages/CronologiaPortugal.

8. For an account of the shared research process that culminated in the inscription of Kola San Jon on the NIICH, see Miguel (2016, 127–66).

9. See https://ich.unesco.org/en/lists?text=&multinational=3&display1=countryIDs #Spain.

10. See https://ich.unesco.org/en/RL/fiesta-of-the-patios-in-cordova-00846.

11. See https://ich.unesco.org/en/RL/valencia-fallas-festivity-00859.

12. Ley 18/2013, de 12 de noviembre, para la regulación de la Tauromaquia como patrimonio cultural.

13. See http://www.culturaydeporte.gob.es/planes-nacionales/planes-nacionales/salvaguardia-patrimonio-cultural-inmaterial.html.

14. For an overview of the 2003 Convention and its impact on legislation and the institutional structure of central government, see Cabral (2011) and Marques (2018). For a detailed account of the implementation of the ICH paradigm and its impact on public policies and institutions between 2007 and 2017, and on the heritagization of Kola San Jon, see Costa (2018).

15. Matriz PCI, see http://matrizpci.dgpc.pt/MatrizPCI.Web/pt-PT/Pages/Apresentacao.

16. A cooperation protocol was signed in 2012 between the General Directorate of Heritage and CRIA (an inter-university research center in anthropology) to promote inscriptions on the NIICH. Training programs in the domain of ICH were launched by the General Directorate of Heritage and by universities, including a postgraduate program offered by the Universidade Lusófona and a PhD program jointly offered since 2013 by the anthropology departments of the Universidade Nova de Lisboa and the Instituto Universitário de Lisboa.

17. An independent committee was appointed for evaluating applications for inscription on the National ICH Inventory. It was headed by the director of the IMC and included the director of IMC's ICH Department, four anthropologists, an ethnomusicologist (Castelo-Branco), and two representatives of the Association of Portuguese Municipalities. The committee met several times to discuss the first application for inscription, but due to administrative changes, it was dissolved a year after its founding.

18. Several ethnomusicologists and graduate students at the Institute of Ethnomusicology-Center for Studies in Music and Dance (INET-md, a transdisciplinary research center based at the Faculty of Social Sciences and Humanities at the Nova University of Lisbon with branches at the Universities of Lisbon and Aveiro, and the Polytechnic Institute of Porto) collaborated in the preparation of the applications for inscription on UNESCO's Representative List of the ICH of fado and the Cante Alentejano (inscribed in 2011 and 2014) and on the NIICH of the following: Kola San Jon (inscribed in 2013), Cantar os Reis em Ovar (Singing the Reis in Ovar), Construção e Práticas Tradicionais Coletivas dos Bombos em Portugal (The Construction and Traditional Colective Practices of the Bombo in Portugal), and Canto a Vozes de Mulheres (Women's Multipart Singing).

References

Abreu, Regina. 2014. "Dez anos da convenção do patrimonio cultural imaterial: Ressonâncias, apropriações, vigilências." *E-Cadernos CES* 21: 14–32.

Aikawa-Faure, Noriko. 2009. "From the Proclamation of Masterpieces to the Convention for the Safeguarding of the Intangible Cultural Heritage." In *Intangible Heritage*, edited by Laurajane Smith and Natsuko Akagawa, 13–14. New York: Routledge.

Bendix, Regina, Aditya Eggert, and Arnika Peselmann, eds. 2012. *Heritage Regimes and the State*. Göttingen, DE: Universitätsverlag Göttingen.

12. Intangible Cultural Heritage and State Regimes 243

Bortolotto, Chiara. 2017. "Placing Intangible Cultural Heritage, Owning Tradition, Affirming Sovereignty: The Role of Spatiality in the Practice of the 2003 Convention." In *The Routledge Companion to Intangible Cultural Heritage*, edited by Michelle L. Stefano and Peter Davis, 46–58. New York: Routledge.

Brissos, Cristina. 2010. "Instituto Português do Património Cultural-Departamento de Musicologia." In *Encilopédia da Música em Portugal do Século XX*. Vol. 2. Edited by Salwa Castelo-Branco. Lisbon: Círculo de Leitores/Temas e Debates.

Bronner, Simon. 2005. "Contesting Tradition: The Deep Play and Protest of Pigeon Shoots." *Journal of American Folklore* 118, no. 470: 409–52.

Cabral, Clara Bertrand. 2011. *Património Cultural Imaterial: Convenção da UNESCO e seus contextos*. Lisbon: Edições 70.

Carrera Díaz, Gema. 2015. "Propuesta metodológica para la documentación del patrimonio cultural inmaterial como estrategia de desarrollo social y territorial." PhD diss., Universidad de Sevilla.

Castelo-Branco, Salwa El-Shawan. 2013. "The Politics of Music Categorization in Portugal." In *The Cambridge History of World Music*, edited by Philip Bohlman, 661–77. Cambridge: Cambridge University Press.

———. 2022. "Sustainability, Agency, and the Ecologies of Music Heritage in Alentejo, Portugal." In *Music, Communities, and Sustainability: Developing Policies and Practices*, edited by Huib Schippers and Anthony Seeger, 177–95. New York: Oxford University Press.

Castelo-Branco, Salwa El-Shawan, Maria João Lima, and José Neves. 2003. "Perfis dos grupos de música tradicional em Portugal em finais do século XX." In *Vozes do Povo: A Folclorização em Portugal*, edited by Salwa El-Shawan Castelo-Branco and Jorge Freitas Branco, 73–141. Oeiras, PT: Celta Editora.

Comaroff, Jean, and John Comaroff. 2009. *Ethnicity, Inc.* Chicago: University of Chicago Press.

Coombe, Rosemary, and Lyndsey M. Weiss. 2015. "Neoliberalism, Heritage Regimes, and Cultural Rights." In *Global Heritage: A Reader*, edited by Lynn Meskell, 43–69. Hoboken, NJ: Wiley-Blackwell.

Costa, Carla Sofia Queiroz da. 2018. "Património cultural imaterial: Políticas patrimoniais, agentes e organizões. O processo de patrimonialização do Kola San Jon em Portugal." PhD diss., Universidade Nova de Lisboa.

Costa, Paulo Ferreira da. 2013. "O inventário nacional do património cultural imaterial: Da prática etnográfica à voz das comunidades." In *Políticas Públicas para o Património Imaterial na Europa do Sul: Percursos, Concretizações, Perspetiva*, 93–116. Lisbon: Direcção Geral do Património Cultural.

———. 2015. "Inventário nacional do património cultural imaterial: Produção de conhecimento e medidas de salvaguarda." In *Cantar no Alentejo: A Terra, O Passado e o Presente*, edited by Maria do Rosário Pestana and Luísa Tiago de Oliveira, 183–96. Estremoz, PT: Estremoz Editora.

De Cesari, Chiara. 2012. "Thinking Through Heritage Regimes." In *Heritage Regimes and the State*, edited by Regina Bendix et al., 399–413. Göttingen, DE: Universitatsverlag Göttingen.

Diamond, Beverly, and Salwa El-Shawan Castelo-Branco. 2021. "Ethnomusicological

Praxis: An Introduction." In *Transforming Ethnomusicology*. Vol. 1. Edited by Beverly Diamond and Salwa El-Shawan Castelo-Branco, 1–24. New York: Oxford University Press.

Durand, Jean-Yves et. al. 2018. "Em concreto (2): O 'património cultural imaterial no terreno': Expectativas, experiências, perspectivas." *Veduta* 12: 7–9.

Foucault, Michel. 1977. "The Political Function of the Intellectual." *Radical Philosophy* 17: 12–14.

———. 1979. "Governmentality." *Ideology & Consciousness* 6: 5–21.

Garcia, José Luís et al., 2020. *Mapear os recursos, levantamento da legislação, caracterização dos atores, comparação internacional*. Lisbon: Secretaria de Estado da Cultura-Gabinete de Planeamento e Avaliação Culturais.

Geismar, Haidy. 2015. "Anthropology and Heritage Regimes." *Annual Review of Anthropology* 44: 71–85.

Gembero Ustárroz, María. 2005. "El patrimonio musical español y su gestión." *Revista de Musicología* 48, no. 1: 135–81.

González Cambeiro, Sara. 2016. "La salvaguarda del Patrimonio Inmaterial en España." PhD diss., Universidad Complutense de Madrid.

Hafstein, Valdimar. 2009. "Intangible Heritage as List: From Masterpieces to Representation." In *Intangible Heritage: Key Issues in Cultural Heritage*, edited by Laurajane Smith and Natsuko Akagawa, 93–111. New York: Routledge.

———. 2012. "Cultural Heritage." In *A Companion to Folklore*, edited by Regina Bendix and Galit Hasan-Rokem, 500–520. Oxford: Wiley Blackwell.

———. 2014. "Protection as Dispossession: Government in the Vernacular." In *Heritage in Transit: Intangible Rights as Humans Rights*, edited by Deborah Kapchan, 25–57. Philadelphia: University of Pennsylvania Press.

———. 2018. *Making Intangible Culture: El Condor Passa and other Stories from UNESCO*. Bloomington: Indiana University Press.

Harrison, Rodney. 2013. *Heritage: Critical Approaches*. London: Routledge.

Howard, Keith, ed. 2012. *Music as Intangible Cultural Heritage: Policy, Ideology, and Practice in the Preservation of East Asian Traditions*. Farnham, UK: Ashgate.

Jiménez-Esquinas, Guadalupe, and Cristina Sánchez-Carretero. 2018. "Who Owns the Name of a Place? On Place Branding and Logics in Two Villages in Galicia, Spain." *Tourist Studies* 18, no. 1: 3–20.

Kapchan, Deborah. 2014. *Cultural Heritage in Transit: Intangible Rights as Human Rights*. Philadelphia: University of Pennsylvania Press.

Kirshenblatt-Gimblett, Barbara. 2004. "Intangible Heritage as Metacultural Production." *Museum International* 56: 52–65.

"Ley 16/1985, de 25 de junio, del Patrimonio Histórico Español." *Boletín Oficial del Estado* 155 (June 29, 1985). https://www.boe.es/buscar/act.php?id=BOE-A-1985–12534.

"Ley 4/1990, de 30 de mayo, del Patrimonio Histórico de Castilla-La Mancha." *Boletín Oficial del Estado* 221 (September 14, 1990). https://www.boe.es/buscar/doc.php?id=BOE-A-1990–22805.

"Ley 1/1991, de 3 de julio, de Patrimonio Histórico de Andalucía." *Boletín Oficial del Estado* 178 (July 26, 1991). https://www.boe.es/buscar/doc.php?id=BOE-A-1991–19203.

"Ley 2/1993, de 5 de marzo, de Fomento y Protección de la Cultura Popular y Tradicional y del

12. Intangible Cultural Heritage and State Regimes   245

Asociacionismo Cultural." *Boletín Oficial del Estado* 1719 (March 12, 1993). https://www.boe.es/buscar/act.php?id=BOE-A-1993-8975.

"Ley 9/1993, de 30 de septiembre, del Patrimonio Cultural Catalán." *Boletín Oficial del Estado* 1807 (October 11, 1993). https://www.boe.es/buscar/act.php?id=BOE-A-1993-26497.

"Ley 4/2013, de 16 de mayo, de Patrimonio Cultural de Castilla-La Mancha." *Boletín Oficial del Estado* 240 (October 7, 2013). https://www.boe.es/buscar/pdf/2013/BOE-A-2013-10415-consolidado.pdf.

Mármol, Camila del, and Beatriz Santamarina Campos. 2019. "Seeking Authenticity: Heritage and Value within the Intangible Economy." *Journal of Mediterranean Studies* 28, no. 2: 117–32.

Marques, Luís. 2018. *Património Cultural Imaterial: Um olhar Antropológico*. Porto: Edições Afrontamento.

Miguel, Ana Flávia. 2016. "Skopeologias: Música e Saberes Sensíveis na Construção Partilhada do Conhecimento." PhD diss., University of Aveiro.

Miguel, Ana Flávia, and Susana Sardo. 2014 "Classificar o património reclassificando as identidades: A inscrição do Kola San Jon na lista Portuguesa do PCI." *E-Cadernos CES* 21: 52–75.

Mulà, Anna. 2018. "Análisis jurídico, antecedentes y consecuencias de la sentencia 177/2016, del Tribunal Constitucional, sobre prohibición de las corridas de toros en Cataluña." *Revista de Derecho UNED* 22: 407–36.

Norton, Barley, and Naomi Matsumoto, eds. 2019. *Music as Heritage: Historical and Ethnographic Perspectives*. London: Routledge.

Patrix, Pénélope. 2015. "Le fado: 'Patrimoine Imateriel' vivant ou monument?" In *l'Archives das les arts vivants: performance, dance, théatre*, edited by Isabelle Barbéris, 185–202. Rennes: Presses Universitaires de Rennes.

Pestana, Maria do Rosário, and Luísa de Oliveira, eds. 2017. *Cantar no Alentejo: A terra, o passado e o presente*. Estremoz, PT: Estremoz Editora.

Pestana, Maria do Rosário, and Maria José Barriga. 2019. "'Le patrimoine c'est nous': Voix plurielles autour du cante alentejano." *Transposition: Musiques et Sciences Sociales* 8. https://doi.org/10.4000/transposition.3353.

Plata García, Fuensanta. 2017. "Protecting Intangible Cultural Heritage in Andalusia: Legal-Political Competence, Scope and Social Function." *Revista Andaluza de Antropología* 12: 94–116.

Sánchez-Carretero, Cristina. 2012. "Heritage Regimes and the Camino de Santiago: Gaps and Logics." In *Heritage Regimes and the State*, edited by Regina Bendix et al., 141–56. Göttingen, DE: Universitatsverlag Göttingen.

Sánchez-Carretero, Cristina, José Muñoz-Albadalejo, Ana Ruiz-Blanch, and Joan Roura-Expósito, eds. 2019. *El imperativo de la participación en la gestión patrimonial*. Madrid: CSIC.

Sandroni, Carlos. 2010. "Samba de Roda: Intangible Heritage of Humanity." *Estudos Avançados* 24, no. 69: 373–87.

Santamarina Campos, Beatriz. 2013. "Los mapas geopolíticos de la Unesco: Entre la distinción y la diferencia están las asimetrías. El éxito (exótico) del patrimonio inmaterial." *Revista de Antropología Social* 22: 263–86.

Santamarina Campos, Beatriz, and Camila del Mármol. 2017. "Ciudades creativas y pueblos con encanto: Los nuevos procesos patrimoniales del siglo XXI." *Revista de dialectología y tradiciones populares* 72, no. 2: 359–77.

Santos, Maria de Lourdes Lima dos, et. al. 1998. *As políticas culturais em Portugal.* Lisbon: Observatório das Actividades Culturais.

Santos, Paula Assunção dos, and Elaine Muller. 2011. "When ICH Takes Hold of the Local Reality in Brazil." In *Safeguarding Intangible Cultural Heritage: Notes from the Brazilian State of Pernambuco,* edited by Michelle Stefano, Peter Davis, and Gerard Corsane, 213–23. Newcastle: The International Center for Cultural and Heritage Studies.

Schippers, Huib, and Catherine Grant, eds. 2016. *Sustainable Futures for Music Cultures: An Ecological Perspective.* New York: Oxford University Press.

Seeger, Anthony, and Huib Schippers, eds. 2022. *Music, Communities, and Sustainability: Developing Policies and Practices.* New York: Oxford University Press.

Smith, Laurajane. 2006. *Uses of Heritage.* New York: Routledge.

Tauschek, Markus. 2015. "Imaginations, Constructions and Constraints: Some Concluding Remarks on Heritage, Community and Participation." In *Between Imagined Communities and Communities of Practice: Participation, Territory and the Making of Heritage,* edited by Nicolas Adell, Regina Bendix, Chiara Bortolotto, and Markus Tauschek. Göttingen, DE: Universitätsverlag Göttingen.

UNESCO. 2020. "Constitution of the United Nations Educational, Scientific and Cultural Organization." In *Basic Texts,* 5–18. Paris: UNESCO.

UNESCO. 2022. "Convention for the Safeguarding of the Intangible Cultural Heritage." In *Basic Texts,* 1–20. Paris: UNESCO.

13

Sounding the Alentejo:
Portugal's *Cante* as Heritage

SALWA EL-SHAWAN CASTELO-BRANCO

On November 27, 2014, I attended the ninth session of UNESCO's Intergovernmental Committee for the Safeguarding of the Intangible Cultural Heritage[1] (ICH) at the organization's headquarters in Paris. I was seated next to a dozen representatives of Portugal's central government, Alentejo's regional authorities,[2] Portuguese journalists, and scholars. This was the session in which the long-awaited decision on the inscription of Alentejo's *cante*[3] on UNESCO's Representative List of the ICH would be voted on by the Intergovernmental Committee (IC) composed of delegates from twenty-four countries, following the recommendation of the IC's Evaluation Body.[4] The thousand-seat auditorium was filled with delegates, representatives of NGOs, and other observers. The chair and members of the ICH's secretariat were seated on stage. The Secretary officiated the "highly codified institutional ritual" (Bortolotto 2015, 252). He read the application's main points projected on a screen, describing it as "exemplary," proposed the inscription of *cante* on UNESCO's Representative List of the ICH, and asked if there were any objections. Following a brief pause, he declared the adoption of the IC's proposal, sealing the decision with a gavel's stroke. Following applause, the Portuguese ambassador to UNESCO delivered a short speech acclaiming Alentejo's "unique heritage" and proposed a performance by the Grupo Coral Etnográfico da Casa do Povo de Serpa, one of the oldest and most respected choirs in Alentejo. Eighteen men clad in costumes, presumably common in early twentieth century rural Alentejo, slowly walked onto the stage. Two of the singers in the front row unfolded the flags of Portugal and Serpa, the municipality that spearheaded the application, exhibiting them throughout the performance. The choir sang "Alentejo, Alentejo,"[5] a widely disseminated vocal composition (*moda*) exalting rural Alentejo as the nation's granary.

In Portugal, *cante*'s inscription as ICH was widely acclaimed as a "victory," a "consecration," an "elevation" to the "heritage of humanity." At Lisbon's airport, cheering crowds awaited Serpa's choir, a reception usually given to football champions. For months following the inscription, *cante* was broadcast on radio and television, and choirs from Alentejo were invited to perform at the capital's prestigious concert halls, all of which were rare occurrences until the inscription. An official congratulatory message was issued by the president of the Portuguese Republic,[6] and the Portuguese Parliament approved a vote lauding *cante* and emphasizing its importance as "a strong identity element [. . . that contributes to] social and generational unity" (December 5, 2014).[7] A performance by the choir Rancho Coral e Etnográfico da Vila Nova de São Bento in the Parliament's public galleries followed the vote.

One year following the inscription, Serpa's municipality launched the Cantefest, an annual event commemorating *cante*'s recognition by UNESCO. Celebrated in Serpa and in Lisbon's House of Alentejo (a voluntary association, founded in 1923, that promotes the region's cultural and social activities in Lisbon), it mobilizes dozens of *cante* choirs based in Alentejo and the greater Lisbon area to sing on stages, in churches, and on the streets.

These celebratory events on UNESCO's international stage, in Portugal's National Assembly, and among Alentejans in Serpa and Lisbon highlight the symbolic value conferred by state institutions to cante and its practitioners as a result of UNESCO's certification. They also illustrate how governmentality (Foucault 1979b; Rose, O'Malley, and Valverde 2006) intersects with "heritage regimes"[8] (Bendix, Eggert, and Peselmann 2012), as well as the "dynamic triangulation" between "community, state and international authority" (Hafstein 2014, 55).

* * *

What is *cante*? When, how, and why was it configured as "heritage"? As will be explored in this chapter, Alentejo's *cante* is not a newly "invented tradition." Its configuration as the iconic genre of Alentejo, the constitution of an "authenticated repertoire" (Castelo-Branco and Branco 2003),[9] and the selection of choirs with no instrumental accompaniment as the "presentational" mode of performance (Turino 2008) are imbricated in heritage politics. At the same time, in many villages and towns throughout the Alentejo region, and amongst some of its migrant communities in the greater Lisbon area, *cante* has thrived as a powerful expressive practice through "presentational" and "participatory" performance (2008) on stages and in taverns, in fiestas, and in private settings.

Using *cante* as a case study, in this chapter I address the politics that characterize different heritage regimes anchored on distinct ideologies and political systems. I trace the beginning of the interest in rural expressive practices in Portugal back to the nineteenth century. I then address the nationalist political project configured by the authoritarian state established by António de Oliveira Salazar in 1933. I proceed to the heritage regime configured in the democratic era, following the 1974 *coup d'état* that ended authoritarian rule, and its implementation by local governments through grassroots associative movements. I then examine the international heritage regime that was adopted following Portugal's ratification of UNESCO's 2003 Convention for the Safeguarding of the Intangible Cultural Heritage (ICH) in 2008. Drawing on fieldwork and archival research, I discuss the main issues and processes involved in the discursive and performative production of *cante* as heritage. I adopt the Foucauldian perspective of governmentality to gain an understanding of the various powers, agents, and procedures at play in the heritagization of *cante* (Foucault 1979b). I also consider the agency of individuals who engage in the construction of *cante* as heritage. I argue that the resilience of the practice of *cante* in the Alentejo region and among its migrants in Lisbon's metropolitan area through different political and heritage regimes transcends heritage politics. For many Alentejans, *cante* is a performative site of memory, an expressive resource that embodies their identification with the region, and a vehicle for social and emotional bonding.

Defining Heritage

The notion of "heritage" is central to the provisional genealogy of *cante* that is proposed in this chapter, a notion that deserves explication. Critical heritage scholars have pointed out the ambiguity of the concept, its myriad uses in public, political, and commercial discourses, the values and meanings it conjures, and its imbrication with memory, identity, and senses of place (Harrison 2013, 14–20; Lowenthal 1996; Roberts 2014). They also stress that heritage is neither a thing nor an object and that the distinction between natural, material, and intangible cultural heritage promoted by UNESCO's conventions is untenable (Smith 2012, 391). Drawing on the perspectives of critical heritage studies and ethnomusicology (Bendix 2009; Harrison 2013; Kirshenblatt-Gimblet 1995, 2004), I anchor my discussion on heritage in the following working definition that I propose elsewhere: "heritage is the discursive and performative production, by several agents, of selected objects, places, and practices associated with the past to which new meaning and value are ascribed in the present with a vision towards the future" (Castelo-Branco 2022a). As Hill and Bithell argue, the "past" is not a fixed time frame, but rather a "subjective, fragmented, malleable, multidimensional [. . .] multivalent" and "ideologically contingent" temporal reference that serves as a "symbolic resource" (2014, 13) from which those who produce heritage draw selectively, often guided by the ideal of authenticity. As such, heritage production is embedded in power relations: it is informed by, and often serves, political ideologies and systems that exert influence on how heritage is defined, used, and regulated.

Encountering *Cante* in Alentejo

My first encounter with *cante* goes back to the spring of 1986 when I visited the town of Cuba in southern Alentejo. Cuba has become known for its *cante* activities and its highly reputed choir founded in 1933, the Grupo Coral os Ceifeiros de Cuba (hereafter the Ceifeiros).[10] The seat of a homonym municipality, the town is situated amid wheat fields dotted with cork trees and holm oaks. At the edge of town, a tall concrete silo is a reminder of Salazar's "wheat campaign" that promoted single-crop agriculture throughout Alentejo, a policy that favored landowners. During the authoritarian regime, most of the town's resident population, as elsewhere in the region, worked in agriculture under harshly exploitative conditions inflicted by a few landowners of large estates (*latifundia*). Many of my collaborators in the field recalled the hardship of agricultural work, typically lasting "from sunrise to sunset," and characterized by poverty, a lack of access to basic schooling, social inequality, no freedom, and police repression. This situation resulted in social unrest and mass migration mainly to greater Lisbon, especially during the 1960s. Following the 1974 *coup d'état* and the revolutionary process that ensued, Cuba, like the rest of the country, saw major political, social, and economic changes. Agrarian reform was launched throughout Alentejo in 1975 within a political environment that was dominated by the Portuguese Communist Party. Workers occupied the farmland and set up Cooperative Production Units (CPU) run by laborers and small landowners. Cuba had four CPUs. Agricultural reform was short-lived, and by 2000 much of the land was returned to its original owners.

I first heard the Ceifeiros in a rehearsal in Cuba's Casa do Povo,[11] an institution in which the choir had been required to affiliate during the Estado Novo.[12] Twenty middle-aged men stood in two rows, their bodies tightly aligned, and sang several *modas* in a slow tempo, demonstrating what the group's *cante* custo-

13. Sounding the Alentejo   251

dians consider illustrative of Cuba's style and emblematic repertoire. I was struck by the affective dimension in the act of singing together and the "spellbinding quality of the sound as a whole," much as the reaction of outsiders to the Corsican *Paghjella* described by Bithell (2007, 58). The generosity of my interlocutors allowed me to share *cante* with them in moments of conviviality in taverns,[13] where only men socialize and sing, at homes with friends and family, and on festive occasions. I also attended several performance events organized by the Ceifeiros which featured performances by up to a dozen invited choirs hosted by the group (Encontro de Grupos Corais Alentejanos). In all these settings, I witnessed how the practice of *cante* was and still is an integral part of the habitus of many Alentejan communities.

My first encounter with *cante* in Alentejo coincided with a significant year for *cante* in Cuba and for the country. Due to political discord in the aftermath of the revolutionary process, several singers who had been members of the Ceifeiros for several decades seceded and formed a new choir, Os Cubenses Amigos do Cante. As Lortat-Jacob pointed out in the case of the *cantu a tenore* groups in Castelsardo in Sardinia, social harmony and concord on central issues is a necessary condition for enabling "acoustic harmony" (1998, 10). In addition, in 1986 the first women's choir in Cuba, the Grupo Coral Flores do Alentejo, was formed, marking the entry of women into the arena of public performances of *cante* in the town.

This was also the year that Portugal became a member of the European Economic Community (presently the European Union), resulting in major structural changes affecting all sectors of life throughout the country. In Alentejo, the Common Agricultural Policy encouraged intensive farming and capital investment, especially in vineyards and olive groves that relied on seasonal migrant labor, with products destined for the global market. Furthermore, in recent decades, Alentejan authorities have intensified the promotion of tourism as a strategy for the region's economic development, providing villages and towns with a "second life" (Kirshenblatt-Gimblet 1995, 369) as tourist destinations. These efforts have transformed the natural environment, historical monuments, gastronomy, artifacts, and expressive cultural practices, including *cante*, into value-added products for tourist consumption. The effects of the investment in tourism have also been evident in the town of Cuba. New infrastructures were created such as a tourist office, a hotel, and a literary museum bearing the name of the local writer José Fialho de Almeida. *Cante* was occasionally introduced in some restaurants, and tourist itineraries and events were created such as the "*cante* and amphora wine route," the "tavern route," and the newly invented local carnival and "snail fiesta."[14]

Heritage Regimes and the Configuration of *Cante* as Iconic of Alentejo

In Portugal, as in other European countries, the celebration and ethnographic study of the rural world and its expressive practices as the building block of national identity, often characterized by the notion of *cultura popular*,[15] can be traced back to the nineteenth century and have continued through different political regimes up to the end of the twentieth (Leal 2000; Alves 2013). It was within this framework that some of the earliest ethnographic descriptions and musical transcriptions of song and dance genres practiced by men and women in Alentejo were published by ethnographers and music folklorists (Picão 1983 [1903]; Piçarra and Dias Nunes 1899–1904). These publications feature sung poetic competitions (*desgarrada*), religious songs, ballads, and other song and dance genres performed solo or in parallel thirds (*descantes*) to the accompaniment of instruments such as the diatonic accordion (*concertina*), the local guitar (*viola campaniça*), and the square frame drum (*adufe*). From these and other publications, we also learn that "participatory performances" (Turino 2008) of a diversity of music and dance genres, styles, and practices were central to the social life and rituals of Alentejans, from agricultural work to weddings, dance parties (*balhos*), and religious and secular fiestas.

By the mid-twentieth century, music and dance practices in the Alentejo region were transformed. Participatory performances continued in taverns where men socialized, in some fiestas and private gatherings, and during manual agricultural work. At the same time, "presentational performances" (2008) by unaccompanied men's choirs of an "authenticated repertoire" of the local vocal genre *moda*, consisting of a heterogeneous repertoire of dance-songs adapted for two-part singing in parallel thirds, were promoted as iconic of Alentejo both in the country and abroad. Repertoire, performance format, and style came to configure a category labelled *canto Alentejano* (Alentejo's song), *cantar à Alentejana* (singing in Alentejo's style), or more recently *cante*, the regional pronunciation of *canto* (Castelo-Branco and Lima 2018, 32). What accounts for this transformation of music practices in Alentejo? When and why were presentational performances by men's choirs selected and promoted as iconic of the region?

A critical genealogy of the choir movement in the Alentejo region is still under construction. However, it is likely that the choice of men's choirs as iconic of the region was an adaptation of the model of male choral societies, designated *orfeões* (singular, *orfeão*), that was introduced to the north and center of Portugal in the late nineteenth century (Castelo-Branco 2008; Pestana 2015), subsequently spreading to other regions. As I point out elsewhere (Castelo-Branco 2008), this

13. Sounding the Alentejo

adaptation also became aligned with the authoritarian regime's policy of promoting choirs as a medium for "disciplining bodies" (Foucault 1979a), creating a sense of community, staging an apparent social harmony (Vialette 2018), and inculcating the regime's nationalist ideology. The *orfeões* expressed the ideals of fraternity, republicanism, and patriotism through choral singing (Pestana 2015). In Portugal, the earliest *orfeões* were founded at Coimbra's University in 1880 (Ofeão Académico de Coimbra, OAC) and in Porto in 1881 (Orpheon Portuense). New *orfeões* were subsequently founded in other parts of the country. In Serpa, a former law student of Coimbra's University founded an *orfeão* in 1907, and two more followed in 1916 and 1940 (Pestana 2014, 4–6).

The State Heritage Regime under Authoritarian Rule

The discursive and performative configuration of two-part singing by men's choirs as the iconic representation of Alentejo was part of the strategy of António de Oliveira Salazar's authoritarian regime (1933–1974). This strategy sought to instrumentalize expressive culture to inculcate the regime's nationalist ideology and to construct a national identity through objectified and stylized representations of an idyllic rural world, which were targeted at the urban middle classes and foreign elites and used to project Portugal's image abroad (Alves 2013; Melo 2001).

Salazar's authoritarian regime, dubbed the New State, was characterized by traditionalist and corporatist nationalism, state economic interventionism, and colonial imperialism (Monteiro and Costa Pinto 2011, 65). The regime's cultural policy, designated *política do espírito* ("politics of the spirit"), was designed by António Ferro (1895–1956), an intellectual and journalist, to forge a national identity grounded in the regime's ideological cornerstones: nationalism, Catholicism, ruralism, and traditionalism. The "politics of the spirit" configured a heritage regime that emphasized the value of rural culture as the essence of the nation. Ferro's plan for culture was implemented during the 1930s and 1940s by state agencies. These agencies included the Secretariat for National Propaganda (Secretariado de Propaganda Nacional), founded in 1933; the National Foundation for Joy at Work (Fundação Nacional para Alegria no Trabalho), founded in 1935; and the National Radio (Emissora Nacional), founded in 1935 (see Chapter 6). They exercised control over expressive culture by defining aesthetic ideals and modeling, institutionalizing, promoting, and regulating expressive practices. In addition, control was exerted over all cultural activities by Censorship Services.

Through the above-named institutions, the state promoted a wide-ranging program in different cultural domains that aimed to inculcate the regime's ideology and to advance state propaganda. This included sponsoring ethnographic research and publication and institutionalizing and regulating folklorized representations of an authenticated repertoire of songs and dances by formally structured institutionalized groups (choirs in southern Alentejo and folklore groups[16] in the rest of the country). The New State also launched and organized festivals, competitions, fairs, invented fiestas, and exhibitions in Portugal and abroad, exalting the rural world and the country's historical achievements and colonial legacy. As Vera Alves shows in Chapter 3, one of Ferro's most ambitious projects was the founding of a professional dance company, the *Bailados Portugueses Verde Gaio*, that performed a repertoire evoking estheticized rural ambiances and historical narratives. Within the framework of National Radio, the State commissioned popular and art music compositions that materialized the regime's aesthetic ideals. In short, musicians, dancers, and visual artists fabricated a nationalist idiom modelled by the regime's official aesthetics, effectively staging an imagined "modern" nation grounded in its glorious history, rural essence, and imperial legacy.

In Alentejo, as in other regions, the agency of individual actors (folklorists, Catholic priests, tradition custodians, among others) was also central to the configuration of *cante* as the expressive mode that represented the region, in the constitution of an authenticated corpus of *modas* and *cantigas*, in the composition of new repertoire,[17] and in the regulation of the choir movement. As I discuss elsewhere (Castelo-Branco and Lima 2018), three seminary-trained Catholic priests and folklorists who resided and worked in the region played an important role in Alentejo's choir movement: António Marvão (1903–1993), Joaquim Roque (1913–1995), and José Alcobia (1914–2003). All three collected and published transcriptions or recordings of local repertoire, founded and directed Alentejan choirs, selected and adapted repertoire for these groups, and contributed to shaping performance styles and aesthetics. Marvão's claim that *cante* had originated in the fifteenth-century religious practice of *fauxbourdon* (1966) was influential in legitimizing the authenticity and value of the local two-part singing practice, a perspective that was in tandem with the ideology of the conservative, Catholic-oriented authoritarian regime (Castelo-Branco 2022b).

Starting in 1946, Alentejan choirs were also regulated through annual competitions organized by the governor of Beja, in collaboration with local folklorists and prominent musicians (Castelo-Branco and Lima 2018, 27–30), as well as through visits to choirs by representatives of state institutions such as the National Foundation for Joy at Work. Notwithstanding the authoritarian regime's disciplining of expressive practices, singing informally continued to be central to the conviviality and social and emotional bonding of Alentejans in

13. Sounding the Alentejo

homes, taverns, on festive occasions, and on the streets of towns and villages. *Cante* became the main expressive mode in the region and most of the other song and dance genres fell out of use or were relegated to isolated communities.

The State Heritage Regime in the Democratic Era

Following the *coup d'état* in 1974 and the revolutionary process that enabled freedom and democracy in Portugal, a new heritage regime was institutionalized. This regime privileged the safeguarding and valorizing of the country's cultural heritage as one of the pillars of national identity and promoted amateur musical activity at a local level as a vehicle for the maintenance of social cohesion (Santos et al., 1998), as detailed in Chapter 12. The associative movement that was tightly controlled by the authoritarian state expanded considerably, providing the framework for myriad local activities, including musicking and dancing. The sponsorship and regulation of local amateur music and dance groups (including folklore groups, wind bands, and choirs) were transferred from central government to its regional delegations and to municipal governments. Regulation became essentially the purview of voluntary associations and the groups themselves. The National Institution for the Occupation of Workers' Leisure Time (INATEL), which replaced the Estado Novo's National Foundation for Joy at Work, has provided occasional funding and "technical advice" to folklore groups and wind bands. A voluntary association for Alentejan choirs, MODA-Associação do Cante Alentejano, was formed in 2000 with the aim of representing Alentejan choirs and safeguarding, valorizing, and promoting *cante*. An actor in the Alentejan choir scene, MODA has been playing an important regulatory role and has forged an "authorized heritage discourse" (Smith 2006) among Alentejan choirs, articulated in cooperation with state and international heritage regimes (Castelo-Branco 2022b).

Contrary to the expectations of cultural politicians and intellectuals, the choir movement in Alentejo and the folklore movement in other parts of the country, which were institutionalized and promoted by the authoritarian regime, have expanded considerably since democracy (Castelo-Branco and Branco 2003, 15). Once an expression of national identity under the auspices of Salazar's regime, these groups have become rooted in local and regional indentity-building projects, thriving through the financial support of municipalities and the commitment of individual actors, extended families, and local social networks (Holton 2003). Furthermore, the migration of large numbers of Alentejans in the 1960s and 1970s extended the practice of *cante* to Lisbon's metropolis where dozens of choirs were founded. According to a survey conducted in 1998 by the Ethnomusicology Institute of the NOVA University of Lisbon, more than 75 percent of active choirs that year were founded following the establishment of democracy (Castelo-Branco, Lima, and Neves 2003). While most of the groups surveyed in southern Alentejo were men's choirs, since the late 1970s women's choirs were also formed and have multiplied during the last two decades, launching women into public performances of *cante* (Cabeça and Rodrigues Santos 2010).

During the revolutionary years following the 1974 *coup d'état*, Alentejo's choir movement was entangled in ongoing political processes, including the agricultural reform that affected the region, with some choirs splitting due to political discord (as was the case with the Ceifeiros) and new lyrics with political content set over extant melodies (Simões 2021). Since 1974, the performance events organized by the State were largely replaced by a new type of event hosted and organized by the choirs and supported by the municipal governments: the Encontro de Grupos Corais Alentejanos (The Meeting of Alentejan Choirs). These events include staged performances of *cante* by choirs that are often followed by a street parade (*desfile*) in which all participating choirs sing as they parade to the *moda*'s regular tempo. Following a meal offered by the host choir, guests and invited choirs join in singing a shared repertoire. These events provide an arena of self-regulation and conviviality among choirs and local populations and create and reinforce a social network based on solidarity and reciprocity (Simões 2017, 76–78).

While there has been a crystallization of the performance format institutionalized by the authoritarian regime, *cante* has become resignified in the democratic era. It embodies the memory of an idealized rural past in Alentejo and a sense of community that extends to the region's migrants in greater Lisbon. An expressive discourse through which southern Alentejo is represented to the outside world, *cante* is also part of a local web of social relations, friendships, and political alliances. In Alentejo, singing together is not possible without a set of dense social relationships into which the practice is embedded. In Alentejan choirs, comradeship, friendship, and agreement on political issues are all necessary conditions for collective singing. Many choir members also emphasize their emotional involvement with and commitment to *cante* and abstain from singing during the mourning period (*luto*) that can last up to two years following the death of a family member.

The significance of *cante* is also linked to the vital relationship between performance and memory. As many scholars have emphasized, heritage practices are an affective, material, symbolic, and performative site of memory. Similarly, several music researchers have explored how music, dance, and other expressive practices produce individual and social memory (Cidra 2015; Feld 1996; De Nora 2000). Indeed, the practice of *cante* and its centrality in the social lives of

13. Sounding the Alentejo

Alentejans is imbricated in the politics of memory of many of its practitioners, embodied through biographical narratives as well as through the poetry and the aesthetics of *cante*, a theme that I plan to pursue in a separate publication.

Despite the vitality of *cante*, many of my aging collaborators expressed their concern about its sustainability due to the advanced age of most choir members.[18] Up to the end of the twentieth century, most young Alentejans eschewed joining choirs, even though some had learned the repertoire through family circles. Many young Alentejans associate *cante* with the memory of exploitative rural work and poverty, materialized through sound and the rural costumes, presumably going back to the beginning of the twentieth century. Such dress was required by the authoritarian regime's regulatory institutions and has been worn by many choir members up to the present. The disinterest of young people in joining choirs was seen by my research collaborators and other *cante* custodians as a threat to the sustainability of this expressive practice. Furthermore, the intergenerational transmission of *cante* was one of the main subjects of debate in the First Congress on Cante organized in 1997 (Pereira 2005) and in the regular meetings of the MODA association.

Starting in the late 1980s and 1990s, three processes were implemented that created the conditions for *cante*'s rejuvenation and sustainability: the introduction of *cante* instruction in primary schools sponsored by several municipalities in Alentejo and in the Greater Lisbon area; the revival of the *viola campaniça* in the municipality of Castro Verde, an instrument that was taken up by young people in other Alentejan municipalities as well, and its use as a pedagogical tool for teaching *cante* in schools and for accompanying the rehearsals of selected choirs (Rodrigues 2017; Castelo-Branco 2022b); and the inscription of *cante* on UNESCO's Representative List of the ICH, which granted significant symbolic capital.

UNESCO's International Heritage Regime

Cante's inscription on UNESCO's Representative List of the ICH (hereafter, inscription) in 2014 brought unprecedented national and international visibility to *cante* performed by selected Alentejan choirs, especially during the months following the official announcement. Inscriptions on UNESCO's lists are political acts that are embedded in the structures and processes of governmentality (Foucault 1979b), a fundamental "organizational principle of UNESCO" (Di Giovine 2015, 88). According to Tauschek (2011, 49), UNESCO's ICH paradigm is a tool of global governance that has produced more governmentality and expanded the institutional dimension of the state. However, this governmentality has at times triggered friction and conflict among the actors involved (De Cesari 2012,

407) and has often ignored the participatory principle of community involvement emphasized by the 2003 UNESCO Convention.

A critical examination of the motivations, political processes, institutions, and actors who were involved in *cante*'s inscription is necessary to understand the workings and impact of UNESCO's international heritage regime at a local level. The preparation of *cante*'s proposal for inscription was a long and conflicted process, as is reported in other cases (De Cesari 2012; Macchiarella 2011; Samson 2015). The idea to seek a UNESCO seal for *cante* was initially launched in 1999 by Évora's municipality, more than a decade following the inscription of the city's historical center on UNESCO's List of World Heritage Sites in 1986 (Castelo-Branco and Lima 2018, 29). The aim was to promote tourism in the city and the region by seeking UNESCO's certification through the program of the Proclamation of the Masterpieces of the Oral and Intangible Cultural Heritage of Humanity that had been approved by UNESCO's Executive Board in 1998. However, due to a change in the municipality's administration, the plan did not go forward.

During the following decade, several state institutions expressed interest in promoting *cante*'s inscription, but no action was taken. In 2011 and 2012, Serpa's municipality spearheaded the preparation of *cante*'s application for inscription, following fado's successful and widely publicized UNESCO ICH seal in 2011. The preparation of *cante*'s application was financially supported by Alentejo's Tourist Board as part of a wide-ranging project of rebranding that promoted the region as a tourist destination (ERT 2014–2020). This process involved the creation of infrastructure and new events for tourists as well as the conversion of local expressive practices and other local goods into value-added products for tourist consumption. Serpa's municipality commissioned a consulting firm that specializes in communication, marketing, creative industries, and tourism, among other expertise, to prepare the application. Based in Lisbon, the firm's main strategy was to market *cante*'s inscription, seeking the support of politicians and cultural elites. The application was initially rejected by the Portuguese National Commission of UNESCO, the institution at the Ministry of Foreign Affairs that validates and submits applications to UNESCO's programs on behalf of the Portuguese government. It was rejected on the grounds that it did not involve the communities of *cante* bearers and did not reflect solid knowledge of the genre's practice. In 2012, Serpa's municipality founded a heritage institution, the Casa do Cante (House of Cante), renamed Museu do Cante Alentejano (Alentejan Cante Museum) with the aim of safeguarding and promoting this expressive practice. Preparation of the application was entrusted to its then director Paulo Lima, an anthropologist and "heritage specialist" who has a longstanding record

13. Sounding the Alentejo

as a scholar of, and advocate for, expressive practices in the region and in other parts of the country.

What was the impact of UNESCO's heritage regime on the practice and meaning of *cante*? As many scholars have pointed out (Howard 2012; Norton and Matsumoto 2019), the repercussions of UNESCO's ICH paradigm on expressive practices and their communities are complex and diverse, and they need to be assessed critically and collaboratively with the actors involved, a task which is beginning to be carried out in the case of *cante*. The following preliminary reflections draw on my observation of the different phases of the preparation of *cante*'s application, my participation in some of the meetings of the MODA association and other interested parties prior to the inscription, my role in the committee[19] that drafted the final proposal for UNESCO, interviews and conversations with research partners, as well as the evaluation of the impact of the inscription by other scholars (Balbino 2021; Branco 2017; Mareco 2017; Pestana and Barriga 2019; Simões 2021). As several heritage scholars have noted, the global field of heritage politics and the different roles assumed by researchers pose epistemological, methodological, and ethical challenges that warrant reflexive critical assessment and take into account recent transformations in anthropological and ethnomusicological praxis (Bortolotto 2015; Castelo-Branco 2022b; De Cesari 2012; Diamond and Castelo-Branco 2021; Hafstein 2014; Samson 2015).

According to a survey conducted by the Casa do Cante,[20] in 2020 there were over one hundred ninety active *cante* choirs in Alentejo and among Alentejans in the greater Lisbon area. Over 3,750 men and women composing these choirs zealously rehearse and perform a poetic and musical repertoire that materializes their identification with the region and their emotional bonding. The choirs are supported financially and logistically by the municipalities in which they are based. While recognizing the symbolic capital accrued from UNESCO's certification, many choirs and their municipalities felt excluded from the process that led to *cante*'s inscription and the media attention that followed and contested Serpa's legitimacy as the sole representative of *cante*. As Bortolotto points out, despite the "participatory heritage governance" (2015, 251) promoted by UNESCO, empowering communities as the central agents in heritage making has been problematic, in part due to the lack of a definition of "community" and of best practices for community engagement in the 2003 UNESCO Convention (De Cesari 2012). In practice, anthropologists, ethnomusicologists, and other heritage "specialists" have played an important role in most heritage-making processes, serving as mediators between communities of practice and among local, national, and international heritage institutions.

UNESCO's certification inscribes *cante* in an archive of "national" artifacts and cultural practices that are of "universal" value and therefore should be safeguarded. As Stuart Hall argues, heritage is the "material embodiment of the spirit of the nation," an archive for the various "national" arts and artifacts, and "one of the ways in which the nation slowly constructs for itself a sort of collective social memory" (2005, 22–23). The discursive construction of *cante* as "intangible cultural heritage" (*património cultural imaterial*) or more broadly as heritage (*património*), and its commodification for the tourism industry, has tended to dissociate this expressive practice from the "subaltern pasts" of many of its Alentejan practitioners, a past that is entangled with the aesthetics and poetics of *cante*. The "otherness" of Alentejo and Alentejans, often emphasized in anecdotal references to the "Alentejan character" and scholarly literature on the region, is gradually giving way to a new image of the region as a rich reservoir of natural landscapes, local gastronomy, and "authentic" cultural practices, an image that is forged by the neoliberal agenda, promoted by the tourism industry, and supported by the "authorized heritage discourse—AHD" (Smith 2006). As critical heritage scholar Chiara Bortolotto points out, AHD "marginalizes different understandings of heritage produced by subaltern communities or lay people and assesses the 'authenticity' of their cultural expressions against criteria seen as objective by heritage professionals" (2015, 249). Within the heritage-making process, the much-valued diversity of *cante* and of Alentejan choirs (each with its distinct historical trajectory, notables, poets, composers, singers, and singing style) is glossed over and homogenized into a certified product, Alentejo's *cante*, to be packaged as a value-added commodity for the global tourist market.

The inscription of *cante* on UNESCO's ICH List has not directly benefitted most of the choirs that zealously maintain and disseminate the practice. At the same time, while most choirs did not accrue the economic benefits and national visibility that they expected, the symbolic value conferred by UNESCO's seal has raised *cante*'s prestige and its practitioners' self-esteem, and according to the above-mentioned survey, catalyzed the formation of over fifty new choirs. It also motivated young people who had previously shunned *cante* to join established choirs and to form their own groups. While maintaining the conventional performance model, singing style, and repertoire of Alentejan choirs, they abandoned the rural costumes, replacing them with contemporary informal attire. Some young Alentejans are also exploring new performance formats, replacing the choir with a handful of singers accompanied by the recently revived local guitar, the *viola campaniça*, or by other musical instruments. Most of these new groups are aspiring towards professionalization and gaining

13. Sounding the Alentejo 261

access to the popular-music market. At the same time, several art and popular-music composers have made arrangements or recreations of *cante*'s repertoire, composing new music inspired by the genre or mixing *cante* with other musical styles (Castelo-Branco and Lima 2018).

Cante Matters

The practice of *cante* has remained resilient through different political, social, and economic transformations and heritage regimes. Institutionalized by the authoritarian state's heritage regime in the 1930s, Alentejan amateur choirs expanded during the democratic era, transforming into a significant grassroots movement in the Alentejo region and among its migrants in the greater Lisbon area and bringing women into the public arena of choir performance. By the end of the twentieth century, the sustainability of *cante* was a major issue due to the advanced age of choir members and the lack of interest of young people in joining. UNESCO's certification in 2014 introduced *cante* to the global arena and resignified it as ICH, an "ideologically grounded symbolic construct" (Castelo-Branco 2013, 661) that tends to dissociate this expressive practice from its subaltern roots.

Transcending heritage politics, Alentejan men and women have constituted *cante* as a powerful expressive resource that has been central to their individual and social lives. Despite the crystalized performance format in which Alentejan choirs were cast and the perpetuation of an authenticated repertoire, they represent a powerful grassroots social movement that empowers individuals, sustains communities, resists oblivion, and contributes to "creating and sustaining social relations through music," as Caroline Bithell has argued in the case of amateur natural voice and world song choirs in the UK (2014, 295). Choir rehearsals and presentational and participatory performances create spaces that promote conviviality, social intimacy, emotional bonding, the expression of emotions, and a sense of belonging to an imagined community of Alentejans.

Notes

1. For a brief characterization of UNESCO's 2003 ICH Convention and its implementation in Portugal, see Chapter 12. For UNESCO's definition of ICH, see Article 2 of the 2003 Convention: https://ich.unesco.org/en/convention.

2. Alentejo is the largest and most sparsely populated region in Portugal with an aging resident population (www.ine.pt). Located south of the Tagus River (as its name indicates, Alem-Tejo, literally beyond the Tagus), it borders the Algarve mountain range to the south, the Atlantic Ocean to the West, and the autonomous region of Extremadura

in Spain to the East. It is divided into four territorial units: northern, central, coastal, and southern Alentejo. Expressive culture, including music and dance, has been central in the symbolic geography associated with this territory.

3. *Cante* is a polyphonic vocal genre sung in two parts mostly by single-gender choirs. Discourse surrounding *cante* associates the genre with southern Alentejo. However, *cante* choirs are also disseminated in central and coastal Alentejo, as well as among Alentejan migrants in the greater Lisbon Area. For a characterization of the repertoire, styles, and performance format of *cante*, see Castelo-Branco (2008, 24–32).

4. For the constitution and functions of the Intergovernmental Committee for the Safeguarding of ICH, see https://ich.unesco.org/en/functions-00586. For the Evaluation Body, see https://ich.unesco.org/en/evaluation-body-00802.

5. Composed by José Lopes Gato in the 1960s, this *moda* has been promoted by the municipality of Serpa in southern Alentejo since 2000 as a "regional anthem" on the "Day of Cante" celebrated by the municipality.

6. See https://anibalcavacosilva.arquivo.presidencia.pt/?idc=18&idi=88341.

7. See https://tinyurl.com/CanteVote.

8. As argued by Castelo-Branco and Sánchez-Carretero in Chapter 12, critical heritage scholars mobilize the concept of "regime" as a tool for analyzing the politics of heritage and the multiple ways in which heritage intersects with "government" in the broader sense of Foucauldian governmentality (Foucault 1979b).

9. Authenticated repertoire refers to the corpus collected by folklorists and ethnographers, textualized in song books, documented in sound recordings, and/or selected by choir masters for presentational performances (Castelo-Branco and Branco 2003).

10. For historical accounts of the Ceifeiros, see Moniz (2007) and Balbino (2021). For historical and recent annotated sound recordings of the Ceifeiros and other Alentejan choirs, see Castelo-Branco and Lima (2018).

11. The Casas do Povo (CP) are a network of institutions created by the Estado Novo in 1933 (Decree Law 23 051, 23–09–1933). Integrated within the regime's corporatist structure, their stated aim was to contribute to the economic, social, and cultural development of local communities, defending the interests of rural workers and administering the social security of local residents. In practice, the CPs exercised control over local populations. In 1982, the Casas do Povo ceased to exist as governmental institutions and were transformed into voluntary associations that aimed to promote the wellbeing of local populations (Decree Law no. 4/82, 11–01–1982). See also Melo (2001).

12. In 1959, the Ceifeiros affiliated with the state agency Fundação Nacional para Alegria no Trabalho, started rehearsing at Cuba's Casa do Povo, changed their name from Grupo de Cantadores de Cuba "Os Ceifeiros" to Grupo dos Ceifeiros da Casa do Povo de Cuba, and replaced their Sunday attire during performance to that used by harvesters (Moniz 2007, 62–65).

13. For an ethnographic account of informal singing in taverns in Cuba, see Balbino (2021, 151–81).

14. For a discussion of the use of *cante* in venues and events targeted at tourists in Cuba, see Balbino (2021, 183–98). For the uses of *cante* for tourist promotion, see Simões (2017 and 2021).

15. The concept of *cultura popular* and its qualifiers such as *música* or *arte popular* have been central in the "authorized heritage discourse" (Smith 2006) of Portuguese

13. Sounding the Alentejo 263

intellectuals, ethnographers, and cultural politicians since the nineteenth century and have been resignified by different political regimes and agents (Castelo-Branco 2013; Castelo-Branco and Cidra 2010).

16. Known as *ranchos folclóricos*, folklore groups are constituted by dancers, singers, and instrumentalists who perform an authenticated repertoire of local dances or dance-song genres in costumes, presumably going back to the beginning of the twentieth century. A dance-song genre was selected as an iconic representation of each region, for example, the *vira* for the Minho, the *fandango* for the Ribatejo, and the *corridinho* for the Algarve (Castelo-Branco et al., 2010).

17. Local practitioners usually avoid references to the composers and poets of *cante* as they associate authenticity with the anonymity of authorship.

18. For a survey of the age profile of Alentejan choirs in 1998 and its update in 2014, see Castelo-Branco, Neves, and Lima (2003) and Lima (2014).

19. Alongside my own participation, the committee consisted of a representative from each of the associations that represent choirs (MODA and the Confraria do Cante), the president of the House of Alentejo, a representative of the municipality of Serpa, and the anthropologist who directed the Casa do Cante.

20. Email communication with the current director, June 30, 2021.

References

Alves, Vera Marques. 2013. *Arte popular e nação no Estado Novo: A política folclorísta do Secretariado da Propaganda Nacional.* Lisbon: Imprensa de Ciências Sociais.

Balbino, Carlos. 2021. "Qui commande le cante a Cuba? Une analyse des jeux d' autorité et de legitimité autor du cante esponâneo, dans une ville rurale portugaise." MA thesis, Université Paris Nanterre.

Bendix, Regina. 2009. "Heritage between Economy and Politics: An Assessment from the Perspective of Cultural Anthropology." In *Intangible Heritage*, edited by Laurajane Smith and Natsuko Akagawa, 253–69. New York: Routledge.

Bendix, Regina, Aditya Eggert, and Arnika Peselmann, eds. 2012. *Heritage Regimes and the State.* Göttingen, DE: Universitätsverlag Göttingen.

Bithell, Caroline. 2007. *Transported by Song: Corsican Voices from Oral Tradition to World Stage.* Lanham, MD: The Scarecrow Press.

———. 2014. *A Different Voice, A Different Song: Reclaiming Community through Natural Voice and World Song.* Oxford: Oxford University Press.

Bortolotto, Chiara. 2015. "UNESCO and Heritage Self-Determination: Negotiating Meaning in the Intergovernmental Committee for the Safeguarding of the ICH." In *Between Imagined Communities and Communities of Practice: Participation, Territory and the Making of Heritage*, edited by Nicolas Adell, Regina Bendix, and Markus Tauschek, 249–72. Göttingen, DE: Universitätsverlag Göttingen.

Branco, Jorge Freitas et al., 2017. "Mesa redonda—O cante: Práticas, memórias e património." In *Cantar no Alentejo: A terra, o passado e o presente*, edited by Maria do Rosário Pestana and Luísa Tiago de Oliveira, 197–246. Estremoz, PT: Estremoz Editora.

Cabeça, Sónia, and José Rodrigues Santos. 2010. "A mulher no cante Alentejano." In *Actas da Conferência de tradición oral: Oralidade e património cultural.* Vol. 2, 31–38. Ourense, ES: Concello de Ourense.

Castelo-Branco, Salwa El-Shawan. 2008. "The Aesthetics and Politics of Multipart Singing in Southern Portugal." In *European Voices: Multipart Singing in the Balkans and the Mediterranean*, edited by Ardian Ahmedaja and Gerlinde Haid, 15–37. Vienna: Bohlau Verlag.

———. 2013. "The Politics of Music Categorization in Portugal." In *The Cambridge History of World Music*, edited by Philip Bohlman, 661–77. Cambridge: Cambridge University Press.

———. 2022a. "Interrogating the Politics and Ethics of Musical Heritage." In *Encounters in Ethnomusicology: Essays in Honor of Philip V. Bohlman*, edited by Michael A. Figueroa, Jaime Jones, and Tim Rommen, 67–74. Zurich: Lit Verlag.

———. 2022b. "Sustainability, Agency and the Ecologies of Music Heritage in Alentejo, Portugal." In *Music, Communities, and Sustainability: Developing Policies and Practices*, edited by Huib Schippers and Anthony Seeger, 177–95. New York: Oxford University Press.

Castelo-Branco, Salwa, and Rui Cidra. 2010. "Música popular." In *Enciclopédia da música em Portugal no século XX*. Vol. 3. Edited by Salwa Castelo-Branco, 875–78. Lisbon: Círculo de Leitores/Temas e Debates.

Castelo-Branco, Salwa El-Shawan, and Jorge Freitas Branco, eds. 2003. *Vozes do povo: A Folclorização em Portugal*. Lisbon: Celta Editora & Etnográfica Press. https://books.open edition.org/etnograficapress/537.

Castelo-Branco, Salwa El-Shawan, Maria João Lima, and José Neves. 2003. "Perfis dos grupos de música tradicional em Portugal em finais do século XX." In *Vozes do povo: A Folclorização em Portugal*, edited by Salwa El-Shawan Castelo-Branco and Jorge Freitas Branco, 73–141. Oieras, PT: Celta Editora.

Castelo-Branco, Salwa El-Shawan, and Paulo Lima. 2018. *Cantes*. 4 vols. Lisbon: A Bela e o Monstro, Edições/Público.

Castelo-Branco, Salwa et al., 2010. "Ranchos folclóricos." In *Enciclopédia da música em Portugal no século XX*. Vol. 3. Edited by Salwa Castelo-Branco, 1097–1101. Lisbon: Círculo de Leitores/Temas e Debates.

Cidra, Rui. 2015. "Politics of Memory, Ethics of Survival: The Songs and Narratives of the Cape Verdean Diaspora in São Tomé." *Ethnomusicology Forum* 24, no. 3: 304–28.

De Cesari, Chiara. 2012. "Thinking Through Heritage Regimes." In *Heritage Regimes and the State*, edited by Regina Bendix et al., 399–413. Göttingen, DE: Universitätsverlag Göttingen.

De Nora, Tia. 2000. *Music in Everyday Life*. Cambridge: Cambridge University Press.

Di Giovine, Michael. 2015. "UNESCO's World Heritage Program: The Challenges and Ethics of Community Participation." In *Between Imagined Communities and Communities of Practice: Participation, Territory and the Making of Heritage*, edited by Nicolas Adell, Regina Bendix, Chiara Borttolotto, and Markus Tauscheck, 83–110. Göttingen, DE: Universitätsverlag.

Diamond, Beverly, and Salwa El-Shawan Castelo-Branco, eds. 2021. *Transforming Ethnomusicology*. 2 vols. London: Oxford University Press

ERT-Turismo do Alentejo. 2014–2020. *Documento estratégico turismo do Alentejo, 2014–2020: Visão, prioridades estratégicas e eixos de intervenção*. Beja, PT: ERT-Turismo do Alentejo. https://www.visitalentejo.pt/fotos/editor2/pdfs/alentejo2014_2020_documento_estrategico_turismo.pdf.

13. Sounding the Alentejo

Feld. Steve. 1996. "Waterfalls of Song: An Acoustemology of Place Resounding in Bosavi, Papua New Guinea." In *Senses of Place*, edited by Steven Feld and Keith Basso, 91–136. Santa Fe, NM: School of American Research Press.

Foucault, Michel. 1979a. *Discipline and Punish: The Birth of the Prison*. Hammondsworth, UK: Penguin.

———. 1979b. "Governmentality." *Ideology & Consciousness* 6: 5–21.

Hafstein, Valdimar. 2014. "Protection as Dispossession: Government in the Vernacular." In *Heritage in Transit: Intangible Rights as Humans Rights*, edited by Deborah Kapchan, 25–57. Philadelphia: University of Pennsylvania Press.

Hall, Stuart. 2005. "Whose Heritage? Un-settling 'The Heritage,' Re-imagining the Post-Nation." In *The Politics of Heritage, The Legacies of Race*, edited by Jo Littler and Roshi Naidoo, 21–32. New York: Routledge.

Harrison, Rodney. 2013. *Heritage: Critical Approaches*. London: Routledge.

Hill, Juniper, and Caroline Bithell. 2014. "An Introduction to Music Revival as Concept, Cultural Process, and Medium of Change." In *The Oxford Handbook of Musical Revival*, edited by Caroline Bithell and Juniper Hill, 3–42. New York: Oxford University Press.

Holton, Kimberley. 2003. *Performing Folklore: From Lisbon to Newark*. Bloomington: Indiana University Press.

Howard, Keith, ed. 2012. *Music as Intangible Cultural Heritage: Policy, Ideology and Practice in the Preservation of East Asian Traditions*. Farnham, UK: Ashgate.

Kirshenblatt-Gimblett. Barbara. 1995. "Theorizing Heritage." *Ethnomusicology* 39, no. 3: 367–80.

———. 2004. "Intangible Heritage as Metacultural Production." *Museum International* 56, no. 1–2: 52–65.

Leal, João. 2000. *Etnografias portuguesas (1870–1970): Cultura popular e identidade nacional*. Lisbon: Publicações Dom Quixote.

Lima, Maria João. 2014. "Cante Singing Groups: A Portrait from Two Extensive Surveys." In *The Alentejo: Voices and Aesthetics*, edited by Maria do Rosário Pestana, 70–93. Vila Verde, PT: Tradisom.

Lortat-Jacob, Bernard.1998. *Chants de passion, au coeur d'un confrérie de Sardaigne*. Paris: Les Editions du Sèrf.

Lowenthall, David. 1996. *Possessed by the Past: The Heritage Crusade and the Spoils of History*. New York: Free Press.

Macchiarella, Ignazio. 2011. "Dove il tocco di Re Mida non arriva: A proposito di proclamazione, UNESCO e musica." *La Ricerca Folklorica* 64: 61–80.

Mareco, Susana. 2017. "A nova geração do cante e as manifestações sobre o cante Alentejano." In *Cantar no Alentejo: A terra, o passado e o presente*, edited by Maria do Rosário Pestana and Luísa Tiago de Oliveira, 59–88. Estremoz, PT: Estremoz Editora.

Marvão, Antonio. 1966. *Origens e características do folclore musical Alentejano*. Author's Edition.

Melo, Daniel. 2001. *Salazarismo e cultura popular: 1933–1958*. Lisbon: Imprensa de Ciências Sociais.

Moniz, Jorge. 2007. "A folclorização do Cante Alentejano: Um estudo de caso do Grupo Coral Os Ceifeiros de Cuba (1933–2007)." MA thesis, Universidade Nova de Lisboa.

Monteiro, Nuno, and António Costa Pinto. 2011. "Cultural Myths and Portuguese National Identity." In *Contemporary Portugal: Politics, Society and Culture*. 2nd ed. Edited by António Costa Pinto, 55–72. Boulder, CO: Social Science Monographs.

Norton, Barley, and Naomi Matsumoto, eds. 2019. *Music as Heritage: Historical and Ethnographic Perspectives*. London: Routledge.

Pereira, J. F. 2005. *Que modas? Que modos? 1º Congresso do cante: Actas*. PT: Faialentejo--Organização Cultural.

Pestana, Maria do Rosário. 2014. "Introduction." In *The Alentejo: Voices and Aesthetics in 1939/40: A Critical Edition of Armando Leça's Sound Recordings*, edited by Maria do Rosário Pestana, 2–19. Vila Verde, PT: Tradisom.

———. 2015. "Introdução: Cantar em Coro em Portugal (1880–2914): Práticas, contextos, ideologias." In *Vozes ao alto: Cantar em coro em Portugal—Protagonistas, contextos e percursos*, edited by Maria do Rosário Pestana, 5–46. Lisbon: Movimento Patrimonial pela Música Portuguesa.

Pestana, Maria do Rosário, and Maria José Barriga. 2019. "'Le patrimoine c'est nous': Voix plurielles autour du cante alentejano." *Transposition: Musiques et Sciences Sociales* 8. https://journals.openedition.org/transposition/3353.

Picão, José Silva. 1983 [1903]. *Através dos campos: Usos e costumes agrícolas-Alentejanos*. Lisbon: Publicações Dom Quixote.

Piçarra, Ladislau, and Manuel Dias Nunes, eds. 1899–1904. *A Tradição: Revista Mensal d'ethnographia Portugueza*. 6 vols. Serpa, PT: Câmara Municipal.

Roberts, Les. 2014. "Talkin bout my generation: Popular Music and the Culture of Heritage." *International Journal of Heritage Studies* 20, no. 3: 262–80.

Rodrigues, Joana. 2017. "'Pelo Toque da Viola': Um estudo etnomusicológico sobre o revivalismo da viola campaniça em Castro Verde." MA thesis, NOVA University of Lisbon.

Rose, Nikolas, Pat O'Malley, and Mariana Valverde. 2006. "Governmentality." *Annual Review of Law and Social Science* 2: 83–104.

Samson, Guillaume. 2015. "Maloya Music as World Cultural Heritage: The Cultural, Political and Ethical Fallout of Labelling." *Translingual Discourse in Ethnomusicology* 1: 27–43.

Santos, Maria de Lourdes Lima dos. et al., 1998. *As políticas culturais em Portugal*. Lisbon: Observatório das Actividades Culturais.

Simões, Dulce. 2017. "A turistificação do cante alentejano como estratégia de 'desenvolvimento': Discursos políticose práticas da cultura." In *Cantar no Alentejo: A terra, o passado e o presente*, edited by Maria do Rosário Pestana and Luísa Tiago de Oliveira, 76–78. Estremoz, PT: Estremoz Editora.

———. 2021. *Imaginação, utopia e práticas de resistência: A cultura expressiva na Raia do Baixo Alentejo*. Lisbon: Colibri.

Smith, Laurajane. 2006. *Uses of Heritage*. New York: Routledge.

———. 2012. "Discussion." In *Heritage Regimes and the State*, edited by Regina Bendix, Aditya Eggert, and Arnkia Peselmann, 389–98. Göttingen, DE: Universitätsverlag Göttingen.

Tauschek, Markus. 2011. "Reflections on the Metacultural Nature of Intangible Cultural Heritage." *Journal of Ethnology and Folkloristics* 5, no. 2: 49–62.

Turino, Thomas. 2008. *Music as Social Life: The Politics of Participation*. Chicago: The University of Chicago Press.

Vialette, Aurélie. 2018. *Intellectual Philanthropy: The Seduction of the Masses*. West Lafayette, IN: Purdue University Press.

14

Flamenco Heritage and the Politics of Identity

CRISTINA CRUCES ROLDÁN

The connections between acts of reclaiming traditional culture and nationalist movements have been the subject of significant theoretical consideration in the last few decades and are often related to concepts such as the "imagined community" (Anderson 1983) and the "invention of tradition" (Hobsbawm 1984). In the case of Spain, the construction of a national identity was a lengthy process that peaked during the nineteenth century, and that was characterized by the difficult coexistence of diverse projects that coalesced around the idea of a "collective we." Contradictions between the romantic image of Spain that arose in industrialized Europe and the "autochthonous and indigenous" (*costumbrista* and *castiza*) image promoted in Spain clashed with the political struggles between conservatives and reformists, creating a "problematic identity" for the country throughout the twentieth century (Juliá Díaz 2004; Álvarez Junco 2003).

Although flamenco was an essential element in these contradictory images of Spain, it only held a peripheral position in debates around the "essence" of Spain. For Andalusian folklorists such as Antonio Machado Álvarez (otherwise known as "Demófilo"), flamenco embodied a collective soul perceived to be at the brink of extinction due to the risqué atmosphere of the *café cantantes* and a loss in its authenticity (Machado y Álvarez 1996). In contrast, the critical currents of thought that emerged in the wake of the collapse of Spain's colonial empire in 1898—fed by both prejudiced ideas from outside of Spain as well as internal negative images (Calvo Serraller 1995; Andreu Miralles 2016)—adopted an approach to flamenco that was closer to contempt than to the Herderian *Volkgeist* or nationalist extolling. Literary quotes from Pío Baroja, José Martínez Ruiz "Azorín," Miguel de Unamuno's essays, and especially the incendiary texts by Eugenio Noel (1914, 1916) are particularly pertinent in this respect. Not surprisingly, in the context of the 1922 Granada competition, a group of poets and intellectuals tried to restore *cante jondo*'s attributes of purity and lyricism that had been alienated by previous anti-flamenco criticism. As in many other contexts of flamenco's history, the competition regarded authenticity as an absolute category rather than a contingent one.

Is the complex and convoluted image of flamenco today a result of these polarized debates? In part, the answer is yes. From the second half of the nineteenth century—arguably the period in which the genre was born—flamenco has been caught up in difficult tensions between appreciation and rejection as well as tradition and modernity. Flamenco continues to be an art form that evokes *Gitano* identity and is rooted in discourses about primitivism and the perceived otherness of Andalusia as an Orient in Europe. Yet the real experience of staged flamenco is that of an art recreated for daily consumption, far from the entertainment of privileged *señoritos* (referring to landowners and aristocrats) and libertines and from the dishonor of the flamenco lumpen.

Over the past four decades, scholarly trends confirm the growing recognition of flamenco as an artistic expression and/or an instrument of identity-making as well as an object of the heritagization politics of the Andalusian government. The Junta de Andalucía—the region's government—owes its approach to the new heritage paradigms that arose from the Convention for the Safeguarding of the Intangible Cultural Heritage (UNESCO 2003). The postulates of heritagization in this context favor values such as significance, relevance, and representativity as the defining characteristics of intangible cultural heritage against those of exceptionality, monumentalism, and scarcity (Abric 1994; Ballart 1997; Ribeiro 1998). Rather than simply support "conservation," the Convention embraces the notion of "safeguarding" (UNESCO 2003, Article 2.3) and regards heritage as a socially dynamic concept, devoid of essentialism. The Convention follows the direction previously adopted by the Franceschini Commission in 1964, regarding the need to establish a compatible relationship between changes introduced in the tradition, processes of transmission, identity formations, and expressions of diversity (Article 2.1) (Cicerchia 2002). More importantly, the Convention ascribes fundamental value to the collective agents of transmission, which it no longer regards as objects of preservation but rather as necessary subjects and as active agents in the process of heritagization. The role of nation-states within this framework is oriented towards defining, administering, and regulat-

14. Flamenco Heritage and the Politics of Identity 269

ing this heritage but not without the prior, free, and informed consent of those communities. At the same time, UNESCO operates at a supra-national level, where it promotes "cultural diversity and human creativity" (2003, Article 21) while evaluating the applications submitted by entities such as the *comunidades autónomas* (autonomous communities) in Spain.

Although the theoretical underpinnings of the Convention are widely accepted, there has also been criticism of the "double decision" management system whereby states have the final word on selection, inventory, safeguarding, and the selection of submissions to UNESCO. Situations of conflict have been reported, provoked by the reduction of consent to a mere formality, the lack of monitoring of state responsibility, and the use of heritage to acquire political prestige or as an instrument of propaganda. These conflicts arise from the imbalanced distribution of power between, on the one hand, the states and institutions that possess decision-making capacities and the bulk of the material and intellectual resources, and, on the other hand, the limitations that communities face, whose heterogenous nature makes it difficult for them to reach consensus on key issues (Kirshenblatt-Gimblett 2004; Peralta and Anico 2006; Bortolotto 2011; Harrison 2013; González Cambeiro and Querol Fernández 2014). From a very critical perspective, decolonial theorists warn of the subordination of the goals of the communities to the state politics of representation (Melé 2005; Fanon 2009; Mignolo 2010; Sousa Santos and Meneses 2014). Sen (1999) proposes that the actors directly concerned should choose the modes of development that they want and the cultural traditions that they value. Several authors problematize the idealization and reification of communities involved in processes of administrative objectivation and note that the UNESCO Convention seems to place individuals, groups, and communities in positions that are foreign to their internal hierarchies and heterogeneity (Waterton and Smith 2010; Hertz 2015; Tauschek 2015). Local research demonstrates that UNESCO objectifies the idea of community, often facilitating contradictory views about the same heritage (Villaseñor Alonso and Zolla 2012; Quintero Morón and Sánchez Carretero 2017).

In November 2010, flamenco was included in UNESCO's Representative List of the Intangible Cultural Heritage of Humanity. However, twenty-first-century flamenco has inherited historical controversies in which intellectual reflection, debates about purity, the exchange of views between the agents involved, and the implementation of political and institutional action coexist. This chapter discusses the recent integration of flamenco in public policies in Andalusia and examines the institutional process that led to the preparation of the UNESCO candidature and its campaign of support. Based on the results of interviews I carried out with thirty-four professional dancers, it also analyzes the extent to which the communities, groups, or individuals referred to in the submission agree with the official discourse, their roles prior to the candidature, what reactions followed, and how they perceived the heritagization process.

The Instrumentalization of Flamenco:
From "España cañí" to Regional Autonomy

Franco's centralist agenda introduced substantial changes into an art that was still clinging to French *espagnolade* (exotic representations of Spain). From the beginning of the Franco dictatorship (1939–1975), regional folklore was drawn upon to resolve the contradictions between unity and diversity, thus turning it into "an aesthetic and emotional element, whereby regional diversity [became] an unproblematic aspect in the composition of a national picture" (Ortiz García 2012, 2). A new process of nationalization (referred to by the term *nacionalflamenquismo*) turned flamenco into an icon of Spanishness. Flamenco was thus whitewashed, as it was deprived of any links to regionalization and dispossessed of its original attachments to class, ethnicity, and culture.

During the 1940s and 1950s, the *ballet español* was disseminated widely, a highbrow genre that added a patina of morality to the less virtuous *baile flamenco* and that avoided the radical, antihegemonic connotations of resistance that flamenco had gained. During the Cold War, Franco pursued a two-pronged strategy, namely, a move towards the institutionalization of flamenco in Spain and its use in the construction of diplomatic ties abroad. He thus organized receptions at La Granja de San Ildefonso palace, as well as the heterogenous *Festivales de España*, and tours of the regime's favorites such as Antonio and Pilar López's touring companies. The academic and stylized *bailes-danzas* of such touring groups helped polish the pathos and tragedy of the *cante jondo* (deep song) and transformed the libertarian *fiesta*, packed with *bulerías* and *tangos*, into a decorative and unengaged form void of social references. Singing trends such as crooner-style *canzonetismo*, *fandango*, and *cantes de ida y vuelta* ("roundtrip songs"), all of which had already been in vogue for decades, continued to feature in Andalusian-inspired theatrical and film comedies until the 1960s. Inside and outside the country, representations of Spanishness used flamenco as a metonym for a patriotic and *tipista* (localist) image of Spain. In the same way as other art forms, flamenco was co-opted into the interventionist policies of Franco's successive governments, into the government-controlled, hierarchical entertainment-industry union, and into the development-oriented subsidized policies, which were applied to all artistic productions "of national interest." At

14. Flamenco Heritage and the Politics of Identity 271

the same time, the echoes of *jondismo* barely scraped by and were relegated to private parties in inns, corner shops, and salacious taverns, contexts in which *cante gitano* began to be marginalized.

The technocratic turn of the 1960s facilitated the renovation of Francoism's flamenco façade. Between 1959 and 1964, the Stabilization and Economic Liberalization Plan and the Economic and Social Development Plan of Laureano López Rodó dispelled the shadows of post-war autarchy and interventionism. Certain diplomatic and, particularly, commercial barriers that had been present since Franco's Italo-German alliance during the Second World War were finally opened: in 1953 Spain signed bilateral agreements with the United States and, in 1964, it subscribed commercial agreements with the European Economic Community despite the latter's reticence to legitimize the regime. A new kind of politics characterized by economic flexibility and industrial development accompanied the tertiarization of the Spanish economy and the shift of agricultural labor to new economic sectors (García Delgado 2013; Vizcaíno Ponferrada 2015). Tourism spread during the 1960s, a decade marked by emigration abroad, rural-to-urban migration, industrial development, rising consumption, and growing income. With the mass arrival of tourists, flamenco was transformed on the stages of *tablaos* (performance venues for flamenco). As Holguín points out, "Once the Franco regime transformed the Spanish tourist industry into one of its top priorities, flamenco became a chief economic engine of Spain's tourist economy and served to solidify flamenco as a major component of Spain's national identity" (2019, 248–49). Meanwhile, the regime cleaned up the image of Spain's backwardness by presenting to German, British, Soviet, and North American audiences attending the International Fair in New York (1964–1965) the flamenco companies of María Rosa, Antonio and Lucero Tena, using them as business cards in an international context increasingly benevolent with the Franco dictatorship.

This political instrumentalization of flamenco coexisted with a more intellectual and engaged strand developed among fans. A few voices called for the rehabilitation of "traditional" flamenco, a style that was behind the making of the films *Duende y misterio del flamenco* (1952) by Edgar Neville and *Antología del cante flamenco* (1954) from Hispavox. Two decades later, the now iconic television series *Rito y geografía del cante* (also *del cante y del toque*) (1971–1973) revived the ethnographic spirit of these two films. The traditionalist approach to flamenco was secured regionally at first and mainly thanks to the landmark publication of *Flamencología* (1955) by Anselmo González Climent, the organization of the *Concurso Nacional de Arte Flamenco de Córdoba* (1956), in which *cantaor* Fosforito achieved a resounding victory, and the awarding of the *Llave de Oro* ("Golden

Key") to singer Antonio Mairena (1962), who co-authored *Mundo y formas del cante flamenco* (1963). These publications and events created a canon of flamenco through a process that could be considered, in Eric Hobsbawm's words, an "invention of tradition." *Mundo y formas del cante flamenco* fell into the same contradiction that characterized the dictatorship's discourse at the time: they both promoted a vision of flamenco anchored in the past but as a salvation for their own "vision of the future" (Bonachera 2015, 212).

Despite the reactionary character of some of its initiatives, the traditionalist revival changed course with the arrival of Spain's transition to democracy following the death of Franco (1975). The rigors of *Mairenismo*, referring here to the influence of Antonio Mairena, had to contend with the modernization of customs and urban cultures and the rise in influence of the mass media from the end of the 1960s. *Mairenismo* also occurred concurrently with the gradual engagement of flamenco with other musics, giving rise to genres such as "rock andaluz," and "blues flamenco," the latter of which was performed by *Gitanos* from marginalized communities in Andalusian cities. As argued by Bethencourt, "there is value in thinking about flamenco during and after the transition not as 'retraditionalised' (or, in Biddle and Knights's terms 're-andalusianized') but as taking up a more fluid (but no less committed) relation to the idea of tradition" (2011, 6). During the Transition, flamenco was freed from its traditional corset thanks to the unprecedented impact of performers such as Paco de Lucía, Camarón de la Isla, and Enrique Morente, born in Andalusia but seasoned in Madrid's *tablaos*.

Following the passing of the Spanish Constitution of 1978 and the promulgation of Andalusia's first Statute of Autonomy in 1981, this region confirmed its status as a "historic nationality." Flamenco became a site of struggle for the pursuit of autonomy in Andalusia and an arena for conflicting interpretations. A section of progressive intellectuals retracted from any cultural expression associated to the dictatorship, including *copla* and flamenco, while the common people, who were hungry for freedom, turned away from certain Andalusian stereotypes. I remember the feeling of dressing up as *flamenca* for the Feria de Sevilla in the late 1970s and how it did not seem "modern" for a woman in her early teens. However, while flamenco was still perceived as a remnant of the past, it was also gradually losing its previous attachments to Spanishness. Left-wing political organizations hired politically engaged singers to enliven their rallies in Andalusia and constructed a type of discourse in which "the people" were represented as the true creators while issuing calls to open centers for the study and the dissemination of flamenco.

14. Flamenco Heritage and the Politics of Identity

The 1970s and 1980s saw the blossoming of associations under the protection of laws of freedom of association and the growth of grassroots social movements. Local *peñas flamencas* (flamenco clubs) were either bound to a neighborhood, a performer, or a theme. Together, they established a network of spaces for the preservation and the dissemination of flamenco in Andalusia as well as the areas of Spain where Andalusian immigration was rife. Pre-democracy institutions such as the Chair of Flamencology in Jerez (1958–1960) were reinforced through new initiatives, such as the privately-funded Fundación Andaluza de Flamenco (1985). Summer festivals flourished thanks to local public investment, restoring the dignity of artists who thus gained economic stability, while larger events such as the Bienal de Arte Flamenco de Sevilla presented attractive programs that combined continuity and change. Meanwhile, researchers and scholars turned flamenco into a topic of intellectual discussion. A rise in the production of discographies led to the publication of collections of classic *cante*, young innovators, artists who embraced the *Gitano* brand, as well as the flamenco-protest artists such as José Menese, El Cabrero, and Manuel Gerena, who appealed to field laborers and denounced the inequalities experienced by agricultural workers.

Between Public Investment and Collective Identity

In 1984, competencies around cultural and heritage-related policy were formally transferred from the Spanish state to the Autonomous Community of Andalusia. From this moment on, flamenco gained more importance than ever before in the design of public policy. This process has been studied with reference to the meanings of flamenco's institutionalization process, its relationship with power, its exploitation of the past (Washabaugh 2012), its contribution to regionalism and localism (Machin-Autenrieth 2017), and the effect of identity politics at supranational, national, and regional levels (Cruces Roldán 2014). Furthermore, Aix Gracia (2014) has studied the transition from revalorization to institutionalization, showing the ways in which flamenco has become a part of official cultural policy, and has examined the festivalization of the cultural offerings of different Andalusian cities.

The public sector was the crucial agent of this flamenco awakening. From the 1980s, local and provincial councils, as well as the Junta de Andalucía, invested in the awarding of grants to support the promotion and diffusion of flamenco. The policies aimed at the development of flamenco that have been implemented during the four decades of socialist government in Andalusia (1978–2019) have, for the most part, been maintained following the victory of the center-right in the 2018 and 2022 elections. From the 1980s to the 2010s, a number of institutions have been established, including the Consultancy Office of Flamenco Activities of the Andalusian Government (1982), the Andalusian Centro for Flamenco (1993)—formerly the Andalusian Foundation for Flamenco; currently known as the Andalusian Center for the Documentation of Flamenco—and the creation of the Andalusian Dance Company (1995), which today is the Flamenco Ballet of Andalusia, representing the most recognized form of Andalusian dance on international stages.

In 2005, the Andalusian Agency of Flamenco was created, and after multiple transformations in the public administration, it culminated in the Andalusian Institute of Flamenco. In 2010, the Advising Committee on Flamenco was established. In strictly heritage terms, the Junta de Andalucía listed the shellac recordings of *Gitana* singer Pastora Pavón Cruz, known as "Niña de los Peines," in the General Catalog of Andalusian Historical Heritage as *Bien de Interés Cultural de Andalucía* ("Asset of Cultural Interest of Andalusia") in 1997. Between 2011 and 2019, the *fiesta de verdiales*,[1] the *Escuela sevillana de baile* ("Sevillian dance school style"), the *Escuela bolera* ("*Bolera* dance school style"), the *zambombas*[2] of towns Arcos and Jerez de la Frontera, and the *fandango de Huelva* were all listed in this catalog. In addition, the Junta pursues other long-term initiatives such as the awarding of grants to flamenco productions, festivals, flamenco networks, book and record publications, festivals such as Flamenco Viene del Sur (Flamenco Comes from the South), the inclusion of flamenco in the conservatory curriculum, and the Flamenco Law of 2022. As Machin-Autenrieth points out, "While flamenco has, in the past, been constructed as a Spanish musical tradition [. . .], its relevance for Andalusian identity has moved to the foreground" (2013, 321).

Two further events fostered the heritagization of flamenco in Andalusia in the early 2000s. The first was the inclusion of flamenco in the reformed *Estatuto de Autonomía* of Andalusia ("Statute of Autonomy" 2007). Articles 37 and 68 assign to the Autonomous Community of Andalusia the role of safeguarding "the conservation and valorization of cultural, historical, and artistical heritage of Andalusia, especially of flamenco," and "the exclusive competency (*competencia*) in terms of knowledge, conservation, research, training, promotion and dissemination of flamenco as a singular element of Andalusian cultural heritage." These articles received little commentary from artists and the public but have nevertheless captured the attention of intellectuals, who have either supported or dismissed the initiative, depending on their beliefs. The second event was the inclusion of flamenco in UNESCO's Representative List of the Intangible Cultural Heritage (2010). Branded as opportunist by many, the application consolidated

14. Flamenco Heritage and the Politics of Identity

Andalusia's position in the Spanish state's policy on heritage. This process of consolidation had begun in the 1990s when the first Law of Andalusian Cultural Heritage (1991) introduced a clause on Ethnographic Heritage and created the category of Place of Ethnological Interest. Further modifications to the law took place in 2007, including the introduction of the category Activity of Ethnological Interest. From the mid-1980s onwards, a complex administrative structure developed within the Department of Culture of the Junta de Andalucía, with the establishment of the General Directions of Cultural Assets and Institutions, the constitution of the Andalusian Commission of Ethnology, and the Andalusian Institute of Cultural Heritage, which publishes the Intangible Cultural Heritage Atlas of Andalusia.

Following the principles of UNESCO's 2003 Convention, in 2004 the Andalusian administration started the process leading to flamenco's nomination, that, if successful, would be interpreted as an administrative success for the autonomous government. Two lengthy documents were prepared in 2004 and 2005 with the intention of submitting them to the Proclamation of the Masterpieces of the Oral and Intangible Heritage of Humanity. The first document was a wide-ranging collection of reports that would never be submitted; the second, *Flamenco y Música Andalusí*, was a joint submission from Algeria, Andalusia, Morocco, and Tunisia and, although submitted, was turned down. The failure of the initiative as described in the UNESCO report was more focused on the insufficiencies in the drafting and justification of the candidature than its appeal to the living character of an expanding art form that, at least in its commercial form, was not at risk of disappearing, as was publicized in the political discourse (Mellado Segado 2017). The intricacies of political and partisan conflict between institutions that held differing stances—namely, the Spanish Ministry of Culture and the Department of Culture of the Government of Andalusia—also contributed to the failure of the candidature.

However, Andalusia's interest in achieving UNESCO recognition for flamenco never disappeared. The growing enthusiasm of some institutional representatives was met by UNESCO's creation of the Representative List of the Intangible Cultural Heritage. The List is an open repository encompassing all cultural expressions that help illustrate the diversity of intangible heritage and that contribute to a wider awareness of its importance. The new call for applications (2009), which simplified the application procedure and forms notably, made it easier for flamenco to be included within the List. The defense of flamenco's suitability to be included in the List did not face any obstacles because the tradition aptly responds to the definition of intangible heritage proposed in the 2003 Convention and meets the expectations as required through the establishment of categories in the form: oral traditions and expressions, including language conceived as a vehicle for the transmission of intangible cultural heritage; performing arts; social practices, rituals and festive events; knowledge and practices concerning nature and the universe; and traditional craftmanship (Article 2.2 of the Convention). Flamenco's inscription in the List allowed, at last, the joining of the cultural and collective aspects of this heritage with its performative character, precisely as required by UNESCO's guidelines.

In a gesture that acknowledged flamenco's optimal suitability for inscription in the List, the Junta de Andalucía looked for inter-regional alliances that allowed flamenco to be promoted in the hierarchy established by UNESCO, which considers both national and multinational nominations. The Andalusian government led a joint submission with the bordering autonomous communities of Extremadura and Murcia (whose presence in the document is rather anecdotal), which required work on three fronts: political (to align the different wishes of multiple administrations, such as proposing motions in regional parliaments and the Spanish Congress as well as motions of support in local councils and meetings between the departments of culture); administrative (with the writing of the submission according to the template established by UNESCO); and social (searching for community support).

The submission of flamenco to the List generated consensus between the committed institutions, the communities, and the actors involved to a greater extent than the consensus around the mention of flamenco in the *Estatuto*, which was only mildly received. None of the institutions and actors had any strong expectations or agendas, or lobbied in any particular direction, but rather proceeded according to the circumstances. The writing process for the application was quite specific. A basic form had to be completed and put together with a list of available resources, measures and plans for safeguarding, and the agreement of the seven communities involved—*Gitanos*, flamenco families and dynasties, *peñas* and associations, artists, critics and researchers, flamenco schools and academies, and flamenco cultural industries—which in fact consisted of about thirty letters of support and references to meetings that justified the demand for flamenco's nomination (Macías Sánchez 2019). The drafting of the nomination file was coordinated by the then director of the Andalusian Agency for the Development of Flamenco, Francisco Perujo, and was presented to UNESCO's office in Paris in August 2009 (Junta de Andalucía 2009).

The following months in the Andalusian political cycle were turbulent, with the replacement of several government officials and the departure of Perujo, but this had little impact on the UNESCO nomination as the framework for the support campaign was already in place. María de los Ángeles Carrasco took over

14. Flamenco Heritage and the Politics of Identity

direction of the new Andalusian Institute of Flamenco in June 2010, after being promoted from her former role as coordinator of the same institution, and she managed an effective institutional campaign. Initially the flamenco communities did not organize themselves into interest groups, but, over time, *flamencos*, public cultural figures, and members of civil society grew more enthusiastic and became increasingly involved in the project. An important factor in this growing involvement was the dynamism of the *Flamenco Soy* initiative. It was launched in January 2010 to garner as much support as possible for flamenco's nomination as well as to select the signatories of various actors, such as local figures, those with greater symbolic power, and big names of the flamenco industry. The mobilization of music celebrities and prominent figures from the cultural sector, such as Daniel Barenboim, Alejandro Sanz, Antonio Banderas, and Paris Mayor Anne Hidalgo, all of whom enthusiastically joined the campaign, was just as important. Public presentations in flamenco venues, political headquarters, and relevant theaters such as the Liceu in Barcelona and the Teatro Real in Madrid demonstrated the success of the campaign's management. The guitarist Paco de Lucía offered a concert at Madrid's Teatro Real in support of the campaign. Four decades earlier, he had had to endure the disdain from part of the audience at that same theater, which at the time was reluctant to admit the merging of flamenco with lyrical and symphonic music. Finally, flamenco was registered in the UNESCO List at the fifth session of the Intergovernmental Committee for the Safeguarding of Intangible Cultural Heritage of UNESCO in Nairobi (UNESCO 2010), together with other submissions presented by Spain: the Catalan *castells*, the *Sibila* chant of Mallorca, the Mediterranean diet, and falconry.

Flamenco Heritage and the Artistic Community

> What I know is dancing, not planning a project. My projects are here [touches head], and I bring them out when I am dancing, not on paper. True flamenco cannot be written in a project, flamenco is an art that you have, that has to come out; and it has to come out at a fiesta. And if you are a professional it also comes out well on a stage, and when that is the case, it is the art that must be paid for. If you are a politician and want to say that flamenco is heritage, I am fine with it, but don't make me write papers. Here I am, what more papers do you want?[3]

Thus spoke a well-known flamenco dancer during a conversation that we had on November 16, 2010, in the patio of the Andalusian Institute of Flamenco in the Santa Cruz neighborhood of Seville. *Gitano* and non-*Gitano* artists, scholars, *peñistas*, teachers, politicians, and cultural managers gathered there to await the UNESCO verdict and were subsequently able to celebrate flamenco's inclusion in the List with a spontaneous *fiesta por bulerías*. However, in less than a year, some of those at this *fiesta* and other professionals that the press described as "*flamenco indignados*"—all of them artists with long careers and who advocated for traditional flamenco—met on the first floor of that very same building to present a series of demands to the then Head of the Department of Culture of the Junta de Andalucía, Paulino Plata. Although the inclusion of flamenco in the school curricula was one of those demands, the fundamental claim was far more practical: to achieve greater equality in the distribution of public resources, particularly in matters directly procured by the Junta. This demand entailed a complete rejection of the model in force, which was based on open competitive grants, and whose calls for applications were seen—as the quote above shows— more as obstacles than guarantees of procedural transparency.

These demands were also raised during a context critical for the making of flamenco identity, in which artists chose three ways to approach the tensions inherent in the binary opposition between tradition and innovation: first, to preserve the aesthetic normativity of what is considered to be "pure flamenco"; second, to take limited risks by introducing certain innovations within a relatively standardized flamenco aesthetic; and third, to introduce experimentalisms that would bring about a true "breakdown of representation" (Rampérez 2004). Since the 1990s, artists born between the mid-1960s and the early twenty-first century revised canonical forms of flamenco dance, employing creative languages and grammars that established new semantic relationships in flamenco, especially in the dance. Relevant figures such as Eva Yerbabuena, Israel Galván, Rocío Molina, Andrés Marín, and Belén Maya, and after them younger cohorts of female and male dancers, have transformed what we know as "*baile flamenco*" from a traditional form to a reconfigured visual and musical language. The theoretical grounding of this phenomenology, shared globally with other cultural movements, has prompted the use of the term "neoflamenco" to identify this redefinition of the art form.

Although it is not possible to discuss in detail the full contents of the thirty-four interviews I carried out, it should be noted that the understanding of flamenco heritage and the attitude towards the heritagization produced heterogeneous discourses.[4] The interviews were designed according to three different types of male and female dancers. First, ten informants subscribe to a somewhat conservative position when responding to the question of what can be understood by flamenco heritage. They resist innovation and safeguard their *savoir faire*, in turn defending the creative aspirations and expectations of traditional audiences. Second, nine other interviewees lie at the opposite end of the spectrum: they praise a form of flamenco that embraces reflexive intellectualization,

14. Flamenco Heritage and the Politics of Identity 279

formal technification, and a type of professional versatility that, while anchored in tradition, is also free from it, because it has abandoned conventional references and performance practice. Last, fifteen informants forming a majority adopt an intermediate position: they call for a reinterpretation or rereading of the past that brings what they consider to be tradition back into the present.

When seven informants from the first conservative group were asked about the utility of flamenco's inclusion in the Representative List, their statements were unanimous. They congratulated the achievement, but they asked the administration to pursue what they thought was a fundamental goal: to safeguard traditional parameters. They condemned what they called "negligence" or "blame" by inaction towards "pure" flamenco and the excessive promotion of avant-garde creative projects (Statements 1 and 2). Some included specific demands, with proposals that ranged from the establishment of quotas to pedagogical measures and the preservation of oral memory or reclaimed the specificity of flamenco as an art that should not be academicized in dance conservatoires (Statement 3).

> S1. The UNESCO thing seems fine to me, but they should invest X amount—I don't know, half of the grants or more—in real [traditional] flamenco performances. Because now it's difficult to go to a show and see a dancer doing a *farruca* the way Antonio Gades used to do them, or [a kinetic] arrangement like Mario Maya's. Now they dance with a hen on their head, or inside a coffin.[5]

> S2. Only the youngsters work. The "authentic ones," the masters, they are not hired. They are at home, with all that they know and have lived, and still with energy, but left high and dry. That's where the Junta should have started.

> S3. What should not happen is that, in the conservatoires, the dance teachers are not *bailaores* [flamenco dancers] because they are told that they don't have a degree—but in flamenco dance that's not how things work. That's where the Junta should be defending a heritage that is ours, and: "No, this flamenco class is going to be taught by so-and-so, despite not having a degree, because they're the ones that really know how to dance."

Oddly enough, the most iconoclastic dancers did not suggest that the concept of "flamenco heritage" or heritagization policies be changed according to their own conceptions of the art as a space of hybridization. They agreed on the need to safeguard heritage legacies and at the same time to reclaim a space for creation; or rather, they considered the Representative List as an opportunity to preserve the normative canon (Statement 4) against alternative flamenco, which, they believed, would find support on its own in international markets. Although no informants declined collaboration with the administration in the flamenco heritagization process, and they all valued the safeguarding actions that had been agreed, they did not show any enthusiasm about creating interest groups to develop concrete aspirations—aspirations in any case that were subsequently thwarted by the collapse of the professional market due to the effects of COVID-19. Before the pandemic, prevailing attitudes had focused more on defending the right to rejuvenate the performance style and aesthetics of dance. This attitude was symptomatic of conceptualization of dance that was understood not as a scholarly heritage held back by transmission and continuity but as a heritage that is open, creative, emancipated, and plural (Statement 5).

S4. For me [the UNESCO List] should stop the flamenco of the past from being lost, because when you go to theaters and festivals outside of Spain, that's not what people want (expect for two or three).

S5. I know that there are things that we cannot do. For instance, the rounding of the arms, or the point-heel [movement], or to lie on the ground; but I like to search for what is risky and forbidden. My body is not prepared for those exercises, but my head thinks about them and wants to do them.

The participants made references to geographies, genetic ties, style, sexuality, and race, regarding the construction of collective identities in flamenco. They also made reference to a range of legitimating communities: families, neighborhoods, *Gitano* communities, and the unique aesthetics of localized traditions, such as the "school of Jerez song." However, twenty-three interviewees claimed that artists should hold the role of tradition-bearers and be the main means of transmission. In this way, they placed themselves above other flamenco communities considered by UNESCO, such as fans, critics, *peñistas*, or scholars. They felt authorized to establish the boundaries of flamenco and claim that they should be consulted on the design of cultural policy (Statements 6 and 7). By contrast, eleven younger dancers who participated in more transgressive cultural projects did not establish any hierarchy between the different agents (communities) involved in the transmission and formation of flamenco. For these artists, flamenco is a free space and their occupation is an additional layer of identity attachment (Statement 8).

S6. When they did the UNESCO thing, why didn't they ask us? The politicians did it and then they called us to sign, but they included anything and everything, and flamenco is not just anything [i.e., it has precise boundaries].

S7. Flamenco is like a certificate of origin, and [we] artists know what flamenco is and what it isn't.

S8. [Who does flamenco heritage belong to?] To Whom? To everyone, to anyone who likes it [. . .] [Where can flamenco go then?] Wherever someone wants it to

14. Flamenco Heritage and the Politics of Identity   281

go—I don't know—or that *we* want it to go; well, wherever we want to take it, the artists first of all; but don't kid yourself, there is also a producer, a director, a journalist [. . .] And the audience, of course, because it's the audience that pays, isn't it? Although often they are people that have no idea of flamenco really.

A prominent aspect of these interviews was the statements by *Gitano* dancers, who were much more critical and more engaged about their own role in heritage activities than the rest of the interviewees. The submission to UNESCO recognizes that the *Gitano* ethnicity (*etnia gitana*) has played a key role in the shaping and development of flamenco. *Gitano* associations and artists signed letters of support and obtained exclusive agreements through the submission. However, *Gitano* artists did not create their own platform for the claiming of heritagization rights through the submission. Out of the eighteen statements collected from *Gitano* informants, only ten made spontaneous references to UNESCO, an organization that informants knew only superficially. Eight of them considered the inclusion of flamenco in the Representative List as an anecdotal matter, to which they had not contributed, and that they believed had no visible effect on their community (Statement 9):

> S9. If flamenco is UNESCO's cultural heritage, [we] the *Gitanos* must have had something to do with it, don't you think? But I don't see any changes, there aren't any more jobs, nor are *Gitanos* in a better position thanks to it.

Conclusion

The study of flamenco poses a theoretical and a methodological challenge and shows that intangible cultural heritage can be approached from multiple perspectives: as a rich concept, as a component of cultural policies, or according to the understandings of tradition-bearing communities responsible for its transmission. From the nineteenth century on, institutional forces have taken various approaches to bringing about the resignification and even reinvention of flamenco alongside other popular expressive arts while promoting its heritagization as a form of national culture. Although the canon of flamenco established during 1950s and 1960s would dominate throughout the second half of the century, following the arrival of democracy and the restructuring of autonomous communities, the cultural management of flamenco heritage, and the selection processes formerly located at a supranational level have been relocated to Spain. In the context of UNESCO, the successive proposals for flamenco's recognition as intangible cultural heritage did not arise from the communities themselves. Moreover, from the moment flamenco was included in the Representative List of the Intangible Cultural Heritage of Humanity, the individuals, groups, and communities involved in the administrative process and in the signing of agreements leading to the nomination have stopped being involved in the evaluation, protection, research, training, and promotion of flamenco. The prestige associated with the recognition of flamenco as heritage, or as an art form that has long been dismissed, may have fostered satisfaction privately. The artists' statements explored above, however, seem to indicate that neither a sentimental attachment nor a utilitarian advantage have been produced through the actions, forms of consent, and expectations fostered by the incorporation of flamenco in the Representative List. This situation highlights the conflicting set of interests that, in the twenty-first century, characterizes networks of heritage representativity such as UNESCO, the nation-states, regions, and communities involved in processes of heritagization.

A decade after the inclusion of flamenco in the Representative List, flamenco artists have witnessed with a certain bewilderment the closure of theaters and *tablaos*, the imposition of restrictions on capacity in venues, and a recession in cultural consumption forced by the COVID-19 pandemic, which unsettle the continuity of the flamenco trade itself. In this context, the flamenco sector has become fragmented, forming a disconnected network of nodes that advance collective strategies only for particular utilitarian purposes. This is the case with the newly established association Unión Flamenca in Cádiz, which reclaims its position as an official interlocutor between the different public administrations and entities. Founded by first-class artists such as Eva Yerbabuena, Arcángel, Marina Heredia, Dorantes, Andrés Marín, Rocío Molina, and Rocío Márquéz, Unión Flamenca seeks to represent professional flamenco artists, defend their rights and interests, and demand a legal framework to protect artists against precariousness.

Regarding what the community of artists understands as flamenco heritage, the statements expressed in our interviews reveal conflicting understandings of the nature of flamenco heritage, of what is and is not "authentic" or acceptable, and about whether it is possible to speak of *"pureza"* (purity) in flamenco. In sum, these debates revolve around the elements that determine flamenco's differences with other expressions. Moreover, these statements illustrate a paradox: the concept of heritage and the traditionalist imaginary around a "rooted" (*de raíz*) flamenco art gestures towards the idea of "legacy," while the experimentation carried out by contemporary artists poses a provocative challenge for the continuation of habits, repertoires, and aesthetics of an inherited flamenco art form.

14. Flamenco Heritage and the Politics of Identity 283

Notes

This chapter was translated from Spanish by Dr. Raquel Campos. The editors would like to thank Raquel for her hard work with the translation.

1. A folk tradition that combines music, dance, and singing in a proto-fandango modal system, with multiple regional sub-modes.

2. A form of Christmas flamenco fiesta where the *zambomba* (a drum that has a stick inserted through the skin) is incorporated. Sometimes it includes *villancico* lyrics and other flamenco-influenced Christmas carols.

3. All translations are from Spanish.

4. Conducted by the author between 2016 and 2020, the interviews took place in seven interactive observation environments and addressed fields of information such as flamenco, profession, and work; tradition and change in the canons of dance; criteria of belonging and identity; and assessment of the patrimonialization processes. They had a semi-structured, directed format, and the testimonies were recorded or transcribed in field notebooks. Secondary selection variables were applied according to gender, age, ethnic identity, professional recognition, and length of professional career.

5. Here the interviewee is referring to *Tuétano* by Andrés Marín (2012) or *El final de este estado de cosas* by Isarel Galván (2008), two performances that emphasize the ruptures with traditional practice that characterize contemporary flamenco.

References

Abric, Jean Claude. 1994. *Prácticas sociales y representaciones*. Coyoacán, MX: Ediciones Coyoacán.

Aix Gracia, Francisco. 2014. *Flamenco y poder: Un estudio desde la sociología del arte*. Sevilla: Iberautor Promociones Culturales.

Álvarez Junco, José. 2003. *Mater dolorosa: La idea de España en el siglo XIX*. Madrid: Taurus.

Anderson, Benedict. 1983. *Imagined Communities: Reflections on the Origins and Spread of Nationalism*. London: Verso.

Andreu Miralles, Xavier. 2016. *El descubrimiento de España: Mito romántico e identidad nacional*. Barcelona: Taurus.

Ballart, Joseph. 1997. *El patrimonio histórico y arqueológico: Valor y uso*. Barcelona: Ariel.

Bethencourt, Francisco. 2011. "Rethinking Tradition: Towards an Ethnomusicology of Contemporary Flamenco Guitar." PhD diss., Newcastle University.

Bonachera García, José M. 2015. *Teoría y juego del mairenismo*. Sevilla: Renacimiento.

Bortolotto, Chiara. 2011. *Le patrimonione culturel immatériel: Enjeux d´une nouvelle caté-gorie*. Paris: Maison des Sciences de l'Homme.

Calvo Serraller, Francisco. 1995. *La imagen romántica de España*. Madrid: Alianza Editorial.

Cicerchia, Annalisa. 2002. *Il bellisimo vecchio: Argomenti per una geografia del patrimonio culturale*. Milano: Franco Angeli.

Cruces Roldán, Cristina. 2014. "El flamenco como constructo patrimonial: Representaciones sociales y aproximaciones metodológicas." *Pasos. Revista de Turismo y Patrimonio Cultural* 12, no. 4: 819–35.

Fanon, Frantz. 2009. *Piel negra, máscaras blancas*. Barcelona: Akal.

García Delgado, José Luis. 2013. "Nacionalismo y crecimiento económico en la España del siglo XX: El turno del franquismo." In *Historia de la nación y del nacionalismo espa-ñol*, edited by Antonio Morales Moya, Juan Pablo Fusi Aizpurúa, and Andrés de Blas Guerrero, 761–78. Barcelona: Galaxia Gutenberg.

González Cambeiro, Sara, and Querol Fernández, Mari Á. 2014. *El patrimonio inmaterial*. Madrid: Catarata-Universidad Complutense.

Harrison, Rodney. 2013. "Forgetting to Remember, Remembering to Forget: Late Modern Heritage Practices, Sustainability and the 'Crisis' of Accumulation of the Past." *International Journal of Heritage Studies* 19, no. 6: 579–95.

Hertz, Ellen. 2015. "Bottoms, Genuine and Spurious." In *Between Imagined Communities and Communities of Practice: Participation, Territory, and the Making of Heritage*, edited by Nicholas Adell, Regina F. Bendix, Chiara Bortolotto, and Markus Tauschek, 25–57. Göttingen, DE: Universitätsverlag Göttingen.

Hobsbawm, Eric J. 1984. "Inventing Traditions." In *The Invention of Tradition*, edited by Eric Hobsbawm and Terence Ranger, 1–14. Cambridge: Cambridge University Press.

Holguín, Sandie. 2019. *Flamenco Nation: The Construction of Spanish National Identity*. Madison: University of Wisconsin Press.

Juliá Díaz, Santos. 2004. *Historias de las dos Españas*. Madrid: Taurus.

Junta de Andalucía. 2009. Formulario ICH-02 de candidatura para la inscripción en la Lista Representativa. Sevilla: Consejería de Cultura.

Kirshenblatt-Gimblett, Barbara. 2004. "Intangible Heritage as Metacultural Production." *Museum International* 221–22, no. 56: 52–65.

"Ley 1/1991, de 3 de julio, de Patrimonio Histórico de Andalucía." *Boletín Oficial del Estado* 178, (July 26, 1991). https://www.boe.es/buscar/doc.php?id=BOE-A-1991–19203.

"Ley Orgánica 2/2007, de 19 de marzo, de reforma del Estatuto de Autonomía para Andalucía." *Boletín Oficial del Estado* 68 (March 20, 2007). https://www.boe.es/buscar/act.php?id=BOE-A-2007–5825.

"Ley 14/2007, de 26 de noviembre, del Patrimonio Histórico de Andalucía." *Boletín Oficial del Estado* 38 (February 13, 2008). https://www.boe.es/buscar/doc.php?id=BOE-A-2008–2494.

Machado y Álvarez, Antonio. 1996. *Colección de cantes flamencos, recogidos y anotados*. Sevilla: Portada Editorial.

Machin-Autenrieth, Matthew. 2013. "Andalucía flamenca: Music, Regionalism and Identity in Southern Spain." PhD diss., Cardiff University.

———. 2017. *Flamenco, Regionalism and Musical Heritage in Southern Spain*. Abingdon, UK: Routledge.

Macías Sánchez, Clara. 2019. "El flamenco en la Unesco: Expediente de candidatura para su inscripción en la Lista Representativa del Patrimonio Cultural Inmaterial de la Humanidad." *Ciencias Sociales y Humanidades* 6, no. 1: 9–25.

Melé, Patrice. 2005. "Conflits patrimoniaux et régulations urbaine." *ESO Travaux et Documents* 23, 51–57. https://halshs.archives-ouvertes.fr/halshs-00005717.

Mellado Segado, Andrés. 2017. "Flamenco y música andalusí: Candidatos a obra maestra de la humanidad en 2005. Análisis de una declaración fallida." *Revista PH Instituto Andaluz del Patrimonio Histórico* 92: 170–90.

Mignolo, Walter. 2010. *Desobediencia epistémica: Retórica de la modernidad, lógicas de la colonialidad y gramática de la descolonialidad*. Buenos Aires: Ediciones del Signo.

14. Flamenco Heritage and the Politics of Identity

Noel, Eugenio. 1914. *Escenas y andanzas de la campaña antiflamenca*. Valencia: F. Sempere y Cía Editores.

———. 1916. *Señoritos, chulos, fenómenos, gitanos y flamencos*. Madrid: Editorial Renacimiento.

Ortiz Garcia, Carmen. 2012. "Folclore, tipismo y política: Los trajes regionales de la Sección Femenina de Falange." *Gazeta de Antropología* 2, no. 3. http://hdl.handle.net/10481/22987.

Peralta, Elsa, and Marta Anico, eds. 2006. *Patrimónios e identidades: Ficções contemporâneas*. Oeiras, PT: Celta Editoria.

Quintero Morón, Victoria, and Cristina Sánchez Carretero. 2017. "Los verbos de la participación social y sus conjugaciones: contradicciones de un patrimonio 'democratizador.'" *Revista Andaluza de Antropología* 12: 48–69.

Rampérez, Fernando. 2004. *La quiebra de la representación: El arte de vanguardias y la estética moderna*. Madrid: Dykison.

Ribeiro, Eunice. 1998. "Cultura, patrimonio y preservación." *Revista Alteridades* 16: 131–36.

Sen, Amartya K. 1999. *Desarrollo y libertad*. Barcelona: Planeta.

Sousa Santos, Boaventura, and Maria Paula Meneses, eds. 2014. *Epistemologías del sur: Perspectivas*. Madrid: Akal.

Tauschek, Markus. 2015. "Imaginations, Constructions and Constraints: Some Concluding Remarks on Heritage, Community and Participation." In *Between Imagined Communities and Communities of Practice: Participation, Territory and the Making of Heritage*, edited by Nicholas Adell, Regina F. Bendix, Chiara Bortolotto, and Markus Tauschek, 291–306. Göttingen, DE: Universitätsverlag Göttingen.

UNESCO. 2003. Convention for the Safeguarding of the Intangible Cultural Heritage. Paris. https://unesdoc.unesco.org/ark:/48223/pf0000132540.

———. 2010. Nomination File No. 00363 for Inscription on the Representative List of the Intangible Cultural Heritage in 2010. Nairobi. https://ich.unesco.org/doc/src/07533-EN.pdf.

Villaseñor Alonso, Isabel, and Emiliana Zolla. 2012. "Del Patrimonio Cultural Inmaterial o la patrimonialización de la cultura: Cultura y representaciones sociales." *Revista del Instituto de Investigaciones Sociales* 6, no. 12: 75–101.

Vizcaíno Ponferrada, María L. 2015. "Evolución del turismo en España: El turismo cultural." *International Journal of Scientific Management and Tourism* 4: 75–95.

Washabaugh, William. 2012. *Flamenco Music and National Identity in Spain*. Burlington, VT: Ashgate.

Waterton, Emma, and Laurajane Smith. 2010. "The Recognition and Misrecognition of Community Heritage." *International Journal of Heritage Studies* 16, no. 1–2: 4–15.

Contributors

RICARDO ANDRADE is a researcher at the Instituto de Etnomusicologia-Centro de Estudos em Música e Dança (INET-md) at the Universidade Nova de Lisboa. His research interests concentrate on several musical domains in Portugal, including pop-rock music and the protest song movement. He completed his PhD dissertation in 2021 about the "boom of Portuguese rock" phenomenon in the early eighties. With Hugo Castro, he is working on a book about singer-songwriter José Mário Branco. He is also a member of the Associação Lopes-Graça board of directors, the Associação José Afonso board of directors, a curator of the José Mário Branco Research and Documentation Centre, and an executive committee member of the Observatory of the Protest Song.

SALWA EL-SHAWAN CASTELO-BRANCO is Professor Emerita of Ethnomusicology at the Universidade Nova de Lisboa, Portugal. She received her doctorate from Columbia University and taught at New York University (1979–1982). She was visiting professor at Columbia University and Princeton University; Tinker Professor at the University of Chicago; Overseas Visiting Scholar at St. John's College, Cambridge University; and Gulbenkian Visting Professor at the University of California, Berkeley. She carried out field research in Portugal, Egypt, and Oman, resulting in publications on cultural politics, musical nationalism, identity, music media, modernity, heritagization, and music and conflict. Recent publications include *Transforming Ethnomusicology* (co-editor and author with Beverly Diamond, 2021) and *Portugal and Spain: Experiencing Music, Expressing Culture* (co-author with Susana Moreno Fernández, 2018).

Contributors

HUGO CASTRO is a researcher at the Instituto de Etnomusicologia-Centro de Estudos em Música e Dança (INET-md) of the Universidade Nova de Lisboa. He completed his undergraduate degree in anthropology at the Universidade de Coimbra, and his master's degree (2012) and PhD (2022) in ethnomusicology at the Universidade Nova de Lisboa. His research focuses on the relationship between music and politics, protest song practices, music industries and music and heritage. He is a member of the executive committee of the Observatory of the Protest Song and of the Associação José Afonso board of directors. He is currently a curator of the José Mário Branco Research and Documentation Centre at the Universidade Nova de Lisboa.

IGOR CONTRERAS ZUBILLAGA is Juan de Cierva (Incorporación) Research Fellow at the Complutense University of Madrid. His research focuses on the relationship between music and politics in Francoist and post-Francoist Spain. His books include the monograph *"Tant que les révolutions ressemblent à cela": L'avant-garde musicale espagnole sous Franco* (2021), and the edited volumes *Music and Resistance: From 1900 to the Present* (2023), *Composing for the State: Music in Twentieth-Century Dictatorships* (2016), *À l'avant-garde! Art et politique dans les années 1960 et 1970* (2013), and *Le son des rouages: Représentations*.

CRISTINA CRUCES ROLDÁN is Professor in Social Anthropology at the Universidad de Sevilla. Specialist in the study of heritage and flamenco, she wrote the plan for the inclusion of flamenco in UNESCO's Representative List of the Intangible Cultural Heritage of Humanity (2005) and technical documentation for the declaration of the songs of Pastora Pavón as "asset of cultural interest" (*Bien de Interés Cultural*). She is technical advisor to the Andalusian Museum of Flamenco and is author of *Flamenco, negro sobre blanco: Investigación, patrimonio, cine y neoflamenco* (2017), *Antropología y Flamenco* (2002, 2003), *El flamenco como Patrimonio* (2001), *El flamenco: Identidades sociales, ritual y patrimonio cultural* (1996), and "Flamenco" in *The Encyclopedia of Popular Music of the World* (2017).

PAULO FERREIRA DE CASTRO studied musicology in France and the UK and holds a PhD from Royal Holloway, University of London. He has written musicological essays on the history and aesthetics of nineteenth- and twentieth-century music in France, Russia, and Portugal. Ferreira de Castro is currently Associate Professor and Department Coordinator at the Universidade Nova de Lisboa and a researcher at Centro de Estudos de Sociologia e Estética Musical (CESEM), with a special focus on theories of musical meaning, intertextuality, and the ideologies of modernism and nationalism, subjects on which he frequently gives lectures in Europe, Russia, North America, and Brazil. He is a member of the IMS Directorium, and a former chairman of the Portuguese Music Research Association.

Contributors

HÉCTOR FOUCE teaches semiotics and communication theory in the Department of Journalism and New Media at the Universidad Complutense de Madrid. He has been professor of ethnomusicology at the Conservatorio Superior de Música de Aragón and consultant on music industry and popular culture at the Universitat Oberta de Catalunya. He is the editor of *Made in Spain: Studies on Popular Music* (2013) and the author of *El futuro ya está aquí: Música pop y cambio cultural* (2006). Fouce has served as president of the SIBE Society for Ethnomusicology (2010–2014) and has been visiting scholar at Colorado State University and the University of Cambridge.

DIEGO GARCÍA-PEINAZO is Associate Professor of Music at the Universidad de Córdoba (Spain). Previously, he was Lecturer in Musicology at the Universidad de Granada. He received his PhD in musicology at the Universidad de Oviedo (FPU-Research Fellowship, 2011–2015), with honors (Degree Award, PhD Award). He was awarded first prize in the competition Otto Mayer-Serra Award for Music Research (Center for Iberian and Latin American Music-UCR, University of California-Riverside, 2020). He was also awarded the *Premio de Musicología* (Musicology Award) in 2016 (Sociedad Española de Musicología) for his book *Rock Andaluz: Significación musical, identidades e ideología en la España del tardofranquismo y la Transición (1969–1982)*. He currently teaches graduate and postgraduate courses about popular music, music analysis, history of western art music, and flamenco.

SAMUEL LLANO is Senior Lecturer in Spanish Cultural Studies at the University of Manchester. He specializes in the music and sound cultures of Spain from a transcultural perspective. He is the author of *Whose Spain?: Negotiating "Spanish Music" in Paris, 1908–1929* (2012), winner of the Robert M. Stevenson Award of the American Musicological Society, and *Discordant Notes: Marginality and Social Control in Madrid, 1850–1930* (2018). With Tom Whittaker, he has co-edited a special issue of the *Journal of Spanish Cultural Studies* entitled "Spanish Sound Studies" (2019). He is currently writing a book titled *The Empire of the Ear: Music, Race, and the Sonic Architecture of Colonial Morocco*, arising from the European Research Council (ERC)-funded project "Past and Present Musical Encounters Across the Strait of Gibraltar" (2018–2023) for which he was Senior Researcher.

LEONOR LOSA is a researcher based at the Center for Twentieth Century Interdisciplinary Studies (CEIS20) at the Universidade de Coimbra. Her work focuses on the politics, aesthetics, and discourses of the recording industry and changes in the field of popular music in Portugal. She is the author of *Talking Machines: Recorded Music in Portugal at the Beginning of the 20th Century* (2014). More recently her work focuses on the intersubjective processes of creativity; on how the past is claimed and produced through music; and on the relationship of different expressive geographies with the production of historicity, especially inquiring how they are made palpable through composing and interpreting the urban musical poetic genre of fado.

MATTHEW MACHIN-AUTENRIETH is Lecturer in Ethnomusicology at the University of Aberdeen. Following PhD studies at Cardiff University, he undertook a Leverhulme Early Career Fellowship (2014–2017) at the University of Cambridge. He was then appointed to the role of Senior Research Associate following the award of a European Research Council Starting Grant for the project "Past and Present Musical Encounters Across the Strait of Gibraltar" (2018–2023). His research focuses on flamenco, regional identity, heritage studies, postcolonial studies, and Hispano-Moroccan musical exchanges. He is the author of *Flamenco, Regionalism and Musical Heritage in Southern Spain* (2017).

VERA MARQUES ALVES received her PhD in anthropology from the Instituto Universitário de Lisboa (ISCTE) in 2008. Her thesis examined the nationalist uses of folk culture during the Portuguese New State. She has taught several anthropology courses at the Universidade de Coimbra. She has also developed postdoctoral research at the Center for Research in Anthropology (CRIA-UC), and at the Interuniversity Center for the History of Science and Technology (CIUHCT-UL). Her main research interests include the history of anthropology; museum anthropology and material culture; national identity, folklore and popular arts and cultural history in the twentieth century. She is the author of several journal articles and book chapters and has published the book *Arte popular e nação no Estado Novo: A política folclorista do Secretariado da Propaganda Nacional* (2013). Currently she is a researcher at the Institute of Contemporary History at the Universidade Nova de Lisboa.

JOSEP MARTÍ earned his doctorate in 1985 from the Philipps-Universität of Marburg after having studied music and cultural anthropology in Barcelona and Göttingen. Since 1989 he has been working as a researcher at the Spanish Council for Scientific Research in Barcelona. Throughout his professional career, his research has centered on the fields of new social meanings of intangible cultural heritage, collective identities and culture (ethnicity, multiculturalism), anthropology of beliefs, and anthropology of the body and expressive culture, especially music. Currently he is interested in exploring the epistemological potential of new theoretical posthumanist approaches by applying their conceptual schemes to anthropology.

EVA MOREDA RODRÍGUEZ is Reader in Musicology at the University of Glasgow. A specialist in Spanish music of the twentieth century, she is the author of the monographs *Music and Exile in Francoist Spain* (2015), *Music Criticism and Music*

Contributors

Critics in Early Francoist Spain (2016), and *Inventing the Recording: The Phonograph and National Culture in Spain, 1877–1914* (2021). The latter monograph was completed with the support of an Arts and Humanities Council Leadership Fellowship, and she has also received grants from the British Academy, the Leverhulme Trust, and the Carnegie Trust for the Universities of Scotland.

PEDRO MOREIRA holds a degree in musicology and a PhD in ethnomusicology from the Universidade Nova de Lisboa, where he also concluded his postdoctoral research. His main research topics are popular music, radio, cultural policy, and the uses of folklore during the Portuguese dictatorship (1930s and 1940s). He is an integrated researcher at the Instituto de Etnomusicologia-Centro de Estudos em Música e Dança (INET-md) and teaches at several universities as invited professor. He also collaborates regularly with Portuguese musical institutions writing program notes.

CRISTINA SÁNCHEZ-CARRETERO is a tenured researcher at the Institute of Heritage Sciences (INCIPIT), Spanish National Research Council (CSIC), where she coordinates the anthropological team. Her research focuses on two lines: the analysis of the relationship between participatory methodologies, conflict, and heritage and the creation of emergent forms of heritage. She has published extensively on these topics and is president of the Spanish Association of Anthropology (ASAEE) and holds a PhD from the University of Pennsylvania through the Center for Folklore and Ethnography.

FERNÁN DEL VAL received his PhD in sociology from the Universidad Complutense de Madrid and is Assistant Professor at the Universidad Nacional de Educación a Distancia (UNED). Previously he was postdoctoral researcher at the Universidade do Porto (Portugal). He has published several articles, in Spanish and in English, about popular music, youth, media, and politics in Spain. He is author of *Rockeros insurgentes, modernos complacientes: Un análisis sociológico del rock en la Transición (1975–1985)* (2017).

Index

"academic crisis" in Portugal, 138, 149n4

affective atmospheres, 207, 211

Afonso, José "Zeca," 16, 43n23, 136, 138–148, 176

Afonso III, 9

Afonso XIII, 51, 56

Aix Gracia, Francisco, 273

Alabarces, Pablo, 166

Alameda, 157, 160, 163

Albalat, Sebastián, 132n14

Albéniz, Isaac, 11

Alcantud, José Antonio González, 158–159

Alcobia, José, 254

Alegre, Manuel, 139–140

Alentejo region, 18, 261n2; *cante* music in, 18, 20, 240, 247–261

Algazzi, L., 67

Allanbrook, Wye, 31

Alonso, Francisco, 93

Amanecer en los Jardines de España (Sunrise in the Gardens of Spain) (Halffter, 1937), 51–52

Amaral, 199

Andalusia: Andalusian autonomy, 272; Andalusian identity, 158–159, 166, 272; exoticism of, 167n5; flamenco music and, 18, 166, 268, 272–277; historical heritage laws and, 230–231; Junta de Andalucía, 163, 268, 273–276, 278; musical regionalism in, 17; *rock andaluz* (RA) music and, 156–160, 163–167; UNESCO's ICH list and, 275–276

Andalusian Center for the Documentation of Flamenco, 274

Andalusian Institute of Flamenco, 274

Anderson, Benedict, 29

Andrews Sisters, 127–128

Anglés, Higini, 12

anti-austerity movement (Spain), 195–196, 198–201

Antología del cante flamenco (Hispavox, 1954), 271

Antonio, José, 53–54

Arabian Rock, 163

Arana, Lucrecia, 92

Arcángel, 282

Ar de Rock (Veloso, 1980), 179–180

Arrieta, Emilio, 84, 86

Arte & Ofício, 175–176

As cores da bandeira (The Flag's Colors), 35

assemblages, 209

Assemblea Nacional Catalana (Catalan National Assembly), 208

Até ao Pescoço (Up to the Neck), 146

authenticity, 11; *cante* music and, 254, 263n9; flamenco music and, 158–159, 167n6, 267–268, 282; heritagization process and, 238, 250, 260; Portuguese popular music and, 129–130, 138; *rock andaluz* and, 159, 162–163

authoritarian regimes, 14–16; agriculture and, 250; heritage regimes and, 253–255; music in Franco's Spain, 15–16, 270–272; music in

294   Index

authoritarian regimes (continued)
   Portugal's Estado Novo, 14–15, 253, 261. See
   also Estado Novo; Franco regime
"authorized heritage discourse," 229–231, 240,
   241n1, 255, 260, 262n15
"Avante Camarada!" (Cília), 150n8
Azaña, Manuel, 50
Aznar, José María, 199
Azores autonomous region, 139, 232, 238

Báez, Joan, 214
Bailados Portugueses Verde Gaio (VG), 15, 67–
   69, 72–73, 78, 254; regional folk dance and, 76
baladeiros, 146, 150n11
ballet español. See flamenco music
Ballet of Andalusia, 274
Ballets Russes, 64, 67, 69–75
La Banda de los Hermanos Cruz, 160
Banda do Casaco, 178, 186n14
Banderas, Antonio, 277
Barbieri, Francisco Asenjo, 85, 91
Barcelona 1992 Summer Olympics, 194
Barenboim, Daniel, 277
Baroja, Pío, 268
Barrionuevo, José, 194
Barros, Luís Filipe, 179, 181
Barthes, Roland, 65
Basque country, 8, 21n3; Basque Radical Rock,
   193, 197, 202n5; folk music research in, 12;
   historical heritage laws and, 230–231; musi-
   cal regionalism in, 17
Beaumont, Cyril, 71–72
Beaupoil, Auguste de, 55
Beka, 104, 107–110, 112
Belo Marques, José, 127, 129
Bendix, Regina, 5
Benevides, Francisco da Fonseca, 33
Berger, Harris, 175
Bergeron, Katherine, 3
Bergés, Eduardo García, 96n29
Berliner, Émile, 103, 105
Bethencourt, Francisco, 272
Bey, Hakim, 191
Bezares, Rafael, 90
Bienal de Arte Flamenco de Sevilla, 273
Bithell, Caroline, 250–251, 261
Björk, 214
Blackmore, Richie, 161
Blanquier, Bernardino, 96n30
blues flamenco, 272

La Bohème, 89
Bohlman, Philip V., 4, 30, 48
Bonet, Maria del Mar, 208
Borges, Paulo, 178
Born, Georgina, 162
Bortolotto, Chiara, 259–260
Boswell Sisters, 127
Box, Zira, 53
Branco, José Mário, 140–141, 143, 145–146,
   148, 176–177
Branco, Luís de Freitas, 10, 120
Branco, Pedro de Freitas, 120
Brassens, Georges, 136, 140, 150n10
Brillant, Maurice, 69
British Broadcasting System (BBC), 121–122,
   131n4, 131n6
British Gramophone Company, 104
British Ultimatum, 10, 34, 114n2
Brito, Tozé, 175
Buch, Esteban, 47
bullfighting, 13, 236

El Cabrero, 273
caceroladas, 210, 212, 216–217, 219n10
Caetano, Marcelo, 40, 135, 142
Camões, Luís de, 140
Canção de Coimbra, 138–139, 149n5
canção ligeira, 131n1, 143
canção popular, 16
canción de autor, 16–17
Canclini, García, 166
Canções da Cidade Nova (Songs from the New
   City), 144
Canções Heróicas (Heroic Songs), 137
Canções Regionais Portuguesas (Portuguese
   Regional Songs), 137
cançonetas, 111–112
Cantalupo, Roberto, 52
"Cant de la Senyera," 208, 219n7
"El Cant dels Adéus," 213, 220n17
"Cant dels Ocells," 212, 213, 220n14, 220n15
Cante Alentejano, 239, 240, 242n18
cante genre, 18, 248–261, 262n3; authenticity and, 263n17; author's experience of,
   250–251; in democratic era, 255–257; dur-
   ing Estado Novo, 253–255, 261; heritage
   regimes and, 252–261; institutionalization
   of, 18, 256, 261; intergenerational transmission of, 257, 261; UNESCO's ICH list and,
   247–249, 258–261

Index

cante jondo, 11, 268, 270
Cantigas do Maio (Afonso, 1971), 145–146
cantores de intervenção, 135
canzonetismo, 270
"Cara al sol," 51–55, 58
Caravana (Quentin Gas & Los Zíngaros), 165
Cardenal, Amparo, 96n31
El Cardo (magazine), 89, 91–92
Cardoso, Geraldes, 147
Cardoso, Miguel Esteves, 184
Carlism, 8, 51
Carmen (musical group), 159
Carrasco, María de los Ángeles, 276–277
Carrión, Miguel Ramos, 86
Casals, Pau, 212, 220n14
Casas do Povo (CP), 262n11
Castello Branco, José, 107–109, 111–112
castells, 214, 220n20
Castro, Fernanda de, 66–68, 76
Castro, Sérgio, 182
Catalonia: Catalan independence movement, 8, 17, 197, 205–219; folk music research in, 12; historical heritage laws and, 230–231; as historic nation, 8; musical regionalism in, 17; September 2017 protests in, 206–212, 219n3; Spanish opposition to independence, 216–217
"Cavalos de Corrida" (UHF), 172, 180
censorship: Estado Novo (Portugal) and, 14, 120, 137, 141, 143, 147–148, 150n9, 150n12, 173, 177, 185n5, 253; of protest songs, 14–15, 17, 141, 143, 147–148; of rock lyrics, 177, 185n5; in Spain, 15, 17, 53, 208; Spanish anti-secession movement and, 218
Centro de Preparação de Artistas (Center for Preparing Artists), 127
Chair of Flamencology, 273
chanson française, 146, 150n10
Le Chant du Monde, 140
Chapí, Ruperto, 84, 86
Charles III, 48
Château d'Hérouville recording studio, 145
"Chico Fininho" (Veloso), 172, 179–180, 182
chirigotas, 217, 220n22
Chomsky, Noam, 214
Christo, Fernando Homem, 122
Chueca, Federico, 50
Cília, Luís, 140–141, 145, 150n8
Clayton, Michelle, 70

Clemente, Luis, 166
Coelho, Dias, 148
Coelho, Rui, 10, 122
Coimbra Song Tradition (*Canção de Coimbra*), 138–139, 149n5
Colaço, Alexandre Rey, 10
Columbia Gramophone, 115n6
Columbia Phonograph, 104
Comisaría de Música, 15
commodification, 20, 103, 196, 260
Communist Party (Portuguese), 138, 140–141, 150n8, 250
"Cómo hacer crack" (Nacho Vegas), 200
Compagnie Française du Gramophone (CFG), 106–107, 110
Companhia Franceza do Gramophone, 106–107
compases de doce, 161, 168n12
Concierto de Aranjuez (Rodrigo, 1939), 15
Concurso Nacional de Arte Flamenco de Córdoba (1956), 271
Conde, Mario, 202n6
Consultancy Office of Flamenco Activities of the Andalusian Government, 274
Convention Concerning the Protection of World Cultural and Natural Heritage (WCNH), 229
copla, 157, 159, 168n9, 216, 272
Coral Vallisoletana, 49
Cordoba, patios of, 235
Coros y danzas de España, 16
Correia de Oliveira, Adriano, 16, 138–145, 148, 176
Côrte-Real, Maria de São José, 136
COVID-19 pandemic: flamenco music and, 280, 282
Crámer, Ivo, 73
Cruces Roldán, Cristina, 158
Cruz, Nando, 197
Cruz, Nono, 160
Cruz, Pastora Pavón, 231, 274
cultural heritage (Portugal), basic laws, 233–234, 237
cultura popular, 11–12, 149n3, 252, 262n15

Darby, Sinkler, 105
De Cesari, Chiara, 239
Deep Purple, 161–162
de la Rosa, Jesús, 164
Deleuze, Gilles, 209

democratization of Iberian Peninsula, 16–18, 173. *See also* Spanish Transition to Democracy

Denning, Michael, 84

Derby Motoreta's Burrito Kachimba, 164

La deriva (Vetusta Morla, 2014), 200

Designation of Origin (PDO), 165

deterritorialization, 235–236

Diaghilev, Sergei, 67, 69–71, 75

Dias, Fausto Bordalo, 145, 148

Dias Nunes, Manuel, 252

Díaz, Gema Carrera, 231, 235

Díaz de Vivar, Rodrigo "El Cid," 49

Disco Exprés, 161–162

Discos Simplex CB, 108–109, 112

Dofus, 159–160

Dorantes, 282

Duarte, António, 177, 183–184

Duende y misterio del flamenco (Neville, 1952), 271

Dundes, Alan, 77–78

Edison, Thomas Alva, 103

Edison Phonograph Company, 87, 104

Eggert, Adiyta, 5

Eksteins, Mordir, 75

Elgenius, Gabriella, 47

Eliminator, Jr., 200

Ellis, Katharine, 3

"Els Segadors," 208, 212–214, 219n7

Enciso, Jorge, 71

Encontro de Grupos Corais Alentejanos, 251, 256

Encuentro Internacional de la Canción Protesta de Casa de las Américas (International Meeting of the Protest Song), 141

Englund, Björn, 105, 111

Escobar, Manolo, 216

"L'Estaca," 212–213

Estado Novo (Portugal), 173–174, 253; agriculture in, 250; *cante* genre and, 18; Casas do Povo (CP) and, 262n11; censorship and, 14, 120, 137, 141, 143, 147–148, 150n9, 150n12, 173, 177, 185n5, 253; cultural policy of, 14; ending of, 136, 148; fado music and, 185n6; folklore dances and, 73–74; heritage regime and, 253–255; *música popular* and, 149n3; *política do espírito* and, 253; Portuguese national anthem and, 40; Portuguese rock and, 183; protest songs against, 16, 43n23,

135–149, 177; radio and, 119–124, 131n3, 142–144; Secretariat of National Propaganda and, 63, 65, 78n4; Verde Gaio and, 68–69

Estatuto de Autonomía of Andalusia, 274, 276

ethnomusicology, 101; heritagization and, 5, 228, 242n18, 249, 259; protest music and, 136–137

European Economic Community, 180, 192, 251, 271

European Union, 251

Exhibition of the Portuguese World (*Exposição do Mundo Português*, 1940), 14, 65–66, 68

Exposição de Arte Popular, 71

Eyck, F. Gunther, 31

Eyerman, Ron, 136

fado, 13, 17; "A Portuguesa" and, 42n20; Estado Novo and, 185n6; National Radio (NR) and, 131n10; Portuguese rock and, 174–175, 184; recordings of, 113, 143; UNESCO's ICH list and, 239–240

Os Faíscas, 177–178

Falange party: 1936 coup and, 46–47; "Cara al sol" and, 53–55; "Marcha granadera" and, 47, 51–57, 59

Falla, Manuel de, 10–12

Fanhais, Francisco, 142–145, 148

feminism, 199

Ferdinand VII, 8, 50

Fernández de San Miguel, Evaristo, 50

Ferrat, Jean, 136

Ferreira, David, 179

Ferreira, Joaquim Duarte, 112

Ferreira, José Gomes, 140

Ferreiro, Iván, 199

Ferro, António, 14, 16, 64–77, 253; Bailados Portugueses Verde Gaio (VG) and, 67–68; Ballets Russes and, 69–71, 73; National Radio and, 118–119, 121–130, 131n10; "Portuguesification" of music and, 124–126, 129–130; regional folk dance groups and, 73–74; Salazar and, 124

Festivales de España, 270

Fialho de Almeida, José, 251

15-M Movement, 190, 196–197, 202

Figuerola, Manuel, 90

El final de este estado de cosas, 283n5

financial crisis of 2008, 20, 183, 189, 194–197, 202

First National Conference of Radiotelephony

(I Congresso Nacional de Radiotelefonia), 120

First Portuguese Song Meeting, 148

flamenco, 11, 12–13, 18, 168n11, 267–282; Andalusian identity and, 272–274; authenticity and, 158–159, 167n6, 267–268, 282; decentralization and, 18; defined as "traditional music," 156–157; films and books about, 271–272; flamenco hybridity, 155–156, 165–167, 279; flamenco jazz, 158; Franco regime and, 157–159, 167n3, 270–272; *Gitano* (Roma) people and, 12, 167n7, 268, 272–273, 276–277, 280–281; historical heritage laws and, 231, 240; *ópera flamenca*, 167n6; as protest music, 157, 273; *quejíos* in, 168n14; recording of, 89; relationship to artistic community, 277–282; *rock andaluz* and, 157–161, 272; rock music and, 155–160, 162, 166, 190–191, 272; Spanish national identity and, 267–268, 270–271, 273; The Storm and, 161–162; tradition *vs.* innovation in, 278–279, 282; transition to democracy and, 272–273, 281; UNESCO's ICH list and, 17, 163, 268–269, 274–282

Flamenco Soy initiative, 277

Flamenco y Música Andalusí, 275

folklore movement (Portugal), 17, 255

folkloric dancing, 64, 69, 78, 254; regional folk dance troupes, 73–77; Verde Gaio and, 67, 72, 76. *See also* Secretariat of National Propaganda

folk music: Catalan independence movement and, 214; commercialization of, 13–14; Lopes-Graça and, 137–138; musical nationalism and, 11–12

Foucauldian governmentality, 227–228, 249, 262n8

Foxá, Agustín de, 54

Franceschini Commission, 268

Franco, Francisco, 52; cult of personality, 47–48, 57; death of, 21n7, 159

Franco regime, 8, 14, 18; Falange party and, 55; flamenco music and, 157–159, 167n3, 270–272; modernity and, 192, 194; Spanish national anthems and, 47–48, 51–52, 55–59

Freire, Manuel, 142–144, 148

Freitas, Frederico de, 39

Freixas, Cesk, 214

Fulcher, Jane, 3

Fundación Andaluza de Flamenco, 273

gabinetes fonográficos, 84, 87–91, 96n17, 96n27; contrasted with gramophone, 87, 92

Gabriel, Peter, 214

Gades, Antonio, 279

Gaisberg, Frederick, 105

Galicia, 8; historical heritage laws and, 230

Galván, Enrique Tierno, 192

Galván, Israel, 278, 283n5

Galvão, Henrique, 121–123

Garcez, António, 175–176

García Lorca, Federico, 11, 158

Garratt, James, 136

Gelbart, Matthew, 3, 64

General Catalog of Andalusian Historical Heritage, 274

General Directorate for Cultural Heritage-GDCH (Direcção-Geral do Património Cultural), 232–233

General Education Act (Spain, 1970), 58

género chico, 84–86, 88–94, 95n8

Gerena, Manuel, 273

"Germanists," 10

Giacometti, Michel, 138

Gigantes y cabezudos, 89

Gil, Tito, 159

Giménez, Gerónimo, 90, 95n8

gitanismo, 158, 167n7

Gitano (Roma) people, 8; flamenco music and, 12, 167n7, 268, 272–273, 276–277, 280–281

Godinho, Sérgio, 141, 143, 145–146, 148, 176–177

"God Save the King/Queen," 30–31, 38

Gong-Movieplay (record label), 157

González Climent, Anselmo, 271; *Flamencología* (1955), 271

Gorostidi, Juan, 56

Graça, Francis, 73, 75

Grajeda, Toby, 103

Gramophone (company), 84, 91–93, 95n1, 104–107, 115n6; artists recorded by, 97n38; "ethnic" recordings and, 93, 97n39; Portuguese branch of, 106

gramophone recording technology, 84, 87, 91–94, 95n4

Granados, Enrique, 11

"Grândola, Vila Morena" ("Grândola, Swarthy Town"), 43n23, 136, 146, 148

"Grecas" (Derby Motoreta's Burrito Kachimba), 164–165

Las Grecas, 164

Index

Gronow, Pekka, 105, 111
Grupo Coral Etnográfico da Casa do Povo de Serpa, 247–248
Grupo Coral os Ceifeiros de Cuba, 250–251, 256, 262n12
Grupo de expertos Solynieve, 191, 199
Guadalquivir, 161, 163
Gualda, Jolís, 160
Guerra, João Paulo, 147

La Habitación Roja, 198–199
Halffter, Ernesto, 51–52
Hall, Stuart, 260
Herderian cultural nationalism, 12, 64
Heredia, Marina, 282
heritage regimes, 2–3, 5, 7, 17, 20, 227–228, 240–241, 262n8; in Andalusia, 274–277; authoritarian governments and, 2, 20, 253–255; "authorized heritage discourse," 229–231, 240, 241n1, 255, 260, 262n15; *cante* and, 252–261; defining "heritage," 249–250; following 2003 UNESCO convention, 234–241; heritage governmentality and, 228; international, 5, 17, 20, 227, 231, 240, 249, 257–259; memory and, 256; in Portugal, 231–234, 237–240, 249, 252–261; prior to 2003 UNESCO convention, 230–234; in Spain, 20, 230–231, 234–237, 240; UNESCO and, 20, 227–228, 257–261. *See also* UNESCO's Representative List of the ICH
heritagization, 5, 163–165, 227–228; of *cante*, 20, 248–249, 258–261; ethnomusicology and, 5, 228, 242n18, 249, 259; of flamenco music, 18, 268, 274, 278–279, 282; of *rock andaluz*, 163–165; UNESCO and, 257–261. *See also* heritage regimes; UNESCO's Representative List of the ICH
Hermanas Arveu, 127, 132n14
Hermanas Russell, 127, 132n14
Hernández, Esteban, 195
Heróis do Mar, 183–184
Hesmondhalgh, David, 162
Hess, Carol, 10
Hidalgo, Ann, 277
Hill, Juniper, 250
Hilmes, Michele, 119
"Himno de Riego," 50
"Hino da Carta" ("Hymn of the Charter"), 32–33, 37

"Hino Patriótico" ("Patriotic Hymn"), 32–33
Historic Heritage of Castilla-La Mancha law, 231
Hobsbawm, Eric, 272
Holguín, Sandie, 271
Homokord, 104, 107–109, 112
House of Portugal, 67, 78n5
Hugens y Acosta, 87, 96n17, 96n27
Huguet, Josefina, 97n38
Hume, David, 77
hybridity: flamenco hybridity, 155–156, 165–167, 279
hyperphonography, 164

Ibañez, Paco, 140
Iberian Peninsula. *See* Portugal; Spain
Iberian studies, 6
Iglesias, Iván, 127, 158
indie rock, 20, 190–191, 197–202; Internet and, 195; origins of, 190; political content of, 198–201
Indignados Movement, 20, 190, 196
Institute of Museums and Conservation (Instituto de Museus e Conservação, IMC), 234
institutionalization: flamenco music and, 163, 270, 273–274; of music studies, 3; of national anthems, 18, 47–48, 59; Portuguese culture and, 18, 118–119, 126–127, 130, 232, 253–256, 261; UNESCO's ICH list and, 237
Instituto Español de Musicologia, 15
International Talking Machine GmbH, 104
Irmãs Meireles, 119, 127–130, 132n15
Irmãs Remartinez, 127
Irmãs Santos, 127
irredentism, 8
Isidro, Júlio, 180
Isla, Camarón de la, 191, 272
"Italianists," 10
Iturralde, Pedro, 158
Iturrioz, Teresa, 197

Jamison, Andrew, 136
"Japanese rock," 175
jota, 93
Jota, 191
Joyce, António, 121–122
Junta de Andalucía, 163, 268, 273–276, 278

Katz, Mark, 103

Index

Keil, Alfredo, 10, 33–38, 42n10
Krausism, 12

Lacasse, Serge, 164
Lage, Francisco, 74, 77
Landowski, W. L., 67
Lenore, Victor, 198; *Indies, hipsters y gafapas-tas* (2014), 198
León Benavente, 199
Letria, José Jorge, 142–143, 145–146, 148
Lindström AG, 104, 110, 115n6
Llach, Lluis, 17, 208, 213
Llano, Samuel, 64, 156
Llave de Oro, 271–272
Llobera, Josep, 197
Llorca, Peris, 198, 200
Löfgren, Orvar, 63
Lole y Manuel, 164–165
Lopes de Mendonça, Henrique, 33–40
Lopes-Graça, Fernando, 14–15, 125, 137–138
López Rodó, Laureano, 271
Lorca, Federico García, 11, 158
Love of Lesbian, 195, 199
Lucía, Paco de, 272, 277
Luna, Pablo, 93

Machado, Augusto, 10
Machado Álvarez, Antonio, 267
Machin-Autenrieth, Matthew, 159, 274
Madeira autonomous region, 232
Madrid Scene (*La movida madrileña*), 192–193, 197–198
Magalhães, Pedro Ayres, 183
Maggie, Dinah, 67
Magny, Collete, 136, 140
Mairena, Antonio, 167n6, 271–272; *Mundo y formas del cante flamenco* (1963), 272
mairenismo, 158, 167n6, 272
Malawi, 10
Los Manolos, 216
Manrique, Diego, 166
Le Mans (band), 197
Manta Ray, 200
"Mãos ao Ar!" ("Hands Up!"), 141
La Maravillosa Orquesta del Alcohol (La M.O.D.A.), 201
"Marcelista Spring," 142–143
"Marcha de Cádiz," 50
"Marcha granadera," 47–59; established as

national anthem, 48; Falange party and, 47, 51–57, 59; Franco and, 55–57; institution-alization of, 47, 59; lyrics of, 49–50, 57–58; Otaño and, 56–57; paradoxes of, 57–58
"Marcha real," 48–51, 55
"Maria da Fonte," 42n18
Marín, Andrés, 278, 282, 283n5
Marina (Arrieta), 84, 86–87, 89–90, 93, 95n9, 96n28
Mar-Molinero, Clare, 7
Maronda, 199
Marques, Silva, 129
Márquéz, Rocío, 282
Marquina, Eduardo, 49; *Las hijas del Cid* (*El Cid's Daughters*, 1908), 49
"La Marseillaise," 31–32, 36, 38, 41n2
Martí, Josep, 12, 20
Martínez Ruiz, José "Azorín," 268
Marvão, António, 254
Mas, Artur, 197
Maya, Belén, 278
Maya, Mario, 279
McDonald, David, 136, 146
MC Tempz, 212
mediatization of music, 3, 5, 19, 111; of protest songs, 141–142
Medina Azahara, 157, 160, 163
"Mediterráneo" (Serrat), 216–217
Meireles, Cidália, 128–129, 132n15
Meireles, Emilia "Milita," 132n15
Meireles, Rosária, 132n15
Meireles sisters. *See* Irmãs Meireles
Menese, José, 273
"Menino do Bairro Negro" ("Boy from the Black Neighborhood"), 139–140
Minamida, Katsuya, 175
Minas & Armadilhas, 177–178
Miranda, Aníbal, 181–182
Misteri d'Elx, 230
MODA-Associação do Cante Alentejano, 255, 257, 259, 263n19
moda genre, 252, 254
modernity, 3, 5, 7, 102, 114; flamenco and, 155, 165, 268; Francoism and, 192, 194; heritage regimes and, 227; Portuguese folk culture and, 66, 149n3; post-Franco Spain and, 191, 193–194, 198, 201; recording industry and, 102–103, 109, 112, 113–114; rock music and, 174, 178, 182

Index

Molina, Rocío, 278, 282
Mondo Sonoro, 165
Montenegro, Roberto, 71–72
Moore, Allan F., 162
Moreno Luzón, Javier, 50, 57–58
Morente, Enrique, 191
Morresi, Guglielmo, 73
Morrissey, Steven Patrick, 214
Moshe Naim, 140
Mota, José Viana da, 10
Moura, José Barata, 144, 148
La movida madrileña, 192–193, 197–198
Mundo da Canção (World of Song), 143
Murillo, Gerardo, 71
Museu do Cante Alentejano, 258
Museum of Folk Art (Portugal), 66
música ligeira, 118, 131n1, 174, 185n3
musical mobilization, 217–218, 219, 220n21
musical nationalism, 205–206; *cante* and, 253;
    Catalan independence movement and,
    205–206, 212–214, 216–218, 219n7; National
    Radio (NR) and, 122, 130; opera and, 42n10;
    in Portugal, 9–10; singing groups and,
    128–129; in Spain, 10–13, 15–16, 50, 58; *zarzuela grande* and, 84, 88. *See also* national
    anthems; protest music
Musical Studies Bureau (Gabinete de Estudos
    Musicais-MSB), 126
música natural, 12. *See also* folk music
música popular, 11–12, 149n2; in Portugal, 16,
    135, 149n3
Mussolini, Benito, 120
Mystery Play of Elche, 235, 241n2

nacional-cançonetismo, 174
national anthems, 29–40, 41n1; archetypes
    and, 30–32; British, 30–31; Catalan, 208,
    212, 219n7; French, 31–32; Portuguese,
    9–10, 30, 32–40, 183; role of, 29–30; Spanish, 11, 47–59, 212, 216
National Defense Act (Spain, 1931), 51
National Foundation for Joy at Work (Fundação Nacional para a Alegria no Trabalho
    FNAT), 120, 127, 233, 253–254
national identity, 5, 7, 63–64; *cultura popular*
    and, 12, 252; fado music and, 17–18; flamenco music and, 267–268, 270–271, 273;
    heritage regimes and, 232, 253, 255; immigration and, 1; national anthems and, 38;

popular/folk music and, 5, 12, 64, 71, 149n3,
    158–159; Portuguese independence and, 9;
    Portuguese National Radio and, 123; Portuguese New State and, 14, 63, 65, 123, 149n3,
    253, 255; recording industry and, 19, 83–84,
    88, 94; Spanish Transition to Democracy
    and, 10, 191–192, 196, 201–202; *zarzuela
    grande* and, 14, 83, 88, 94
National Institute for the Occupation of
    Workers' Leisure Time (INATEL), 233, 255
National Inventory of ICH (NIICH), 234,
    237–239, 242nn16–17
National Museum of Ethnology (Portugal), 237
National Radio (NR) of Portugal, 118–130,
    253; directors of, 121–123, 130; Estado Novo
    and, 119–124; fado music and, 131n10;
    Ferro as leader of, 123–125; international
    music and, 126; musical nationalism and,
    122, 130; "Portuguesification" of music and,
    119, 124–126, 129–130; programming for,
    126–127; propaganda and, 120–121; singing
    groups and, 127–129
Navarro, Inocencio, 92
neoflamenco, 278
neoliberalism, 192, 198–199, 201, 260
Neville, Edgar, 271
New State (Portugal). *See* Estado Novo
New York World's Fair (1939), 65
La Niña de los Peines, 231, 274
Niños Mutantes, 199
Niza, José, 147–148
Noche en los jardines de España (Falla), 51
Noel, Eugenio, 268
Nova Cançó movement, 17, 208, 216, 220n18
"El novio de la Muerte," 216
Nuevo Flamenco, 165

occidentalism, 102
Ochs, Phil, 200
Odeon, 104, 107–110
Las Odio, 199
Oliveira, Carlos, 140
Òmnium Cultural, 208
"On estan les paperetes?," 213
opera, 84–85; contrasted with *zarzuela grande,*
    84, 86, 88, 91, 93, 95n9; *género chico* and, 85,
    95n8; musical nationalism and, 42, 84–85;
    national anthems and, 35; recordings of, 87,
    89–90, 93, 96n24, 97n38, 113

Ordovás, Jesús, 161
orfeões, 252–253
Orfeu (record company), 16, 144–145, 147
"Oriamendi," 51
Orquestra Ligeira (Popular Music Orchestra), 127
Orquestra Típica Portuguesa (Portuguese Typical Orchestra), 127
Ortiz, Carmen, 47
Otaño, Nemesio, 47, 55–58, 60n5

Pacheco, Duarte, 121
Página Um (radio broadcast), 143, 148
Palacio, Guillermo, 90
Paredes, Carlos, 148
Paris International Exhibition (1937), 65
Parkhurst, Shawn S., 7
parodic songs, 213–214
Partido Popular (Spain), 236
"Passi-ho bé," 213
Pathé Phonograph Company, 87, 104, 106–107
À Patria (To the Fatherland), 10
Patrie! (Kiel), 34–35, 42n13
Pedrell, Felipe, 12
Pedro, Dom, 32–33
Pelayo, Gonzalo García, 157
Pemán, José María, 49–50, 58
peñas flamencas, 273
Peña y Goñi, Antonio, 85, 91
Pereira, Mota, 127
Peret, 216
Pérez, Lucrecia, 194
periodicals: Portuguese rock and, 179–180, 183–184; protest songs and, 143–144, 146; rock journals, 160–161, 165; *Se7e* (magazine), 179–180, 183–184
Perujo, Francisco, 276
Peselmann, Arnika, 5
Pessoa, Fernando, 140
Piçarra, Ladislau, 252
Pieterse, Jan N., 166
Pinho, António, 178–179, 186n5
Pinto, Pedro Feytor, 148
Pla, Albert, 214
Los Planetas, 190–191, 198
Plata, Paulino, 278
Plataforma de Afectados por la Hipoteca (PAH, Platform for People Affected by Mortgages), 200

Política do Espírito, 14, 124, 253
Polvorado (Nacho Vegas), 200
Pony Bravo, 199
Portugal, 9, 100–101; agriculture in, 250–251; authoritarian regimes in, 14–16, 119–120, 250; British Ultimatum and, 10, 34, 114n2; *cante* in, 248–261; colonial empire of, 10, 138; Communist Party of, 138, 140–141, 150n8, 250; *cultura popular* and, 11–12; European Union and, 251; fado music and, 17; heritage regimes in, 20, 231–234, 237–240, 249, 252–261; Iberian studies and, 6–7; musical nationalism in, 9–10, 15; national anthem of, 9–10, 32–40; National Radio (NR) of, 118–130; during nineteenth century, 41n6, 41n8, 42n18; "Portuguese rock," 19, 172–185; protest songs in, 16, 43n23, 135–149, 149n1, 176–178; recording market in, 101–102; Secretariat of National Propaganda, 63–68, 70, 72–78, 121, 123–125, 130; transition to democracy in, 16–17, 21n7, 231–232, 251, 255–256; UNESCO's ICH list and, 231–234, 237–240, 247–249, 257–261. *See also* Estado Novo
Portugal, Marcos, 32, 41n3
"A Portuguesa" (Keil/ Mendonça, 1911), 10, 30, 32–40; fado music and, 42n20; "La Marseillaise" and, 36–37; lyrics of, 37, 42n22; Portuguese republicanism and, 39–40, 42n14; writing of, 33–35
Portuguese Institute of Cultural Heritage (Instituto Português do Património Cultural, IPPC), 232–233
Portuguese Institute of Museums (Instituto Português de Museus, IPM), 233–234
"Portuguese rock," 19, 172–185; *Ar de Rock* and, 179–180; English lyrics and, 175–176, 180–181, 185; Portuguese lyrics and, 177–180, 184–185, 185n5; "Portugueseness" of, 181–184; protest music and, 176–178; record industry and, 178–181
"Portuguesification" of music, 119, 124–126, 129–130
Potter, Pamela, 3–4
Prado, Pedro de Oliveira Leitão do, 131n11
Prado, Pedro do, 126
Primo de Rivera, Miguel, 8, 46; Spanish national anthem and, 49–50
Prior Examination Act (Portugal), 147

Processo Revolucionário em Curso (Ongoing Revolutionary Process, PREC), 21n7

Proclamation of the Masterpieces of the Oral and Intangible Heritage of Humanity, 229

protest music, 16, 43n23, 135–149, 149n1; Catalan independence movement and, 212–219, 220n22; censorship of, 14–15, 17, 141, 143, 147–148, 150n9, 150n12; "flamenco protesta," 157, 273; important composers of, 137–140; *La movida madrileña* and, 193; mediatization of, 141–142; musicological scholarship on, 136; parodic songs as, 213–214; Portuguese protest singers in Paris, 140–141; "Portuguese rock" and, 176–178; radio and, 140, 143–144; record industry and, 144–147; recording technologies and, 145–146

Puelles y Puelles, Antonio María de, 57

Puigdemont, Carles, 213–214

punk rock, 177–180, 193

Queen (rock band), 161

quejíos, 165, 168n14

Quentin Gas & Los Zíngaros, 164–165

radio: Estado Novo and, 119–124, 131n3, 142–144; Portuguese language and, 181; Portuguese rock and, 179; propaganda and, 120–121; protest songs and, 140, 143–144, 148; radio orchestras, 131n5; singing groups and, 127–129; Spanish Civil War and, 123, 131n5; World War II and, 123–124. *See also* National Radio (NR)

Rádio Clube Português, 123–124

Rádio e Televisão de Portugal (RTP) Song Festival, 174, 185n4

Rádio Renascença, 123–124

ranchos folclóricos, 9, 16, 263n16

record industry, 114n1; economic relations and, 101–102; Irmãs Meireles and, 128; modernity and, 103, 113–114; in Paris, 140; in Portugal, 104–114; Portuguese rock and, 178–181; protest songs and, 139–140, 144–147

recording technologies, 84, 95n1; "ethnic" recordings, 93, 97n39; *gabinetes fonográficos,* 84, 87–91, 96n17, 96n27; Gramophone recording technology, 84, 91–94, 95n4; invention of phonograph, 103; modernity

and, 103; protest music and, 145–146; of protest songs, 139–140; recording "expeditions," 105

regeneracionismo, 88–89

Regev, Motti, 157–158

Register of Good Safeguarding Practices, 234–235

"Representative Manifestations of ICH" *(Manifestación Representativa del Patrimonio Cultural Inmaterial),* 235–236

Resina, Joan Ramón, 6

Ribeiro, António Manuel, 175, 177–178

Ribera, Sigfredo, 132n14

Riego, Rafael del, 50

Rio de Janeiro Independence Centenary International Exposition, 71

rock andaluz (RA), 17, 156–167, 272; Andalusian identity and, 158–159; flamenco hybridity and, 19, 156, 166–167; heritagization of, 163–165; The Storm, 160–163

rock con raíces, 157, 159, 162

rock music, 156, 174, 181–182; authenticity and, 181; flamenco music and, 155–160, 162, 166, 190, 272; Internet and, 195; languages used, 172, 175–176, 181, 185n5; modernity and, 174; as protest music, 176–178, 193; recording industry and, 144–145, 179; regional identity and, 161, 163–165, 181–185; rock "canon," 157. *See also* indie rock; "Portuguese rock"; *rock andaluz* (RA)

Rock radikal vasco, 17

Rodrigo, Joaquín, 15

Rodrigo, Pablito, 155

Rodrigues, Nuno, 178, 186n5

Rodríguez, Moreda, 15

Roldán, Luis, 194

Romanos, Eduardo, 196

"Ronda do Soldadinho" ("Soldier's Round"), 141

Roque, Joaquim, 254

Roseman, Sharon R., 7

Ruiz, Diego, 162–163

rumba catalana, 216

Sagi-Barba, Emilio, 92–93

Salazar, Adolfo, 10, 17, 21n7

Salazar, António de Oliveira, 14, 119, 121, 249; *cante* and, 253; National Radio and, 121–123; protest songs against, 135. *See also* Estado Novo

Index

303

Sampedro, Victor, 197

Sánchez, Marta, 216

Sanchis, Ramon Pelegero "Raimón," 17

Santo, Couto dos, 121

Santos, Ary dos, 148

Santos, Joly Braga, 39

Santos, Pavão dos, 73

Sanz, Alejandro, 277

Saramago, José, 140

Sassetti (record company), 144–146

saudade, 42n21

Savall, Jordi, 214

Scotland, 64

Se7e (magazine), 179–180, 183–184

Secretariat of National Propaganda (Secretariado da Propaganda Nacional, SPN), 63–68, 70, 72–78, 120–121, 123–125, 130, 253; ethnographic campaign of, 65–66; Exhibition of the Portuguese World (Exposição do Mundo Português) and, 65–66; folkloric dance and, 67–68, 78n4; founding of, 65; international exhibitions and, 72; National Radio and, 120–121, 130; "Portuguesification" of music and, 124–125; regional folk dance groups, 73–77. *See also* Bailados Portugueses Verde Gaio (VG)

Segurola, Andrés Perelló de, 97n38

Seixas, Núñez, 50, 57–58

Semana Santa celebrations, 236

Sérgio, António, 179

Serrana (Kiel, 1899), 42n10

Serrat, Joan Manel, 214, 216–217

Siete70, 199

Silva, Viera da, 142

Sinfonía (Quentin Gas & Los Zíngaros), 165

singer-songwriter movement, 16–17

Smith, Angel, 7

Os Sobreviventes (The Survivors), 146, 148

Socialist Party (PSOE) of Spain, 192, 194

Solnado, Raúl, 150n11

Los Solos, 159

Sopeña, Federico, 15

A Sound of Thunder, 214, 218

Spain, 7–8; 1936 coup in, 46–47, 52; 2008 economic crisis in, 20, 183, 189, 194–197, 202; 2011 protests in, 189–190, 196–197, 202; anti-austerity movement in, 195–196, 198–201; anti-secession movements and, 216–218; authoritarian regimes in, 14–16, 46–48, 192, 270–272; Basque provinces of, 8; Catalan region (*See* Catalonia); civil war in, 47–48, 52; feminism in, 199; flags of, 53, 55, 57, 59n2; flamenco music and, 12–13, 18; folk music in, 12; heritage regimes in, 20, 230–231, 234–237, 240; Iberian studies and, 6–7; indie rock in, 190–191, 197–202; irredentism in, 8; judicial independence in, 220n25; middle classes in, 193–194; musical nationalism in, 10–13, 15–16, 50, 58; national anthem of, 11, 47–59; radio orchestras in, 131n5; *rock andaluz* (RA) in, 156–167; Spanish Republic, 220n24; transition to democracy in, 16–18, 21n7, 156, 158, 167n1, 190–192, 194, 196, 202n1, 202n4, 272; UNESCO's ICH list and, 230, 231–234, 241n2

Spanish civil war, 47–48; music in, 51–53, 59; radio in, 123, 131n5

Spanish Constitution of 1978, 241n4, 272

Spanish Historical Heritage Law, 230–231

Spanish Transition to Democracy, 21n7, 156, 158, 190–192, 194, 196, 202n1, 202n4; flamenco music and, 272; Spanish Constitution of 1978, 241n4, 272; "Transition Culture," 193

Spanu, Michael, 175

Steingress, Gerhard, 11, 165

The Storm, 160–163

Street Kids (rock band), 180

Supersubmarina, 199

Surfin Bichos, 198

Swidler, Ann, 162

Tamberlick, Enrico, 86

tamborradas, 235

Tantra (rock band), 176, 178–179

"Es tanzt ein Bi Ba Butzemann," 213–214, 218

Taruskin, Richard, 41n1

Tavares Belo, Armando, 127–129

Taylor, Timothy, 103

Tê, Carlos, 179–180

Teatro Circo de Parish, 86–87

teatro de revista, 13, 74, 106, 109–111, 113, 115n5

Teatro Novo (New Theater), 75

Teatro Real (Spain), 84, 86, 277

television, 143–144; *Zip-Zip* (television program), 143–144, 148, 150n11, 176

Tellería, Juan, 54

Index

La tempestad (Chapí), 84, 86–87, 89–90, 93
Tempo Zip (radio broadcast), 148
La Tempranica (Giménez, 1900), 95n8
Théâtre des Ambassadeurs, 67
Tordo, Fernando, 148
Trabalhadores do Comércio, 182–183
transphonography, 164
Triana, 157–158, 160–161, 163–165
Trindade, Arnaldo, 144–145, 147
Trindade, Jorge, 175
Trio Lescano, 127, 132n13
Trio Meireles. *See* Irmãs Meireles
"Trova do Vento que Passa," 139, 149n6
Tuétano, 283n5

U2 (band), 214
UHF (band), 172, 175, 177–178, 185n1
Unamuno, Miguel de, 26
UNESCO's Representative List of the ICH (Intangible Cultural Heritage) of Humanity, 17–18, 163, 228–230, 240, 268–269, 274–282; bullfighting and, 236; *cante* and, 247–249, 258–261; criteria for selection, 269; fado and, 17; flamenco and, 17, 163, 268–269, 274–282; heritage regimes and, 227–228; Portuguese heritage regimes and, 231, 234, 237–240, 249; Portuguese music and, 17, 247–249, 257–261; Representative Manifestations of, 235–236; Spanish heritage regimes and, 230, 234–237, 240. *See also* heritage regimes
Unión de Ofensiva Nacional-Sindicalista, 53
Unión Flamenca, 282
Unión Patriótica choir, 49
Universal Exposition of Seville (Expo '92), 194

Valentim de Carvalho, Rui, 178–179, 181
Valtonyc, 218
Valverde, Joaquín, 50
"Os Vampiros" ("The Vampires"), 139–140
Vasconcelos, Francisco, 179–180

Vegas, Nacho, 199–200
Vela, Luisa, 92–93
Veloso, Rui, 172, 177, 179–180
Venham Mais Cinco (Afonso, 1973), 145
Venn, Couze, 102
Ventura, Luís, 180
Verde Gaio (VG). *See* Bailados Portugueses Verde Gaio (VG)
Veroli, Patrizia, 70, 75
Vetusta Morla, 200
Victor Talking Machine, 104, 115n6
Viera, Ernesto, 33
Viñuales, Rodrigo Gutiérrez, 72
viola campaniça, 252, 257, 260
"Virolai," 208, 219n8
"Y Viva España," 216
Vives, Amadeu, 93
"Vuelve la canción protesta" ("The Protest Song Returns"), 191, 198
Vuillermoz, Émile, 66–68

Walden, Francis and Ruth, 72
wax cylinders, 84, 87, 95n14, 103
Wheeler, Duncan, 193
world music, 17–18, 155
World War I, 10
World War II, 123–124

Yerbabuena, Eva, 278, 282

Zaguán, 164
Zahara, 199
zambomba, 274, 283n2
zarzuela grande, 83–95; *gabinetes fonográficos* and, 87–91; gramophone recordings of, 91–94; before recording technologies, 84–87
Zimbabwe, 10
Zip-Zip (television program), 143–144, 148, 150n11, 176